SYMBOLS FOR COMMUNICATION

STUDIES OF DEVELOPING COUNTRIES (formerly *Non European Societies*)

edited by

prof. dr. L. H. JANSSEN S. J. (Tilburg), prof. dr. A. J. F. KÖBBEN (Amsterdam), prof. dr. R. A. J. VAN LIER (Wageningen), prof. dr. G. W. LOCHER (Leiden) and prof. dr. J. D. SPECKMANN (Leiden).

1 dr. ANNEMARIE DE WAAL MALEFIJT, The Javanese of Surinam. Segment of a plural society

2 prof. dr. A. J. F. KÖBBEN, Van primitieven tot medeburgers

3 V. F. P. M. VAN AMELSVOORT M. D., Culture, stone age and modern medicine. The early introduction of integrated rural health in a non-literate society. A New Guinea case study in medical anthropology

4 dr. J. D. SPECKMANN, Marriage and kinship among the Indians in Surinam

5 dr. L. M. SERPENTI, Cultivators in the Swamps. Social structure and horticulture in a New Guinea society (Frederik-Hendrik Island, West New Guinea)

6 dr. D. G. JONGMANS, Anthropologists in the Field

7 dr. R. A. M. VAN ZANTWIJK, Servants of the Saints. The social and cultural identity of a Tarascan community in Mexico

8 dr. CORA VREEDE-DE STUERS, Parda. A Study of Muslim Women's Life in Northern India

9 dr. CORA VREEDE-DE STUERS, Girl Students in Jaipur

10 dr. J. TENNEKES, Anthropology, Relativism and Method

11 prof. dr. J. VAN BAAL, Symbols for communication. An introduction to the anthropological study of religion

SYMBOLS
FOR COMMUNICATION

An introduction to the anthropological study of religion

BY

J. VAN BAAL

Professor of Cultural Anthropology
University of Utrecht

Assen, 1971

Van Gorcum & Comp. N.V. - Dr. H. J. Prakke & H. M. G. Prakke

ISBN 90 232 0896 X

Printed in the Netherlands by Royal VanGorcum Ltd.

See how the skies proclaim God's glory, how the vault of heaven betrays his craftsmanship. Each day echoes its secret to the next, each night passes on to the next its revelation of knowledge; no word, no accent of theirs that does not make itself heard, till their utterance fills every land, till their message reaches the end of the world.

Ps. 19 : 1-5 (The Knox Translation)

For A.M.J.

Preface

Religion is a rather neglected field of study in cultural anthropology. During the last fifty years anthropologists showed more genuine interest in the social aspects of culture and the forms and conditions of culture change than in the problems presented by the multifarious expressions of religious thought and behaviour. A general theory attuned to modern anthropological concepts and theories is as sadly lacking as a comprehensive survey of the numerous theories which are of interest for the anthropologist who wishes to make a study of the religious aspect of a culture or of culture generally. The present book is an effort to meet both requirements.

In the first place it is a textbook of anthropological theories of religion and of theories which are either not strictly anthropological or, though anthropological, not specifically concerned with religion and yet of interest for the anthropologist who wishes to devote himself to the study of religious phenomena. Existing handbooks dealing with the religions of preliterate peoples pay more attention to the description of religious variety and the analysis of its correlations with divergent social conditions, than to the theoretical discussions raised by the various efforts to find suitable explanations for religious phenomena. Such descriptions are as valuable as they are indispensable, but they fail to meet the student's need for a more comprehensive survey of the various theories of religion and for a critical discussion of their value and impact.

In the second place the book offers a theory of religion. It is based on the view that religion is a system of symbols by which man communicates with his universe. These symbols enable him to overcome the inner solitude which is the inescapable result of his inability to solve the existential problem ensuing from the fact that he is a subject opposed to and separate from his universe, as well as a part of that same universe and functioning in it. The theory is expounded in chapters X and XI. Readers more interested in these chapters than in the preceding survey of theories might be advised to include in their reading the Introduction, sections 4 and 5 of chapter VI, section 3 of chapter VII, and sections 3 and 4 of chapter IX.

I wish to express my very sincere thanks to Mrs. Sylvia Broere-Moore

VII

B. Litt. for reshaping and correcting the numerous imperfections in my English. She applied herself to this task with great understanding for what I wished to say in all those cases where I did not succeed in expressing myself in appropriate form in a language not my own. Equally grateful I am for her assistance in reading the proofs.

I am much indebted to Mr. W. E. A. van Beek of the Department of Cultural Anthropology at Utrecht University for his willingness to read the text and for giving me his frank and valuable criticism.

Important help was given by Mrs. Miriam de Beet-Sterman, who did almost all of the typing work, and Mr. Ed Koster, who drew up the bibliography and the index with great care and diligence. I thank them for their unabated willingness and dedication.

I thank the 'Stichting Film en Wetenschap' at Utrecht for the photograph copied on the cover, and Messrs. Harper & Co., the publishers of W. LLoyd Warner's 'A black Civilization', for their courtesy in permitting me to reprint the lengthy quotation from this book found in the last section of chapter X.

Finally I wish to thank the publishers, the Koninklijke Van Gorcum & Comp. N.V. at Assen, for their obliging co-operation.

J. van Baal
University of Utrecht

Contents

PREFACE   VII-VIII

CONTENTS   IX-XII

I. INTRODUCTION. A DEFINITION OF RELIGION   1- 8

II. PRELUDES TO AN ANTHROPOLOGICAL THEORY OF RELIGION
IN THE 18th AND 19th CENTURIES   9- 29

1. The period of enlightenment (a period of doubt; De Brosses; Meiners) 9- 14

2. The study of myth (concepts and definitions of myth; myth, folktale and
märchen; the discovery of Sanskrit and the origin of comparative linguistics;
the Von Humboldt and Grimm brothers; the study of folklore)   14- 20

3. F. Max Müller (his linguistic theory; his studies of myth; his theory of
religion and the apprehension of the infinite)   20- 26

4. The increase of ethnographic information up to 1870 (books of travel;
Klemm; Waitz; the theory of evolution)   26- 29

III. THE CLASSICAL PERIOD OF EVOLUTIONIST ANTHROPOLOGY   30- 63

1. Tylor and the theory of animism (early publications; Primitive Culture and
the theory of evolution; the doctrine of animism and the higher forms of
religion; the effect of Primitive Culture; Spencer; Wilken)   30- 44

2. W. Robertson Smith and the theory of sacrifice (totemism; the Lectures;
ritual and myth; the social character of religion; the theory of sacrifice) 45- 53

3. J. G. Frazer and the theory of magic (a conjectural history of the human
mind; the Golden Bough; the theory of magic)   53- 58

4. The classical period in retrospect: animism and spiritism (inconsistencies in
the hypotheses of Tylor and Frazer; And. Lang; Alfr. Lehmann; W. James) 58- 63

IV. SUPERNATURAL POWER, RELIGION, AND FEELINGS OF DE-
PENDENCE   64- 93

1. The concept of mana (Codrington; F. R. Lehmann; R. Firth) 64- 66

2. R. R. Marett (pre-animistic religion; critique of Frazer; a theory of magic; mana and taboo) 66- 71

3. More forms of belief in mana. Soul-substance and dynamism in the theories of A. C. Kruyt (wakanda, orenda and manitou; Kruyt on soul-substance and magical power) 71- 75

4. K. Th. Preusz (Der Ursprung von Religion und Kunst; Die geistige Kultur der Naturvölker) 75- 77

5. Mediators, supreme beings and mana (K. Breysig; P. Ehrenreich; N. Söderblom) 77- 82

6. The religious sentiment in the works of two American authors (R. H. Lowie, P. Radin) 82- 86

7. The phenomenologists (R. Otto; a category sui generis; G. van der Leeuw) 86- 91

8. K. Th. Preusz, continued 91- 93

V. HISTORICISM AND ITS INFLUENCE IN GERMANY AND ELSEWHERE 94-108

1. Introduction. Early anthropologists in Germany (Bastian, Wundt, Ratzel) 94- 97

2. The founders of the historical school (Frobenius; Graebner and Ankermann on Kulturschichten; Graebner's Methode der Ethnologie) 97-100

3. Pan-babylonism and pan-egyptianism (Winckler; Elliot Smith; Perry) 101-102

4. Father Wilhelm Schmidt S.V.D. (his works; primeval monotheism; the Kulturkreis-concept; Schmidt on religion) 102-108

VI. ANTHROPOLOGICAL THEORY OF RELIGION IN FRANCE AND THE PROBLEM OF TOTEMISM 109-143

1. Emile Durkheim (Division du Travail social; Règles de la Méthode; primitive forms of classification; the introduction to Les Formes élémentaires) 109-114

2. The earlier contributions of the French school of sociologists: Hertz, Hubert, Mauss (Hertz on the right hand; Hubert and Mauss on sacrifice and magic) 114-118

3. Les Formes élémentaires de la Vie religieuse 118-122

4. A critical comment 122-126

5. Other contributions of French students of religion (Hertz on the dead;

X

Lévy-Bruhl and the theory of primitive mentality; Bergson's Les deux Sources
de la Morale et de la Religion)   126-133

6. The rites of passage (H. Schurtz; A. van Gennep; the term crisis-rites) 133-139

7. The concept of totemism critically examined by Goldenweiser and Van
Gennep   139-143

VII. THE STUDY OF SYMBOLS; THE WORKS OF FREUD, JUNG
AND CASSIRER   144-164

1. Sigmund Freud and his school (the sub-conscious; Totem und Tabu;
Mozes and Monotheism; G. Roheim; Malinowski's Sex and Repression;
evaluation)   144-154

2. C. G. Jung   154-157

3. Man the Symboliser (Cassirer's Philosophy of Symbolic Forms; a classification of symbols; the limitations set to human expression and the use of models) 157-164

VIII. RELIGION IN ANTHROPOLOGICAL THEORY AFTER 1920   165-181

1. Functionalism (Malinowski; field studies of religious belief; Radcliffe-Brown) 166-173

2. Historicism and the phenomenological school of thought (Bornemann;
Jensen; Eliade)   173-178

3. Anthropological theory in the United States (Margaret Mead; E. Sapir;
Linton; Bateson; Ruth Benedict)   178-181

IX. STRUCTURE AND STRUCTURALISM   182-213

1. The Concept of Structure (a controversial concept; Mauss, Essay sur le Don) 182-185

2. The beginnings of structuralism (J. P. B. de Josselin de Jong; Locher;
Held; Radcliffe-Brown; Stanner)   185-189

3. Claude Lévi-Strauss. Introduction (Simonis; Les Structures élémentaires de
la Parenté; thinking in oppositions; dualism; the signifying and the signified;
the concept of mana; magic, medicine-man and psychiatrist)   189-200

4. Lévi-Strauss on classification and myth (Le Totémisme aujourd'hui; La
Pensée sauvage; the 'bricoleur'; the structure of myth; myth and music; the
transmutations of myth)   200-213

X. THE HUMAN FOUNDATIONS OF RELIGION   214-241

1. The major characteristics of religion   214-219

2. The fundamental contradiction of the human condition (the effect of symbolising; the human subject and the necessity of being a part; means and limitations of communication) 219-227

3. Conflict, misfortune and comfort (personification and apprehended intentionality; the conditions of life in primitive society; ascriptive thinking; symbols for communication; a state of harmony) 227-241

XI. SYMBOLS FOR COMMUNICATION 242-280

1. Introduction (introduction; the religion of the Marind-anim; the religion of the Ngad'a) 242-258

2. The belief in the efficacy of the magic rite. Spell and Prayer (the transposition of the symbol and the symbolised; the formula; spell and prayer; faith and doubt; elaborations on a central theme) 258-267

3. The animistic complex. The belief in the persistence of the soul and the power of the dead (the death of the other as the point of departure; the primacy of the ascriptive worldview; the independent origin of the ancestor-concept) 267-272

4. Myth and ritual in two religious systems. Conclusion (Marind-anim myth and ritual; conscious systematisation; sorcery and ascriptive thinking; the limited role of the spirits of the dead among the Ngad'a; the supreme being; sacrifice; conclusion) 272-280

BIBLIOGRAPHY 281-293

INDEX OF AUTHORS 294-295

XII

I

Introduction
A definition of religion

Religion to the anthropologist is a cultural phenomenon, an expression of the human mind conditioned by a cultural context. The anthropologist does not ask whether there is divine truth in religion. Though as a private person he may be interested in problems of divine revelation, he is well aware that such questions fall outside the scope of anthropology and of the science of religion generally. If they are scientific questions at all, they are questions of theology. To the anthropologist the point of interest is not the truth or the fallacy of any form of religious belief, but the fact that representations, labelled as religious, occur in all societies. Important to him as a scientist is their actual content, not their truth. Their truth is a matter of belief and the believer is a participant in a religion, whereas the anthropologist is an observer who is an outsider, a student of human behaviour carefully trying to keep aloof from inner identification, even when he applies the method of participant observation.

However, it is not an easy task to steer clear of religious prejudice. Among the various definitions of religion proposed by successive students of religion, there are many which bear the clear traces of preconceptions which we now recognise as forms of ethnocentrism, i.e. as formulations based on prescientific notions current in our own culture. One of the most persistent forms of ethnocentrism is the trend to define the religious as characterised by attitudes of dependence on superhuman power. Notions of this kind go straight back to early nineteenth century theology, to Schleiermacher, who defined the religious as "das Gefühl der schlechthinnigen Abhängigkeit". Frazer and many others, including his critics, have simply followed the lead given by the consensus of theological thinking of their time by accepting feelings of dependence and humility as distinctive characteristics of the religious category. The inevitable conclusion was that magic could not be accepted as a form of religion. In all forms of magic early investigators noticed an element of compulsion or automatic effectiveness due to the skilful manipulation of esoteric knowledge, which has so little to do with humility or dependence on supernatural beings that it seemed appropriate to make a strict distinction between religion and magic and present

1

the two as opposites. The distinction has had a harmful effect. Since its introduction into anthropological theory it has never ceased to produce confusion. It soon became apparent that many forms of so called magic had typically religious traits as well, and that many manifestations of the religious were profoundly contaminated with magical acts and expectations. This confusion culminated in the acceptance of the contradictory term 'magico-religious'.

Ethnocentricity, however, is not the only error with which early theorists of religion can be upbraided. They committed another and even more serious error as well. While accepting feelings of humility and dependence as characteristic of the religious category, they did not accept characteristics borrowed from the realm of the 'is', but from that of the 'ought'. When theologians claim that feelings of humility and dependence are the essence of religion, they are not talking about religion as it presents itself in observable human behaviour, but they are saying what religion ought to be. Their definition of the religious is of the ideal-typical, and not of the descriptive kind. Anyone who is not too irregular a churchgoer can easily find out for himself how widely religious practice differs from religious theory. Every time the sermon deals with prayer — the heart and core of the themes of humility and dependence — the faithful are exhorted not to pray in a compelling way, and it may well happen that the preacher warns them that prayers of the more compelling kind should be discarded as word-magic. It is the theologian's good right to posit that praying in a compelling manner is no longer true religion, but the anthropologist is poorly served with an approach which involves him in problems of true and false religion. Questions of true and false are not his concern. The allegedly false is as important and as true to him as the allegedly true.

The anthropologist needs a definition of a descriptive character, a description which is free from religious or philosophical preconceptions, confining itself to indicating the limits of a specific field of human thought and behaviour, distinguishing it from other fields by summing up the distinctive traits in which this field differs from all others. In the course of this book we shall discuss many efforts made to formulate such a definition and we shall find that none of them has been left undisputed. Although it is fairly generally agreed that the term supernatural contains the most important characteristic of religion, even in this case there are still too many objections against its use and its content to justify accepting this term as the basis for our discussions. In fact, the debate on the definition of religion still goes on. A few years ago an entirely new one was presented by Clifford Geertz (in Anthropological Approaches to the Study of Religion p. 4): "a system of symbols which acts to establish powerful, pervasive, and long-lasting moods and motivations in men by formulating conceptions of a general order of existence and clothing these conceptions with such an aura of factuality that the moods and motivations seem uniquely realistic".

2

Though the formula has important assets as a definition of what religion is, it leaves us dissatisfied, our main objection being its lack of specificity, its abandonment of any effort to find a directly observable, formal characteristic which is universally applicable as a means of identifying the religious. The rather general tendency to agree on the use of the term supernatural as a very important indicator should encourage us not to give up too quickly in our efforts to find an operational circumscription of religion, based upon one or two easily observable characteristics which are specific to this field.

To that end the most convenient thing to do is to make a fresh start and begin by drawing up an inventory of the various terms which, according to common usage, have a religious connotation. The easiest and most objective manner of collecting them is by consulting the sub-headings of the card-index of a documentation centre or the index of a book on comparative religion. Once we have drawn up such a list, we can find out whether or not a common denominator can be found. Without any pretence of being complete the following list is variegated enough to include the most divergent forms and aspects of religious life and representations: gods, polytheism, monotheism, pantheism, atheism, angels, ghosts, souls, the dead, spooks, spirits, elves, dwarves, goblins, demons, devil, satan; underworld, upperworld, nether world, heaven, hell, eternity, karma; prophet, seer, teacher, shaman, priest, preacher, monk, medicine-man, witch-doctor, sorcerer, witch; trance, possession, prayer, sacrifice, meditation, mystery, mysticism, ascetism, fast, apparition, ecstasy, revelation; omen, divination, prophetism, fetishism, animism, animatism, totemism; fas, nefas, sacred, profane, holy, damnation, blessed, mana, taboo; myth, fairy-tale, initiation, rite, exorcism, conjuration, charm etc. The list can easily be extended.

All the various concepts and activities listed here have one thing in common: they refer directly or indirectly to something which is either embodied in the concept or presupposed in the activity. In turn, that something refers to matters or states which are beyond normal human experience, and which are impervious to scientific experiment. Therefore we define religion or the religious as: *all explicit and implicit notions and ideas, accepted as true, which relate to a reality which cannot be verified empirically.*

Some comment seems appropriate here. First of all, take the words 'accepted as true'. If a clause of this kind were lacking, then the purely literary fairy tale (such as "Le Petit Prince" by De Saint-Exupéry) and all the works of science fiction would come into this category. In the second place the words 'explicit and implicit': they have been inserted in order to exclude any doubt which might be raised as to the religious character of a ritual act performed either in silence, or without any direct reference to a non-empirical reality. If a notion of a non-empirical reality is implicit in the act, this suffices to characterise the act as religious, i.e. as a rite.

More important is the limitation to representations which cannot be veri-

3

fied empirically or experimentally. The presence or absence of such representations is a matter of fact and open to impartial observation. We can state that some people believe in spirits, in eternal bliss or in hell. We can also state that nobody can prove that spirits, heaven, or hell exist. It is true that some people have tried to demonstrate by empirical methods that spirits and the aftermath do exist, but none of the proofs presented by the partisans of the spiritist hypothesis is convincing enough to persuade a moderately critical mind of the veracity of spirits and spirit manifestations. Even the arguments brought forward by philosophy are not convincing. The proofs for the existence of God presented by traditional theology are no more than arguments which one is free either to accept or reject. These proofs lack the compelling power proper to the evidence which shows that the specific gravity of iron is higher than that of water.

At first sight our definition seems a bit clumsy. Would it have made any difference if we simply had stated that the category of the religious includes all notions regarding the supernatural and all acts implying such notions? It certainly would; the supernatural is a well-known category and to most people it is more or less self-evident, and easily accepted as a matter of fact. The wording we choose reveals that, after all, the religious is anything but a self-evident category. Why of all things should man occupy himself with what is open neither to proof nor to experiment? Of all beings man is most richly prepared to experiment and to make an empirical investigation of his universe. He has the senses of sight, hearing, smell and touch. Moreover, he is able to reason, and he is capable of devising instruments to measure his experience and control his experiments. Why should he grope for a reality which can neither be proved by reason nor demonstrated by experiment? And yet man believes that such a reality exists, and he does not do so occasionally or individually but almost universally. Man's belief in a reality transcending the empirical is neither a matter of exceptional circumstances, nor a belief in a something which may be true or not true, but it is a belief on which he has set his soul. Often his whole way of life is guided by that belief, and there is ample proof that for the sake of it he is prepared to make great sacrifices, and that in some cases he will even sacrifice his life. Important expectations are connected with this belief, ranging from assistance in difficulties to eternal bliss. The faithful feel quite sure that their belief is well-founded; the Heidelberger Cathechism claims that faith is not only a firm confidence but even a sure knowledge (cf. the 7th 'Sunday'). Others again abandon every effort to rationalise and simply agree with Tertullian: 'credo quia absurdum'.

In fact, from the standpoint of pure reason the absurdity of religion is undeniable, and it is this very fact which gives reason for reducing all phenomena referring to such a non-empirical reality to a common denominator, and accepting that they all belong to one and the same category, the religious. This definition highlights the most specific peculiarity of the reli-

4

gious category. When we call it an absurdity the term is not used in a pejorative sense. The unprovable is not by definition untrue or irrelevant. On the contrary, the few truths which are humanly relevant are, without exception, believed truths, not proven ones, and this again must sound like an absurdity, as, in fact, it is. Once we accept the absurdness of the situation we are cautioned, cautioned not forthwith to reject religion as an illusion, but to concede that apparently we are up against something important[1]. Religion is a phenomenon so widely spread that it may well-nigh be considered to be universal. An absurdity of this magnitude is utterly incomprehensible unless it is rooted in very fundamental human needs. For the time being we need only confine ourselves to the matter of fact statement that here is a category of phenomena which raises a twofold problem: the problem of its foundation in the human condition and existence, and that of its function in human life. Had we contented ourselves with adopting the term supernatural we should have had a long way to go before arriving at our present vantage point.

Quite apart from this, the term supernatural has serious disadvantages when it comes to applying it to religious notions foreign to us. To the believers themselves their notions seem quite natural. Various scholars have argued that primitive man does not make a difference between the natural and the supernatural. Although the argument seems a lot stronger than it really is, it is wiser to avoid the term, even if we feel that it is up to the student, and not to the native informant to decide what should be listed as supernatural and what not. By substituting the term 'referring to a non-empirical reality' for 'supernatural' all problems resulting from the possibility of the informant's views merging with those of the student are avoided, because the formula chosen clearly stresses the observer's point of view. Even then, problems may still arise when it comes to deciding whether or not a specific notion or act must be categorised as religious. But at least the decision cannot then be obscured by subjectivistic arguments on the content of the term supernatural.

One of the more serious objections usually raised against our definition is that it is too wide because it includes magic as well as an important part of metaphysics. One might be inclined to reply: so what; but that is a crude and rather unsatisfactory answer. Nevertheless, as far as metaphysics is concerned, would it do any harm if we admitted that metaphysical concepts are religious when they refer to a non-empirical reality? Is there any

[1] In this context Sir Peter Buck's views are relevant: "As an anthropologist, I see religion as an essential part of the culture of any people. The things man has created with his mind and worshipped in the spirit are as real to him as the material things he has made with his hands. The belief in the supernatural and in the immortality of the soul must be accepted as real facts that have led to action and results. I am not concerned as to whether they can be proved scientifically. As a student of the manners, customs and thoughts of peoples I am concerned with their beliefs" (P. H. Buck (Te Rangi Hiroa), Anthropology and Religion, 1939 p.94).

sense in denying that metaphysics and religion repeatedly go hand in hand? Often metaphysics is simply religion, even if it is religion in a very specific, intellectualised and speculative guise. Neo-platonism and medieval scholasticism are good examples. So is classic Buddhism of the small vehicle. Should we not be satisfied that our definition gives us a sound reason for classifying Buddhism as a religion even if it is a philosophy as well? And why should we deny the religious character of some modern forms of metaphysics? It might contribute substantially to our understanding of religion in general if we could admit that some undefined part of the modern intellectual's armchair philosophy enters the realm of the religious, more especially so when he is speculating upon problems of ultimate reality.

The fact that our definition includes magic in the category of the religious, raises more problems than in the case of metaphysics. These problems do not derive from any doubt regarding the religious character of so-called magic. In the course of this book we shall demonstrate that 'magic' actually is a very important form of religion, allowing us to define magic as *simple rites performed for the purpose of concrete ends*. Rites being religious acts, the definition clearly recognises the religious character of magic. We shall not enter into discussion here whether or not it is advisable to differentiate between prayer and magic formula. In religious practice the two often merge, and the relevance of the distinction is open to question. The real difficulties with regard to the religious character of magic do not arise from its similarity to other religious categories, but from the fact that there is a broad No-Man's-Land between magic and erroneous thought. How should we classify the belief that certain herbs are effective provided they are picked when there is a full moon? Or the notion that the knife which cut your finger should be carefully cleaned lest the wound inflame? What should we think of the old lady who puts the hood over her sewing machine when there is a thunderstorm in order to prevent the lightning from striking the house? And what about so many household medicines which derive their main effect from the patient's firm confidence in their adequacy?

In some cases the problem of how to classify these acts can be solved easily. If the picking of the herbs at full moon must be combined with the recitation of certain formulas, there is no doubt that we are dealing with a rite, i.e. with religion. In other cases the position is less clear, and any decision taken to classify these acts is arbitrary. There is a good reason for the frequent occurrence of this kind of border-line cases. As we shall see later, magic rites are based on the belief that in and behind the things manipulated there works a mysterious power of some kind. Usually the believers are well aware that the power concerned is of another order than that of the workaday world, in other words that it makes part of what we called a non-empirical reality. Whenever this is the case the performance of the act leaves no doubt that the performer realises that he is dealing with something transcending this profane world. Sometimes however, every sign of this

6

awareness is sadly absent; the 'supernatural' has merged into the natural and lost its specific character. Where and whenever this happens, the performer equates the so-called magical act with a technical act, and in such cases the religious rite turns into a simple act of routine. There is little sense in elaborating on this; the one important point is the fact that the 'magical world-view' favours the perpetuity of religious acts in the guise of superstitions and symbolic actions, consciously or subconsciously classified by their performers as just natural, using some term denoting the profane. It is a fact we have to accept. There is not one theory or definition which can remedy the confusion ensuing from it. Whether we like it or not, we simply have to be aware of the fact that human behaviour is not always consistent with our efforts to categorise it. The definition is not impaired by the fact that certain acts or notions sometimes tend to lose their religious character because people are no longer aware that they refer to a non-empirical reality. On the contrary, this definition has many advantages, one of them being the obviation of the endless dispute on the non-existing contrast between magic and religion, a contrast which caused chronic confusion as is well testified by the introduction and frequent use of such contradictory terms as magico-religious.

Finally a few observations must be made with regard to the specifically anthropological character of the present work. Anthropologists are more particularly concerned with folk-societies which are perhaps best defined as preliterate societies. The so-called primitive religions are the anthropologist's primary interest, at least if he is at all interested in studies of religion. Yet, the restriction to religion in folk-societies is not a hard and fast rule; it is more a matter of focal interest. The study of religion as such cannot be restricted to a study of so-called primitive religions exclusively. Similarly cultural anthropology cannot be limited to the field of folk-societies either, and in exactly the same way as cultural (or, if preferred, social) anthropology has very close connections with sociology, so the anthropological study of religion is related to the science of comparative religion. The two belong together and share the principle that they study religion as a human phenomenon. They do not ask whether one religion is more true than the other; they are interested in religion as an expression of the human mind in various cultures and under the most diverse conditions. On more than one occasion we will have to refer to the works of scholars who were not anthropologists at all.

In anthropological theory of religion the significance of culture as a specific determinant of religious phenomena is particularly emphasised. Religion to the anthropologist is primarily a cultural phenomenon. He does not deny that there are individual forms and utterances of religion. He simply insists on the fact that these forms and utterances are conditioned by culture to a far greater extent than some people care to admit. This preference for studying religious acts and notions in their cultural setting has its advantages as well as its drawbacks. An advantage certainly is the anthropologist's readiness to admit the social nature of religion; a drawback is that he tends to neglect the study of individual variations within a culture in favour of emphasising the impact of religion on society and of the influence of social factors on religious behaviour and belief.

The anthropologist usually deals with other cultures than our own. One of the interesting aspects of his studies of the cultural setting of religion is that, in the course of these studies, the theories developed to explain the specific peculiarities of other cultures unwittingly give highly interesting information on the more recent development of our own culture as well. The historical sequence of the various theories of religion presented in the following chapters mirrors the development of western thinking on religion in general.

II

*Preludes
to an anthropological theory
of religion in the
18th and 19th centuries*

1. The period of enlightenment

A firm belief that religion is the product of divine revelation does not create a favourable climate for the study of other religions, and certainly not for a study enquiring into the foundations of religion in the human condition. The human element in religion need not be denied, but the theological viewpoint is paramount where and whenever divine revelation stands unchallenged. What matters is the divine word, and everything deviating from it is necessarily explained as corruption, caused by sinful lust or the instigations of satan. In western thinking on non-christian religions condemnation of these religions prevailed until well into the 18th century. Yet, in spite of their religious bias our more learned ancestors were never entirely consequent. Even their Christian world had a pagan legacy which they appreciated, the classics. An acrimonious criticism of Greek and Roman religion did not exempt the student of the Latin school from the duty of acquiring an extensive and thorough knowledge of the classic pantheon.

When firm faith in divine revelation weakened and theological certitudes began to fade, religious belief, once a source of certainty and inspiration, became a problem. The question arose: what has man contributed to the form and content of his religion? In other words, what is the human element in religious belief? Raising the question did not yet imply scientific interest or activity. The question simply expressed a wavering doubt that many ideas and experiences traditionally attributed to God or to divine inspiration, might after all be nothing more than the products of human wisdom or fantasy. The most important change was the admittance of the possibility that other religions too may contain a kernel of truth, an idea eloquently brought out by Lessing in "Nathan der Weise". The three rings of Nathan effectively symbolise the end of the Western world's unshaken belief in the superiority and ultimate truth of Christian religion. Scepticism is taking the place of faith, and doubt prevails over certainty.

Nevertheless, 18th century scepticism and doubt were not as radical as its contemporaries were apt to believe. Lessing kept to the idea that all religions hold a kernel of truth; the notion that they might all be false did not arise, or if it did it was rejected. The philosophers of the Enlightenment might be in doubt about the truth of revealed religion, but they did not doubt the value of religion as such. Diderot (1713-1784), one of the most radical minds of his time, summarised his criticism in the statement that all revealed religions are merely heresies of natural religion. Few people doubted the validity of natural religion and its three main truths: the existence of God, the natural code of morals, and the immortality of the human soul. Goethe, who was certainly not a professing Christian, firmly believed in the immortality of the soul. In his "Gespräche mit Eckermann" he was clearly outspoken on this point. At a distance of two centuries the Enlightenment philosophers' conflict with traditional religion does not seem to differ very widely from the conflict of any new religion with its predecessor, and yet there is an important difference. This time the new religion does not refer to a new revelation, but it makes an appeal to reason. This is a new standpoint, since it emphasises the importance of the human element in religion. Reason is human; and it remains human even when deified by a number of enthusiastic revolutionaries.

Once the human origin of religion had been accepted as a serious possibility, another approach vis-à-vis non-christian religions came within reach. Divine revelation was no longer an obstacle on the way towards recognising the human element in these religions. On the contrary, by now these religions might serve to demonstrate the altogether too human nature of religion generally. Of course, this again is not sufficient to constitute a really scientific approach. Initially, the point of interest was not to find out what these religions are and how they can be explained as human phenomena, but how they may supply data which confirm the ideas of current philosophy. However, even this biased interest was an important step forward; it implied that a study of these religions might contribute to the knowledge of man and that it was worthwhile to pay more attention to them.

A more scientific approach begins when and where religions are compared to each other. To that end data are needed. During the 18th century information on non-christian religions was decidedly poor. The classics still were the main source of information, supplemented with books about the travels of 17th and 18th century merchants and missionaries. This was a kind of information which, in all its imperfection, expanded rapidly. The 18th century was a time of keen and inquisitive curiosity about the unknown parts of the globe. The travels of Cook and De Bougainville were followed with great interest, and in England, France and Holland the latest travel-books found a ready market. The data available might be poor enough, but contemporaries were inspired by them and used them in their works, including their works on religion. Needless to say, these works give us more information on the religious ideas of their authors than on the religions discussed therein; but this is less important than the fact that a first beginning was made with the study of foreign peoples, however prejudiced and uncritical these scholars set about it.

One of the best and most frequently quoted among these early studies is the book published in 1760 by Charles de Brosses, "Du Culte des Dieux fétiches" with its curious subtitle: "Parallèle de l'ancienne Religion de l'Égypte avec la Religion actuelle de la Nigritie" (285 pp. in duodecimo). 'Nigritie' is a fairly unusual term which can best be translated with Negroland. The context makes clear that it refers to West Africa, at that time the only part of Africa about which more extensive information was available. De Brosses consulted the works of Atkins, Bosman and Des Marchais, sources which are fairly poor in content in spite of their volume. For America he had a more reliable guide in Lafitau's communications on the Iroquese, and for Siberia he had taken refuge to the four volumes of the "Recueil des Voyages au Nord", a well-known compendium often referred to until well into the 19th century. He borrowed his information on Egypt from the classics, such as Herodotus, Strabo and others. In 1760 the stone of Rosette had not yet been discovered, let alone deciphered.

De Brosses introduced the term fetishism by which he meant the worship of animals and unanimated objects which are deified. A fetish can be anything selected for consecration by a priest. It may be a piece of wood, a pebble or a shell, as well as the tail of a lion, a plant or an animal, and even a tree, a mountain, or the sea. The fetish is described as a deity, an amulet or a sacred object; it may be carried around in processions, it may be worshipped, or simply used as a means of divination to find out the truth about something. One of the cases illustrating animal worship is the description of a really perplexing snake-cult in Guinea centring around a sacred snake served by consecrated virgins and priestesses.

De Brosses' concept of fetishism was a very broad one, broad enough to cover all the forms of archaic religion which came to his notice. The sacred bull, cat and ibis of ancient Egypt were good cases in point, and De Brosses did not hesitate for a moment to present an ingenious theory about their origin. At the time the Nile valley was still wooded and its sparse population lived in small, isolated communities, each and every group had its own group-fetish which the group regarded as sacred and which none of its members was allowed to eat. It is interesting to note that for a century-and-a-half similarly unwarranted hypotheses about the origin of human customs and beliefs of all kinds were destined to play an immense role in the human and social sciences, most evidently so in the science of religion.

The same is the case with some of the arguments presented by De Brosses to explain the origins of fetishism in more detail. The uncultivated and unreasoned mind of the savage prevents him from seeing the true relations between certain causes and their consequences. Savages are like children; they live in an uninterrupted state of childhood and never pass the level of the four year old. Children too imagine that their dolls are animated and they treat them accordingly. The origin of fetishism is fear, and fetishism he found everywhere, in Egypt as well as in the manitu of the Iroquese and in the religious ideas of Asian tribes. He further argued that it takes many centuries of barbarism before a deeper understanding emerges. The rule of conservatism is an immense obstacle to change and to the dissemination of more advanced ideas. Yet, all peoples — advanced nations as well as savages — are aware of some supreme power because human weakness is common to all. The human feelings and emotions inspired by this notion of the presence of some supreme power are four in number: fear, admiration, gratitude and reason. The two last mentioned are the privilege of higher civilisation. Savages have only notions of fear and of admiration. In the explanations presented by De Brosses fear predominates. Uncommon events, calamities, sickness and wars induce terrified man to personify the disasters afflicting him, and to represent them as fetishes which can be called upon to save him. In a later phase of development conjurers, recognising the opportunity to use this belief to their private profit, elaborate on the system even further. Very little is said about admiration as a source of religious belief. De Brosses confined himself to the statement that admiration is the cause of 'sabéism', the veneration of the celestial bodies.

In De Brosses' expositions, various later theories can be recognised in an incipient form. The idea of progressive development, the childish mind of the savage, fear as a source of religion, the primacy of emotions like fear and admiration over rational considerations as sources of religious notions, even the fraud of priests, were all destined to play a part in the further development of the theory of religion. It would be wrong to conclude from it that De Brosses was a scientific genius. Actually, it is the other way round. The fact that so many of these theories were presented in an incipient form by De Brosses holds a serious warning, viz. that they all have a common source in popular notions. That does not imply that these theories are always wrong. Popular notions are not always wrong either, but they are suspect. It is important to be aware of the share which such notions have had in the development of religious theory.

The reflections presented by De Brosses are interesting historically but their scientific value is small. On one point he even did much harm. He introduced the term fetishism, a term which has caused a great deal of confusion. The word is derived from the Portuguese 'feitiço', something which is made, more specifically an amulet. Portuguese sailors, well supplied with amulets themselves, were quick to recognise a similar usage in Africa where it has a very specific and well developed form. The term fetish should be reserved to that specific African form[2].

[2] Cf. below sub Söderblom, p.80. We note in passing that De Brosses' own etymology of the word feitiço differs widely from the one presented here, which has been borrowed from Max Müller.

Yet, De Brosses' book had its merits. It was an important stimulus to further studies and in spite of the author's loose and unconvincing reasoning, De Brosses had a sound point of departure which, if applied, must lead to a really scientific study of religion. He formulated it at the end of his book. "Ce n'est pas dans les possibilités, c'est dans l'homme même qu'il faut étudier l'homme: il ne s'agit pas d'imaginer ce qu'il aurait pu ou dû faire, mais de regarder ce qu'il fait". Tylor was impressed by these words; he quoted them as a motto on the title-page of his "Primitive Culture". Unfortunately, De Brosses did not stick to his principle; it took more than a century before scientists thought it really worth while to go and look at what man does in primitive communities.

We mention only one of the other books belonging to this period, viz. Conrad Meiners, "Allgemeine kritische Geschichte der Religionen", a work in two volumes which appeared in 1806/07. To a certain extent, it belongs to a later period since the symptoms of the rising tide of Romanticism can be recognised in the stress laid upon such concepts as 'Verehrung', 'höheren Naturen' and the effects of human phantasy. In its main trends, however, the author, a professor of philosophy of Göttingen University, conforms to the ideas characteristic of the period of Enlightenment. He keeps fairly close to De Brosses. The most obvious difference between the works of the two authors is in size, for Meiners' work is some 1300 pages. Meiners consulted a greater variety of sources than De Brosses; extensive references are made to the writings of Garcilaso de la Vega on Peru, of Dobrizhoffer on Brazil and of Cook and his companions on the Pacific, apart from those already used by De Brosses. Another difference between the two authors is that Meiners is interested in spirits of the dead as a specific category of religious phenomena. However, the attention paid to these spirits is small in comparison to the emphasis laid on fetishism which is also the really important concept for Meiners. We are indebted to the latter for recording the story which was destined to be the case of fetishism par excellence for many years to come. A negro village suffers a sudden attack from its enemies. The headman flies and in his flight he hurts his foot on a small stone. He bends down to pick up the stone and hurries on. He saves his life and makes the stone his fetish[3].

We need not dwell long on all this nor on Meiners' theory of the role human phantasy plays in the further development of religious concepts. A few words suffice. In the larger nations natural objects, which were initially worshipped without the use of images, gradually became represented by images. In the course of time, such representations were more and more humanised until they took the shape of profoundly human gods, to each of whom mythology imputed a history of his own. The real cause of this

[3] For a caustic criticism of the value of the story by Max Müller, see below, p.25.

fallacy is the lack of knowledge and understanding which prevails until a fairly high level of civilisation has been realised.

In retrospect we must state that there is precious little in Meiners' work which is intrinsically new. Methodologically it does not bring us one step forward, in spite of the critical approach announced in the title, and in spite of the various efforts of the author to effectuate this criticism in the course of his expositions. Actually, these expositions, based on an accidental quantity of equally accidental knowledge, are merely speculative reflections on how things could have thus developed.

2. *The study of myth*

There is one field in which the early 19th century took a special interest and to which it paid a more systematic attention, viz. the study of mythology. Since the early middle ages one generation after another had been confronted with the problem of myth. The classics, as studied in monastic and latin schools, abounded with allusions to ancient mythology. For a very long time during and after the Renaissance period it was *bon ton* to make use of the names of Greek and Roman deities for symbolic references in poetry and formal speech. The fact that other religions had preceded Christianity was constantly brought to mind. The records of the early history of western and northern Europe kept alive yet another pagan legacy, the myths and sagas concerning the gods and heroes of the German, Nordic and Celtic pantheon. The reality of the occurrence of other religions was inescapable and invited reflection.

Reflection on myth has a long history. The Greek already struggled against a mythology in which belief had grown impossible, because it depicted a pantheon which was incompatible with a more rational worldview. Once such a worldview got the upperhand and belief in a divine principle underlying the universe was accepted in one form or another, the discarded pantheon and its mythology had to be 'explained', i.e. it either had to be harmonised with the new schools of thought, or it had to be exposed as fraud or superstition. Classic scholars employed three different lines of reasoning to that end, viz.:

a   Myths are allegories of specific human gifts and properties such as reason, simplicity, love, etc., or of the struggle of the elements between themselves. Poets embellished these allegories and thus contributed to the creation of a pantheon. In part the theory is supported by fact. Undoubtedly some of the gods are personifications of certain aspects of nature or they are associated with human properties and occupations; thus Poseidon and Neptune are associated with the sea, Helios is the sun, Diana is the goddess of hunting and Pallas Athena that of wisdom.

b   Myths are legends echoing the power and wisdom of venerated princes who lived in bygone days. These princes were deified by later generations.

Again the theory is supported by fact; Alexander had himself deified during his lifetime, and the Caesars, from Augustus onwards, did the same. The theory is attributed to Euhemeros: hence the term 'euhemerism' to indicate explanations of this kind.

c   Myths are the products of fraud committed by princes and priests who took advantage of the superstition of the masses to keep them under control.

The apologetics of the Christian faith drew freely on the sources stemming from philosophical scepticism to demonstrate the childishness and obnoxiousness of pagan religion. Euhemerism was their particular favourite, until the Renaissance with its keen interest in the classics and its passion for poetry gave a new impetus to the school of allegorical explanation. Poets were restored to their earlier position as reputed myth-makers, and in the genesis of myth poetical imagination was attributed a more or less equal share with the supposed heroes of euhemerism. Nevertheless, the greater appreciation of the aesthetic qualities of myth contributed fairly little to a more balanced opinion on its intrinsic value for those who had once believed in its truth. Then and later a myth was regarded as a story which, though presented as truth, is untrustworthy; in common usage it is still the usual connotation of the word myth. This approach to mythology is meaningless to the anthropologist. His problem is not whether a myth holds truth or not, but why people believe a myth — their myth — is true or, at the very least, has meaning for them. A definition of myth which stresses its untrustworthiness or its poetic value is not operational in an anthropological context. Anthropologists are dealing with people who believe in myths and in such a context myth should be defined primarily as religious truth in story-form. This is how mythology functions in the religious faith of many peoples. They need not be primitive peoples. Myth thus defined is what the Bible is to Christians who confess that the scripture is the word of God, and what the Koran is to the orthodox Moslem.

Yet, such a definition of myth has its disadvantages. If applied it is necessary to find out in each and every case whether a story dealing with religious ideas is really believed to be true, before accepting it as a myth. In a rapidly changing world like ours this is hardly feasible. Many modern Christians seriously object to accepting the whole Bible — the Christian myth — as divine truth. The ethnographer working among so-called primitives meets with comparable reactions among his informants. Thus, for example, older observers of the Marind-anim in New Guinea make mention of the atmosphere of mysterious awe created by the narrator of a myth. He and his auditors do not foster the slightest doubt in the veracity of the story. Even to-day myths may be presented in that way, provided the story is brought in their own language. To the outsider who does not know Marindinese and who must make do with a rendition in Indonesian, the same story is brought in a perfectly different manner, often as a very amusing story causing great hilarity. It may be that those who have no objections to using the Indonesian language (as some of the older men actually had) are more sophisticated, but it is also possible that the narrator just pretends to be sophisticated because he wishes to forestall the observer's criticism. It is impossible to decide which is true and the only thing we know for certain is that until recently the story was accepted as religious truth by the members of the community. Must we conclude that to-day the story is no longer a myth or that it is a myth only for a rapidly dwindling generation? If we do, the term myth is rendered useless because it can only be applied under the proviso that people believe in its truth, and this is something that no outsider, and indeed not even an insider can know for certain. Obviously, a story which was respected as a myth until a few years ago should still be called a myth to-day. We do the same with Greek and Roman myth though there is not a single living person who accepts them as religious truth. Therefore we must add to our definition and reformulate it as follows: *a myth is a story which, within the framework of a given religion, once was or still is valid as religious truth.*

The definition thus formulated comes closer to current usage of the term in other disciplines, notably in philology, even though an anthropologist will rarely feel at ease with the philologist's use of the term. To philologists a myth is more often a form of literature (either a genre or the elaboration of a specific motif which can be traced in the literary products of other nations) rather than part of a people's religious faith during a certain period. Accordingly the definitions of the concept of myth as applied or presented by philologists are vague and ambiguous. The anthropologist consulting a current handbook of mythology such as the one written by Jan de Vries, "Forschungsgeschichte der Mythologie" (1961), will be impressed by the wide difference in approach between the two disciplines, a difference which cannot simply be explained by the fact that the author of this particular handbook was a belated romanticist. The philologist's focus of interest is different from that of the anthropologist.

The latter's interest in myth as a source of knowledge about religious belief raises its own set of problems. How do we know that a story has validity as religious truth within the framework of a given religion, especially when there is no rite connected with the myth? The question is complicated by the fact that the oral literature of an illiterate people is often rich with folktales dealing with religious matters. Some of the people concerned accept these stories as religious truth, whereas others prefer to adopt a more sceptical attitude. A story relating the adventures of a man meeting a supernatural being may fit perfectly well in the existing framework of the religion in question. It may be believed by some, because the main character of the story was a man still remembered by the senior members of the community, and doubted by others because they feel that such an encounter could hardly have taken place. The mythology of preliterate peoples is not

16

codified, and it is rare to find that myths and folktales are differentiated terminologically. Mythology is surrounded by a broad borderland of folktales elaborating on religious themes. Such folktales are not explanations of ritual or cosmology as the more important myths are, but they may give valuable information on popular religious belief and practice. Whether these stories should be accepted as myths or classified as folktales depends primarily upon the attitude of the people concerned, if at all known. Belief has its gradations and a clear distinction is well-nigh impossible without some form of official pronouncement on the part of the leaders of the religious community as to what the faithful are obliged to believe or disbelieve.

Pronouncements of this kind are extremely rare. Christianity is one of the few codified religions and even this codification fails to solve all problems. Various denominations made divergent decisions with regard to the apocrypha. In addition, there is a vast literature recommended as edifying reading. It includes the works of the church-fathers as well as the legends of the saints. Belief in them is not mandatory and yet they constitute part of the total system of religious notions embodied in the church. A hard core of truths which are firmly believed in, is surrounded by a fringe of notions oscillating between the likely and the doubtful, a situation which is also found in primitive religious communities. The main difference here is that traditional Christian religious lore covers a wider area.

In our culture traditional religious literature is equalled by a vast array of non-religious traditional literature. Together the two encompass what might be called the folktales of western culture in which various specific genres can be discerned, such as the fairy-tale, the legend, the saga, the fable, the classic myth and the 'Märchen'. The various categories overlap extensively and we shall not try to unravel the differences, but an exception must be made for the 'Märchen' which had an important impact on early studies of myth and religion.

Märchen is a German word for which English has no equivalent. At least three different kinds can be distinguished, viz.
a   folktales embroidering on a theme reaching back to pre-Christian times, notably old Germanic mythology, such as the story of Little Red Riding-hood;
b   folktales of which a mythological origin of some sort is improbable;
c   fairy-tales and fables, more especially stories about animals, which may or may not have functioned as myths in an unknown past and have since spread over the greater part of the world as pure literature, such as the stories from the great Indian fable-book, the "Pantja-tantra".
The märchen have in common that quite peculiar, undefinable atmosphere which includes the miraculous. They have a specific appeal to humanity and some modern authors have engaged in composing perfectly new ones, one of the few really successful efforts being "Le petit Prince" by De Saint-Exupéry. The traditional märchen however has no known author. It is a

real folktale and the mythical elements contained in a number of them, attracted the attention of the mythologists at a fairly early stage.

The study of myth and märchen has not been restricted to studies of their religious meaning. Some scholars concentrate on the historical content which can be abstracted from myth. This is not the place to explain that the historical value of myth is easily overestimated, even though true historical characters play a role in the story as happens to be the case in the 'Nibelungen Lied'. Other scholars again devote themselves to research into the distribution of mythical plots and motives in various parts of the world, studies which are important for our knowledge of culture contact and diffusion, as well as for a more penetrating knowledge of the predilections of the human mind in general. The number of mythical plots and motives is not unlimited; some of them are extraordinarily widespread and recur with an almost astounding frequency. In some cases close resemblance in the structure of the plot goes hand in hand with a great difference in content. The study of myth, then, has been approached from various angles and for divergent purposes. Here, however, we shall restrict ourselves to the impact of the study of myth and folktale on the study of religion during the period preceding the rise of a properly scientific anthropological discipline. The last quarter of the 18th and the first of the 19th century are important periods for these studies, which were greatly favoured by the coincidence of the 'discovery' of the Sanskrit language and the growth of romanticism.

We put the term discovery in quotation-marks. That a Sanskrit language existed was known long before then. The first European student of the language was probably an Italian Jesuit, Father Roberto de Nobili. He went to India in 1597 as a missionary, where he devoted himself to the conversion of members of the Brahman castes. It may be concluded from his letters that he acquired a thorough knowledge of Sanskrit (cf. A. J. de Jong, p. XIX of the introduction to his edition of a 17th century missionary's book on the idolatry of the East-Indian pagans). The early students of Sanskrit did not pay specific attention to the similarities between the Sanskrit and the European languages. According to Jespersen (Language p. 33) the first who realised the importance of Sanskrit for comparative linguistic studies was another Jesuit father, Coeurdoux, who discussed the point in a memoir written in 1767 but published forty years later. In the meantime the credit for the discovery of the close linguistic affinity between Sanskrit and European languages went to the British judge Sir William Jones who, in 1796, made the following statement: "The Sanscrit language, whatever be its antiquity, is of a wonderful structure; more perfect than the Greek, more copious than the Latin and more exquisitely refined than either; yet bearing to both of them stronger affinity ... than could possibly have been produced by accident; so strong, indeed, that no philologer could examine them all three without believing them to have sprung from some common source

..." (quoted by Jespersen, loc. cit.). Sir William even noted that Sanskrit has affinities with Gothic, Celtic and old Persian, but he refrained from giving a follow-up to his discovery.

The follow-up was made in Germany, which at that time was a centre of bustling scientific and spiritual activity[4]. Scholars such as Von Schlegel, Bopp, Schleicher, and Von Humboldt inaugurated the new science of comparative linguistics. Part of their inspiration was drawn from the writings of the old Indian grammarian Panini, but they did not restrict themselves to the study of Sanskrit only. Other languages too were drawn into the orbit of their studies. The sterile efforts of previous generations to derive all languages from the Hebrew definitely came to an end with the successful classification of languages into linguistic families. One of the most outstanding contributors to the study of language was Wilhelm von Humboldt, author of a voluminous work, posthumously edited, "Ueber die Kawisprache auf der Insel Java" (1836-40). For several reasons interest in his writings has increased in the course of the present century, his fame for a long time having been overshadowed by that of his younger brother, Alexander, the geographer and geologist.

Another famous pair of brothers must also be mentioned in this context, the brothers Grimm, Jacob and Wilhelm. Jacob too was a linguist. He is the author of the "Deutsche Grammatik", a book which is not, as the name suggests, a grammar of the German language, but a comparative grammar of germanic languages. In its kind it is a novum; the author does not endeavour to state how a language should be spoken or written, but tries to find out how a language is actually used. It is the first descriptive grammar. Jacob Grimm must have been a good listener, as is well demonstrated by the "Kinder- und Hausmärchen". This book was written in collaboration with his brother Wilhelm, and the work has made them famous up to the present day. The first two volumes, published in 1812 and 1815 were followed in 1822 by a volume of explanation and comment which was in part a comparative study of motives and plots of märchen all over the world. Whilst the märchen had been noted down by the brothers straight from living oral tradition, the comparative study was a learned work, for which the data had to be compiled from published sources. In spite of their relative paucity Wilhelm, the main author of the 'Märchen', succeeded in collecting an impressive amount of information on European non-Germanic märchen and on märchen from India, Persia, Arabia, and even from Africa and America. The study is Germanic-centered and Wilhelm comes to the conclusion that parallels are most frequent among Indo-germanic peoples. Arabian parallels are explained because of contact with Persia but the sporadic occurrence of parallels in Africa raises problems which wisely he did not try

[4] A good review of the German school of early linguists is to be found in Jespersen, Language, chapter II.

to solve. The absence of parallels in American märchen may have strengthened his conviction that his starting-point — the German märchen — was correct, an idea which we cannot easily agree with, because it is too narrowly ethnocentric. The imperfection is of small account when compared to the outstanding merit that the work laid the basis for a new branch of scientific activity, the comparative study of myths and folktales.

The inspiration for this new activity, which was sparked off by the study of Sanskrit and comparative linguistics, came from the romantic movement. Romanticism greatly stimulated interest in the past and more particularly in national traditions, 'das Volkstümliche'. The political counterpart of the movement is the surge of nationalism which swept over Europe at that time under the stimulus of the patriotic reactions called for because of the Napoleonic wars. The "Kinder- und Hausmärchen" are an important marker on the way to further studies of the national and local past which within a few decennia engendered a real zeal for the study of folklore. These folkloristic studies culminated in the work of W. Mannhardt, the author of the "Wald- und Feldkulte" (1875/77), which for a long time was a frequently quoted standard work on European folklore. The interest taken in folklore stimulated interest in mythology, a field in which Max Müller, a younger contemporary of Mannhardt, became the great 19th century authority.

3. F. Max Müller (1823-1903)

Friedrich Max Müller, born in 1823 at Dessau in Germany, was in the most literal sense a son of romanticism. His father was the poet who wrote many of Schubert's Lieder, his godfather was Felix Mendelssohn Bartholdy. Young Müller very nearly decided to study music instead of literature. He finished his studies of Sanskrit in Germany and after a short period in France he settled in England where the British East India Company granted him the financial aid which he needed for his translation of the Rig Veda Samhita with Sayana's commentary. In those days the East India Company was no longer a governing body but in its capacity as an advisory body it took the opportunity to promote scientific studies on India.

This work shouldered by Müller took a long time to complete. The first volume of his translation appeared in 1849, the sixth and last in 1873. In the meantime Müller had found a position at the University of Oxford. He acquired British nationality and became one of the leading men in British 19th century scientific life. He was a prolific author, but probably the more enduring service he paid to the development of science was editing the Sacred Books of the East. During the years of his editorship some 50 volumes appeared. In this context, however, his publications on mythology and religion are more immediately relevant, notably his essay "Comparative Mythology" (1856; reprinted in Chips from a German Workshop II pp.

1-143); "Greek Legends" (1867, Chips II pp. 156-171); "Introduction to the Science of Religion" (1873); and "Lectures on the Origin and Growth of Religion as illustrated by the Religions of India" (1878; the first of the Hibbert Lectures).

Max Müller was a brilliant writer who became famous at an early age because of his publications on the history of language and the development of mythology. However, he is best remembered for his studies on myth. His mythological studies cannot be discussed separately from his linguistic theories, theories which do not find a single defender to-day. Language is a faculty which, in Max Müller's views, is posterior to thought. Man had to pass through a prolonged period of linguistic growth before he succeeded in developing language into an adequate instrument for the expression of thought. Language originated in action and the first elements of language, the roots, are mono-syllabic expressions of action, or signs for concrete things. "They are all substantives, they express something substantial, something open to sensuous perception. Nor is it in the power of language to express originally anything except objects as nouns, and qualities as verbs" (Comparative Mythology, Chips II pp. 53, 54). The linguistic expression of general concepts and abstracts necessarily gave rise to extreme difficulties. "As long as people thought in language, it was simply impossible to speak of morning or evening, of spring and winter, without giving to these conceptions something of an individual, active, sexual, and at last, personal character" (ibid. p. 55). We shall pass over the effect attributed to the grammatical gender in this early essay; in his later works he brought it in a more attenuated form, apparently because the argument places the origin of grammatical gender in an extremely early phase of linguistic development (cf. Lectures on the Origin and Growth p. 189). The main argument is that "language breaks out first in action" (Lectures Origin and Growth p. 183): "When everything that was known and named had to be conceived as active, and if active, then as personal, when a stone was a cutter, a tooth, a grinder or an eater, a gimlet, a borer [and we must for the sake of clarity add from a preceding passage, the moon a measurer] there was, no doubt, considerable difficulty in dispersonifying, in distinguishing between a measurer and the moon, in neutralising words, in producing in fact neuter nouns, in clearly distinguishing the tool from the hand, the hand from the man; in finding a way of speaking even of a stone as something simply trodden under foot. There was no difficulty in figuring, animating, or personifying. . ... Our problem is not, how language came to personify, but how it succeeded in dispersonifying" (Lectures Origin and Growth pp. 188 f.).

The development of language was complicated by the early outburst of synonymy which in turn gave rise to a proliferation of homonyms. Since most nouns were originally appellatives or predicates, objects could be and actually were named after more than one of their attributes. In the course of time most of these synonyms were discarded, while others lost their original metaphorical and poetical meaning and developed into what may be called the proper names of the objects concerned. The superfluous terms, however, were not simply forgotten. Some of them lingered on in conversation, understood in their original meaning by the older generation but misunderstood by the younger, who interpreted these terms, which were still full of bold metaphorical meaning, as personal names. Thus the Sanskrit 'Dyaus' and Greek 'Zeus', once names for the sky, gradually turned into proper names (Comparative Mythology, Chips II pp. 71 f.).

They turned into proper names, i.e. names of persons who lived in a long bygone past and who were characterised by the activity embodied in their names, thus giving rise to the birth of mythology, "an inevitable phase in the growth of language" (Greek Legends, Chips II p. 162): "Everything, while language passes through that peculiar phase, may become mythology. Not only the ideas of men as to the origin of the world, the government of the universe, the phenomena of nature, and the yearnings and misgivings of the heart, are apt to lose their natural and straightforward expression, and to be repeated in a more or less distorted form, but even historical events. . . may be spoken of and handed down to later ages in a form decidedly mythological. After the laws that regulate the growth and decay of words have once been clearly established, instead of being any longer surprised at the breaking out of mythological phraseology, we almost wonder how any language could have escaped *what really may be called an infantine disease,* through which even the healthiest constitution ought to pass sooner of later. The origin of mythological phraseology. . . is always the same; *it is language forgetting herself*" (ibid; the present author's italics in both cases).

A disease of language; it is a favourite theme with Müller (and even more so with his opponents!) who often returned to the inflictions on thought caused by the imperfections of language. "I do not hesitate — Müller states in a lecture of 1871 on the philosophy of mythology (cf. Introduction Science of Religion p. 355) — to call the whole history of philosophy, from Thales dówn to Hegel, an uninterrupted battle against mythology, a constant protest of thought against language". To Max Müller mythology was, essentially, a corruption of the mind caused by the imperfections of language. Language suffered from mythology (Lectures Origin and Growth p. 44). In spite of all this, Müller had a genuine love of mythology because of its poetic qualities. Mythological language is poetical language, produced during the period which he called the mythopoetic age of language, when thought had to be expressed in active and personifying forms. "Poetry is older than prose, and abstract speech more difficult than the outpouring of a poet's sympathy with nature. It requires reflection to divest nature of her living expression. . ." (Comparative Mythology, Chips II p. 57). "Why should we wonder at the ancients, with their language throbbing with life and revelling in colour, if instead of the grey outlines of our modern thought, they threw out those living forms of nature, endowed with human powers, nay with powers more than human..." (ibid. p. 59). Poetical language prevailed and we can still find the traces of this mode of expression in Sanskrit and old Greek. "Hence, the mythe — 'The heroic maid Kyrene, who lived in Thessaly, is loved by Apollo and carried off to Libya'; while in modern language we would say, — 'The town of Kyrene, in Thessaly, sent a colony to Lybia, under the auspices of Apollo' " (Comparative Mythology, Chips II p. 68).

Myths are poetic renderings of events and natural phenomena, partly distorted because the names once used for natural bodies or specific objects were misinterpreted as names of living persons. A careful analysis of these names is required in order to explain a myth. The etymology of the name is the key to the interpretation of the story, and to that end Müller summons up the whole apparatus of comparative linguistics. Sanskrit in particular is exploited as a means of deriving etymological inferences regarding the names of the gods and the meaning of their history. One of his best known etymologies — and one of the few which still hold — is that of 'Jupiter' from the Greek 'Zeus-pater' and the Sanskrit 'Dyaus pitar'. It is not the place here to give a review of Müller's activities in this field. Suffice it to state that to him the main theme of mythology is a poetic rendering of the course of the heavenly bodies among which the sun is the most important. The reader is presented with a host of names for the rising and the setting sun, the dawn of morning and evening, the sky at various times of the day, the moon, the stars and the earth. Müller's contemporaries were deeply impressed and no wonder. Müller made a strong appeal to their romantic feelings of nature-love, and his colourful descriptions and penetrating comment contributed greatly to the persuasiveness of his argument. Actually, some of his explanations were acute enough, such as the following one: "if we find in Homer that Helios had seven herds of oxen, fifty in each herd, and that their number never grows and never decreases, surely we can easily discover in these 350 oxen the 350 days of the primitive year. And if then we read again, that the foolish companions of Ullysses did not return to their homes because they had killed the oxen of Helios... his companions wasted their time, or killed the days, i.e. the cattle of Helios" (Greek Legends, Chips II p. 165).

Here, however, appreciation must stop. A few successful explanations do not make up for serious errors in method and in linguistic philosophy. The separation of language and thought postulated by Müller does not constitute an operational basis for a theory of language. Neither does the hypothesis that roots are the first elements of language, nor his supposition that the oldest forms of language were inadequate expressions of the experiences of their speakers. Equally poorly founded is the supposition that the history of language is such a young one that the early Aryans spoke a language still in its initial phases of development at the time preceding the migration of one Aryan branch to the west and another to India. There is not a single linguist to-day who subscribes to any of these theories, and the same may be said of the great majority of the elaborate etymologies on which he wasted both his wit and his time. Nevertheless, during the 19th century his influence was deep and widely spread, and whereas his theories have been forgotten his belief in the heuristic value of etymologies still finds its supporters among those who are not professional linguists. A *caveat* is well in place here. An etymology may of course be helpful if it is a well-founded one. Unfortunately, well-founded etymologies are rare and one of the first lessons the student of mythology has to learn is that there is very little certainty in etymologies. Most of them never rise above the level of possibilities, and only a few of them are more than probabilities.

One aspect of mythology has thus far passed unnoticed, viz. its religious meaning. It is an important aspect because Max Müller was one of the early students of religious phenomena whose views carry weight in the history of the science of religion. His more important works in this field are his "Introduction to the Study of Religion" (1873) and his Hibbert Lectures "On the Origin and Growth of Religion as illustrated by the Religions of India" (1878). The latter is undoubtedly the best of the two, as it is the product of ripe and thoughtful consideration. Religion was a problem to Max Müller for more than one reason. In the first place there is the close connection between myth and religion; the foolishness of myth clashes with the sublimity of religion. Max Müller undoubtedly was a pious Christian himself, though contemporaries may have criticised him as a dangerous modernist. Here was another reason for his interest in the subject; the pious devotion of the Hindu had made a deep impression on him and he needed a broader basis for his thinking on religion than that offered by Christian theology. He found this basis in Kantian philosophy to which he added his own views, at least as far as religion is concerned. "Religion is a mental faculty which, independent of, nay, in spite of sense and reason, enables man to apprehend the infinite under different names and under various disguises" (Introduction Science of Religion p. 17; Lectures Origin and Growth p. 23). It is a faculty to apprehend, not to comprehend (Lectures Origin and Growth p. 52), an important distinction, because the 'potential energy of faith' is a specific faculty which must be well discerned from sense and reason and accepted as one of the fundamental faculties of man (ibid. p. 27). The infinite is present in all the finite which refers to it as it were. To Max Müller the infinite is the necessary and inescapable background of all experience to which all things refer.

The discussion of the subject as presented by Max Müller in the first of his lectures, is neither very clear nor very convincing. Nevertheless, it is worthy of our attention, because the argument that the visible things refer to the invisible is neither new nor outmoded. If it had been presented less as a declaration of faith and more as a matter of fact, Max Müller's argument might have offered a better basis for scientific enquiry than many theories thereafter.

Even so Max Müller's theory enabled him to construct a fairly closely-reasoned argument. First of all he turned to fetishism which, to most of his contemporaries, was the oldest form of religion. The etymology of the word (and this time his etymology is well-founded) suggests that fetishes are man-made objects, just like the amulets of the superstitious Portuguese sailors who coined the word (above, p. 12). These amulets of the Portuguese refer to the Saints; could not the fetishes of the African negroes refer to higher beings? Quoting Waitz and a number of other authors, he argues that higher forms of religion are by no means absent in Africa and he brings the point home when he refers 'inter alia' to the story of the man who in his flight picked up a stone which then became his fetish (above, p. 13). He raises the question: "How do these people, when they have picked up their stone or their shell, pick up at the same time the concepts of a supernatural power, or spirit, of god, and of worship paid to some unseen being?" (Lectures Origin and Growth p. 125).

The lecture on fetishism is interesting for other reasons as well. Here he brings up the concept of *mana*, first mentioned by Codrington in a letter dated July 7, 1877. He hails it — and not wholly unrightly so — as a Melanesian term for the infinite. The same chapter also gives him an opportunity to complain about the insufficiency and shallowness of the available ethnographic data, and again we must agree that, after all, his preference for data borrowed from Indian sources is understandable, even though we seriously doubt their value when in later chapters they must serve to demonstrate that a notion of the infinite was present at the dawn of history. We shall not enter into his argument in any detail. The one point of interest is that myth, in spite of its clumsiness, carries something of that notion of the infinite which filled the heart of the early beholder of nature when he burst out in poetic language to express his awe and admiration. The expression is strongest when he is contemplating objects intangible or half-tangible, and it is these objects which are first turned into objects of veneration of some sort because of the infinite apprehended in them. In a word like *déva*, originally meaning bright and used as "an epithet applicable to the fire, the sky, the dawn, the sun, also to the rivers and the trees, and the mountains" (Lectures Origin and Growth p. 214) the invisible and infinite takes shape until at last it becomes the terminus technicus for deity, i.e. for the manifestation of the infinite.

In his commentary on the Indian pantheon Max Müller coined a new term, *henotheism;* its literal meaning is the same as monotheism but the notion conveyed is a different one. Henotheism refers to the practice of regarding the deity invoked or venerated as the one and only god at the moment of worship. Another day a different deity may be worshipped in precisely equivalent terms. For the worshipper the deity is at that moment the only one, or at least the one who counts more than anyone else. The term was short-lived and it has never found general acceptance, probably because, as Wilh. Schmidt noted, the term refers to a specifically Indian practice of a late date.

Max Müller, once a man of great renown, amply survived his fame. He lived to see his theories rejected and much of the work of his later years is devoted to the defence of these theories against the attacks of his opponents, among whom Andrew Lang was one of the most spirited and indefatigable. Yet, these years were not without consolation. In 1898 he even became a member of the Privy Council, an unprecedented honour for the foreigner who published four volumes of "Chips from a German Workshop". In spite of the production of so many ill-founded and rightly rejected theories, the tribute was well-deserved; Max Müller has been one of the most outstanding promotors of religious and ethnographical studies of the 19th century.

4. The increase of ethnographic information up to 1870

The 18th century stood witness to an unprecedented growth of interest taken in distant peoples. Anyone who rummages among old books will discover the most unexpected evidence of this curious interest. Books of travels and descriptions of other peoples' customs must have been immensely popular. Expensive folio editions in many volumes found a ready market. Even in a small country like Holland with a very restricted number of readers, the authors of voluminous works succeeded in finding editors willing to print their works, and illustrate them with magnificent copperplates. These editions were not restricted to the works of famous travellers like Capt. Cook or De Bougainville; the minor ones too had their works printed in perfectly edited and well illustrated books. In addition, numerous compilations and extracts were published from the end of the 18th century. Anthropology was announcing itself; there was a new interest in the races of mankind and their different ways of life. The scientific value of most of these works is limited. Very few of them come up to the standard of Lafitau's description of the Iroquois. Most of the information they contain is haphazard and superficial. Nevertheless, they sufficed to enable a man like Meiners to write two volumes "Allgemeine kritische Geschichte der Religionen" at the early date of 1806 (see above, p. 13). In the course of the 19th century the stream of information steadily increased. In many respects the descriptions are superficial and defective, but they answered the apparent needs of all those readers who wished to increase their knowledge of foreign races. Moreover, some of these books were far more than mere descriptions or itineraries. One of the best was written in the shape of a picaresque novel, "The Adventures of Hajji Baba of Ispahan" by James Morier (1824), a real master-piece which combines extensive and really relevant

26

information with exquisite entertainment. During these years anthropology and art still go hand in hand, though a trend towards more strictly scientific methods is evident, as is well demonstrated by the works of Alexander von Humboldt. A first effort to classify this knowledge is Gustav Klemm's "Allgemeine Cultur-Geschichte der Menschheit", a work in ten volumes which appeared between 1843 and 1852. He paid much attention to material culture; he was a great collector himself and he repeatedly referred to the collections of his museum at Leipzig. Another topic which held his interest was that of the diversification of the human races. However, the scientific value of his observations is small. A distinction between culture and race is as lamentably lacking as one between acquired and hereditary properties. A good case is the following quotation (from Part I p. 196): "Man musz aber, wenn von einer Nation oder einer Rasse die Rede ist, diese als ein Individuum, als ein groszes gegliedertes Ganze auffassen, dessen eigenthümliches Gepräge sich nicht blosz aus seiner körperlichen Erscheinung, wie am Einzelnen, sondern namentlich in seiner Sitte, seinem Glauben, seiner Sprache und seiner Geschichte deutlich herausstellt". The basic confusion presented here was further complicated by his division of the races into active and passive ones, a dichotomy which opened the way to much prejudice in the discussion of his data.

Some twenty years later Klemm's theories were elaborately criticised by Theodor Waitz (1828-1864) in vol. I of his "Anthropologie der Naturvölker" (1859), the first of a work in 6 volumes, four of them written by Waitz himself, and the last two volumes by G. Gerland after the author's death. The work of Waitz is undoubtedly more modern and more systematic; in this more or less comprehensive general ethnography of the whole world the author made a serious attempt at systematic description. For many years the "Anthropologie der Naturvölker" was a frequently consulted and often quoted book which brought the author great fame. Tylor highly appreciated his work, and in 1937 a scholar like Robert Lowie hailed the first volume of Waitz's book as a worthy forerunner of Boas' "The Mind of Primitive Man" (History of Ethnological Theory p. 17). In his discussion of race Waitz is, indeed, liberal and rational, but his confidence in the heredity of acquired properties is just a bit too substantial to allow him much credit for it. Nevertheless, certain elements in his extensive comment on the natural talents of the various races are worth while, even to-day. These natural talents, he says, are not invariable; in part they are influenced by living conditions. The appreciation we owe him makes the methodological shortcomings all the more sharply felt. Waitz is a forerunner of anthropological science, not a founder. His work is a compendium of all the information which can be gathered from printed sources; it does not give a theory which makes clear distinctions and which systematises the various data. Anybody who delves into the works of Klemm and Waitz first, and then switches over to Tylor, will appreciate how much we owe to the clear and systematic approach of this founder of anthropological theory and — through Tylor — to Darwin and his theory of evolution which for the first time in history presented a clear picture of the early history and development of mankind, constructed on the basis of a plausible, all-embracing hypothesis. It is the great merit of the 'doctrine' of evolution that it supplies a model for the orderly arrangement of data. As such it has been an important stimulus for increasing precision in observation and analysis.

The idea of evolution was not Darwin's discovery. It had been in the air for almost a century when, in 1858, Darwin's "The Origin of Species by means of natural Selection" offered a valid hypothesis for the explanation of the biological process which made the idea of evolution operational. The stimulus emanating from it was enormous. The various data favouring the idea of evolution which had been collected in the course of the century now seemed to fall into place. A notorious case is the discovery made in 1838 by Boucher de Perthes that human beings using stone implements must have lived as early as the pleistocene period. Boucher de Perthes' conclusion was sound enough but it was not until 1858, the year of Darwin's famous publication, that it met with acknowledgement and acceptance.

Between 1860 and 1870 evolutionism made definite progress in the field of anthropological studies. Nevertheless, not all of the progress made can be ascribed to the influence of biological science. Since the idea of evolution had been broached for quite some time, it had a development of its own in other disciplines, inter alia in historical inquiries such as the study of the classics and of law, the latter under the stimulus of the historical school of thought initiated by F.K. von Savigny (1779-1861). With authors such as H. J. S. Maine (1822-1888), the author of "Ancient Law" (1861), and N. D. Fustel de Coulanges (1830-1889), who wrote "La Cité Antique" (1864), the influence of Darwinism is minimal, if it had any influence at all. Both authors give an outline of the development of ancient society and its legal institutions, taking Greece and Rome in the first place. In their reconstructions they confine themselves to verifiable historical facts ordered in an evolutionary sequence.

J. J. Bachofen (1815-1887) went a step further. In "Das Mutterrecht" (1861) he presented a theory of social evolution in which a hypothetical state of promiscuity preceded that of matriarchy which, in turn, was succeeded by that of patriarchy. The basic idea is evolutionist, but Bachofen did not take his inspiration from biological science but from his classical studies, his own rather confused mysticism, and his dislike of contemporary historiography. It is only with authors such as McLennan, Morgan and Tylor that the influence of Darwinistic thought makes itself really felt in anthropology. Of the three, the first (1827-1881) is at best a precursor. Lewis Morgan (1818-1881) on the other hand is really one of the founders of anthropological science; his "Systems of Consanguinity and Affinity of the human Family" (1871), an outstanding contribution to our knowledge of primitive society, was based on carefully and diligently collected data, which were partly the result of the author's own fieldwork. Yet, this study, important as it is, is confined to a selected aspect of culture. This is exactly where he differs from Tylor, who was the first to recognise human culture as a category of its own. Tylor presents culture as the all-embracing concept, including all the various aspects that previous authors had treated as items belonging to various separate disciplines such as law, comparative religion, classical studies, linguistics or archaeology. The concept of culture laid the foundation for a completely new discipline, viz. the study of man and of human development as the study of culture and cultural growth.

III

The classical period of evolutionist anthropology

1. Tylor (1832-1917) and the theory of animism

Edward Burnett Tylor was a self-made man. As the son of a well-to-do Quaker he was not allowed to visit the University, since Quakers did not go there. When he was 16 years of age he became an employee in his father's business until ill-health forced him to travel abroad. For a time he stayed in the south of France and then he went to America where he visited Mexico (1855/56). Here an older friend aroused his interest in Mexican archaeology, and Mexican archaeology became the subject of the first book he wrote (1861). Four years later, in 1865, the book followed which established his reputation as a scholar, viz. "Researches into the early History of Mankind". His principal work, the one which brought him world fame, was edited in 1871, namely "Primitive Culture, Researches into the Development of Mythology, Philosophy, Religion, Language, Art and Custom". Among his later publications there is only one book, "Anthropology, an Introduction to the Study of Man and Civilization" (1881). It is the first introduction to the new science of anthropology, which for an important part was the author's own creation.

Tylor's reputation and career did not suffer from the fact that he missed the benefit of a university education. Before he was forty years old (1871) he was made a member of the Royal Society. In 1883 he was nominated keeper of the University Museum at Oxford and in 1884 he became reader, and in 1896 the first professor of anthropology at Oxford University.

In a sense, "Researches into the early History of Mankind" is a prelude to "Primitive Culture". The author's purpose is clear: "In studying the phenomena of knowledge and art, religion and mythology, law and custom, and the rest of the complex whole which we call civilization, it is not enough to have in view the more advanced races, and to know their history... The explanation of the state of things in which we live has often to be sought in the condition of rude and early tribes" (p. 1). In a dozen essays dealing with various aspects of culture, he constantly returns to his main theme, viz. that there is a line of development connecting modern civilisation with primitive culture. Much attention is paid to gesture language and word language, to picture writing and word writing, and throughout the modern reader is impressed by the author's careful avoidance of daring theories. He gives much factual evidence on material culture and technical growth, and except for the unattractive comparison of savages to grown-up children (chapter VI), the book makes highly interesting reading. Modern students are inclined to think that evolutionists believed in a very strict and monolinear scheme of development which every culture has to live through. The accusation holds true for various evolutionists but not for Tylor. He definitely took account of the possibility of divergent development, and above all of culture change by contact and historical accident. Not only the mere possibility but also the probability of diffusion was recognised and even emphasised and demonstrated. The chapter dealing with the geographic distribution of myths is quite instructive in this respect.

Tylor returned to the theme in "Primitive Culture", a work in two volumes. We may safely state that it initiated a new era in anthropology, in particular in that branch which concentrated on problems of religion and mentality[5]. The argument is clear and straightforward. The opening sentence is of a lucid directness: "Culture or Civilization, taken in its wide ethnographic sense, is that complex whole which includes knowledge, belief, art, morals, law, custom, and any other capabilities and habits acquired by man as a member of society" (Primitive Culture I p. 1). Without any ado he claims that culture is not a matter of biological heredity but of acquired forms of behaviour originating in and from social conditions. He continues by stating that the study of culture is a subject "apt for the study of laws of human thought and action", and then summarises the basic principles of his approach in the following words: "On the one hand, the uniformity which so largely pervades civilization may be ascribed, in great measure, to the uniform action of uniform causes: while on the other hand its various grades may be regarded as stages of development or evolution". In less than a page the method and program of his scientific activity are presented in the most simple and unequivocal terms.

His statement is more than a simple statement of fact; here Tylor takes a position on two important issues of his day and he is well aware of it. The first is whether human thought and action are subject to laws, the second whether primitive culture is really primitive, i.e. culture at the very beginning of development, or the product of degeneration. About 1870 these issues were burning questions. If human action is subject to law what is left of free will? Does not the belief in creation imply that at his creation man was endowed with at least some of the fundamentals of culture? For Adam spoke when he was in paradise and gave names to all cattle and fowl and to

[5] References are to the 4th edition. There is a paperback edition edited in 1958 by Radin (Harper's Torchbooks) which is an exact reprint except that vol. II opens with chapter XI, which was the closing chapter of vol. I in the earlier editions.

every beast of the field, even before he had a companion in Eve.

Tylor does not enter into philosophy. To those who wish to deny that human will is subject to law, he holds out that in daily practice everybody takes account of the motivations supposed to define other people's acts. We base our expectations on our knowledge of these motivations. This implies that, up to a degree, human activities are predictable, a property implied in the notion of law. Quoting the remark of a Bechuana chief that one event is always the son of another, and we must never forget the parentage (ibid. pp. 4 f.), he argues that it is exactly this parentage which is important. Historians study the connections between events, we ought to study the similarities in human cultures and institutions. Our knowledge is wholly inadequate to predict the course of history or to make a design of the future, but what we can do is to compare similarities of institutions and implements in order to find out what we can learn about the course of their development.

This leads him to the issue of evolution or degeneration. To solve the question he raises two points which are methodologically relevant. Ignoring the theological argument he first of all dissects culture into its parts. "A first step in the study of civilization is to dissect it into details, and to classify these in their proper groups" (ibid. p. 7). Thus, weapons can be classed under spear, club, sling, bow and arrow; textile arts under matting, netting and weaving, etc.; in rites we can discern sacrifices made to the ghosts of the dead and other spiritual beings, the purification of moral uncleanliness by water or fire and so forth. There are hundreds of items, and the ethnographer studies their distribution just like the biologist studies the distribution of species, both apart and in combination with other species. "Just as the catalogue of all the species of plants and animals of a district represents its Flora and Fauna, so the list of all items of the general life of a people represents that whole which we call its culture" (ibid. p. 8). The various items are for the ethnographer (we would say anthropologist, but Tylor has a preference for ethnographer) what the species are for the biologist.

The second step of methodological relevance is the ordering of items into series demonstrating how one type evolved from another. A first instance presented to the reader is that of the history of firearms; the wheel-lock was replaced by the flint-lock which, in turn, gave way to the percussion-lock. Their history is well documented, while the history of the fire-drill is not. Yet, no one can doubt that the drill worked by a cord or bow is a later improvement on the primitive instrument twirled between the hands (ibid. p. 15). Everywhere we meet with progressive development. The stone age is older than the bronze age which was followed by the iron age. Although development is not strictly unilinear and backslides do occur, for example when people return to older, more primitive techniques, the general trend of history is one of progressive development. He strongly opposes the theory of degeneration, *inter alia* by pointing out that whenever we start digging for artefacts, the deeper we go the more simple and primitive the artefacts we find. We never find the finer, better and higher developed items in the lower strata.

The clinching argument of his reconstruction of developmental history is his theory of survivals. Survivals "are processes, customs, opinions, and so forth, which have been carried on by force of habit into a new state of society different from that in which they had their original home, and they thus remain as proofs and examples of an older condition of culture out of which a newer one has evolved" (ibid. p. 16). There are thousands of instances of survivals: midsummer bonfires, the Breton peasants' All Souls' supper for the dead, as well as so many other things, which all confirm that there is a progressive development and stand witness to the fact that our own society was once similar to so many primitive societies to-day. "Civilization may be looked upon as a general improvement of mankind by higher organization of the individual and of society, to the end of promoting at once man's goodness, power and happiness" (ibid. p. 27).

The weak spot of Tylor's theory of survivals is obvious. No one to-day would subscribe to the idea that customs or opinions are 'carried on by force of habit'. Habit has not enough force of itself to have that effect. Yet, however defined, nobody can deny that we are surrounded by traces of older phases of our culture reminding us of the past. Bow and arrow, the discarded weapons of the hunter and warrior, are still in use as toys. Written sources testify to the fact that there is a continuous development, and where such sources are lacking, comparative studies and archaeological excavations confirm that an unbroken chain of evolutionary growth links modern civilisation with primitive culture.

In the early 19th century customs and notions reminiscent of primitive ways of thought were not as uncommon among the less educated classes of Europe as they are to-day. Tylor gives numerous instances. "The Hessian lad thinks that he may escape the conscription by carrying a baby-girl's cap in his pocket — a symbolic way of repudiating manhood. Modern Servians, dancing and singing, lead about a girl dressed in leaves and flowers, and pour bowls of water over her to make the rain come. Sailors becalmed will sometimes whistle for a wind; but in other weather they hate whistling at sea, which raises a whistling gale" (ibid. pp. 118 f.). Customs and notions of this kind are survivals, originated in an age of low intellectual development. The obvious parallels to these notions are found in the magical arts of primitive peoples.

Magic, and occult science in general, is based on a faulty manipulation of the association of ideas. "Man, as yet in a low intellectual condition, having come to associate in thought those things which he found by experience to be connected in fact, proceeded erroneously to invert this action, and to conclude that association in thought must involve similar connexion in reality" (ibid. p. 116). The Jeypore witch in Orissa "lets down a ball of thread through her enemy's roof to reach his body, that by putting the other end in her own mouth she may suck his blood" (ibid. p. 117). "The Zulu may be seen chewing a bit of wood, in order, by this symbolic act, to soften the heart of the man he wants to buy oxen from, or of the woman he wants for a wife" (ibid. p.118). The symbolism implied is of the same kind as that applied by the Hessian lad and the Servian rainmakers.

Tylor did not elaborate on his theory of magic. He had done this already in his "Researches" (chapter VI). Twenty years later Tylor's theory was taken up again by Frazer in his "Golden Bough" (below, pp.56 f.). Our author paid far more attention to mythology. Foremost among the factors which transfigure daily life and experience in terms of myth is the childlike state of the mind of early man, which recognises the operation of personal life and will in every detail of his world (Primitive Culture I pp. 284 f.). A more detailed survey of the various forms of animism and their origin will be given below; for the present it is sufficient to refer to Tylor's opinion that the personifications of myth have their close parallels in the personifications given to objects by young children in their play. In primitive culture these personifications have a very powerful sense of reality; far from being a matter of poetic fancy they are experienced as perfectly real. In the further analysis of mythological thinking Tylor points out that the origin of myth must be sought even farther afield than in the development of animism. The mythological explanation of the course of nature "is but a part of a far wider mental process. It belongs to that great doctrine of analogy from which we have gained so much of our apprehension of the world around us . . . Analogies which are but fancy to us were to man of past ages reality" (ibid. pp. 296 f.). The reference to his theory of magic is obvious, and if Tylor stressed animism as the most original form of religion, he was nevertheless well aware of the effects of the peculiar ways of thought which are responsible for magical thinking, or primitive mentality as it came to be termed later. The erroneous interpretation of the association of ideas and of allegory are part and parcel of his theory of primitive thought.

Tylor's interpretation of myth differs substantially from Max Müller's, a fact cautiously formulated in his courteous statement: "I am disposed to think (differing here in some measure from Professor Max Müller's view of the subject) that the mythology of the lower races rests especially on a basis of real and sensible analogy, and that the great expansion of verbal metaphor into myth belongs to more advanced periods of civilization" (ibid. p. 299). Of course, Tylor does not deny that many myths are nature-myths. On the contrary, a whole chapter is devoted to this category. However, he has more reservations than Müller, and he warns explicitly against rash explanations, taking as one of his instances the case of Julius Caesar. If we did not know better, Caesar's life-history could very easily be interpreted as a solar myth: "his splendid course as in each new land he came, and saw, and conquered; his desertion of Cleopatra; his ordinance of the solar year for men; his death at the hand of Brutus. . .; his falling. . . shrouding himself in his cloak to die in darkness" (ibid. pp.319 f.). Though honesty requires us to admit that Max Müller once sounded a similar warning (Greek Legends, Chips II p. 169), Tylor is certainly the more cautious of the two. Neither does he restrict the field of mythology to nature-myths. On the contrary, he introduces a number of other categories besides, such as philosophical myths, geological myths, myths of the relation of apes to men, myths attached to legendary or historical persons, etymological and eponymic myths, fables, and so forth. His compass is wider, the sources of the myth-making mentality he mentions are more variegated, and above all related to the more fundamental dispositions of the human mind. Without sharing Tylor's views it is certainly evident that he made a great step forward. Where Müller reduced myth to error, Tylor went back to general dispositions. Unfortunately, the course he steered ultimately led him to a theory subject to just the same objections, viz. that he reduced religion to erroneous thought.

The repeated references to animism and the impact of personification emphasised in Tylor's treatment of mythology, imply that myth is seen as part of the realm of religion, the subject to which the greater part of his work is devoted. His definition of religion is brief and formal: *"the belief in spiritual beings"* (ibid. p. 424; italics ours). It is a minimum definition, exactly the kind of definition he needed for including the more rudimentary forms of religion of the lower races as well as of the highest, i.e. those of modern society (loc. cit.). He does not dwell long on the reasons for chosing this definition; he simply states that the belief in spiritual beings is universal and found among even the most primitive peoples — at least as far as his own information showed. A survey of the data concerning those peoples reported to have no religion at all, reveals that these reports are denied by fact. In all these cases belief in spiritual beings of some sort is evident (ibid. pp.417-424). Of course, this does not prove that non-religious savages do not exist or have not existed, but the hypothetical condition of man before he arrived at the religious stage of culture cannot be brought forward as an argument in a theory of the natural evolution of ideas, since such a theory must be based on factual evidence (ibid. p.425). For years to come, the question whether or not non-religious peoples do occur remained a much disputed point, but this need not concern us here.

Animism was the name Tylor gave to the belief in spiritual beings. He might have chosen the word spiritism but as the term had already been monopolised by a particular modern sect, he preferred the term animism to designate the various forms of belief in spiritual beings in its world-wide sense (ibid. p.426). This animism is described as "the deep-lying doctrine of Spiritual Beings, which embodies the very essence of Spiritualistic as opposed to Materialistic philosophy (ibid. p.425). "Animism characterizes tribes very low in the scale of humanity, and thence ascends, deeply modified in its transmission, but from first to last preserving an unbroken continuity, into the midst of high modern culture" (ibid. p.426). "Animism in its full development, includes the belief in souls and in a future state, in controlling deities and subordinate spirits, these doctrines practically resulting in some kind of active worship" (ibid. p.427). Rather extensively he dwells on the fact that the moral element, so important in higher forms of religion, is "little represented in the religion of the lower races" (loc. cit.). It is not that a moral sense is lacking among these races — the proofs to the contrary are more than sufficient — but that the conjunction of animistic philosophy and ethics is made at a later stage of development.

Before we enter into details a cautionary note must be made. Animism is called a philosophy as well as a doctrine, "a world-wide philosophy, of which belief is the theory and worship is the practice". It would be entirely wrong to take these expressions for a metaphor; Tylor must be taken at his word. Animism is a system, though in various stages of development, but still a system, and the word doctrine ought to be taken literally. Very consistently the author speaks of the two great dogmas of animism, the first "concerning souls of individual creatures, capable of continued existence after the death or the destruction of the body; [the] second concerning other spirits upward to the rank of powerful deities" controlling the material world and man's life hereafter (ibid. p.426).

The first point to be considered is the origin of the belief in souls on which that in spirits has been modelled. Apparently thoughtful men were arrested by two groups of biological problems. "In the first place, what is it that makes the difference between a living body and a dead one; what causes waking, sleep, trance, disease, death? In the second place, what are those human beings which appear in dreams and visions?" (ibid. p.428). The first problem raises the notion that there is something in man which could be called life. The second, even more difficult, suggests that during the dream something in man leaves the body to visit other places, a something resembling a shade or phantom, because the apparitions in dreams are shady. The problem is all the more real because primitive man has not the slightest reason for sharing our opinion that dreams are empty.

The next step for our primitive philosopher (a favourite expression with Tylor) must have been to combine the two notions, that of the life and the phantom. Each of them is a manifestation of the body; why should not they belong together as forms of one and the same soul? If considered as united, "the result is that well-known conception which may be described as an apparitional soul, a ghost-soul. This, at any rate, corresponds with the actual conception of the personal soul or spirit among the lower races, which may be defined as follows: It is a thin, unsubstantial human image, in its nature a sort of vapour, film, or shadow; the cause of life and thought in the individual it animates; independently possessing the personal consciousness and volition of its corporal owner, past or present; capable of

36

leaving the body far behind, to flash swiftly from place to place; mostly impalpable and invisible, yet also manifesting physical power, and especially appearing to men waking or asleep as a phantasm separate from the body of which it bears the likeness; continuing to exist and appear to men after the death of that body; able to enter into, possess and act in the bodies of other men, of animals, and even of things" (ibid. p.429).

The picture given is illustrated and exemplified step by step by a host of instances, systematically collected from all over the world. We shall not follow Tylor in this and instead consider the case the late A. W. Nieuwenhuys, an inveterate Tylorian and my first teacher of anthropology, preferred to give to his students as an illustration of the belief in the peregrinations of the soul during the dream, a case which he probably borrowed from Wilken. Two men in western Java pass the night together. One is awake and sees a mouse leaving the open mouth of his sleeping comrade. The mouse enters the rice-barn nearby and after some time she returns and re-enters the mouth of his friend who now wakes up and tells that he has had a terrible dream. During his sleep he visited an enormous granary from where he was chased by a big, ferocious tiger. Needless to say that the mouse had met the cat kept in the rice-barn.

An important point is that the soul is not 'tied' to the body. The soul lives in the body but can leave it at will, a fact which may result in the owner's sickness or even death. The independence of the soul from the body is apparent at death; the soul lives on and continues to appear to the living in dreams and visions. In case of sickness the soul may be conjured up by a shaman who has to enter into trance, either to meet the gods or to find the soul. The variations are legion and we should carefully avoid conceiving of souls and their actions in a too dogmatic or uniform way. Some peoples even believe that every individual has more than one soul. Others again believe that some souls are werewolves, attacking and devouring the souls of their fellow-men during their sleep. Particularly active are the souls of the recently dead, who often appear in dreams and visions. Specific attention is paid to dreams. The information presented by dreams and visions may be evaluated so highly that they come to be stimulated by fasting or by the use of narcotics.

The notions on future life are widely divergent. Representations concerning the fate of the soul after death are most elaborate among peoples living in the barbaric stage, the second of the three stages discerned by Tylor. The first of them is the savage stage, that of hunters and collectors living mainly in the stone age. The barbaric stage is characterised by primitive agriculture (horticulture) and/or husbandry. Civilised life, the third stage, begins with the discovery of writing (cf. Tylor, Anthropology p.18). The classification is a rather crude one which has never been strictly and uniformly applied, neither by Tylor nor by anybody else. Malinowski for example, classified his Trobrianders as savages, though they are able horticulturists.

The Batak of Sumatra who are literate and can boast their own script, have never been classified as civilised. Fortunately, in the present context a strict classification is hardly relevant. The main point is that in the barbaric stage the representations concerning the dead and their way of life are more variegated and more elaborate than in both the preceding and the following stage. In the last stage these representations lose much of the detail and certainty of the barbaric phase. Among savages the notions of the hereafter are extremely vague and variable. Life in the land of the dead usually resembles that on earth, sometimes it is considered to be better, then again to be worse. A connection between life after death and good behaviour before is lacking. Punishment and reward of sins and virtues respectively are the products of a higher stage of civilisation. Among savages the relations between religion and ethics are insignificant and the notion of a last judgement is lacking.

The doctrine of souls, once developed, offered the native in his "early childlike philosophy... the direct key to the understanding of nature at large", by referring its phenomena "to the wilful action of pervading spirits" (Primitive Culture II p.108). The solution is not the outcome of spontaneous fancy but of "the reasonable inference that effects are due to causes" (ibid). Primitive man, even in his savage state, did not lack the notion and power of rationality. *"Spirits are simply personified causes"* (ibid; italics ours).

In this brief and clear statement Tylor is again at his best. To prove his point, he refers to the apparent similarities between souls and spirits. Just like souls, spirits are able to enter into man, thus causing the phenomenon of possession. Demoniacal possession occurs more frequently than possession by souls, and an exorcist or a shaman is needed to cure the patient. A special case of 'incorporation' is that of fetishism, a term applied by Tylor to "the doctrine of spirits embodied in, or attached to, or conveying influence through, certain material objects". He continues: "Fetishism will be taken as including the worship of 'stocks and stones', and thence it passes by an imperceptible gradation into Idolatry" (ibid. p.144). Heavenly bodies such as the sun can also become fetishes, if it is thought that they 'incorporate' spirits.

The acceptance of the term fetishism and the new content given to the concept must be condemned as a regrettable lapse. It is one of the rare occasions that Tylor can be accused of adding to confusion, in this case to the confusion round an already confusing concept. In many other respects Tylor's argument is a marvel of lucidity. We shall refrain from enumerating the various categories of spirits discussed and classified in Tylor's book. The great variety need not raise problems provided we keep in mind "first, that spiritual beings are modelled by man on his primary conception of his own human soul, and second, that their purpose is to explain nature on the primitive childlike theory that it is truly and throughout 'Animated Nature" (ibid. p.184).

There is often a difference in rank and importance between the various categories of souls and spirits. Among the souls a difference is made between those of ancestors and other souls. The former are protectors and helpers, rewarding those who respect the traditions, and punishing trespassers. The worship of the 'manes', the ancestors, is an important form of religion.

Spirits, too, are differentiated, both according to their character and their importance. There are good and evil spirits, the latter being called demons. Even among savages some spirits rank above the others because of their importance. Thus among the Australians "Biam gives ceremonial songs and causes disease, and is perhaps the same as Baiame the creator" (ibid. p.249). Biam is one of Tylor's many examples of "mythic figures of higher divinity" (loc. cit.). A very important category is that of the fetish-deities, the spirits of sun and moon, heaven and earth, rain, thunder and fire. Another major class is that of the deities who have certain functions to perform, for example in agriculture, in the land of the dead, and in war. The ancestors too may become deities; sometimes the first ancestor even ranks as a kind of supreme deity.

Special attention is paid to the frequent occurrence of a dualistic organisation of the deities; in the lower societies it is a dualism not of good and evil, but one of cosmological oppositions such as heaven and earth, or sun and moon. In a more progressive state of civilisation the gods constitute a kind a pantheon in which one of them may gradually become more powerful than the others. Tylor proceeds with great caution in his discussion of the evolution of animism into forms of polytheism and ultimately into monotheism. The development he sketches does not by any means resemble the monolinear kind of scheme so often presented as the essence of his theory. He is well aware of the wide range covered by divergent forms of religion, even at the lower stages of civilisation. "If the monotheistic criterion be simply made to consist in the Supreme Deity being held as creator of the universe and chief of the spiritual hierarchy, then its application to savage and barbaric theology will lead to perplexing consequences", as the belief in a Supreme Creator is found among various peoples pertaining to the lower stages of cultural development (ibid. p.332). The term monotheism must be reserved for those cases in which the distinctive attributes of deity are assigned to none save the Almighty Creator. In this "strict sense, no savage tribe of monotheists has been ever known. Nor are any fair representatives of the lower culture in a strict sense pantheists. The doctrine which they do widely hold. . . is polytheism culminating in the rule of one supreme divinity. High above the doctrine of souls, of divine manes, of local naturespirits, of the great deities of class and element, there are to be discerned in 'barbaric' theology shadowings, quaint or majestic, of the conception of a Supreme Deity, henceforth to be traced onward in expanding power and brightening glory along the history of religion" (loc. cit.; italics ours).

In some cases these foreshadowings of higher religion among savage and barbaric peoples are due to missionary influences, but in others they have to be recognised as genuine. In the civilised state these concepts may lead to the notion of "a heavenly pantheon arranged on the model of an earthly political constitution, where... the King is the supreme Deity" (ibid. p.335). "Among thoughtful men whose theory of the soul animating the body has already led them to suppose a divine spirit animating the huge mass of earth or sky, this idea needs but a last expansion to become a doctrine of the universe as animated by one greatest, all-pervading divinity, the World-Spirit. Moreover, where speculative philosophy grapples with the vast fundamental world-problem, the solution is attained by ascending from the Many to the One, by striving to discern through and beyond the Universe a First Cause" (ibid.).

Here at last we enter the region of transcendental theology which pertains to the world's great religions. These religions still retain clear traces of former stages of development, of the belief in spirits and souls and of the dualistic opposition of powers of good and evil. These traces, most manifest among the lower classes of the peoples involved, confirm that these higher religions are the products of evolution, and not the lower ones of degeneration. The elements of higher religion occurring at the lower stages are products of natural religion which "in no way transcend the powers of the low-cultured mind to reason out" (Primitive Culture II p.336). "In the higher animism these doctrines [of lower forms of animism] are retained side by side with other and special beliefs, of which the religions of the lower world show scarce a germ" (ibid. p.357). The development from lower animism to higher, from souls to spirits, to gods and supreme being is presented as a very gradual one. The successive grades overlap to such an extent that transition marks are obliterated. The impression of gradualness is enhanced by a lack of distinction in Tylor's terminology. We search in vain for a definition of the difference between spirits, deities and gods. It is evident that deities and gods are 'higher' and more distinctive personalities than spirits, but the exact difference remains undisclosed.

At the end of his sketch of religious evolution, Tylor apologises that "the intellectual rather than the emotional side of religion has... been kept in view", although even among the rudest savages "religious belief is associated with intense emotion, with awful reverence, with agonizing terror, with rapt ecstasy when sense and thought utterly transcend the common level of daily life" (ibid. pp.358 f.). The apology should not be taken too seriously. On the same page he continues: "My task has been here not to discuss Religion in all its bearings, but to outline the great doctrine of Animism... and to show its transmission along the lines of religious thought". When all is said and done, to Tylor the doctrine is the essence of religion. It is a doctrine common to all peoples.

The rationalist line of thought, implied in the emphasis on the doctrine, is paramount too in Tylor's discussion of rites and ceremonies. We confine our survey to prayer and sacrifice. Prayer is "the address of personal spirit to personal spirit" (ibid. p.364). "Prayer is a reasonable and practical act... It has not indeed been placed everywhere on record as the necessary outcome of animistic belief, for especially at low levels of civilization there are many races who distinctly admit the existence of spirits, but are not positively known to pray to them. Beyond this lower level, however, animism and ceremonial prayer become nearly coterminous" (loc. cit.). The data borrowed from ethnography "agree with an opinion that prayer appeared in the religion of the lower culture, but that in this its earlier stage it was unethical. The accomplishment of desire is asked for, but desire is as yet limited to personal advantage. It is at later and higher moral levels, that the worshipper begins to add to his entreaty for prosperity the claim for help toward virtue and against vice, and prayer becomes an instrument of morality" (ibid.).

Sacrifice is closely connected with prayer. "As prayer is a request made to a deity as if he were a man, so sacrifice is a gift made to a deity as if he were a man" (ibid. p.375). Its prototype is the gift presented to a chief when making a petition for help. In its first stage of development the offering is a gift, accepted by the deity out of appreciation for the gift itself. Later making sacrifices acquires the meaning of an act of homage towards the deity, and in its highest phase the offering becomes an act of abnegation, the sacrificer denying himself the benefit of something precious to him. The most striking cases are found in human sacrifice, as among the Phoenicians, who sacrificed their dearest children to propitiate the angry gods (ibid. p.398).

The practice of sacrifice raises a host of problems. How can men imagine that the spirits or the gods are in need of anything? According to Tylor the problem did not arise at a low stage of civilisation. The wish to make a gift prevailed, and the problem as to whether the deity really availed himself of the offering, could hardly have arisen at all: for example when a sacrifice was made by throwing the offering into the sea; or when the priest ate the offering as a substitute for the deity. Often only part of the gift is dedicated to the gods, preferably the blood which seeps into the earth or, in case of a holocaust, the smoke of the burned offering. Many peoples — in Africa, Indonesia, Polynesia and the Caribbean Islands — solved the problem by accepting that the gods take the spiritual essence of the offering, leaving the material part for the sacrificer to enjoy.

"Through the history of sacrifice, it has occurred to many nations that cost may be economized without impairing efficiency" (ibid. p.399). "In Madagascar the head of the sacrificed beast is set up on a pole, and the

41

blood and fat are rubbed on the stones of the altar, but the sacrificers and their friends and the officiating priest devour the whole carcase" (loc. cit.). More convincing cases are those in which one animal is substituted for another — for example a goat offered as a sacrifice is said to be a cow; or when the offering consists of cakes of dough or wax in the shape of the beasts for which they are presented as symbolic substitutes. Elsewhere a human sacrifice is forestalled by offering a finger, or — in case a child should have been offered — by substituting a lock of hair. Human sacrifice looms large in Tylor's work as it did in that of all 19th century anthropologists. Theoretically of greater interest is the value attached to the gift-theory, which is brought forward as the rational and fundamental explanation of sacrifice.

In his conclusion Tylor stresses the practical value of our new knowledge of the evolution of civilisation "as a source of power destined to influence the course of modern ideas and actions" (ibid. p.443). The science of ethnography, while confirming the essential correctness of the doctrine of evolution, has a practical function of making known to all concerned what, in our own culture, is "received on its own direct evidence, what is ruder ancient doctrine reshaped to answer modern ends, and what is but time-honoured superstition in the garb of modern knowledge" (ibid. p.445). Theology should apply the results of ethnography and adapt its doctrine to the exigencies of modern scientific thought. The ethnographer is called upon to set his mind on the advancement of civilisation, inter alia by exposing "the remains of crude old culture which have passed into harmful superstition, and to mark these out for destruction. Thus, active at once in aiding progress and in removing hindrance, the science of culture is essentially a reformer's science" (ibid. p.453). The final admonition which marks the end of the work, did not pass unheeded.

Rarely has a scientific work been welcomed as eagerly as Tylor's Primitive Culture. When a second edition appeared two years later, the book had already been translated into German and Russian. Nobody took offence at Tylor's strongly rationalistic approach, or noted the discrepancy between his theory of magic and the sound method of reasoning displayed by his primitive philosopher who at one time goes ahead in childlike fashion and at another like a fully mature person. On the contrary, for years on end the way shown by Tylor was followed without hesitation and with a minimum of criticism by all students of religion. They had good reason to do so; initially the new theory of religion found strong support in the results of ethnographic research carried out between 1870 and 1890.

Unfortunately, this favourable result was not the effect of improved methods of fieldwork. Tylor and his contemporaries paid very little attention to research methods. This is not as strange as it seems at first sight. The early students of culture were not primarily interested in the description of specific cultures, but in classifying the facts noted in a great variety of cultures into an all-inclusive, stratified system of development, valid for all tribes and peoples. It was more important to bring together data on selected subjects from all over the world for comparative purposes than to collect information on a single culture and to investigate its consistency. This predilection for widespread data militated against circumstances favourable for research by trained experts whose investigations must necessarily be restricted to a single area. It took many years before this inevitable restriction was really accepted, and before experts well prepared for their task set out to make detailed studies of single cultures. That does not mean that these experts were trained anthropologists in the sense attached to the term today. Most, if not all of them, had specialised in another branch of science; it was these specialists who, toward the end of the century, set new standards of research, and introduced better methods of investigation. Here the names must be mentioned of Franz Boas in the U.S.A., Baldwin Spencer in Australia, and the members of the Cambridge Expedition to Torres Straits, Haddon, Rivers, Seligman and Ray, in Britain.

Observers trained to have a more critical attitude soon found out how easily suggestive questions provoke answers confirming the belief in the most classic forms of animism. The danger of falsifying data was brought home to me years ago, when I did fieldwork in Lombok, Indonesia. With a few people we walked through a forest, somewhere in the southwest of the island. Suddenly our guide gesticulated that we should be silent. He pointed to an open spot. It was a sacred place which had to be approached in silence. If I had asked whether a spirit lived there, they would have answered in the affirmative, even though this was not how they saw it. To them the sacred place simply meant that they should be silent and nothing more. Scores of observers have, by questioning, contributed substantially to the number of spirits, even encouraging their informants to create new ones according to the pleasure of the inquisitive gentlemen. Older observers also tended to explain all sorts of taboos from the spirit-hypothesis. Even mourning for the dead and the use of mourning-dress were explained by it: extensive mourning as an act to please the ghost of the deceased, mourning-dress as a disguise in order not to be recognised by him. As long as detailed knowledge of other aspects of the people's behaviour is lacking, explanations of this kind will do. However, they become untenable as soon as more and better information becomes available, for example when it is found out that the 'disguised' mourner is camping day and night on the deceased's grave where he is sure to be found by the haunting ghost.

If the defective state of ethnography favoured Tylor's theory, its strongest support was borrowed from the contemporary trend of positivistic evolutionism of which Herbert Spencer (1820-1893) was the leader in Britain. Spencer's authority, although not undisputed in orthodox circles, was great, and his 'Principles of Sociology' were widely read. In Part I (1876) he advanced theories which were greatly akin to those of Tylor's. Spencer too found among all peoples a belief in the survival of the dead which provides the basis for the worship of the ancestors, the form of religion from which higher forms of religion developed.

Spencer's contemporaries looked to him as an important authority in anthropology, mainly because of his fame as a philosopher. From the point of view of ethnography the Dutchman G. A. Wilken (1847-1894) is of greater interest. His 'Verspreide Geschriften' (edited in four volumes by F. D. E. van Ossenbruggen in 1912) give much information on Indonesia where he was born, the son of a missionary. As a young man he obtained a great deal of first-hand experience as a junior member of the civil administration, before he became professor at Leiden where he held the chair of 'land- en volkenkunde van Nederlandsch-Indië', i.e. geography and ethnography of the Netherlands-Indies, a chair instituted in the early sixties for the training of future civil servants of the colonial administration. His more widely known works are the series of articles edited under the title of "Het Animisme bij de Volken van den Indischen Archipel" (Indische Gids 1884, 1885) and "Über das Haaropfer und einige andere Trauergebräuche bei den Völkern Indonesiens" (Revue Coloniale 1886, 1887). Wilken was an ardent supporter of Tylor and a typical representative of the school of thought which used animism as a master-key for the explanation of all problems presented by primitive custom. The Ambonnese gardener, who goes through the motions of coitus with his naked body pressed against the stem of his clove-tree, urging the tree to greater fertility by repeatedly crying out 'more cloves', is supposed to believe that the tree is animated. According to Wilken he ascribes to the tree a personality with human properties and impulses including the sexual ones, which only need to be excited in order to stimulate the tree into fertility (Verspreide Geschriften III pp. 45 f.) The interpretation obviously goes beyond the facts; although the personification of the tree is evident, it is not personified to the extent that Wilken suggests. He fails to appreciate the meaning of symbolism, the phenomenon which characterises the act. In the interpretation of this and of other similar cases, Wilken bases his interpretation of the facts not on their cultural context, but on the notion that certain customs belong to a given stage of cultural evolution. Animism is a doctrine, and those who accept it apply it in a doctrinaire way.

Tylor's influence was far-reaching. It also extended — in conformity to his wishes — to the world of theologians. The bible-critical school, usually heralded by the names of Kuenen and Wellhausen, openly sympathised with his ideas. An outstanding case is that of Tiele (like Kuenen, professor of theology at Leiden), one of the founders of the discipline of the history of religion as taught in the faculty of theology. However, there is one theologian who is far more important than those who followed in Tylor's wake, viz. Robertson Smith. He steered his own course — one significant enough to exert a lasting influence.

2. *W. Robertson Smith (1846-1894) and the theory of sacrifice*

W. Robertson Smith was a man of many talents. He studied theology, Semitic languages and mathematics. At the age of 24 he became professor of Eastern (i.e. Semitic) languages and Old Testament studies at Free Church College in Scotland. His contributions on the Old Testament for the new edition of the Encyclopaedia Britannica brought him into conflict with his church. A five year long process resulted in his summary removal from his chair (1881). Two years later he was appointed professor of Arabic at Cambridge. Among his works there are two which are relevant to anthropologists, viz. "Kinship and Marriage in early Arabia" (1885) and "Lectures on the Religion of the Semites" (1889). The latter is the really important one of the two, but the former cannot be ignored since it brought up the subject of totemism. Before 1885 very little attention had been paid to totemism, and it must be discussed at some length before we can proceed with Robertson Smith's more specific contributions to the science of religion.

Totemism can be defined as the belief in some sort of a supernatural relationship between a group of people — in some cases an individual — and a species of animals or plants or some material object. In substance our formulation does not differ very widely from the one given two years after the publication of Robertson Smith's "Kinship and Marriage" by J. G. Frazer in his "Totemism" (1887): "A totem is a class of material objects which a savage regards with superstitious respect, believing that there exists between him and every member of the class an intimate and altogether special relation" (p.3 of the reprint in Frazer, Totemism and Exogamy I). The word totem is an American Indian word, appearing in print for the first time in 1791 as 'totam' in J. Long, "Voyages and Travels of an Indian Interpreter". J. F. McLennan devoted three articles to the subject in the Fortnightly Review of 1869/70 under the title of "The Worship of Animals and Plants". He refrained from putting forward a theory about its origin, as did Tylor in his "Primitive Culture" (II p.235). The latter, calling it an obscure and complex subject, showed that he was well aware of the difficulties involved.

Herbert Spencer was more daring. Soon after McLennan's articles in the Fortnightly Review, he published in the same journal a theory on the origin of totemism, in which he followed in Max Müller's footsteps. He thought that the custom must be derived from the imperfections of early language. A man who was called by the name of an animal during his lifetime, would be worshipped as an ancestor after his death. Subsequent worshippers, no longer aware that the animal name of their ancestor was only a name, believed that their ancestor had really been an animal and consequently proceeded to worship the species as well. The theory is one of a series of fables, invented one after another to explain the origin of totemism. They all share the same merit and the same weakness: inventiveness and incredibility. These early theorists erroneously took totemism for just another doctrine, composed of a number of associated but separate dogmas. We shall not dwell here on any of their divergent speculations; we shall return later to some of them. Here the one thing we need is a concise survey of the various forms of totemism which occur among primitive people in different parts of the world. We shall start with its most common form — clan-totemism.

A clan is a unilineal, usually exogamous kingroup, the members of which trace their descent back to a common traditional ancestor. A more precise definition runs as follows: a unilineal, usually exogamous kingroup, the members of which derive their identity from a common symbol, often by descent from a common, traditional ancestor or group of ancestors. The latter definition is also applicable to totem-clans, a totem being such a common symbol as is inferred here. Totem-clans are found in many parts of the world; their members claim to have a specific relation to a certain species of animals or plants, sometimes to a material or immaterial object. The nature of this relationship is highly divergent in content, but invariably it has a supernatural component of some sort. All the members of the clan consciously share in it; often they express this by saying that the totem belongs to them. Fairly often the clan derives its name, or one of its names, from the totem. Sometimes clan members and totem-species derive their descent from a common ancestor. Such an ancestor may be believed to have been both a human being and an animal or plant of the totem-species, either combining features of both in one, or manifesting himself in one shape or the other alternately. In other cases the ancestor had both human and animal offspring, or the ancestor is the originator of the species, or simply got involved in some kind of adventure with the totem. It is even possible that the relation with the totem is not warranted at all by any explanation or myth.

The specific relationship between clan members and their totem has divergent forms of expression. Sometimes the clan is symbolised by an emblem which is also the emblem of the totem. Such an emblem may play an important role in ritual. In many instances clan members are not allowed to kill, eat or injure their totem. However, the reverse may also be the case. Sometimes clan members boast that their ancestor created a highly appreciated food, and they consume their totem with as much pleasure as anyone. In such cases it is not uncommon that the totem-clan concerned has the duty of performing special rites to increase the fertility of the totem.

Totems are not exclusively animals or plants. The sun and moon may be totems, or sometimes certain mountains, and rivers, or a material object like an axe or a bow; even a specific act may be referred to as a totem. The va-

46

riety is enormous, which often can be attributed to the fact that clans may have more than one totem. Sometimes clans have quite a number of totems and in such cases one or two of their totems are the principal ones which may be used as clan symbols. Where this occurs, as happens to be the case among the Marind-anim of South New Guinea and a number of Australian tribes, the whole of nature is more or less distributed between the clans. The technical term for this form of totemism is 'multiple totemism'. Wherever it occurs, clans are usually organised in moieties and phratries[6]. The result is a classification of nature into as many classes as there are overall-groups. Ordinarily dualism prevails, and prevails to such an extent that it is doubtful if any classification of nature on the basis of multiple totemism can be found which does not show traces of an underlying dualism. A good case of classificatory dualism is that of the Marind-anim where one moiety is associated with *inter alia* the southeast, dry monsoon, sun, moon, the coastal region, dry ground and plants growing there, initiation rites and sodomy; and the other with the northwest, rainy season, the interior of the territory, water, sea, swamp and swamp plants, headhunting, feasts, sorcery and heterosexual intercourse.

Classificatory systems of this kind are by no means rare, and each of them is based on dualistic principles of its own. The diversity is great, so great that even the reverse of this type of classification occurs. Among the Southern Massim in the far east of New Guinea, each clan has four totems: a bird, a snake, a fish and a plant (cf. C. G. Seligmann, The Melanesians of British New Guinea p.435). The main totem is always a bird. Here each clan is associated with all the four principal aspects of nature.

It is obvious that the forms of totemism are highly divergent. The same is the case with the nature of the groups associated with a totem. Usually the totem-group is a clan, but also subclans, sections, phratries and moieties may have a totem or totems of their own. This is the case especially in Australia where every kind of group tends to associate itself with a totemic symbol. Here even each of the sexes may have its own totem, for example bat and owl. Among the Kurnai (S.E. Australia) killing the totem of the opposite sex is an insult which necessarily calls for action, i.e. a fight between the two sexes, a fight which, as is only natural, ultimately leads to a number of marriages being concluded afterwards.

An even more deviant form of totemism was discovered first amongst some of the North American Indians, viz. individual totemism. Here an individual acquires a totemic relation with a species by means of a vision on the occasion of the so-called vision-quest. With these tribes it is mandatory for every boy or young man (sometimes also for girls) to retire into solitude until, after prolonged fasting, he has a vision from which his individual

---

[6] A phratry is here conceived of as a group of associated clans. Phratries may occur where moieties are absent. However, where phratries are combined with the occurrence of multiple totemism, dualism predominates.

totem can be derived. Later individual totemism was also found among Australian medicine-men who, of course, have their own methods of acquiring such a totem.

The difference between group-totemism and individual totemism is great. In group totemism the relation with the totem is established by birth, either on grounds of descent or sex, i.e. on the natural order of things, whereas in individual totemism it is based on a specific experience. Yet, the difference between the two seems more important than it really is. Toward the end of the century Spencer and Gillen reported a new variety of totemism from Central Australia where the totem of the child is determined by a specific experience of its mother. When during her pregnancy she feels for the first time the motions of the child in her womb, she tells the old men where this happened to her. The men then determine the identity of the totem-ancestor who is responsible. They believe that the motion in the womb is caused by a germ sent out by or embodying a totem-ancestor, who is thus reincarnated in the child. This kind of totemism is called 'conceptual totemism'. Elsewhere the totem is defined by a dream of the child's father and then the term 'dream-totemism' is applied. In both cases, however, the woman's pregnancy is ascribed not to the father but to the totem-ancestor. The father's role in procreation is denied. Though he is not the genitor, there is nevertheless a close tie between father and child. Later research, *inter alia* by Meggitt among the Walbiri, gives evidence that whatever the dream- or conception-totem of the child, the relations with his father's patri-clan are maintained. Later the child, if a boy, will participate in the ritual of his father's cult-totem. The dream- or conception-totem just provides the child with an extra-relation with nature, unless this totem coincides with the father's cult-totem, in which case he may later play a leading role in the concomitant ritual.

All these details were unknown during the days of Robertson Smith; the information available was confined to the occurrence of clan-, sex-, and individual totemism and even this information was of the scantiest. The meagreness of the information left wide scope for unfounded opinions such as the idea that the clanmates looked upon their totem as a kind of deity. The interest taken in totemism, however, was not primarily inspired by its possible significance for knowledge about primitive religion, but by the supposition that totemism might have had an impact on the most ardently discussed problem of the time, viz. the origin of exogamy. Since the totem-clan was normally exogamous, scholars fostered the futile hope that the study of totemism might afford a better insight into the foundations of exogamy. Robertson Smith contributed to the discussion in his book "Kinship and Marriage in early Arabia", in which he pleaded on shaky grounds that the early Arabians had known the institution of totemism. The arguments which he produced to support this view were so poor that even Frazer, never loath to accept a conjecture, could not favour the hypothesis. "Kinship and Marriage" would have been forgotten long ago if it had not served as a spring-board for the theory of sacrifice forwarded in the "Lectures".

The "Lectures on the Religion of the Semites" make perfect reading; what is more, they still make sense even though the data on which they are based are long since obsolete. Actually, the data are hardly important; it is the ideas which count and these ideas differ profoundly from those of Tylor. The latter had found the essence of religion in a doctrine and he applied this doctrine to explain ritual. Robertson Smith, whose personal experience with doctrine had been discouraging to say the least, reversed the argument. The idea, that belief and dogma are more important for the knowledge of religion than ritual, is a mistake springing from the predilection for dogmatic controversy in Christian religion which values questions of doctrine extremely highly. This predilection makes us blind to reality. Actually, ritual is fixed and immutable, whereas its interpretation changes repeatedly. The ancient Greek did not bother about interpretation. Everybody was allowed to think of the meaning of the rites as he liked, provided the ritual was performed as prescribed. The myth explaining the rite is not an essential part of the ritual. The ritual is obligatory, not the belief. "So far as myths consist of explanations of ritual their value is altogether secondary, and it may be affirmed with confidence that in almost every case the myth was derived from the ritual, and not the ritual from the myth" (Lectures p.19).

We must pass over his comment on myths not connected with ritual. These he considers to be of minor importance, regarding them as products of speculative thought which are not purely religious. The one point which should be stressed is that Robertson Smith's argument is stronger than it seems to be at first sight, though in the present author's opinion it is too absolutist to be subscribed to. If Robertson Smith had wished to do so, he could have brought up a good number of cases to support his view. For instance, he might have referred to the following passus in Tylor's "Primitive Culture" (II p.121): "It is well known that Romulus, mindful of his own adventurous infancy, became after death a Roman deity propitious to the health and safety of young children, so that nurses and mothers would carry sickly infants to present them in his little round temple at the foot of the Palatine. In after ages the temple was replaced by the Church of St. Theodorus, and there Dr. Conyers Middleton, who drew public attention to its curious history, used to look in and see ten or a dozen women, each with a sick child in her lap, sitting in silent reverence before the altar of the saint. The ceremony of blessing children, especially after vaccination, may still be seen there on Thursday mornings".

Another and hardly less important novum in Robertson Smith's approach to the problems of religion is his explicit emphasis on the social function and meaning of religion[7]. Ritual is part of the organised social life of the group in which the individual is born. Everybody takes part in the fulfilment of religious duties, complying with greater or lesser zeal, according to his own nature, but nobody is strictly irreligious because the performance is a social duty. "Religion did not exist for the saving of souls but for the preservation and welfare of society" (Lectures p.30), a point of view which was adopted later by the French school of sociologists. Robertson Smith extends the social ties between the members of the community to the tribal god as well, who in his turn behaves socially toward the community. "As a father the god belongs to the family or clan, as a king he belongs to the state" (ibid. p.41) but whatever he may be, he is "always placable except to enemies of [his] worshippers or to renegate members of the community (ibid. p.55). "Religion. . . is a relation of all the members of a community to a power that has the good of the community at heart, and protects its law and moral order" (loc. cit.). Having demonstrated the difference in spiritual climate between Tylor and Robertson Smith, we must leave it at this and now turn to the ritual itself, the sacrifice, to which the main body of the "Lectures" is devoted. The theory forwarded here is the third novum brought by the author, whose examples are mainly confined to the religious life of the Semites.

The ancient Semites were pastoralists, says Robertson Smith, and the oldest form of sacrifice among them was animal sacrifice. The relevant sources, in the first place the Old Testament, make mention of three main forms of procedure: the victim is burned and thus really offered to the god; it is consumed by the priests; it is consumed by god and sacrificer jointly in a communal meal. The notion that the gods actually consume the food is "too crude to subsist without modifications beyond the savage stage of society" (Lectures p.212). In essence the meal is an act of communion between the god and his people, the god being offered the blood — the soul as the bible calls it — which is pledged to the soil.

Sacrifice in pre-exilic Israel was of the third type; references to it are found in the Book of Samuel. Robertson Smith presents us with the following description: "A sacrifice was a public ceremony of a township or a clan, and private householders were accustomed to reserve their offerings for the annual feast, satisfying their religious feelings in the interval by vows to be discharged when the festal season came round. Then the crowds streamed into the sanctuary from all sides, dressed in their gayest attire, marching joyfully to the sound of music, and bearing with them not only the victims appointed for sacrifice but store of bread and wine to set forth the feast. The law of the feast was openhanded hospitality; no sacrifice was complete without guests" (ibid. p.236). Having stated that there cannot be a feast

[7] On this point as on that of the importance of ritual Robertson Smith might have found support in the views expounded by Fustel de Coulanges. However, he does not refer to "La Cité antique".

without meat, Robertson Smith continues: "This view is proper to religions in which the habitual temper of the worshippers is one of joyous confidence in their god, untroubled by any habitual sense of guilt, and resting on the firm conviction that they and the deity they adore are good friends, who understand each other perfectly and are united by bands not easily broken" (ibid. pp.237 f.).

Some imagination is needed to extract this magnificent description from the Book of Samuel. Yet, personally I am impressed. I saw such a celebration with my own eyes in 1941, when attending the annual feast at Gangsa in the district of Tandjung in northwestern Lombok (Indonesia). Everything was there; the people, the festive attire, the music, the beasts to be sacrificed in redemption for promised vows, the meal, the stores and the wine as well as the guests enjoying themselves. I was one of them. Robertson Smith could not know that reality; he never saw what he described. He was what a scientist should never be, a visionary, and yet as a scientist he was more acute in analysis than any of his contemporaries.

Robertson Smith's attention focused on the victim. It must be a beast from the herd or from the flock and without blemish. Once it enters the place of sacrifice, the beast becomes sacred and its meat must be consumed within the precincts. Since the beast is sacred the participants must be consecrated too. They must become sacred as well. The mourners and the sick are excluded. Whence the sacredness of the victim? It is a sacredness reminiscent of the sacredness of the totem animal. At this point Robertson Smith took a decisive step: the sacrificial animal has taken the place of the totem animal. Originally a sacrifice was made as a means of participating in the divinity of the god by the ceremonial eating of the totem animal, i.e. of the god himself. The solution he presented is as daring as it is far-reaching and unexpected. It is evident that in the background of the author's line of thought the idea of the Christian communion loomed[8]. It is as if he wished to say to his audience: "Look, the ritual is immutable. It has always been the deity who is consumed. It is only the interpretation which changes". The conclusion is so obvious that Robertson Smith could not have failed to draw it himself. However, he was not out to hurt the feelings of his fellow-men and, although toward the end he came very near to making his conclusion explicit, he refrained from pronouncing it, carefully avoiding to scandalise the Christian world. It took more than twenty years before another scientist, viz. Freud, uninhibited by a 'sentiment de respect', took upon himself the task of formulating the inevitable conclusion in terms which even the slowest wit could not misunderstand.

The theory of sacrifice, presented by Robertson Smith, explains why he exerted himself so much to prove that the early Semites had once known

[8] With regard to the Christian communion the reader may be referred to 1 Corinthians 11: 23-26. It is in the New Testament.

totemism. He needed it for his explanation of sacrifice. Unfortunately, his arguments were weak and the strongest among them presuppose the validity of his theory rather than proving it. A good instance is the argument which he derived from the fairly inconclusive indication that among certain circles sacrifices of pigs, dogs, mice and fish had occurred, animals which were considered impure in pre-exilic Israel. Robertson Smith jumps to the conclusion that these animals must have been totem animals. If they were sacrificed at all, the fact itself does not prove anything with regard to totemism. The one and only real argument which Robertson Smith could produce, is the story told by Saint Nilus, an anchorite living in the Sinai district during the third century A.D. When there is a severe famine the local Arabs, who otherwise would never kill a camel, slaughter their camels, one for each clan or group. The animal is tied up and put down on a crude altar of stones. The tribesmen walk around it three times, singing all the time. Then the leader inflicts the first wound and hurriedly drinks the blood. The other men follow and hack the victim to pieces, hastily devouring the raw flesh. The act has to be completed between the rise of the morning-star and the time the sunlight makes it invisible (Lectures pp. 263 jo. 320).

This amazing case of an emergency slaughter has all the decisive traits of a ritual and Robertson Smith accepts for certain that the act is the survival of an age-old sacrificial procedure. The deity must be consumed raw to confirm the mystic unity between god and man. The unifying element between god and man is the life of the holy animal, the beast of the herd which took the place of the totem animal which is a relative of god and man equally.

The life of the animal is concentrated in its flesh but most of all in its blood. Blood is the principal *res sacramenti*. Drinking each other's blood is a ceremonial act of communion performed on the occasion of a formal declaration of blood-brothership. In a later stage of development, when the victim is no longer a totem animal but a beast of the herd or flock and its meat is no longer consumed raw, the blood is kept apart and offered to the deity by letting it flow away. Nevertheless, the animals of the herd are still sacred, so sacred that god and man may consume them together. This is the phase of the pre-exilic sacrifice depicted in the Book of Samuel.

From this point two lines of development are possible, one of a continued degeneration, the other of renewed intensification. The first, degeneration, is in part caused by the fact that game becomes more and more scarce. If people wish to eat meat, an animal of the flock must be slaughtered. However, it is not just killed; it is offered as a tribute to the god and the eating of meat is confined to ceremonial occasions. In the long run the association with ceremony becomes more and more tenuous and the sacredness of the animal correspondingly passes into oblivion. In the days of St. Paul the meat of animals killed as a sacrifice used to be sold in the market. Finally all that remains of the sacrificial act is ritual slaughter as prescribed by Moslem law; the blood must still run away and the animal is killed in the name of God the all-Merciful.

An example of the second possibility, renewed intensification, is the piacular sacrifice, the sacrifice for the atonement of sin. The victim now becomes so sacred that only the priest may consume it — if it be consumed at all and not burned in its totality. The sacrificer may touch the victim only once, viz. just before it is killed. This development is the curious consequence of the desacralisation of the herd. Originally, the beast of the herd stood equal to a member of the tribe and thus could be sacrificed to reconfirm the relation between the god and the members of the tribe. When the herd lost its sacred character a reinterpretation of sacrifice was called for. In this reinterpretation the sacrificial beast was considered to be a substitute for the sacrificer. A man should have been sacrificed instead of the beast, because man had become more sacred than the beast of the herd and thus was a more suitable victim. Various peoples, including some of the Semites, have indeed come to this conclusion, and have switched to human sacrifice. Others however used the beast as a substitute. Where the latter solution was chosen, the consumption of the victim by the sacrificer and his group became impossible. Because it is improper to eat a member of the tribe, it is also improper to consume his substitute. Thus the burning of the sacrifice became a necessity. Specific attention is paid by Robertson Smith to the fact that a holocaust with a human victim had to be performed somewhere outside (ibid. pp.354 ff.). A similar rule held for criminals; they were carried outside the town to be killed (ibid. p.401). Here the parallel with the doctrine of the Passion of Christ intrudes once more, and again the author keeps the relevant data separate, and refrains from making the conclusion explicit.

The 'Lectures' make wonderful reading even to-day, in spite of the fact that their conclusive force is minimal. Far too much has been loaded on the hump of St. Nilus' poor camel, said one of his critics. There is no denying it. Robertson Smith's merit lies elsewhere, in the freshness of his ideas and in his deep awareness of the value of a communion between god and man in religion. Methodologically Robertson Smith cannot be compared to Tylor but his ideas surpassed the rather shallow rationalisations of the latter both in depth of insight and in originality. In spite of the weakness of his data Robertson Smith has exerted a lasting influence on the theory of religion.

3. J. G. Frazer and the theory of magic

Sir James George Frazer (1854-1941) is the third outstanding anthropologist of the classical period. A professional classicist, all his work is typical of a learned armchair scholar who always keeps to his study, writing one voluminous work after another in the cultivated style of a man of letters, occasionally spicing his interminable treatises with the wisecracks of an accomplished mid-Victorian Tory.

The fundamental theme of his scientific activity was the construction of a conjectural history of the human mind. He once proposed to discard the term social anthropology in favour of mental anthropology (cf. A. R. Radcliffe-Brown's "In Memoriam" in Man, 1942). It should be emphasised that the kind of history Frazer had in mind is exactly as he called it, conjectural history, a history hypothesised on the basis of evolutionism. His works abound with conjectures, but conjectures being what they are it is not to them that Frazer owes his fame. He is remembered far more for the unbelievable quantity of data he amassed and conveniently arranged in such a way, that they could easily be consulted by the non-anthropologist without incurring the obligation of making a more detailed study of specific cultures. Frazer is the most prolific writer of the history of anthropology; even Bastian and Schmidt are only second to him. Any work which he took up rapidly took on almost unmanageable dimensions. His first essay was prophetic of the passion for exhaustiveness which more and more took possession of him. He had been invited to write an article on totemism for the Encyclopaedia Britannica. Only an excerpt could be accepted; the essay itself was published in 1887 in book form under the title "Totemism" and numbered more than 100 pages. In 1910 it was reprinted with other essays in "Totemism and Exogamy", a work in four stout volumes, followed by a supplement in 1937. Between 1890 and 1910 Frazer put forward three different, mutually exclusive theories on the origin of totemism. They need not be discussed here as all these theories are very hypothetical, in fact typical specimens of conjectural history. Only one of them, the second, has a certain degree of plausibility. The specific merits of "Totemism and Exogamy" are not the republication of these shaky theories, but the extensive collection of data. In addition to "Totemism and Exogamy" and Frazer's main work, "The Golden Bough", mention should be made of "Folk-Lore in the Old Testament" (1918, 3 vols) and "The Belief in Immortality and the Worship of the Dead" (1913-24, 3 vols). This list is by no means exhaustive.

"The Golden Bough" is essentially a brilliant book. It appeared in 1890 in two volumes and has been re-edited twice, the second time between 1911 and 1915. The third and last edition consisted of 12 volumes and was followed by a thirteenth, an Aftermath, in 1936. In the meantime an abridged edition of 700 closely printed pages had appeared in 1922. The title of the book refers to "that golden bough which, at the Sibyl's bidding, Aeneas plucked before he essayed the perilous journey to the world of the dead" (Golden Bough p.3 of the abridged edition from which all references and quotations in this book have been taken).

The theme of the book is an attractive one, that of the priest-king who with a drawn sword in his hand, guarded a certain tree in the sacred grove of Nemi in the Alban hills near Rome. Whoever succeeded in breaking a bough from that tree could try his own strength against that of the royal guardsman and, if he managed to kill him, become Rex Nemorensis in his place. It is the theme of the divine king who embodies the fertility of the land and therefore may grow neither old nor infirm. A king is not in the first place a ruler (even though he may be a ruler as well) but a priest, and as a priest even a god. The Rex Nemorensis is such a king. He is the incarnation of Virbus, the hero worshipped in the sanctuary of Nemi. Virbus is the same as the Greek hero Hippolytus who escaped from Hades and was protected against the wrath of Zeus by Diana who hid him at Nemi where she entrusted him to the care of the nymph Egeria, the mistress of the wise king Numa of Rome. Frazer discusses the symbolism of the story very extensively. The grove is a wood of oak trees, and the oak is a symbol of fertility as well as the symbol of the Roman kings. The pontifex maximus, who is always the king, adorns his head with oak-leaves. The oak is also associated with the May-tree, the symbol of the rejuvenating spring and exactly such a symbol of renewed and rejuvenated kingship as the new Rex Nemorensis who slew his predecessor. The most remarkable historical details are brought in. Once every year offerings are brought to Diana at Nemi because it is Diana who blesses barren women with children. This is done on the 13th of August, the day of Saint Hippolyte's death who, like his Greek namesake venerated as Virbus in the sanctuary, was trampled on by horses.

The discussion of the symbolism involved makes highly interesting reading even though the arguments are not always as conclusive as the author believes them to be. There is a wealth of information on divine kingship of which Western civilisation has retained only a last, weak shadow in the formula "Sovereign by the Grace of God". A few hundred years ago the last vestige of the priestly functions of the king disappeared in Britain when William III, raised in Calvinist tradition, refused to make use of the gift which folk-belief ascribed to the kings of England, to heal scrofula, the king's sore, by his touch. The fundamental problem is how it is possible that such a great influence on the fertility of the land is ascribed to the king's vitality and virility, as is the case in those countries where the king is killed as soon as he shows signs of impotence (the Shilluk of the White Nile are a good example). It is this question which leads us directly to the underlying theme of the book, the belief in magic and in the efficacy of all sorts of symbolic acts.

We must pause here for a moment, and interrupt our survey of "The Golden Bough". Magic is a dangerous word, more dangerous than magic itself, because it is such a handsome term to cover everything that we fail to understand. The term is used far too often as a vague kind of explanation, but in fact it explains nothing. If used at all, it should be applied in a strictly descriptive manner for *ritual acts, preferably of a simple character, executed to promote the realisation of a concrete end.* For reasons which will become apparent in the course of this book, specific care should be taken to avoid misleading platitudes such as the coercive effect of the magical act. They have served generations of anthropologists (and amateurs) to suggest to their readers as well as to themselves that their unsolved problems were explained.

After this digression we return to Frazer who more than anybody stresses the coercive effect of magic. To him magic has nothing to do with religion. He takes Tylor's explanation as his point of departure; magic is based on an erroneous association of ideas. In essence magic is a false science, based on two principles, the first of which is that like produces like, or that an effect resembles its cause (the Law of Similarity), and the second, that things which have once been in contact with each other continue to act on each other at a distance, after the physical contact has been severed (the Law of Contact or Contagion) (Golden Bough p.11). The Law of Similarity is applied in acts of imitative or homeopathic magic. If a sorcerer wishes to kill one of his fellow-men he may shape a piece of wood into an image of his enemy. The wooden puppet then is buried in a humid place where it rots away. Consequently, the person the puppet represents will fall ill and slowly pass away. The Law of Contagion is applied when a sorcerer makes use of something inadvertently left behind by his prospective victim, preferably a scrap of nail, some excrement, a small pluck of hair or a piece of cloth. When burned or otherwise destroyed by the sorcerer, the victim will fall ill and die.

Imitative and contagious magic can be applied separately as well as in combination. They are classified together by Frazer under the comprehensive name of sympathetic magic "since both assume that things act on each other at a distance through a secret sympathy" (ibid. p.12). The magician implicitly believes that the principles which he applies in the practice of his art are the same as those regulating the operations of inanimate nature; magic "is a false science as well as an abortive art" (ibid. p.11).

Frazer gives a host of instances from which only two will be quoted. Imitation of the totem animal causes the species to prosper. A man who cut his finger with a knife must clean the knife to forestall inflammation. All these positive precepts are called charms. However, "the system of sympathetic magic is not merely composed of positive precepts; it comprises a very large number of negative precepts" as well. The negative precepts are taboos (ibid. p. 19). While the aim of positive magic is to produce a desired effect, negative magic, a taboo, is applied to avoid an undesirable one (loc. cit.).

Frazer strongly insists that the fundamental conception of magic "is identical with that of modern science; underlying the whole system is a faith, implicit but real and firm, in the order and uniformity of nature. The magician does not doubt that the same causes will always produce the same effects, that the performance of the proper ceremony, accompanied by the appropriate spell, will inevitably be attended by the desired result, unless, indeed, his incantations should chance to be thwarted and foiled by the more potent charms of another sorcerer" (ibid. p.49). Magic then, differs fundamentally from religion which assumes that, at the very least, "the course of nature is to some extent elastic or variable and that we can persuade the [superhuman beings who control the world] to deflect, for our benefit, the current of events from the channel in which they otherwise flow" (ibid. p.51). Religion implies the belief in higher powers and the attempt to propitiate or to please them. The religious assumption of a world directed by conscious agents "stands in fundamental antagonism to magic as well as to science" (loc. cit.).

However, even if magic is a science, it is a false science. "The shrewder intelligences must in time have come to perceive that magical ceremonies and incantations did not really effect the results which they were designed to produce. ... The discovery amounted to this, that men recognized their inability to manipulate at pleasure certain natural forces which hitherto they had believed to be completely within their control. It was a confession of human ignorance and weakness" (ibid. p.57). "Our primitive philosopher must have been sadly perplexed and agitated till he came to rest... in a new system of faith and practice, which seemed to offer a solution of his harassing doubts" etc. (ibid. p.58). Since he became aware that magic failed to help him out of his difficulties, man began to ascribe the regulation of events to uncontrollable personal powers.

At first sight it seems as if Frazer's hypothesis contradicts Tylor's, who explained religion as a product of the speculations of primitive philosophers on life, death and dream. Actually, there is little difference between the two; only that Frazer gives substance to the idea that a non-religious era must have preceded the age of animism, and that he adds another argument to explain the origin of religion to those already forwarded by Tylor, viz. the failure of magic; but he explains the workings of magic in exactly the same fashion. Frazer's theory is, in fact, an elaboration of Tylor's comment on magic. There is not the slightest indication that Tylor looked upon magic as a religious phenomenon and we may take it for granted that he too held that magic is older than animism. In this respect his comment on the fundamental role of analogy in the origin of myth (above, p.34) is very suggestive.

At the end of this section a critical note should be added on terminology. Frazer uses the term sorcery as a synonym of positive magic, i.e. any magic. In modern anthropology the terms sorcery and sorcerer are reserved for anti-social or black magic, the magic used to harm a fellow-man. Magic performed for the benefit of people, such as the magical acts for healing the sick or promoting the fertility of animals and plants, is called white magic. If its performer is a professional specialist he is called a medicine-man. The medicine-man may also be a sorcerer making black magic either professionally or privately, but the two functions should be clearly differentiated, even if they are exercised (as often is the case) by the same person. *Sorcery,* in turn, should be distinguished from *witchcraft.* Whereas sorcery must be learned and is always performed deliberately, a witch is a person who has certain harmful qualities which he cannot control, at least not consciously. The witch may be a kind of werewolf whose soul goes out at night to devour the soul of a fellow-man, or he may just have the evil eye. The witch does not do harm on purpose, at least he need not do it on purpose, because his harmful powers derive from some innate defect which he has not necessarily under control. Excellent descriptions of witchcraft are found in E.E. Evans-Pritchard, "Witchcraft, Oracles and Magic among the Azande" (1937). Useful as the distinction between witchcraft and sorcery is, the reader should be aware that transitional forms do occur in which the difference between them simply cannot be made. After all, these distinctions are the result of our attempts to classify phenomena produced by human beings, and human action tends to be more diversified than can be foreseen in our systems of classification.

4. *The classical period in retrospect: animism and spiritism*

The typical representatives of the period are Tylor and Frazer. Though as staunch an evolutionist as they, Robertson Smith stands apart. His own deep religiosity, his awareness of the social aspects of religion and of the comforting value of the idea of communion, create a wide distance between his ideas and the shallow rationalism of his contemporaries. Apparently the latter was more in accord with the prevailing current of the time, otherwise one cannot understand why it took such a long time before criticism arose. No one even noted that if magic must be explained from a disability of reason, and animism from a perfectly rational philosophy, the combined occurrence of magical and animistic notions in practically each and every primitive society raises an unsoluble problem. The two attitudes are exclusive, because contradictory. In a way, Frazer himself seems to have been one of the very few who realised that there was a problem here. He did all he could to reason away the inconsistency with the well-known argument of the graduality of development. Whenever graduality is pleaded there is reason for scrutinising the argument.

The inconsistency just mentioned is not the only weak spot of the theories of Tylor and Frazer. There are at least three others, viz.:
1. the obsolete psychological theory on which they had based their theory of magic;
2. the individualistic approach which led them to ignore the social aspects of religion as well as the internal coherence of the various expressions of religious life and experience within the framework of every single tribal group;

58

3. the mono-linear character of the evolutionist development scheme which left insufficient scope for the possibility of divergent lines of development, and neglected the effect of specific historical events by overstressing the regularity of cultural evolution. (We note, however, that Tylor himself always carefully guarded against extremes in this respect. In his "Researches into the early History of Mankind" he explicitly makes allowance for divergent historical developments).

Each of these weaknesses was destined to give occasion to severe criticism soon after the turn of the century. The first of them was attacked by those who held the opinion that supernatural power is a more general and also more adequate religious notion than soul or spirit; the second by the school of French sociologists, and the third by the American diffusionists under Boas, and the German historicists under the leadership of F. Wilh. Schmidt. These criticisms and the theories advanced in their place will be discussed in the following chapters of this book. Here we shall first pay attention to a few writers who cannot be classified as adherents of any specific school of anthropological thought, and whose works, published in the years round about the turn of the century, mark the first beginning of new trends in the study of anthropology. The one thing they have in common is their interest in modern European animism, namely spiritism. The most conspicuous among them is Andrew Lang.

Adrew Lang (1844-1912) was not a professional anthropologist, but an essayist who made his livelihood by writing literary reviews for The Times. A poet, a novelist, a historian, and well versed in the classics, this prolific essayist was also a dedicated student of anthropology. Initially he concentrated on studies of mythology, and his well developed sense of criticism soon turned him into an ardent opponent of Max Müller. Unmercifully he exposed the weaknesses of the hypotheses on which Müller had founded his etymologies and his interpretations of mythology. A similar fate befell Frazer whose reconstruction of the history of the Rex Nemorensis he severely criticised (cf. A. P. L. de Cocq, Andrew Lang, Ch. IV and p.115). Among his contemporaries Lang was primarily known as a mythologist, but he won a more lasting fame with his book "The Making of Religion" in which he opposed Tylor, though in a somewhat more subtle way than when he criticised Müller and Frazer.

"The Making of Religion", one of the six books he wrote on anthropological subjects, appeared in 1898. It is divided into two parts which seemingly have little in common. However, both parts do raise serious doubts as to the tenability of important points in Tylor's theory of animism, the second part not less than the first, in which he argues that the "savage theory of soul" can and should be explained from motives other than philosophical contemplations on life and dream. This first part is dedicated to the impact of paranormal phenomena on the development of the notions of soul and spirit. Lang was a devoted member of the Society for Psychical Research which, from its foundation in 1882, had organised scientific experiments with media in the various fields of their specialisation. In those years spiritism flourished in England and the critical activities of the Society were by no means superfluous. It is fairly easy to-day to criticise these activities because they were not critical enough. Nevertheless, the Society succeeded on the one hand in exposing a number of quacks, and on the other in contributing substantially to a better evaluation of telepathic phenomena and the impossibility of brushing them aside as deceit. The veridity of a number of telepathic phenomena is not to be denied, though each case in turn should be very carefully examined before it is accepted. The main merit of these studies has been their contribution to the genesis of the notion of the subconscious. Various experiments strongly suggested the influence of a subliminal layer of the mind on human activity.

Not every member of the Society successfully withstood the attractions of the spirit-hypothesis as an explanation of paranormal facts. Lang, anyhow, did not fall for it (De Cocq p.59). Nevertheless, he was impressed, and perhaps slightly more impressed than can be justified. Even so, we can agree with him that the forms and symptoms of animism must be compared with parallel phenomena in Europe, such as those presented by spiritist media. The comparison does not necessarily lead us to subscribe to his conclusion, viz. that there is a rare human faculty or gift, which occurs more frequently among primitives than among the civilised, and that this faculty enables man to gather information by extra-sensory means which definitely transcend the ordinary and controllable methods of acquiring knowledge. Lang argues that it is this faculty which more than anything contributed to the development of the notion of the soul, notably a soul which can move freely out of the body. The question whether these paranormal phenomena are veritable in the sense that the description given of them corresponds with the actual facts, is not at issue here, nor is the undeniable fact that many paranormal phenomena are caused by an activation of the subconscious. The one point which matters is that paranormal phenomena (however explained) do occur and that they occur more often among primitive people than among us. We cannot neglect this fact in our studies of the origin of the notion of soul.

Lang's argument is a sound one. The ethnographic literature abounds with "strong stories" of paranormal events and Lang mentions a couple of really delightful cases. Unfortunately, among the instances quoted there are also a few which cannot bear critical examination. In attributing conclusiveness to these cases the author spoils the force of his argument. This must be deplored. The occurrence of paranormal phenomena in primitive cultures has never been given the attention it deserves in the present author's opinion. Actually, there is a sound reason for expecting a greater frequency of paranormal phenomena there than in modern civilised society. The point is that at the initial phase of a paranormal experiment, the subject is required to have a so-called blank mind. He must surrender to a state of absent-mindedness in which he thinks of nothing in particular. The demand is a fairly difficult one to people who from early youth are educated to be active and always occupied with something or another. In societies with value-systems which do not favour the boundless activity characteristic of our own, the situation is different. There we meet with men and women who still are able to sit down without doing or thinking of anything in particular. A state of blank-mindedness is less distant to them than to us, and we may expect a correspondingly greater openness to paranormal experiences. I do not know of any specific research in this matter and, although a sceptic myself, better knowledge of it would be decidedly welcome.

We must return to Lang's "Making of Religion". The second part of the book discusses the origin of the idea of a supreme being with ethical qualities — according to Tylor a late development of animistic belief. Lang points out that some very primitive peoples recognise such a supreme being. The Firelanders believe in one who evidently has ethical qualities: he punishes the killing of foreigners by sending hail and rain. The Australians have a supreme being whom they call Father. He sees to it that the elders are obeyed, that the women are not molested and that the food taboos are respected.

Numerous cases of primitive peoples recognising an ethical supreme being are mentioned. It is evident that these beliefs cannot really be a late product of evolution; these beings are as old as souls and spirits. From of old there must have been two streams of religious belief, one leading to the idea of a single eternal, moral being who is a creator, the other emanating from the doctrine of souls. In the first edition of "The Making of Religion" Lang states that he is unable to give a theory concerning the origin of this belief. In the preface to the second edition, however, he gives an indication of what he deems probable: "As soon as man had the idea of 'making' things, he might conjecture as to a maker of things, which he himself had not made, and could not make. He would regard this unknown Maker as a 'magnified non-natural man', who is a Maker. The conception being given, his power would be recognised, and fancy would cloth (him) with . . . moral attributes as of Fatherhood, goodness and regard for the ethics of his children. . ." (2nd ed. p. VII, 1900).

The explanation is meagre and does not deserve the name of an explanation at all. The critical part of his argument is stronger, although in his interpretation of the data borrowed from Fireland and Australia he certainly stretches the facts. With the exception of one or two border-line cases they do not really justify the use of the term supreme being. However, the cases put forward from other areas are more convincing and, all things considered, Lang's presentation is better founded than the hypothesis that all these supreme beings are the result of missionary influence, an explanation already rejected by Tylor in his "Primitive Culture". In spite of its weak spots, Lang's critical survey gave sufficient evidence to prove that the evolutionist theory did not fully fit the facts. That does not mean that Lang's book was met with approval. Tylor's cautious definition of monotheism had made his position almost unassailable (cf. above, p.39). It is not surprising that Lang's contemporaries remained sceptical (cf. De Cocq, pp.101 ff.). It took more than ten years before his attack on Tylor's development scheme found support, viz. of F. Wilh. Schmidt. However, the latter's views differed widely from those held by Lang. Schmidt ignored Lang's references to paranormal phenomena as stubbornly as he applauded the latter's emphasis on the originality of the belief in supreme beings.

Alfred Lehmann belongs in this section for very different reasons. A Danish psychologist with great experience in experimental psychology and interested in paranormal phenomena, Lehmann is the author of one of the most delightful books on the history of European spiritism and parapsychological practices and beliefs generally. The book, originally written in Danish in 1893, was published in German under the title of "Aberglaube und Zauberei" (1898; 2nd ed. 1908). Superstition (Aberglaube) is here defined as every general supposition not supported by a recognised religion and conflicting with current scientific views. Lehmann's interest in parapsychology is not the result of vague expectations that, after all, the occult might have more in the offing than hitherto guessed. On the contrary, Lehmann had a clear mind and he did all he could to expose the deceit which he suspected to be at the bottom of most if not of all parapsychological manifestations. We are indebted to him for great refinement in the methods of observation and for a sharp criticism on the lack of methods of many previous observers. He definitely proved that a not unimportant number of manifestations could be deposited on the scrap-heap of ordinary deceit without further ado. However, the data concerning telepathic experience fairly successfully stood the test of his critical and sometimes even hypercritical methods of analysis, a fact almost grumblingly admitted by the author. The analysis of these manifestations brought after all renewed confirmation of the importance of subliminal processes. To the anthropologist the book is of particular interest because it posits the various forms of European occultism and spiritism in the framework of animism generally, and combines the psychological analysis with an interesting survey of historical facts.

William James, the American philosopher of pragmatism, should also be mentioned here. He is the author of "The varieties of religious experience" (1902), a series of lectures held at the university of Edinburgh during the academic year of 1901/02. James is not an anthropologist and he does not venture into the realms of primitive religion. In his 'Varieties' he strictly confines himself to religious experience within the orbit of Christianity. His approach differs widely from that of Tylor and Frazer and their school. On the one hand he dismisses an impressive amount of humbug as the product of chaotic psychic conditions, but on the other he refuses to exclude the possibility that extra-human entities could in some way or other influence the subconscious. Whether this is true or not must necessarily remain undecided because such influences are by definition unobservable. The reservation made by James is not the result of a belief in any specific religious truth but of his appreciation of the contributions made by religion to spiritual strength. Religion meets the private needs of the individual in his subjectivity. Religion has pragmatic value and therefore it cannot simply be rejected as erroneous. James urges his contemporaries to make a sharp distinction between what we can know and what we cannot know. The human mind is too complicated an organism and subject to far too many influences, for its workings to be explained as if they were the product of elementary arithmetics. The theoretical position taken up by James is, of course, tenuous. The pragmatic value of religion is quite another matter than its error or truth, and the two should never be confused. Nevertheless, James' plea in favour of a more cautious approach of religious data was well-founded. The study of parapsychological facts had given additional reasons for recognising that religion touches deeper layers of the mind than most students of primitive religion hitherto had been willing to admit. In the long run these warnings could not fail to affect anthropological theory.

IV

Supernatural power,
religion, and
feelings of dependence

1. The Concept of Mana

Concepts of souls and spirits were succeeded by notions of mana as a main theme of anthropological discussion. The first information on 'mana' came from a letter quoted by Max Müller in 1878. The letter had been written by R.H. Codrington who published an article on the same subject in the Journal of the Anthropological Institute a few years later (1881). Codrington gave additional information in his book "The Melanesians" (1891).

Introducing the concept Codrington writes: "The Melanesian mind is entirely possessed by the belief in a supernatural power or influence called almost universally 'mana'. This is what works to effect everything beyond the ordinary power of men, outside the common processes of nature; it is present in the atmosphere of life, attaches itself to persons and to things, and is manifested by results which can only be ascribed to its operation" (Melanesians pp.118 f.). An important point is that mana is known primarily because of its effect. It is the cause of all success in life which surpasses the ordinary, of excessive fertility, and of all things which in one way or another fall outside the scope of the ordinary and the natural order of things. It is a kind of supernatural power which can be applied in many ways. If a man finds a stone which for one reason or another arrests his attention, he will try to find out whether the stone holds mana by placing it in his garden. If, subsequently, he harvests a rich crop, he feels sure that the stone has mana. Mana is also present in songs and formulas recited with the aim of increasing the yield of the crop. A charm may even be called a mana. All spirits have mana — ghosts very often and also certain people, chiefs and sorcerers in particular. The power they have is their mana. It is as if to these Melanesians power, including human power, is supernatural by nature. A brave and successful warrior must have received mana from a spirit or from a deceased warrior, and he carries it with him in a talisman or in a formula which he has learned by heart. If a man has many pigs or is blessed with a rich harvest of yams, this is so because he has many stones which are rich in mana, the kind of mana conducive to the multiplication of pigs in the one case, and to the growth of yams in the other. Mana is communicable; the performance of certain ceremonies conveys mana to a new canoe, the mana which makes the canoe go fast. Other ceremonies transmit mana to a new fish-net to induce it to catch many fish.

Mana is closely associated with the spirits. Codrington states explicitly that all mana derives from the spirits. No man has mana of his own; in all his work he needs the assistance of spirits and souls. Of spirits it can be said that they are mana, whereas a human being can at best have it. Mana is manipulated in various kinds of magic and it seems justified to conclude that all the activities of these Melanesians are focussed on the acquisition of mana; or in Norbeck's words: mana is "a force existing everywhere which acts in all ways for good and evil and which is of utmost importance for man to possess and control" (Norbeck, Religion p.39).

Codrington's description of the concept of mana with its emphasis on the close relation between mana and spirits could hardly be considered as contradictory to Tylor's theory of animism. He presented mana as a phenomenon concomitant with animism, and initially the implications of the difference between the concept of mana and that of spirit passed unnoticed. We will come to this presently, when discussing the further development of anthropological theory. For the moment we shall give some further consideration to Codrington's book. Much tribute has been paid to it, but it should be noted that it falls short of modern standards of ethnographic research. It it not the result of fully authentic fieldwork in the area described, viz. the southern part of Melanesia, including some of the Solomon Islands and the New Hebrides (Santa Cruz and Banks Islands in particular) — and not the whole of Melanesia as the title suggests. The author was a missionary who lived in the Pacific from 1863 to 1887. He spent most of his time in Norfolk Island, halfway between New Caledonia and New Zealand at a latitude of 29° S. Here he supervised a teacher training institute for students from the islands to which his data refer, and he frankly informs the reader that he owes his information primarily to these teachers. It is evident that he questioned them with great care and diligence, but the result cannot be equivalent to research in loco. What we sadly lack in the description is the direct observation of the role of mana in the daily life of the people. All we have are the opinions and descriptions of teachers; we would prefer texts taken from conversation with the villagers, illustrating the actual use of the word.

In spite of all this, later investigations confirm that Codrington's description of the content of the concept is correct in its main aspects. This is corroborated inter alia by a comparative study of a much later date, the one written by the German Fr. R. Lehmann, "Mana, Der Begriff des ausserordentlich Wirkungsvollen bei Südseevölkern", Leipzig 1922. He points out that mana is a widespread concept, in particular in Polynesia[9]. However, it

[9] In Melanesia it is confined to the southern islands.

is not only a religious concept; the term can also be used in a perfectly profane sense as is the case with the corresponding Indonesian forms 'wenang' and 'menang' (Javanese and Malay, respectively). Lehmann criticises Codrington's statement that spirits are mana whereas human beings only have mana. He argues that an opposition of this kind cannot be made in any Austronesian language because these languages do not know the copula. He is perfectly right when he states that the copula is lacking, as right as he errs when he thinks that the absence of this particular grammatical form makes it impossible to express the opposition implied. Of course it is possible and nobody conversant with any Austronesian language would have any difficulty with it. The irrelevance of the question is manifest since R. Firth published his study "An analysis of mana: an empirical approach" (Journ. Polyn. Soc. 1940; reprinted in Tikopia Ritual and Belief). With the help of a wealth of texts the author demonstrates how the word mana is used, that it belongs to a pragmatic context, and is associated with such matters as propitious fishing, an abundant crop, the cure of sickness etc. Mana is a personal attribute of the chiefs who, in their priestly function, are the mediators between the human world and that of the gods and spirits — the ultimate source of mana, granting mana to the chiefs or withholding it from them. Success and efficacy are proof of the mana of the chief and of the favour of gods and spirits. Firth reminds his readers of Malinowski's warning, that the mana-concept is "an example of early generalization of a crude metaphysical concept" but that on the "empirical material the mana-concept is too narrow to stand as the basis of magic and religion" (Tikopia Ritual pp.176 f.). The warning was well in place because Codrington's discovery of the concept of mana had been followed by reports from other parts of the world, announcing the occurrence of very similar concepts. Within a few years the notion of mana, of supernatural power, had acquired an important status in the science of religion.

2. R. R. Marett

The first attack on Tylor's rationalist and intellectualist interpretations (and a penetrating one) was launched by R. R. Marett, a classicist who later became the successor to Tylor's chair of anthropology in Oxford. An armchair anthropologist like so many early students of primitive culture, he differed from them in this respect that he did not indulge in the habit of writing voluminous books. Marett's influence (and it has been an enduring one) is based on a small number of articles written in the early years of his scientific activity and re-edited in his famous book "The Threshold of Religion". The first edition was in 1909, but the revised and enlarged one of 1914 is to be preferred. We shall confine ourselves to four of these early articles and the introduction to the second edition of 'The Threshold', the later work of Marett being of little importance for our present purpose.

The oldest essay is an address read to the British Association in 1899. It is entitled "Pre-animistic Religion" and won the author the fame of being the founder of the pre-animistic hypothesis. In this essay Marett argues that Tylor's minimum definition of religion is both too narrow and too intellectualistic. "Psychologically, religion involves more than thought, namely, feeling and will as well" (Threshold p.1). We are confronted with such phenomena as religious emotion and religious thrill and with primitive forms of religion manifesting themselves in almost unideated feelings (ibid. p.6). The relevant notions are vaguer and run wider than the notion of soul as defined by Tylor, viz. a spiritual being capable of moving about freely, separate from the body of its owner. The question arises whether "before, or at any rate apart from, animism, ... early man [was] subject to any experience, whether in the form of feeling, or thought, or of both combined, that might be termed specifically 'religious'" (ibid. p.8). The question is closely bound up with yet another one, viz. the fundamentally unexplained problem of the extension of the concept of soul to that of spirit. "How came an animistic colour to be attached to a number of things not primarily or obviously connected with death and the dead?" (ibid. p.9).

From whatever angle the approach is made, in religion we are invariably confronted with "efforts at self-interpretation... whereof the component 'moments' are fear, admiration, wonder, and the like, whilst its object is, broadly speaking, the supernatural" (ibid. p.10). The prevailing feeling called forward by the mysterious supernatural is one of awe which, in turn, gives occasion to the personification of the object. Supernaturalism may, indeed, "be expected to prove not only logically but also in some sense chronologically prior to animism", a particular form of religion which constitutes only a special embodiment of supernaturalism (ibid. p.11).

The English word which expresses the fundamental religious feelings most nearly, is the word awe. Concepts such as mana and its numerous equivalents in other linguistic areas (e.g. 'wakan', 'wakanda', among the Sioux Indians) very clearly convey that vague notion of wonder and awe which lies at the root of religious experience.

Far too many religious phenomena have been explained by animism without sufficient attention being paid to the question if a soul or spirit in Tylor's sense really manifested itself in them. When at the approach of a thunderstorm the inmates of a Kaffir village, led by their medicine-man, rush to the nearest hill to yell at the hurricane to divert it from its course, their action is a simple case of straightforward personification. The idea that there is a spirit living in the storm is absent. We cannot call this a case of animism because there is no spirit. The case differs profoundly from that of the Point Barrow Eskimo who "in order to persuade the river to yield him fish, throws tobacco, not into the river, but into the air, and cries out 'Tuana, Tuana' (Spirit)" (ibid. p.15). Here is full-fledged animism. It is not animism when the Kanakas of Hawaii differentiate their sacred stones into males and females, and firmly "believe that from time to time little stones appear at the side of the parent blocks" (ibid. p.18). However, it certainly is animism when a Banks' Islander says of a big stone with little stones around it, "that there is a 'vui' (spirit) inside it, ready if properly conciliated to make women bear many children and the sows large litters" (loc. cit.).

In those cases where there is a question of personification but not of a spirit, we should not speak of animism, but of *'animatism'*. Animatism is of frequent occurrence and the transitions from animatism to animism are almost imperceptible. When the Cree-Indians catch a fish the like of which they have never seen before, they promptly return the fish to the water and perform a ceremony, because the fish is (a) 'manitu', a word which may mean spirit but which is also used to denote supernatural power. Animatism is also connected with magic which, in turn, is associated with the notion of supernatural power. "There are many animals that are propitiated by primitive man neither because they are merely useful nor merely dangerous, but because they are, in a word, uncanny... in the case of powers such as these, sympathetic magic will naturally suggest the wearing of tooth or claw, bone or skin as a means of sharing the divine potency" (ibid. p.21). Here, however, is also "the chance for animism to step in. Thus a Kennaiah chief, who wishes to wear the skin of the Borneo tiger-cat for luck in war, will wrap himself in it, and before lying down to sleep will explain to the skin exactly what he wants, and beg the spirit to send him a propitious dream" (ibid. pp.21f.). The transition from the one to the other is fluctuating and easy. "A young native of Leper's Island, out of affection for his dead brother, made his bones into arrow-tips. Thereafter he no longer spoke of himself as 'I', but as 'we two', and was much feared" (ibid. p.24). It is evident that the essence of religion should not be sought "so much in the shifting variety of its ideal constructions, as in that steadfast groundwork of specific emotion whereby man is able to feel the supernatural precisely at the point at which his thought breaks down" (ibid. p.28).

If Marett expressed himself rather reluctantly in his first essay, he was more outspoken in an article published in Folk-Lore in 1904. In this essay, captioned "From Spell to Prayer", he defines the object of religion as *"whatever is perceived as a mystery and treated accordingly"* (Threshold p.33; italics ours). Taking this as a vantage point, he attacks Frazer's contrast between magic and religion as well as his thesis that primitive man adopted the belief in mysterious supernatural beings once he discovered that his magic failed to help him out. "The glowing periods in which the history of 'the great transition' is recounted by Frazer are pure rhetoric and we could almost as well say that, when man found he could not make big enough bags with the throwing-stick, he sat down and excogitated the bow-and-arrow" (ibid. p.34).

Frazer's theory of magic is derived from a psychological theory of associations which is wholly obsolete. No psychologist to-day "holds that association. . . suffices to explain anything that deserves the name of reasoning or thought". Association depends on continuity of interest, and thought, instead of merely reconstructing the old, transforms it into something new (ibid. p.37). Therefore, magic "is not merely an affair of misapplied ideas, but must be studied. . . from its emotional side" (ibid. p.29).

So far the argument is sound enough. The same cannot be said of the theory of magic presented in its place, which Marett based on the supposition that a sudden discharge of pent-up emotions and violent passions results in gratifying feelings of relief. As an example he takes the case of the disappointed lover who throws the portrait of his faithless maiden on the fire. He feels that it does him good. It is only a symbolic act but it is near to rudimentary magic because he may believe that his action has an effect of some sort in reality. The psychological effect tends to be projectively transmitted to the real object. Rudimentary magic is to real magic what make-belief is to belief. For rudimentary magic to become magic the symbolic act must be accompanied by a spell which expresses the actor's faith in its efficacy, and combines the symbolic act with the actual, ulterior aim. Hesitatingly Marett forwards the supposition that the oldest form of magic is that of man against man. He is more positive about the spell. He calls it "the crispest embodiment of the 'must', [the] spring and soul of the projection" (ibid. p.55), i.e. the projection of the desire motivating the actor. A good example of it is the following: "In ancient Peru, when a war expedition was contemplated, they were wont to starve certain black sheep for some days and then slay them, uttering the incantation: 'As the hearts of these beasts are weakened, so let our enemies be weakened' " (ibid. p.55).

The argument is unconvincing and suffers from two distinct weaknesses. In the first place, the very starting-point, the beneficial effect of a violent discharge of pent-up feelings: anybody who ever indulged in such an outburst may have found, that the one and only result was that the outburst left him worn-out and perhaps somewhat ashamed of himself. The gratifying feeling which Marett expects as a result, is a myth. The second weak point is the transition from make-belief to belief, from rudimentary to developed magic. This is not explained at all. Primitive people know as well as we do that a wish is not fulfilled by wishing more ardently, and that fair words butter no parsnips. Fortunately, the present essay has other merits than the new theory offered, namely the demonstration of a number of striking instances of the belief in magic, and above all, of new proofs of the well-founded thesis that magic manipulates supernatural power. Magic and religion have the notion of mana in common and the two interpenetrate and transfuse. A beautiful case is that given of the Kei Islands. "When their lords are away fighting, the women, having anointed certain stones and fruits and exposed them on a board, sing: 'O Lord sun and moon let the bullets rebound from our husbands. . . . .just as raindrops rebound from these objects which are smeared with oil' " (ibid. p.67). Here, prayer and spell are inextricably mixed up. The difference between the two is that a prayer is an act of supplication, a spell the expression of the desired effect of a projective act. Magic and religion, characterised by spell and prayer respectively, "must be held apart in thought, from another point of view they may legitimately be brought together" (ibid. p.72).

The theme is taken up again in the essay "Is Taboo a negative Magic?", first published in "Essays presented to Tylor", 1907. It is again a thesis of Frazer's which provides the starting-point of his argument, namely that taboo is not a negative magic but a negative mana. Taboos are based on the apprehended presence of a mysterious power of awfulness. A taboo always implies a sanction in the shape of some suggestion of mystic punishment, but the nature of the punishment is rarely defined and, if specific, "an infinite 'plus' of awfulness will. . . be found, on closer examination, to attach to it" (Threshold p.79). This plus can only be explained by the fact that underlying the taboo is a supernatural power which fills the hearts of men with trepidation. How can we explain "that when an Australian black-fellow discovered his wife to have lain on his blanket he wholly succumbed to terror and was dead within a fortnight? Only a twilight fear, a measureless horror, could thus kill" (ibid. p.95). Sometimes the mysterious power pervades the whole of nature, requiring that all activity should be sustained and the village gates closed as in the case of a 'genna' (general taboo) in the Manipur region. Had the information been available at the time, the Balinese 'njepi' (from 'sepi', silent) could have provided the author with an even better example. On the occasion of the annual 'njepi', the day on which all the witches of Bali are about, even the fires must be extinguished. Somewhere danger is lurking, an unknown danger because it is supernatural by nature.

However conceived or materialised, it is always mana which must be respected. One year later, in his essay "The Conception of Mana" (1908), Marett draws the final conclusion from his reconnaissance in the field of taboos, summing up everything in the statement that mana and taboo together present us with a workable minimum definition of religion in which 'taboo' represents the negative and 'mana' the positive aspect of the supernatural. The supernatural itself is not a moral notion; it is neither "moral nor immoral, but simply unmoral" (Threshold p.114).

We need not enter into Marett's comment on the personal and the impersonal in rudimentary religious thought. We willingly agree that the line drawn between the personal and the impersonal is fluctuating and vague (ibid. p.100). Here we must sum up the effect of Marett's essays on the theory of religion. We do not need many words for it. The main effect has been the recognition of psychological or emotional motives as prime movers in the shaping of conceptions of supernatural powers behind and above the every-day world. Marett does not specify the nature of these motives. Throughout a certain vagueness prevails, which is one of the essential properties of the religious category. This vagueness is typified in the "Introduction" to the (2nd) edition of his "Threshold": "My own view is that savage religion is something not so much thought out as danced out, that, in other words, it develops under conditions, psychological and sociological, which favour emotional and motor processes, whereas ideation remains relatively in abeyance" (p. XXXI). In those days, these views meant an important step forward; it soon became apparent that many students of anthropology had the greatest difficulty in realising their purport.

3. More forms of belief in mana. Soul-substance and dynamism in the theories of A. C. Kruyt

In the meantime ethnographic and linguistic research among the North American Indians had led to the discovery of concepts more or less akin to the Melanesian (or rather Polynesian) 'mana'. One of these is the Omaha term 'wakanda', used to denote supernatural power as well as spirit or deity (cf. in particular Miss A. C. Fletcher in Bull. nr. 30 of the Bureau of American Indian Ethnology, 1910).

In 1902 J. N. B. Hewitt, in a short article entitled "Orenda and a Definition of Religion", A. A. 4(1902) pp.33-46, drew attention to the Iroquois concept of 'orenda'. Unfortunately, he founded his exposition more on considerations of a general theoretical nature than on Iroquoise notions pure and simple. "Welfare is the primary motive underlying all human effort", is the opening sentence of the essay. He further argues that to the mind of primitive man there is a mystic potency of variable efficiency and purpose at work in all things and bodies present in his universe. The Iroquois call this mystic potency 'orenda'. A shaman has 'orenda' as well as a hunter. If the hunter is successful, his 'orenda' has thwarted the 'orenda' of the quarry; if the reverse is the case the 'orenda' of the game was stronger than that of the hunter. The 'orenda' of the cicada summons the heat of the day, because the singing of the cicada is loudest in the early morning of a hot day; the 'orenda' of the rabbit controls the snow, since the rabbit barks the underbrush at a height indicating the depth of the snow which will fall during the winter. Orenda controls the conditions of human well-being, it is active in rites and ceremonies and it is embodied in gods and spirits. Religion is a system of words, actions and devices, employed to ensure a state of well-being through the 'orenda' of other entities, and it is interesting to note that one of the more fundamental connotations of 'orenda' is singing or chanting, activities closely associated with the performance of charm and ritual.

In an article called "The Algonkin Manitou", published in the Journal of American Folk-lore 18(1905), William Jones presented the 'manitou' concept of the Algonkin Indians in terms which are highly reminiscent of those commonly used for the description of the concepts of 'mana' and 'orenda'.

He stresses the impersonal character of 'manitou', calling it a cosmic, mysterious property, believed to exist everywhere in nature. It can become identified with objects of nature but it may also manifest itself in spirit form. It always awakens a sense of mystery and it is closely connected with ritual performance and the recital of myth. The description given is rather interpretative in character and the more personal manifestations of 'manitou' are more or less glossed over. One thing, however, is clear enough, viz. the belief in a pervading, mysterious power closely connected with the spirit world and manifesting itself in the most divergent ways and objects.

Since then, words more or less synonymous with 'mana' have been discovered in many societies. They need not be discussed here, but an exception must be made for Kruyt's 'discovery' of what he called 'zielestof' (soul-substance) among a number of Indonesian peoples. The misconceptions raised by this notion as well as by some of the later work of Kruyt give occasion for a broader discussion of his contributions to ethnological theory, not because of their intrinsic value, but because the misconceptions involved are symptomatic of a widely spread and persistent leaning toward home-brewn rationalist interpretations.

Albert C. Kruyt (1869-1949) had a good reputation as a missionary. In the then uncontrolled interior of central Celebes (Posso) he had applied a new method of missionary approach; he postponed preaching until he had mastered the language and studied the local culture. In 1905 he published a book, called "Het Animisme in den Indischen Archipel", an attempt at a comprehensive description of Indonesian animism. Wilken had previously tackled the same subject in a series of articles which appeared under an only slightly different title in 1884 and 1885 (above, p.44). Unfortunately, Kruyt almost immediately became entangled in the complexity of the Indonesian manifestations of the soul-complex. From Skeat he borrowed the view "that the root idea seems to be an all pervading animism, involving a certain common principle ('semangat') in Man and Nature" (Het Animisme, p.1). Notions of such a vital principle are also found among other peoples than those described by Skeat, and Kruyt was well aware of the important difference between this notion of a vital principle and that of soul in the Tylorean sense of the word — the soul which leaves the body temporarily during the dream or in illness, and survives as a ghost at death. Instead of carefully analysing the various terms which, together, define the soul-complex in each of the Indonesian cultures he studied, Kruyt concluded that throughout Indonesia two notions had to be discerned, the soul which survives as a ghost, and the vital principle just mentioned to which he gave the name 'zielestof', soul-substance. Had he left it at this we would have no reason for complaint other than that of a careless method of description. But Kruyt did not leave it at this. On the contrary; he immediately used his notion of soul-substance as a heuristic principle for the explanation of magic, and wherever he came across a magical act (or one to him incomprehensible anyway) he resolutely regarded such acts as proof of the presence of a notion of soul-substance. A typical case is his comment on the custom of the Olo-Ngadju Dayak in Borneo of offering a gift of rice to grindstone, hatchet and rice-knife (the special knife for cutting the ears) just before the harvest begins: "To-day this act of nourishing has acquired the character of an offering brought to the vaguely personified soul-substance of these utensils. Originally the custom served to make the utensils hard through the addition of the soul-substance of the rice" (Het Animisme p.159). It is obvious that here the notion of soul-substance is not a fact derived from what the Olo-Ngadju said or thought, but the interpretation surreptitiously substituted for the data by Kruyt himself. The actual presence of a notion of soul-substance is an unproved contention.

From the point of view of the science of religion even more objectionable is the philosophy underlying these interpretations. It is foreign to anything resembling Marett's cautious interrogation of fact or his respect of emotional values. Instead, we are straightaway led back to a rationalism even more pronounced than Frazer's. To Kruyt the aim of religion is the collection and increase of soul-substance, an idea which won popular support in many circles. Among professional anthropologists sharing this view, Jensen and his school must be mentioned. They do not use the word soul-substance but 'Schöpfungskraft', a term coined by Jensen. Even as late as 1960 so intelligent an anthropologist as the late C. A. Schmitz distorted the description of religious behaviour in his "Beiträge zur Ethnografie des Wantoat Tales" with explanatory remarks on the collection of 'Partikelchen Schöpfungskraft' (small scraps of creation-power).

A more general term for soul-substance is magical power. Kruyt was one of the first to substitute it for soul-substance, namely in the series of articles published in Bijdragen 74, 75, 76 (1918-1920) under the caption "Measa, eene Bijdrage tot het Dynamisme" (Measa, a contribution to Dynamism). 'Measa' is the Toradja word for ominous, inauspicious. It signifies a bad omen. If a man breaks a pot just before his departure on a long journey, this is a bad omen and he will stay at home. He has had his warning. Kruyt's interpretation exceeds by far the purport of the simple incident. Ignoring the fact that nobody feels anxious if a pot breaks on a day with nothing exceptional on the programme, he turns the event as such into the agent of disaster. The pot has been burnt in the fire and by this act magical power has been piled up in it. This power is set free when the pot breaks into pieces, and then threatens the prospective traveller who is in a magically unstable state himself, because he is at the point of setting out on an important enterprise. A great many cases are interpreted along these lines, cases supplied by the native teachers whom he had summoned up to answer his questions. About 250 pages are devoted to a stream of cases with explanations abounding with analogies borrowed from the theory of electricity. Terms such as magic power, emanation of a magical current, restoration of the magical equilibrium, paralysing of magical power and so on, recur with astounding regularity. At the end we learn to our astonishment that the Toradja is unaware of the proper background of his actions, an ignorance hardly believable after this exposition of an astute intellectualism.

Mana, presented by Marett as the product of a notion of awe, a term covering the manifestations of mysterious or supernatural power (cf. Threshold p.99), is here turned into an energy subject to rationally calculated manipulation. The rules of its manipulation are fixed by a specific doctrine, the doctrine of 'dynamism', a term first proposed (at least as far as I am aware) by Van Gennep in his "Rites de Passage". Dynamism is the doctrine preceding the doctrine of animism. We note, however, that it is only too evident that the doctrine of dynamism does not reflect the ideas fostered by the poor dynamists themselves, because they are supposed to be unaware of their real motives. The doctrine pays very little attention to what primitive people think themselves. In fact the doctrine is hardly more than a simple, heuristic principle applied by rationalist westerners to explain in their own terms what is unintelligible to them in the behaviour of primitive people. The use of this principle reveals more about the opinions of the authors than of the way of thinking of primitive people.

Interpretations like those forwarded by Kruyt are widespread, even today. Of course, professional anthropologists rarely subscribe to them now (although they occasionally do) but in the early years of the century they were readily accepted. Actually, Kruyt's ideas on magic power were taken from F. D. E. van Ossenbruggen who, in turn, had borrowed them from Vierkandt (cf. Van Ossenbruggen, Het primitieve denken, Bijdragen 71, 1916, pp.33 ff.). Fortunately, the term dynamism turned out to be short-lived, but the same cannot be said of magic power, a term of amazing persistence, haunting the works of scientific ethnography with almost undiminished frequency. There are at least two reasons for it. The first is that magic and magic power are highly convenient short-hand expressions which can be so applied as to leave the reader free to interpret them just as he likes. The other is that the problem of the contrast between magic and religion, initiated by Frazer and reduced but not eliminated by Marett, still holds its sway over the theory of religion, the prevailing view being that the two should be discerned as the contrasting poles of a continuum. In essence this is a mock solution which leaves the problem intact.

At the beginning of the century the contrast between religion and magic was strongly emphasised. An often quoted book on the subject is Karl Beth, "Religion und Magie bei den Naturvölkern" (1914). Here the contrast is depicted as well-nigh absolute. The book is not of such quality that we need discuss it here; more important is the apparent fact that by that time magic had turned into the central problem of religious anthropology. There was ample reason for it. The great importance attached by the magician to the precise performance of all the details of the rite, combined with his unrestricted reliance on the efficacy of a well performed rite, strongly conflict with the fact that the powers involved in the rite are by definition superhuman and supernatural. The actions of superhuman beings must be incalculable as such, and their power necessarily invites an attitude of dependence among the believers, an attitude flatly contradicted by a magician's reliance on strict procedure. There is, indeed, reason to suppose that the magicians believe they have some supernatural power of their own; concepts as 'mana', 'wakanda', 'orenda' etc. do suggest that something like a manipulative magic power is not foreign to their thinking. Even if it is admitted that Kruyt's rationalistic interpretation must be false, the problem remains how people can believe in concepts so utterly contradictory, and incompatible with all logical notions of reality as well.

4. Konrad Theodor Preusz (1869-1938)

The problem of magic has been the problem of many authors and one of the most interesting among them is K. Th. Preusz. He was one of those scholars who gradually change and develop their ideas, thus keeping in constant touch with the time, yet without losing continuity with their own past. Preusz was an Americanist, a staff member and later one of the directors of the Berliner Museum für Völkerkunde. Shortly before his first visit to Mexico he published "Der Ursprung von Religion und Kunst", a series of articles which appeared in "Globus" (vols. 86 and 87, 1904, 1905). The main purport of his essay is a new theory of origin. He states that the majority of primitive cult-forms cannot be explained by animistic belief. These forms must be older because they are associated with magic. The central problem is the magic of the ritual, an interesting formula because here magic is neither contrasted to ritual nor set apart from it. The ritual has a magical effect of its own accord. We are confronted with observable acts producing unexplainable effects. The occurrence of such effects is not confined to rites and magical acts. According to Mexican folk-belief the cicadas produce the heat of the early afternoon with their harsh chirping which sets in about noon. In the rain-ritual the imitative act of the tobacco-smoking priest causes the rain to come. But the gods too perform this sort of imitative magic; the god of the clouds is represented as a tobacco-pipe with the clouds forthcoming from the pipe. In all these acts and objects a wonderful force is operating, a 'Zauberkraft' (litt. magic power) which he describes as a substance capable of changing things, effectuating the most heterogeneous transitions. The gods owe their origin to this 'Zauberkraft'; they themselves are the extraordinarily powerful magic substances resulting from and through the rites and their performance.

To explain the origin of the cult and the conceptions ensuing from it, Preusz refers to the difficult circumstances under which early man had to hold his own. No longer able to rely on his instincts as a source of effective action and forced to act rationally instead, he stumbled from one error into another. It was only by following the poor remnants of his instincts and by imitating the events around him, that the earliest human beings succeeded in asserting themselves. The beginnings of religion and art — another activity in which imitation plays a prominent part — emanate from this imitative phase, from this 'menschliche Urdummheit' (human arch-stupidity).

The appeal to this 'menschliche Urdummheit' was a serious slip. Preusz did not succeed in explaining how everything had come about. He never once referred to it afterwards and in his later work he turned more and more away from questions of origin. Yet, for long after the term was held against him. Undeservedly so, because the analysis preceding the final explanation was important enough. His observation that animals, men and gods are endowed with 'Zauberkraft' is as worthy of being given consideration as the hypothesis that the gods owe their origin to ritual, a hypothesis closely related to Robertson Smith's.

The problem of magic held Preusz in its grip, and in 1914 he returned to it in a booklet which for years after served in various countries as an introduction to the study of primitive religion, viz. "Die Geistige Kultur der Naturvölker" (Leipzig 1914). In this book questions of origin are no longer emphasised. The author concentrates on description, and much attention is paid to human needs. A point of interest is his frequent use of the term magico-religious, a term incidentally used before by Marett. It is not a term which can be recommended because it is self-contradictory and contributes more to the preservation of the problem than to its solution. When seen in the context of the time, these objections weigh less heavily because the combination implies a recognition that magic and religion cannot be separated, a point which in those days was well in need of special emphasis.

Preusz stresses the difficulties of primitive man's life. In his never ending daily need his magico-religious rites are a source of comfort and spiritual strength. He does not give an explanation of these religious phenomena, but the fact that he places the religious life in the existential context in which it belongs, certainly constitutes a decisive step forward.

Much attention is paid to the specific modes of primitive thought, a problem raised a few years earlier by L. Lévy-Bruhl (cf. below, pp.127 ff.). According to Preusz the difference between the mental make-up of primitive and modern man is primarily a difference in modes of perception. Among primitives perception is complex, and as a case in point he mentions the Huichol of Mexico who associate deer with peyote. This association is connected with the notion that the stars are the deer of the sun who hunts them at sunrise. The prosperity of the crops depends on the success of the sun's chase, and because of this deer are the sacrificial animals on festive occasions. On such occasions peyote is also needed. It must be brought from the far east, from the land of sunrise. When the expedition in search of peyote arrives there, first of all deer must be shot and thus deer and peyote are associated. They belong together. Similar complex notions can be noted in every-day magic. A disease is represented as an object which must be sucked out. A potsherd of hearth-stone, sewn in the seam of a garment, protects its user because the stone has been hardened in the fire for generations. By resorting to these means man recognises his inability to manage his own affairs to the full, a recognition which leads him into the field of religion. The realisation that supernatural powers are implied grows, and whereas man becomes more and more conscious of his own impotence these powers assume the shapes of gods.

The exposition is more an attempt to describe than to explain. The reference to perception as an important element in the constitution of complex notions can be appreciated as a contribution to a fuller description, but its explanatory value is small. The facts remain as impervious to comprehension as before. On one point Preusz is faithful to his previous views. The gods originate from and are personifications of the powers which man attempts to influence through the cult. In no way they owe their origin to the ghosts, and in this context Preusz presents a new theory on mortuary rites, one which fully suits his ideas about complex notions. The mortuary rites must protect the living against the dead and the nefarious influences emanating from them. The dead participate in the powers of death and decay, and the connections which the living have with them must be severed. Primarily mortuary rites are farewell-rites during which the dead are explicitly sent away to the land of the dead. The worship of the dead must be of a later date; it could not originate until people came to believe that it was the ancestors who had instituted the mortuary rites.

Many years later Preusz returned once more to the problems presented by death and the dead, and by the relations between gods and ritual. However, at that time he also included in his considerations the belief in a supreme being. In the meantime, the nature and origin of the supreme being had been the topic of elaborate discussions and these should be considered before we return to Preusz. The presentation of these discussions in the next section must be incomplete, because we must pass over the theory presented by F. Wilh. Schmidt. It belongs to another chapter for the simple reason that in the latter's theory the concept of supernatural power does not play a part at all. To Schmidt the concept of a supernatural power, which might be of a more or less impersonal nature, is a philosophical and not a religious concept.

5. Mediators, Supreme Beings and Mana

Andrew Lang's plea for paying more attention to the role of supreme beings in primitive religious systems was a first warning that the spirit world of these systems is more complicated than so far had been surmised. Some seven years later discussion arose on yet another category of spiritual beings to which very little attention had been paid, namely that of the mediators between god (or gods) and man. The category is rather heterogeneous in composition; there are saviours, culture heroes and tricksters, but they are all the same in this respect — in one way or another they all mediate between the world of the gods and that of human beings. If from the point of view of ideology the tricksters sometimes seem to be of a rather profane nature, later studies have sufficiently demonstrated that their role in mythology is important enough to admit them to this company of mediators. Besides, even Hermes must be recognised as a trickster and he was an extremely popular god among the Greeks (cf. J. P. B. de Josselin de Jong, "De Oorsprong van den goddelijken Bedrieger").

The discussion was started by Kurt Breysig's essay, "Die Entstehung des Gottesgedankens und der Heilbringer" (1905). Breysig founded his argument on the evolutionist hypothesis that a pre-animistic stage had been followed by an animistic one, and that at the end of the second period saviours (Heilbringer) had originated from the worship in memory of eminent individuals who had distinguished themselves as heroes. The argument is a purely euhemeristic one, also in its sequence. These heroes were supposed to have developed later into gods who subsequently became personifications of nature. The content of the essay is neither convincing nor impressive, and its one noteworthy merit is that it stimulated Paul Ehrenreich to refute the argument in a long article, entitled "Götter und Heilbringer" (ZfE 38 pp.536-610, 1906).

Ehrenreich, a German Americanist, might well be called the last of the nature-mythologists. His principal work in this field is his book "Die allgemeine Mythologie und ihre ethnologischen Grundlagen" (1912) which shall not be discussed here. We confine ourselves to a survey of his rejoinder to Breysig, who had hit Ehrenreich at a point which lay close to his heart. Ehrenreich argued that the principal myths are always nature-myths, in particular the myths of sun and moon, because these heavenly bodies are often symbols of human life and death. Through the cult the heroes of nature-myths developed into gods. However, a nature-god never represents more than a certain aspect of nature. Such a god can never develop into a supreme being of his own accord. The monotheistic trend has another origin. It refers to the medicine-man who brings diseases and cures them, causes and wards off disasters. The supreme being has his origin in a heavenly medicine-man, the projection of an earthly one, who is capable of doing everything which surpasses human power. If this celestial medicine-man develops into an all-powerful Creator-god, he may become too high and elated to continue caring about human beings any more. When this happens people need a mediator who concerns himself with earthly matters. This mediator is the Heilbringer, the saviour, who again is either a kind of glorified shaman or medicine-man, or is associated with one of the heavenly bodies, in particular with the moon. If associated with the latter, the mediator easily turns into an ambivalent, i.e. dual character, who represents in his two manifestations the light and the dark moon respectively. In essence the mediators are not deified human beings, but projections of human nature on the one hand, humanisations of the supreme being on the other.

Ehrenreich's rebuttal of Breysig's exposition is of interest because his nature-mythological approach is better founded than that of Max Müller's. It is not necessary to agree with Ehrenreich that all the principal myths are nature-myths to admit that nature-myths are often very important. Neither is it necessary to subscribe to his theory of the celestial medicine-man to appreciate the possibility of an association between moon and trickster as symbol of the latter's ambivalent nature. It is impossible to enter more fully into these questions. The mediators — saviours, culture-heroes and tricksters — have been discussed by many authors and those interested can find a useful survey of the relevant literature up to 1930 in A. van Deursen, "Der Heilbringer" (Groningen 1931). It is uncertain whether a discussion of this category of supernatural beings can be of any use. Such terms as mediator, Heilbringer, saviour, culture-hero and trickster are our terms, products of our attempts at categorisation. To what extent are we justified in making these categories and bringing them together under the common denominator of mediators? Do they have so much in common, and if they do, can we decide that they really belong together without taking into consideration the function of each of them in its own religious system? I must confess that the relevance of some of these attempts at categorisation is not always clear to me. After all, each religion is a whole and it is not without risk to compare the parts without comparing the wholes. Nevertheless, the discussion had to be mentioned, not the least so because some of the points raised here had an impact on our main concern in this section, Nathan Söderblom's book on the growth of the belief in god.

Nathan Söderblom, "Das Werden des Gottesglaubens" (Leipzig 1916; a Swedish edition appeared in 1914 in slightly different form). Söderblom (1866-1931), former professor in the history of religion at Leipzig and since 1914 Lutheran archbishop of Sweden, made an attempt at synthesising the three main themes which so far had been forwarded in the science of religion, viz. animism, the belief in supernatural power, and the belief in supreme beings and mediators. None of these phenomena occurs in isolation and each of them is elaborately analysed in the book just mentioned.

In his discussion of animism Söderblom emphasises the importance of animatistic phenomena. Personification and the tendency to experience things as live beings are of common occurrence, in particular among children. Söderblom's ideas on this point bear clear traces of the influence of the famous Swedish novelist of his days, Selma Lagerlöf. The main trend, however, is philosophical. The ultimate source of the soul-concept is the self-consciousness of the individual, the consciousness "ein sich selbst be-stimmendes Wesen zu sein", to be a self-defining being.

'Mana' is in the first place vitality; it is connected with life and as such it is correlated with the soul-concept. Various words for soul are, in fact, words for vitality, for the power of life manifesting itself in man. In this context he analyses West-African fetishism. A good example is the 'nkisi', the medicine-bag, a carrying-net stuffed with a collection of the most het-erogeneous objects, such as one or more skins of monkeys or wild cats, with chalk, mica, resin, salt, gunpowder, pepper, hair, animal claws, feathers, teeth, seeds, metal rings, rock-crystals and so on. The bag is anointed with palm-oil and coloured with ochre; rattles and a wooden block are attached on the outside. The 'nkisi' is made by a priest who does all he can to fill it with everything curious or dangerous (sacred roots, leopard-claws and so on) which happens to come his way. Whilst he is at work the villagers as-semble round his hut to sing. Now that the 'nkisi' is consecrated it exerts a mysterious power, it can cure and cause disease, it can harm the enemy, chase away spooks and sorcerers, and protect the owner's property. The question arises whether there is a spirit in the 'nkisi' or not. The question is unanswerable. Primarily it is an impersonal power which manifests itself, but often the contents of the 'nkisi' include a wooden puppet as well, which suggests something personal. Apparently we stand on the threshold of a well-ordered 'Sondergötterreligion', as is confirmed when we turn further north, to Benin, where these puppets are real idols, images of gods. With the 'nkisi' and with fetishism in general, we enter an area which is transi-tional between power and spirit. We may be sure that many spirits of older ethnography are really manifestations of a much vaguer nature. Supernatu-ral power, then, may be combined with spirits. However, not with spirits only, but with gods and even supreme beings as well. 'Manitou' is both su-pernatural power and supreme being. A more generally known case is that of 'Brahma' with the derivative notions of 'brahman' (power) and 'brah-mān' (the caste). A third instance is that of the Japannese concept of 'kami', which sometimes denotes power and extraordinary qualities in men, animals and things, or then again a deity. Power is 'ce qui sort de l'ordinai-re', and is associated with the contrast between the sacred and the ordinary.

Finally there is the category of the 'Urheber', originators, a term which Söderblom probably borrowed from Usener. The originators are the beings who explain the nature of things, their 'so-Sein'. Along with Ehrenreich, Söderblom thought that the prototype of the originator is the shaman or medicine-man, the man who works miracles. The originators are the makers, the institutors and messengers; the Heilbringer (saviours) are also among them. The originators are a category encompassing supreme beings as well as mediators; even the Australian 'alcheringa-beings' (the dream-time beings of more recent ethnography) are included. A strict distinction is made between originators and nature-gods. The latter enjoy a cult, the originators bring one. Söderblom's line of thought differs widely from the one of F. Wilh. Schmidt. The latter's 'Urmonotheismus' is decidedly discarded; according to Söderblom it is turning things upside down to have development start with a supreme being (cf. the relevant section in Werden des Gottesglaubens pp. 150-162).

In his subsequent discussion of the motives of religion Söderblom advances the suggestion that religion owes its origin to plural causation. Souls (and the beings of animism and animatism generally) derive their origin from the wish to express 'what' things really are; in essence they are manifestations of volition; power is associated with the 'how' of things, and reflection on it leads to the idea of the supernatural; the originators, finally, demonstrate 'whence' everything is and lay the foundations of the cosmological and ethical systems.

The theory is an exercise in mild scholasticism rather than an explanation. We do not come far with it and the supposed plural causation is so poorly elucidated, that the need to detect a basic motive common to the divergent forms of religion is all the more sharply realised. Söderblom himself must have had an inkling of it. Passing on to a discussion of magic he states that the basic idea of all religion is 'das Heilige', the sacred in the sense of the holy, fas, as is confirmed by his remark: "Fromm ist der für den es etwas Heiliges gibt" (ibid. p.193). His compass of the holy is wide. The notion of it is present in the attitude adopted where and when people are confronted with mana. It is an attitude in which fear and confidence go combined. The notion of the holy is also present in the manifestations usually labelled as magic. Time and again the performer of so-called magic gives evidence that he is aware of a higher power in which he has confidence, although he also fears it. These acts are religious acts and the use of the term magic should be confined to the various forms of anti-social magic. The latter alone are not religion, because they have nothing to do with the sacred defined as the holy. Contrary to this, white magic should be recognised as religion. Religion does not depend on the belief in gods or spirits alone; identical rites are performed where a belief in spirits and gods prevails as well as where such a belief is absent. Some rain-making rituals constitute a case in point. The essential fact is the notion of the sacred.

The term sacred as used by Söderblom has a different meaning than it has with Durkheim, a fact already apparent by its restriction to the holy. The difference between the two is explicitly emphasised, because in his evaluation of magic Söderblom became aware that he had come so close to Durkheim's views that the difference between their respective philosophies might be obscured. Therefore he stresses that the sacred is not a product of society but derives its origin from an irrationality. What that irrationality is, is hardly specified; it is a point which, two years later, would be taken up by Rudolf Otto in a penetrating analysis of the idea of the holy as a category sui generis.

At the end of this section a few remarks are in place. As a comprehensive theory of the various forms of religion, Söderblom's book is a failure. Nevertheless, it laid the basis for a new approach, that of the phenomenological school. Moreover, as a description it certainly is a valuable book. Among its merits special mention should be made of the comment on fetishism and the proposal to confine the use of the term magic to anti-social acts of sorcery and witchcraft. Söderblom's outstanding merit is that he was the first to be clearly aware that an important part of what is ordinarily called magic is really religion, not only because it is relevant to supernatural power, but in no less degree because the attitude of the performer is a religious one.

The difficulty is how to decide what exactly is a religious attitude. It has been a matter of dispute in anthropological theory of religion for many years. The answers given are sometimes of a psychological nature, then again inspired by idealistic philosophy. In the next section we shall take stock of some later developments of the psychological approach as embodied in the works of two American anthropologists, Lowie and Radin. We shall be led far ahead of the period under discussion, but an evaluation of so evasive a concept as religious attitude or sentiment is impossible without explaining the later development of its role in anthropological theory. Having completed our excursion, we shall return to the second decennium of the 20th century to study the beginning of a more philosophically inspired approach to the problem. Its subsequent elaboration will again lead us well ahead to the years between 1930 and 1940.

6. The religious sentiment in the works of two American authors

R. H. Lowie (1883-1957) is the more cautious of the two authors here to be discussed, the one also whose authority ranks highest. He wrote the most widely read handbook on "Primitive Religion" which, under this title, appeared for the first time in 1924. In the Introduction (p. XVI of the edition of 1960) he defines religion as follows: "Religion is verily a universal feature of human culture, not because all societies foster a belief in spirits, but because all recognize in some form or other awe-inspiring, extra-ordinary manifestations of reality". Lowie does not mention the term Supernatural here which, in the sequence of the book, is the term which he uses alternately with the Extra-ordinary (both words duly written with a capital) to indicate the core-notion of religion. He notes that it may well be that primitive people have no specific words equivalent to our terms, but that does not imply that the notion of the Extra-ordinary or the Supernatural escapes them.

Religion is not a matter of the intellectual recognition of the supernatural. Everything depends on the subjective attitude, not on any objective characteristic: "the dominance of the emotional side of consciousness in religion is universally accepted, and where that phase of mental life is in relative abeyance religion must be considered wanting" (Primitive Religion p.XIII). Elsewhere (ibid. pp.340, 342), he calls "religious thrill" or "mystic thrill" the true characteristic of religion. In all religions we meet with a certain kind of sentiment that, when concentrated on a certain object, creates the supernatural. Science, too, or a philosophy, can be involved in this religious atmosphere. The idea of a 'religious thrill', mentioned already by Marett and suggested by William James, is further emphasised, but an exact description of the thrill is kept in abeyance. Actually, Lowie is less interested in exact definitions or generalisations than in concrete description. The first part of his book is devoted to the description of four religions. One of these is the religion of the Crow Indians with which he was better acquainted than anyone. These Indians display vis-à-vis the universe a humility which sharply contrasts with the personal pride prevailing in their social contacts with tribal fellows. Confronted with the universe, the Crow Indian "evinced that sense of absolute dependence on something not himself, which Schleiermacher and Feuerbach postulate as the root of the religious sentiment" (ibid. p.18). The case is specific and its description is not followed by general theory. Lowie, a pupil of Boas and a typical representative of the Boas tradition, preferred facts and he shrinked from forcing them by theories or generalisations. Even more so than generalisations, theories of origin were anathema to Lowie. The view that such theories offer no certainty at all, was nowhere stronger than among the scholars of the school of Boas.

Paul Radin (1883-1959) goes a step further than Lowie. We shall find occasion to point out that this step is, after all, in many respects a step backward. Radin, who had field-experience among the Winnebago Indians, laid down his views on primitive spiritual life and religion in two books, "Primitive Man as Philosopher" (1927) and "Primitive Religion, its Nature and Origin" (1938). A later work, "Die religiöse Erfahrung der Naturvölker" (1951), did not bring anything substantially new.

"Primitive Man as Philosopher" is a refreshing protest against the current misconception of earlier theorists that in a primitive tribe all people are alike and think alike. Actually, the members of a group of primitive people differ as much among themselves in temperament and individual talents as is the case with us. Not only are they different individually, but they also aspire to be different among themselves. There is much emulation and rivalry between tribal members, the one trying to score off the other. The common notion that primitive people always strictly follow the rules of the tribe, is not true. There are, of course, a number of rules which are rather strictly adhered to, because transgression raises so much communal indignation that harsh punishment is practically always certain, but there are others which are applied or ignored with a marked degree of indifference and sophistication. In conclusion he states: "there is not the slightest indication of the existence of any fundamental difference in [primitive people's] emotional nature as compared with ours. I think we may confidently assume that the same differentiation of ability and temperament holds for them that holds for us" (Primitive Man pp.364, 365).

The differentiation of ability lays the foundation of the dual opposition dominating Radin's argument, the opposition between the man of practice and the thinker. As among ourselves thinkers do not number more than one to a hundred, but it is these thinkers who are the creators of the higher aspects of culture, the philosophers who on the one hand have wisdom, and on the other the taste and capability of philosophising on nature and on the unity of all the various manifestations of religious beings. His 'Primitive Man' abounds with delightful instances of statements forwarded by thinkers from among a great variety of cultures. To the man of practice, however, Radin pays very little attention. He is depicted as a doer who is less concerned with causation than with the practical effect of what he does, and because of this pragmatic attitude he is interested in the magical means which may favour the realisation of his aims. He is not interested in his own inner life as the thinker is, who is more of an introvert as well as a thoughtful observer. The latter, for instance, is aware that the solar disc, the heat, the sunbeams, and the corona of the sun are all one, whereas the man of action thinks that they are different things. In fact, the latter does not give thought to it; he just accepts the ideas presented by the thinkers without understanding them and without discernment. The vagueness and confusion of his thinking are reflected in the ethnographic descriptions produced by students who relied on the information of these men of action, who are so much interested in results that to them a deity is identical with his effect. The deity is valued for its relation and usefulness to man, just like any object.

On the face of it, it is all very interesting, but we are left in the dark as to how this extremely small minority of thinkers manages to stamp its imprint on local culture. Sometimes it seems as if two cultures exist side by side. In chapter XIII, for instance, Radin refers to a couple of inter-related myths, one of which he supposes to be the product of the men of action, the other of the thinkers in the relevant culture. It is all very unconvincing. After all, thinkers and men of action participate in one and the same culture, and the thinkers could not possibly give shape to the society's cultural life if they did not give form to notions on which all the members of the society agree. Besides, the contrast between thinkers and men of action is presented as an absolute one, whereas it can at best be a polar opposition. Reflecting on Radin's preference for thinkers, the reader is beset by the unpleasant feeling that he is being taken in tow by a curious manifestation of the intellectual's pride. The feeling persists when he takes Radin's second book to hand, from which I quote the following surprisingly apposite passage: "The priest-thinkers, with that intellectual arrogance which their later colleagues have inherited, seem to have sensed this and to have looked with commiserating contempt upon their less intellectual fellowmen" (Primitive Religion p.267).

Radin's "Primitive Religion" is a book which hardly should be discussed in this chapter at all, although the definition given of religion on p.3 fits remarkably well in its context. Religion "consists of two parts: the first an easily definable, if not precisely specific feeling; and the second certain specific acts, customs, beliefs and conceptions associated with this feeling. The belief most inextricably connected with the specific feeling is a belief in spirits outside of man, conceived of as more powerful than man and as controlling all those elements in life upon which he lays most stress". The reader who expects an exposition continuing the line of thought inaugurated by Marett and followed by Lowie, will be disappointed. Radin is a Frazer in a modern disguise, adorned with feathers borrowed from Freud and Rudolf Otto. Like Frazer Radin is thoroughly convinced that magic is older than religion, but his explanation of magic is a Freudian one. The essence of magic is coercion in the interest of imperative organic needs (Primitive Religion p.61), born "in the childhood of thought, when thinking was fairly exclusively a form of not-understood coercion" (ibid. p.68). Religion presupposes the belief in spirits but not all belief in spirits is religion. On the contrary: "animism is not a religion at all; it is a philosophy" (ibid. p.198). It can only become religion when it becomes the object of that "easily definable, if not precisely specific feeling" which, in spite of the assertion of easy definability, remains in the mist. Though on p.4 Radin assures us that the feeling manifests "itself in a thrill, a feeling of exhilaration, exaltation, awe, and in a marked tendency to become absorbed in internal sensation", it has nothing specific in itself because he adds: "The condition itself, we may surmise, differs little from such states as intense aesthetic enjoyment or even the joy of living, for example. What distinguishes it from them is the nature of the subject matter calling it forth". This simply sends us back to the notion of spirits.

On the origin of religious concepts Radin is vague. He returns to it in various places without ever once being definite except on the point that they must derive from fear resulting from difficult economic conditions. Thinkers, of course, have paid an important contribution to shaping and elaborating these concepts. In the present book (Primitive Religion) the thinker is usually called by another term, viz. that of religious formulator or of priest-thinker. The earliest religious formulator is the shaman, an individual of neurotic disposition, subject to trances and to fits of unconsciousness (ibid. p.107). The shaman suffers, and in his suffering he gives shape to the suffering of the people at large. In his trances he is confronted with spirits and demons, and elaborating on these experiences the shaman becomes the first religious formulator, overpowered and overwhelmed by awe. Yet he is more than just that. His communications meet with response among the people whose sufferings are, in principle, the same as his own sufferings. He acts as a medicine-man and he cures their ailments. Economically his position is an enviable one and with the remuneration of his services, priestly fraud enters into the history of mankind. It is in the medicine-man's own interest to expand the spirit-world and to stress its power, as in a later phase of development it is to the benefit of the priest. The religious formulators and priest-thinkers represent a curious mixture of religion and imposture. They need not even be genuinely religious individuals themselves; the rewards of the position appeal to intelligent men strongly enough for them to assume the roles of religious formulator and priest even without the proper psychological qualifications. Radin's expositions of the self-interest of medicine-men and priests and their concomitant fraud lead us straight back to Frazer who never tired of this same argument.

Of course, Radin does not pretend that all religious formulators are impostors or religious illusionists. On the contrary, among these formulators there are also the thinkers, the philosophers, and the higher forms of religion undoubtedly present in primitive societies are the products of their contemplation. Where supreme beings are found these beings have emanated from the speculation of religious thinkers who are, in fact, the only ones in the community who believe in these beings. The men of action are content with magical acts and vague representations of spirits, which in one way or another must be induced to give proper assistance to their worshippers. Radin caustically criticises ethnographers who failed to differentiate between the information acquired from thinkers and from men of action, and thus gave a distorted picture of primitive religion. His criticism would have been justified in content (not in tone) if he had succeeded in proving the magnificence of the cleavage separating the thinkers from the men of action, but he has not even seen that there is a problem here, just as he did not see that there is a problem in magic which has been left unsolved. In fact, Radin did not take religion seriously. He first reduced it to a mere feeling which is not even specific, and as if that were not enough, he contrasted religious men to non-religious men, the latter being capable of religious feelings only in times of crisis.

In spite of the book's richness of magnificent instances and inspiring quotations from native informants, it must be condemned as a deplorable step backward. Radin's later work, "Die religiöse Erfahrung der Naturvölker", does not give us cause to alter this view. Although he strongly mitigated his former opinions on priestly imposture (Religiöse Erfahrung p.122 ftn. 27) he tenaciously kept to his division of mankind into thinkers and pragmatists, religious and irreligious men, a distinction which is not very helpful when a general phenomenon is at issue.

7. *The phenomenologists*

The psychological theories discussed so far have one point in common; they all fail to specify the feeling of dependence which is supposed to be the essence of the religious emotion. Moreover, the idea as such is not of anthropological origin but goes straight back to the German philosopher Schleiermacher who defined religion as "das Gefühl der schlechthinnigen Abhängigkeit", the feeling of absolute dependence. Not anthropologists, but Neo-Kantian philosophers who were also students of religion, set themselves the task of giving content to the religious feeling and to the definition of what religion really is. An important contribution to that end was the book of Rudolph Otto, "Das Heilige" (1917). The sub-title of the book shows that we are confronted with an elaboration of Söderblom's suggestion that the idea of the holy is founded on an irrational content: "Über das Irrationale in der Idee des Göttlichen und sein Verhältnis zum Rationalen".

Otto's starting point is theological. Every rational idea of God and every rational religion come to a dead end at the irremediable fact that the rational predicates attributed to God, fail to express the divine essence exhaustively. The divine subject can neither be encompassed nor even touched by these predicates; the subject is and remains an irrational datum. The core of religious experience and religious consciousness is not to be found in rationalisations and explanations, but in the holy. The holy is a notion which in modern usage acquired a predominantly ethical connotation; yet the idea of the holy is more encompassing than the moral alone. It is surrounded by a halo of notions originating from another complex of sensations which originally constituted the very essence of the idea of the holy. These notions were, in principle at least, ethically indifferent as is evidenced by, *inter alia*, the Latin *sacer* and the Hebrew *qadosj*. For this qualifying property of the holy in its older and more original sense he introduces the term *numinous*, from *numen*, the unspecified supernatural.

The numinous is a category *sui generis;* as an elementary concept it is not strictly definable. The meaning of such a concept like the numinous can only be prompted, so that the hearer suddenly grasps the idea and 'sees' it; in Otto's words: "Man kann dem Hörer zu ihrem Verständnis nur dadurch helfen, dasz man versucht, ihn durch Erörterung zu dem Punkte seines eigenen Gemütes zu leiten, wo sie ihm dann selber sich regen, entspringen und bewuszt werden musz" (Das Heilige p.7). An analysis of the numinous reveals that the concept is actually more encompassing than Schleiermacher's 'Gefühl der schlechthinnigen Abhängigkeit' alone; 'Abhängigkeit' involves a relation, whereas vis-à-vis the numinous every real relation is excluded. Confronted with the numinous the human subject loses all its weight and sinks away in its own nothingness, realising that the one true existent is the all-powerful other. The numinous does not prompt a feeling of dependence but of being a mere creature, and the numinous itself is experienced as "schlechthinnige Unnahbarkeit", as absolute unapproachability.

On further analysis the numinous is circumscribed as *mysterium tremendum*, a fear and trembling rousing mystery. The adjective *tremendum* is composed of three main elements, viz.

a fear in the sense of "grauen", of turning goose-flesh all-over;

b majestas, i.e. the exalted august;

c the energetic, i.e. the restless urging, acting, compelling and vital, in its pagan variety best exemplified in Goethe's 'Dämonisches'.

The core of the complex is the mysterium, the unfathomable which transcends understanding because it is the wholly other, 'das Ganz Andere', paradoxical and antinomic in one. As a mystery, however, it is at the same time a *fascinans*, inviting man to do something about it. Primitive man answers its call with shamanistic possession; on a higher stage of civilisation man indulges in mysticism, groping for the beatitude of unification with the divine, experiencing fright over his sinfulness on the one hand, and a need for atonement and reconciliation on the other. The mysticist, speaking of his experiences, can only express himself in negative terms; nevertheless he fully succeeds in transferring a clear notion of what he has in mind.

The holy — and the religious generally — cannot be explained or deduced from other categories. Man discovers the holy in and from himself. Passing through a series of successive sensations, the one prompting the other, he finally arrives at the holy, at "was unser eigener Erkenntnissvermögen, durch sinnliche Eindrücke blosz veranlaszt, aus sichselbst hergibt" (ibid. p.131). *Durch sinnliche Eindrücke blosz veranlaszt: t*he idea of the holy is autonomous, stemming from man himself, not from experience but originating in man as a consequence of his experience — in a way it is his answer to it. Of course it may and even will be elaborated by further interpretations and valuations, but the basis of it is an autonomous source of notions and sensations in the human mind itself. Because of the incommensurability of its content this source should not only be distinguished from Kant's practical and theoretical reason, but should also be taken for deeper and higher than both. In other words, religion is irreducible to any other category, it is *sui generis* and in man. Every man has a natural aptitude for religion, an aptitude which we see in its incipient form in primitive religion, as a religious shuddering over spooks, and gradually rising to ever higher forms of further development.

Otto's book is of a very modest size, an odd 200 pages, but the impression it made was enormous. In 1924 it had already a 12th edition. There was a sound reason for this popularity; by proclaiming religion an irreducible category sui generis, Otto had made religion unassailable. It now became possible to study religion not as an error which had to be explained, but as a normal human phenomenon. No wonder that theologians were enthusiastic and made Otto's ideas the starting-point for their studies of comparative religion as practised in theological faculties. However, before entering into this matter, a few critical remarks are well in place. First of all we note that the concept of religion forwarded here is a normative one. It embodies an elated ideal, inspired by Christian religion, not as it is practised, but as the theologically defined ideal of how it should be practised. Our second remark is, that the anthropologist can hardly feel happy with a theory which presents primitive religion as just an incipient development of the religious category. If there is only a germ of truth in the contention that it is a category sui generis higher and deeper than both practical and theoretical reason together, primitive people of to-day cannot be at the beginning of religious thought but must have elaborated on it in their own way. This, however, is not a principal point; it is an imperfection of the theory which might be mended.

More important — and this is the third point we must make — is the question whether the term category sui generis stands for anything of factual significance or is simply a learned euphemism for 'out-of-bounds'. The present author is not a philosopher and he must confess that he does not know what to do with the expression, just as he does not know what to do with the assurance that the numinous as an elementary concept is not strictly definable. The one thing he remembers is having read that Rickert, discussing elementary concepts, takes the concept of love as an example, arguing that there is no definition of love which can make one any the wiser. It is a statement to which he fully subscribes, but the fact that exactly love is presented as an instance raises the question whether this is perhaps a specialty of notions of an emotional or predominantly emotional nature. These are only questions, and questions far beyond his competence to answer. The one question within it is, whether a caption in latin, presumably meaning out-of-bounds, should prevent him from asking further questions. Here the answer is an unconditional no, in which he feels strengthened by his conviction that any definition of a category of fact should shun every reference to feelings or sensations, in short to anything emotional, the emotional, as Lévi-Strauss very adequately remarked, representing the most vague and unexplored part of the human mind, a part which should be explained instead of being used for explanation (Lévi-Strauss, Totemism p.71). The definition of religion, presented in chapter I, is not the product of a sudden impulse, but a deliberate effort to combine a broad compass with definite and factual description, the kind of description sadly absent where the essence of thought and ideas is sought for in emotions.

The lamp, lighted by Otto, was carried on by G. van der Leeuw, the most prominent scholar among the initiators of the phenomenological school. They accept religion as a human property, the task of the scientist being to understand and to make understood its divergent manifestations. First of all a thorough description of the facts is required. To that end the describer must give himself up to the facts. As far as is humanly possible, he must free himself from his private prejudices and approaches, so that he can take the detached observer's point of view, which alone allows him to keep aloof and recognise the humanly relevant in the phenomena by understanding them in their human meaning. In a more generalising way we might say that the method aims at unsealing what is humanly relevant in religious facts on the basis — or should we say bias? — that the category of the religious is a human universal.

The emphasis on good description is a step forward; it is to the phenomenologists' credit that they wished to steer clear of theories of origin which were in vogue up to 1915, and even later. Not one of these theories could stand the test of critical examination. Nothing was more needed at the time than exactly the thorough description of the religious phenomenon pleaded for in Van der Leeuw's theoretical exposition of methods. Equally desirable was the alleged aim of unsealing the universally human in the religious phenomena, even though it is possible to disagree with him on the formula which is not as exact as might be wished. We need not discuss that formula here; more important is it to know how the phenomenologists applied their method. The reply to this question is necessarily brief: they fell short of their own standards. There is hardly a more disappointing book than G. van der Leeuw's "Phaenomenologie der Religion" (1933). One quick glance through the table of contents suffices to show that this phenomenology is not concerned with religions but with religious phenomena, and the same holds true of the introduction of 1924, republished in 1948 under the title "Inleiding tot de Phaenomenologie van den Godsdienst". The point may be illustrated by the following extract from a part of the table of contents of the "Phaenomenologie":
"Erster Teil, Das Objekt der Religion.
Macht; Theoretische Macht; Ding und Macht; Mächtigkeit, Scheu, Tabu; Die heilige Umwelt; Heiliger Stein und Baum; Heiliges Wasser und Feuer; Die heilige Oberwelt; Die heilige Mitwelt; die Tiere; Wille und Gestalt; die Gestalt der Mutter; Macht-Wille-Heil; der Heiland; der Köning; Die mächtigen Toten", etc. etc.

Throughout the real phenomenon escapes his observation. That real phenomenon is religion, i.e. *a* religion, the religion of a people or a group, observed and described in its totality. The phenomenology of Van der Leeuw is not a true phenomenology. The subclasses, into which facts borrowed from a great diversity of religions have been arranged, are erroneously mistaken for phenomena, whereas they are only subclasses made for the purpose of ordering the mass of incoherent facts, incoherent because it was the classifyer who made them incoherent by plucking them out from their original context. The causes which led to this misconception are obvious; Van der Leeuw failed to make a proper analysis of the conceptual content of the term phenomenon. Worse is that once religion had been recognised as

90

a human universal which has its origin in itself, the problem of religion was relegated to its various forms of expression, and that instead of analysing real facts attention was concentrated on abstracts of dissected facts.

Another point for criticism is the author's inclination to present primitive forms of religion as the products of a mentality structurally deviant from ours. Van der Leeuw was strongly influenced by Lévy-Bruhl and by Jung, and in spite of scattered utterances which suggest that he was well aware of the necessity to hypothesise the fundamental unity of mankind, we are obliged to assume that what he really had in mind were structural differences of a genetic nature. Van der Leeuw's successor in Groningen, Th. van Baaren, has severely criticised him because of these and other obscurities in his comment on primitive religion. Nevertheless, in the main Van Baaren kept to the same method as Van der Leeuw, preferring the study of religious phenomena to that of religions (cf. his 'Wij Mensen', 1960). The same can be observed with other phenomenologists who made primitive religions the object of their study. As anthropologists we cannot say that the phenomenological school has contributed much to our insight in religion as such. The ultimate cause of its failure, however, should be sought in its definition of religion as an ideologically qualified state of mind, i.e. by an assumed cause, instead of as a complex of notions and ideas which are observable facts.

8 K. Th. Preusz, continued

Once more we must return to Preusz, the one and only older anthropologist who, without joining the ranks of the phenomenologists, gave evidence of a certain appreciation of some of their arguments, even though he kept to his usual independence. The appreciation is more particularly apparent in his essay "Glauben und Mystik im Schatten des höchsten Wesens" (1926), in spite of its modest size one of the best discourses on primitive religion of the period.

Religious belief, says Preusz, is not the product of logical considerations but of an inner, mystic experience. The Eskimo who first sewed a sherd of hearth-stone in the seam of his dress, did not do so on logical grounds but because he had had a very specific experience. Without experiences of such a kind religious belief is dead and cannot help primitive man to acquire what his religious belief should bestow on him: "eine übernatürliche Ergänzung seiner nicht ausreichenden kausal-logischen Fürsorge". This belief cannot be understood without putting it in the context of the mystic relationship assumed to exist among things, a relationship which itself is defined by the totality of the relevant religious notions and beliefs. "Der Glauben aus dem die Religion hervorgeht, ist nicht etwas an sich Wahres oder Falsches, es ist nicht in der übernatürlichen Welt an sich gegeben, sondern der Mensch erzeugt ihn aus seinem Innersten, und das Wunderbare der übernatürlichen Schöpfung seines Inneres ist eben, dasz er die mystische

Anlage dazu besitzt". Though a reference to a category sui generis is lacking, his sympathy for the phenomenologists is evident. Man's natural aptitude for religion is accepted.

Pursuing the argument, Preusz points out that the supreme being has an important part to play in religious belief. He is the representative of the cosmic order and he is also the donor of the cult. The cult may be coercive, but it is not performed in pride. On the contrary, it is a matter of obedience to the supreme being. Having arrived at the closing scene of the ritual which influences the course of cosmic events, the Cora-Indians proceed to the altar, solemnly to lay down the right thoughts which the gods inspired in them for the sake of a correct performance of the ritual. The act is not a psycho-pathological but a mystic one; the actors are fully aware of the symbolic character of their action. What matters is the cosmic order, embodied in the gods and more particularly in the supreme being. The latter stands for the universe, for totality, totality taken not as a pure existent, but as a power which is apprehended by man and must be approached and influenced through the medium of the ritual conferred on him by the supreme being. The relation between the supreme being and the ritual is of the closest; rarely has the interrelation between the two found a more penetrating expression than in the following Uitoto-text: "Im Anfang gab das Wort dem Vater den Anfang", in the beginning the Word originated the Father, in which 'the Word' stands for the ritual songs and ceremonies given by the Father. The two are identical.

In this altogether too compact essay Preusz also discusses the dead and their worship, a subject to which he returned in a short paper published in 1930, "Tod und Unsterblichkeit im Glauben der Naturvölker". Here he states that human beings believe in an after-life because it is simply impossible to grasp the idea of being dead. The argument contains an incipient approximation to the existentialist point of view, but Preusz — well aware that the statement as it stands is an unwarranted over-simplification of a very complex psychological situation — immediately mitigates the effect of his pronouncement by warning that people often do not look forward to eternal life, but simply to a life as long as they expect survival to be attractive or at least bearable. Another aspect which is considered in these pages is the interrelation between death and the sexual act. The latter cannot be meaningful unless there is also death, a simple fact of life with which our generation is confronted more poignantly than any generation before.

In this context he returns to an old hobby-horse; the mortuary rites are necessary because the bonds between the dead and the living must be severed. These bonds are dangerous and the mortuary rites are primarily farewell-rites, devised to send the deceased on their journey to the land of the dead. Preusz never discovered that this is at best half the truth; that mortuary rites often aim at installing the dead as active ancestors — this is a point of view which he consistently overlooked.

Finally, mention should be made of a paper published by Preusz in 1933, "Der religiöse Gehalt der Mythen", the only one of the three discussed in this section which is more generally accessible to modern readers, since it has been reprinted in C. A. Schmitz, "Religionsethnologie" (pp. 119-153). He begins with a warning against generalisations such as primitive mentality (Lévy-Bruhl) and 'mythisches Denken' (Cassirer); they have in common that they present religious ideas and notions which by their very nature refer to extra-normal states of affairs, as normal processes of thought in the daily life of primitive people. The dichotomy supposed to exist between magic and religion has strongly favoured this misconception (Schmitz, Religionsethnologie pp.120 f.). Actually, the cult is magical because it is coercive, but the cult has been given by the gods and this fundamental fact is exposed in myth. This exposition is at the same time a verification; the cult is founded in primeval time, at the beginning of things when the present world was ordered for once and for ever. This has raised the problem of primacy; what was first, the cult or the myth? Actually, the problem should not be stated this way; usually there is something which is prior to both, viz. some general concept basic to cult and myth together. He illustrates his point with the theme of death and resurrection common to many initiation rites which give access to sexual intercourse. The founding idea is the correlation existing between death and sexual intercourse, a correlation which must be brought home to the novice (ibid. pp.133 ff.). It is not always possible to discover such a fundamental idea. Without denying the possibility that sometimes the cult is older than the myth, he forwards two cases in which the cult apparently is based on a pre-existent myth (ibid. pp.138 f.). Moreover, the narration of a myth is often a ritual act in itself, which has a salutary effect on the prosperity of man and his crops (ibid. pp.140 ff.).

Myth, however, is not restricted to situations and events which have a bearing on cults and ritual activities. Myth can be connected with anything that is of interest to the life and thought of a primitive people. Projecting its origin and nature into a mythical primeval era (which need not be very long ago), every situation, event or phenomenon is put in the context of what has always been and shall always be, in the mysterious, supernatural background of the universe. It is this mysterious universe and its meaning for man which counts and which finds verification in myth. The paper ends with a protest against psychological and psycho-analytical explanations of myth which are one in ignoring the fundamental fact that myth is a verification and justification of the human universe in its actuality. In all this Preusz is a typical anthropologist, basing his approach not on isolated phenomena, but on the inner cohesion of cultural facts which in each and every case belong to the universe proper to a specific culture.

93

V

Historicism and its influence in Germany and elsewhere

1. Introduction. Early anthropologists in Germany (Bastian, Wundt, Ratzel)

The historical school of the anthropology of religion reached its fullest development in German speaking countries. It is a development which borrowed its first inspiration from *Adolf Bastian (1826-1903)*, the nestor of
German anthropology. Yet, what Bastian had in mind was not history but a
comparative psychology revealing the genesis of human thought, not in the
more or less a-prioristic ways of early evolutionists, but by applying purely
inductive methods of comparison which take the impact of natural surroundings into account. The foundations of human thought are the 'Elementargedanken' (elementary concepts) which can still be found among
primitive peoples (Naturvölker) in the most simple elements of their religious concepts, social institutions, forms of production, aesthetic sentiments
and technical skills. The 'Elementargedanken' are necessarily few in number; they include only the most simple forms of thought. A good instance
are the first weapons, viz. sticks or clubs. They are projections of the human body, extensions of the arm. The 'Elementargedanken' are the same all
over the world. Differentiation is effected by the influence of natural surroundings, 'der geografische Provinz'; the 'Elementargedanken' develop
and become diversified so that they must be called 'Völkergedanken', speci-
fications of human thought testifying to the diversity of opportunities and
capacities for growth and development of the human mind. The next step
of cultural development is that of the exchange of 'Völkergedanken' by
means of contact. Just as the 'Völkergedanken' are determined by the peculiarities of the 'Geografische Provinz', so is intercultural exchange conditioned by the opportunities presented by the natural means of communication embodied in the great 'Geschichtswege der Menschheit', the highroads
of the history of mankind. In the later stages of cultural development the
impact of natural surroundings weakens and a new situation develops. The
earlier stages however offer an opportunity for applying strictly scientific
methods to the study of man as a social being.

There is a great difference between Bastian's ideas and those of the historical schools of the 20th century. Bastian is primarily interested in what cultures have in common in spite of their variety. The borrowing of cultural elements, the transfer of cultural forms, are matters of secondary importance. First of all the 'Elementargedanken' must be traced which should provide the primary basis for explanation. Then attention should be paid to the influence of natural surroundings (the 'geografische Provinz'), and the possibility of borrowing should only be contemplated in the case of cultural similarities which cannot be explained as the result of a universal law or rule of development. A good specimen is the history of the Chinese footbow which has found its way to such outlying places as the Andaman Islands on the one hand, and — through the medium of early Portuguese travellers — to the Congo on the other.

Adolf Bastian was a very exceptional person, *inter alia* in the respect that, in contrast to his contemporaries, he was not an armchair scholar but an indefatigable traveller. He studied medicine at Bremen and Berlin (where he met Virchow, the man who has been a great inspiration to many students) and in 1850 he sailed off as a ship's doctor. After eight years of roaming the seven seas he returned to write his first big work, "Der Mensch in der Geschichte" (3 vols.). In 1861 he went again, this time spending four years in Asia. The result was the 6 vols. of "Die Völker des östlichen Asiens".

In the meantime he had started his most impressive achievement, the Berliner Museum für Völkerkunde — for many years a model for ethnographic musea. With Virchow he organised the 'Gesellschaft für Ethnologie' but his great love was the museum. On behalf of its collections he made one journey after another; on one of these journeys he died at the age of 77. A great man and a tragic man. Always a bachelor he had no other pastime than his work: travelling, collecting and writing, one book after another. Each book in turn was reverentially welcomed, praised and read by an ever decreasing public. But for the descriptive parts which contain a lot of unorganised information, his books are almost unreadable, his writings becoming increasingly indigestible with the years. Interminable sentences are lost in numerous clauses; time and again the argument is interrupted with broad expositions, placed in brackets, in which the author rummages about everything found above, in, and under the earth. He makes quotations in an unbelievable number of languages, refers right and left to an immense variety of authors, but never mentions a place. His obscurity soon became proverbial. And yet he must have had a stroke of genius. He was respected as an important scientist by two of the clearest thinkers of his time, Tylor and Virchow.

No one has ever succeeded in coping with Bastian's ideas. The 'Elementargedanken' are, after all, an unmanageable concept and although the terms he introduced were not forgotten, Bastian never found a following. The one idea which found support for a time, was that anthropology should be primarily 'Völkerpsychologie'. It was Wilhelm Wundt who shouldered the task of developing this idea.

Wilhelm Wundt (1832-1920) was a slightly younger contemporary of Bastian and, in no less degree than the latter, a real monument of scholarship. Wundt owes his reputation to the fact that he was the founder of experimental psychology. Not until he was well over sixty years of age did he take a really active interest in anthropology. In 1900 — when Wundt was 68 — the first volume of his "Völkerpsychologie" appeared, the tenth and concluding volume in 1920, the year of his death. At the time several preceding volumes had already been reprinted, an indisputable token of the popularity his work enjoyed. It certainly had allure; even the linguistic aspect, to which he devoted two volumes, was not forgotten. In spite of all this, the voluminous oeuvre is a work of old age. The scholarship displayed is impressive but does not bring new ideas. Even the concept 'Völkerpsychologie' is not really elucidated. A definition of the subject, 'Volk', is as carefully avoided as the pitfall of reifying the notion of 'Volk' into some sort of mythical subject. Wundt was too accomplished a scholar to make such mistakes. On the other hand, what he gives instead does not bring much news. That language, art and religion are never the products of an individual but have their origin in the interaction ('Wechselbeziehungen') of the various individuals of a community, will not easily be contested.

Anybody wishing to study Wundt will do well to consult the systematical summary of his ideas in his also rather voluminous book of 1912, "Elemente der Völkerpsychologie". Its subtitle, "Grundlinien einer psychologischen Entwicklungsgeschichte der Menschheit", clearly describes the author's intentions. It is a conjectural history of mankind deviating in various points from the usual evolutionist scheme, among others by the importance he attached to totemism, at least to totemism as the author saw it. The book is an instructive manual for readers who are interested in risky speculations on origins of customs and beliefs.

Friedrich Ratzel (1844-1904) deliberately introduced historical thinking into anthropological theory. Ratzel was primarily a geographer, and, as such, a meritorious one. He rejected Bastian's theories; the 'Elementargedanken' were to him an unmanageable concept. Bastian's explanation of culture as a product of 'Völkergedanken' can only hold true if the various nations, after having dispersed, had settled in one place for ever. However, the nations did not settle forever; Bastian's presupposition must be rejected. Nations and tribes are always moving from one place to another. If we wish to explain a people's culture, we must know its history.

This is the one line of Ratzel's argument. The second line is nearer to Bastian's thinking. It is a revision of the latter's observations on the effect of the 'geografische Provinz'. Climate and vegetation may exert a decisive

96

influence, Ratzel argues. The occupants of upland plains are industrious and militant; those of the steppe are nomads and brigands; sometimes they become outstanding conquerors. An equable, hot climate has a flagging effect, and so on. To us, to-day, the generalisations forwarded by Ratzel seem cheap enough. Honesty demands us to admit that Ratzel was well aware of the weaknesses of his ecological theories; he aptly pointed out that, although the factors mentioned play their part, they should not be dissociated from other factors, such as the particular history of a people. Migrations play an important role, and if one wishes to assess their effect on any culture, an intensive study of that culture should be combined with broad comparative studies of their material culture and institutions, as well as with an investigation of the linguistic background and racial composition of the people concerned.

Ratzel's argument is better balanced and more reasonable than that of his followers who founded the so-called historical school. He is, as is only natural from his point of view, interested in similarities between cultural traits occurring in different cultures but, whilst he warns against a too rapid exclusion of the possibility that they are the result of diffusion, he never denies the possibility of repeated invention and independent development of cultural parallels. His followers were less scrupulous in this respect. Of Ratzel's works we mention his "Anthropo-Geographie" (2 vols., 1882, 1891); "Völkerkunde" (first ed. in 3 vols., 1885-1888; the second edition in 2); and "Politische Geographie" (1897).

2. The founders of the historical school

The first impetus towards a closer study of historical contacts between widely separated cultural areas came from Leo Frobenius who in 1898 in his essay "Die Masken und Geheimbünde Afrikas" and in his book of the same year, "Der Ursprung der Afrikanischen Kulturen", pointed to a number of remarkable similarities between West African and Melanesian masks. Scientific support was given by Graebner and Ankermann who, six years later, presented a fairly detailed theory to the 'Berliner Gesellschaft für Anthropologie, Ethnologie und Urgeschichte' in a couple of addresses, the first, by Graebner, on "Kulturkreise und Kulturschichten in Ozeanien", the other, by Ankermann, on "Kulturkreise und Kulturschichten in Afrika" (published in ZfE 37, 1905).

Graebner, the theorist of the new school, stated its central problem as follows. Is it possible, in spite of the total absence of written sources and prehistorical data, to make an assessment with a sufficient degree of certainty of the correct sequence of the successive cultural layers (Kulturschichten) which in a given cultural area overlap each other? Graebner answers the question in the affirmative provided one condition be observed, viz. that a world-wide approach should be avoided. If we confine ourselves to a few culture areas which can be studied in detail, real progress can be made; in particular if attention is focussed on culture elements which are not easily transmittable and which occur throughout the culture area under study. We can thus define what is specific to the area. The next step is to make an inventory of the more easily transmittable culture elements which go with the characteristics already defined as specific. We then have a point of departure for further studies.

Such a starting point he found in eastern New Guinea and western Melanesia. In this area the culture element not easily transmittable is the prevailing system of exogamous matrilineal moieties as found in the New Hebrides, part of the Solomon Islands, eastern New Guinea, New Britain and New Ireland. The more easily transmittable elements combined with this system are secret societies and mask-dances together with such items of material culture as the club, a special kind of shield, the spear-thrower, the pan-flute, tree-houses and a number of others. He gave the complex the name of 'Ostpapuanische Kultur', a culture complex which left its traces in Australia where these traces are found in combination with patrilineal traits originating from another complex, the 'Westpapuanische Kultur', which is characterised by patriliny, a strict dichotomy of the sexes and a host of other traits, which space does not permit us to specify. Apart from elements originating from the East- and West Papuan culture complexes, the Australian culture area also shows traces deriving from three other culture complexes, viz. the Tasmanian, the Melanesian and the Proto-Polynesian. Graebner elaborately specifies the characteristics of each of these complexes and points out how they affected the Australian culture complex.

Ankermann applied Graebner's method and results to African data. The similarities between Melanesia and West Africa which Frobenius had noted were confirmed and their number considerably increased, among others with such items as saddle-roofed houses, wickerwork shields, bark cloth, circumcision, and some musical instruments. These items belong to successive South Oceanian cultural layers, notably the East- and West Papuan, the Melanesian and the Proto-Polynesian culture complexes. Ankermann advanced the suggestion that a 'culture stream' flowing from Melanesia to West Africa passed through Indonesia and Madagascar, finally reaching West Africa through the Zambesi valley. He then turned his attention to those parts of Africa which hitherto had been left undiscussed, and combining the results of this part of the analysis with the former, he succeeded in the construction of the following (compressed) scheme of subsequent culture layers which can in part be identified with corresponding Oceanian culture complexes:

1 The nigritic layer, in substance corresponding with old-Australian culture.
2 West African culture, mainly East Papuan, but combined with younger elements and originating from Indonesia.

3 A layer corresponding to the West Papuan cultural layer and probably also originating from Indonesia.
4 In the western Sudan a layer of unidentified origin, probably deriving from India.
5 A Hamitic or old-Semitic layer in the Sudan, East- and South Africa.
6 A younger Semitic (Arabian) layer in the same areas.

The present survey of the argument proposed by the two scholars amply demonstrates its speculative character. Even the first step taken by Graebner is a perfectly arbitrary one, viz. the choice of the area which served him as a starting-point, New Guinea and Melanesia. In New Guinea, where a profound lack of proper information enabled him to assume a marked degree of cultural homogeneity, two sub-areas are advanced as standard areas for further comparison, as cultural layers which can be demonstrated to exist in other parts of the world as well.

In 1911 Graebner, in his "Methode der Ethnologie", attempted to give his approach a more solid theoretical foundation. Everything depends on the answer we give to the question whether a discovery may be made more often than once. If this happens to be the case, the possibility of parallel development must be admitted. If a discovery is ordinarily made only once, the presence of any culture element outside the location of its origin must be attributed to diffusion. Unfortunately there is no proof of either possibility, and therefore we must make a choice. Graebner opts for the hypothesis that a discovery is made only once. This does not imply that we are free to explain every case of cultural similarity from diffusion. At the very least, diffusion must be demonstrated as probable. To that end he develops a number of criteria which a case must meet before diffusion can be accepted as satisfactorily proven: the criterion of form (similarities which cannot be explained from the function of the instrument or the specific nature of the materials applied); the criterion of quantity (the occurrence of a number of concurrent similarities); and the criterion of continuity (the occurrence of the same traits in areas connecting the areas under comparison).

The criteria mentioned and amply elucidated are sound enough. They have been generally accepted. However, they do not suffice to solve the problem. First of all, what is a discovery? In the theoretical discussion the cases advanced to elucidate the concept are all borrowed from material culture, but in actual practice every change of social organisation or religion may be taken as a case of discovery. If we accept that every discovery is made only once, the possibility of autogeneous culture change is reduced almost ad nihilum, a supposition so eloquently contradicted by fact, that the hypothesis must be rejected. It is not true that a culture persists unaltered unless contact induces change. And yet it is only by hypothesising this unchangeability of culture that 'Kulturschichten', cultural layers, can be recognised. What Graebner called a historical method is not a historical method at all, but a geological one. The identity of this method with the geological even goes so far that cultural layers are said to be characterised by specific cultural 'Leitfossile', guide fossils. As if culture could exist in a fossilised state and were not the expression of the way of life of living men! The fundamental misconception of the notion of culture manipulated by these would-be historians is manifest in the selection of culture elements supposed to characterise the various culture layers, such as the matrilineal system of exogamous moieties of the East Papuans, and the patrilineal organisation with strict sex dichotomy of the West Papuans. Matriliny and patriliny are not the contrasts these older ethnologists supposed them to be; both notions are included in that of kinship. Later research has given irrefutable evidence of the fluctuations of social organisation within any culture area, the East- and West Papuan included. Moreover, the areas just mentioned are by no means the homogeneous culture areas Graebner thought them to be. To mention only this: clubs and tree-houses, supposed to be characteristic for the East Papuans, have since been found among the West Papuans as well. Historical reconstructions of the kind Graebner and Ankermann proposed can only be drawn up on the basis of minimal information, and they run the risk of being overturned by each new item of information provided by further research. These theories raise more problems than they solve.

In spite of all this they met with a fair amount of approval in Germany where a keen interest in historical problems prevailed. Of course not all German ethnologists went to such extremes as Frobenius, Graebner and Ankermann. A scholar like R. Heine-Geldern, also deeply interested in historical problems, was appreciably more cautious. Other German anthropologists, notably Thurnwald, kept aloof from historical problems, whereas Preusz, in his studies of Mexican archaeology, applied perfectly legitimate methods. Nevertheless, the historicism introduced by Frobenius and Graebner has exerted a deep and lasting influence on German anthropology.

Of course, our criticism is not directed against the historical approach as such. On the contrary, any information which can give time-depth to our culture studies is extremely welcome. The synchronic character of the greater part of the available information is a serious handicap. History and ethno-history are legitimate and very useful occupations for an anthropologist, but they should be pursued with legitimate methods. Fr. Boas and his school have made very substantial contributions to the development of such methods. Combining the analysis of ethnographic data with comparative linguistics and archaeological research, they laid a sound basis for gathering as much historical knowledge as can be drawn from the obviously limited opportunity to penetrate into the human past. Only, such historical knowledge is not world history, the history meant to replace the conjectural history of the evolutionists. It is spatially confined; the aims set are of a more modest nature. A good introduction into the methods advanced by American anthropologists is E. Sapir, "Time perspective in aboriginal American culture" (1916).

3. Pan-babylonism and pan-egyptianism

In the early years of the century historicism was in the air. Pan-babylonism is even older than Graebner's theories. It is the fruit of the enthusiasm inspired by the discovery of the Babylonian and Sumerian cultures, and more specifically, of the detailed knowledge of astronomy acquired by the early inhabitants of the Mesopotamian valley. The protagonists were philologists, among whom mention must be made of H. Winckler, the author of the essay "Himmels- und Weltbild der Babylonier als Grundlage der Weltanschauung und Mythologie aller Völker" (1901). He argued that all myths are astral myths, i.e. they refer to the heavenly bodies. These myths are based on a sound knowledge of the motions of these bodies and thus must originate from a country where the relevant knowledge was available. The one country meeting this requirement is Babylonia where the observational techniques and the knowledge of the heavenly bodies were far ahead of those among other peoples. Winckler compares Babylonian myths with old European ones in order to demonstrate that the latter have been borrowed from Babylonia. Deviations of the European myths from the Babylonian model are explained as fallacies caused by misconceptions among the borrowers. By limiting the concept of myth to the astral myth Winckler could ignore all mythological data of a non-astral nature, a limitation which simplified his position considerably. This position was nevertheless difficult enough. In European astral mythology the sun has a leading role. It was not an easy task to explain its connections with Babylonian myths with their preference for moon-myths. A detailed discussion seems superfluous. The reflection that all peoples must have walked in darkness until the Babylonian light came up over them, is sufficient reason for rejecting the hypothesis.

Pan-egyptianism should be rejected on the same ground, and we could leave it at this had not the pan-egyptian thesis been presented with considerably greater scholarship and erudition that the shortlived pan-babylonian one. Pan-egyptianism is a purely British achievement, testifying to the fact that historicism was not the exclusively German affair as might erroneously be concluded from the preceding pages. In Britain too the historicist bias had its partisans and among them so eminent an anthropologist as W. H. R. Rivers who, in "The History of Melanesian Society" (1914), advanced a migrational hypothesis to explain *inter alia* the prevailing moiety system. Rivers however was not among the pan-egyptianists; they were fathered by his friend G. Elliot Smith, a distinguished anatomist. When stationed in Cairo, he had turned into an ardent admirer of ancient Egyptian culture. Advancing the theory that all culture comes from Egypt, some of his presuppositions are more or less the same as Graebner's: "Man is uninventive; hence culture arises only in exceptionally favorable circumstances, practically never twice independently" (Lowie, History p.161). Elliot Smith could safely be forgotten to-day if he had not found a brother-in-arms in W. J. Perry, reader in comparative religion in Manchester University. Perry's outstanding contribution to pan-egyptianism is "The Children of the Sun" (1923), a fascinating book, in spite of the numerous reasons the author gave for disagreement and caustic criticism. Of course Perry shared Elliot Smith's view that all forms of higher culture originated from Egypt. In search of wealth — more specifically of gold, pearls and iron — members of the higher classes, Children of the Sun like the Pharaohs, wandered away from Egypt to the ends of the world, disseminating the techniques of agriculture, the use of polished stone, pottery, metal-working and pearl-fishing, together with dualistic systems of organisation, the cult of the sun and of a mother-goddess, exogamy, totemism, cannibalism and an increase in warfare (Children of the Sun p.306). The original cultures of non-Egyptian peoples were those of food-gatherers in their simplest form; these early food-gatherers did not even practise magic. It is a theory to which nobody will subscribe to-day. Yet, fantastic as the argument is, it is stimulating because the erudite author confronts us with problems which cannot be as easily brushed away as his explanations. One of these problems is the restricted number of religious ideas and ritual practices. Even if we succeed in finding in fundamental human conditions a satisfactory explanation of the basic forms of religious thought and action, there still remain the many details which have very little to do with human condition or universal needs, and nevertheless are widely spread and display a similarity which, in some cases, is simply baffling. We might refer here to man's irrational and fundamentally unexplainable preference for gold and pearls. Here is another surprising case, that of the cowrie shells (ibid. pp.457, 481 e.a.). Cowrie shells from India have been found in the cave of Grimaldi near Mentone; the Egyptians collected cowrie shells; cowrie shells are still an article of wealth in many parts of Africa as well as in the central mountains of Western New Guinea. In the latter area cowrie shells constitute the main form of wealth even to the extent that they function as money. History has many fascinating problems. It is the merit of historicism that it has brought them to our attention, just as historicism is to blame for the fact that these problems became very unpopular among anthropologists because historicists — not historians — bungled the problems they raised.

4 Father Wilhelm Schmidt S.V.D. (1864-1954)

The most outstanding representative of historicism is the late Father Wilhelm Schmidt, a man of great versatility and diligence, a capable organiser and an ardent defender of his viewpoints. Initially he specialised in linguistics and some of his earlier publications were devoted to the relations between the languages of the Southeast Asian continent and the Austronesian languages. He also studied the languages of Australia and Tasmania. Though he never gave up linguistics, anthropology soon got the upper hand. His really important activities were in this field. One of his most enduring contributions was the organisation of ethnographic research by Roman Catholic missionaries. To that end he founded the journal Anthropos in 1906. It offered a rich opportunity for the publication of field data, and for the editor, Father Schmidt, to expound his views, in particular those concerning the belief in a supreme being, which according to the author was the primeval religion of mankind. The thesis was a bold one and Schmidt gratefully took advantage of the fact that ten years earlier Andrew Lang, an authority unsuspected of religious prejudice, had already pleaded the primacy of the belief in a supreme being. Schmidt never became tired of sounding the praise of Lang to the skies, but carefully avoided including the latter's parapsychological excursions in his laudations. Schmidt found another and materially more important support in the descriptions of the religious belief of the African Pygmies which ascribed a leading role to a supreme being. In 1910 he devoted a special study to this subject, "Die Stellung der Pygmäenvölker in der Entwicklungsgeschichte des Menschen".

Schmidt's ideas on primeval religion and the part played therein by a supreme being were first published in a series of articles in Anthropos (1908 and following years) under the title "l'Origine de l'Idée de Dieu". The articles later appeared in German as vol. I of "Der Ursprung der Gottesidee; eine historisch-kritische und positive Studie". "Der Ursprung der Gottesidee" is Schmidt's magnum opus. He finished 12 volumes, each of some 800 to 900 pages. The excessive scope of the work obliged him to write a couple of smaller books summarising the main points of his theory. The best known among them are "Handbuch der vergleichenden Religionsgeschichte" (1930; English translation The Origin and Growth of Religion, 1931) and "Handbuch der Methode der kulturhistorischen Ethnologie" (1937).

To Schmidt religion is the recognition of one or more personal beings who transcend the earthly and the temporal. Buddhism is not a religion but a philosophy, and the same holds true of the concept of impersonal supernatural power. The personal element is essential in religion, so essential that it cannot be the outcome of the belief in souls or spirits; animism itself is the result of a relatively late development and, more important still, of philosophising. Animism is, as Tylor said, a doctrine, a theory. The earliest religion cannot possibly have been a theoretical religion. It must have been one in which intellectual cognition coincided with affection and with acts resulting from a combination of both, as is the case with the sacrifice of the first fruits offered by the African Pygmies to their supreme being. Is this primeval religion knowable? The author answers the question in an unconditional affirmative. We can know it, because the primitive cultures of today are but a "préambule, aujourd'hui pétrifié", of the civilisations of higher developed peoples (l'Origine de l'Idée de Dieu, Anthr. III p.135; cf. also Origin and Growth, p.255).

The statement contains a dogma as well as a programme. The dogma is that primitive cultures are petrifactions, fossils, in which the past, even the remote past, the primeval past, is contained. The programme is that these fossils must be interpreted in order to re-discover primeval religion and to define its historic development. It is up to the science of comparative religion to describe and to classify the religious data, to trace their origin, diffusion and development. The task is a historical, not a psychological one. We just have to find out what happened.

Schmidt never paid much thought to the foundations of religious belief. A good neo-thomist of cardinal Mercier's school, religion was to him a perfectly reasonable affair and he had not the slightest difficulty with Lang's opinion that the belief in a supreme being is the result of intellectual and as such rational contemplation. With Lang he accepted that the primeval belief in a Maker has been obscured by the fantasies of myth which did not emanate from reason but from imagination. Schmidt's position is perfectly reflected in the following statement[10]: "As long as the instinct of causality prevails it effectuates the higher forms of religion, but as soon as imagination takes the lead religion lapses into ridiculous and even obscene forms". The testimony of the rationalism of the neo-thomistic revival is unmistakable. We cannot blame Schmidt for it. On the contrary, when Schmidt posits the primacy of primeval monotheism this is not a matter of biblicism — which he rejects — but the necessary outcome of his unshakable and solid confidence that reason necessarily leads to the belief in a supreme being who is a creator, a first cause, and a father. To him it is evident that the primeval form of worship was a simple one, consisting of prayer and the sacrifice of the first fruits as the natural expressions of the faithful's gratitude vis-à-vis the supreme being. Early man conceived this supreme being on the one hand as invisible, then again as human but of superhuman size and appearance. Often it is called Father, while other names refer to his role as creator, supporter and protector. The supreme being is everlasting, omniscient and good, a guardian of morality who punishes evildoers. All these traits had been noted among the Pygmies who, in addition, had arrested his attention for being monogamists. Apparently monogamy was next to monotheism yet another distinctive trait of primeval culture.

Primeval cultures have been preserved in the most inaccessible parts of the world, in impenetrable jungles and remote areas. Here we still find peoples living by the most simple form of human economy, viz. that of gathering. It is an economy which is combined with a very simple form of social structure; they live in mutually independent, small local groups. Such peo-

[10] The author has to apologise that he cannot mention the place. His endeavours to recover it have sadly failed.

104

ples are found in different parts of the world and Schmidt classifies them in three main groups, the central, the arctic and the southeast Australian primeval culture (Urkultur). The central primeval culture is found in the most isolated parts of the old world, in the jungles of Africa (Pygmies) and Malaya (Semang, Sakai), among the Negrito tribes in the interior of the Philippines, and on the Andaman Islands. A negroid trait is common to almost all of them. The arctic primeval culture — which Schmidt hesitantly associated with 'homo Pekinensis' — is found in Arctic Asia and America (Eskimoes), some Algonkin Indian tribes, the Californian gatherers and the inhabitants of Tierra del Fuego. The third main branch, the southeast Australian (primarily Tasmanian), is no longer a purely primeval culture but has already been mixed with elements deriving from further developed cultures.

Starting from primeval culture three different ways of further development are possible, according to the kind of economic specialisation. Thus originated the three primary cultures, those of the lower agriculturalists or palaeo-horticulturalists, the higher hunters, and the pastoralists respectively. Since agriculture is the primary task of the women, in horticultural societies women have a privileged position, resulting in a matrilineal ('mutterrechtliche') organisation. In these societies the supreme being suffers from female competition; he is joined by a mother-goddess who is associated with the earth and the moon. Accordingly moon-mythology makes its appearance in this culture, in which the development of animism is fostered by the significance which family-ties have for women. Patrilineal ('vaterrechtliche') societies originate where favourable conditions permit the association of hunting for a livelihood with living in more extended communities. Here totemism develops together with a mythology in which the sun has a dominant part. The third possibility, pastoralism, also favours the male sex. The pastoralists become cattle breeding nomads dominating other peoples. Their social structure is patriarchal and patrilineal. Among them the supreme being develops into a typical sky-god.

The three primary cultures outlined here are called the three primary 'Kulturkreise'. The term is untranslatable; its literal meaning is culture area but culture area is a profoundly different concept as shall be demonstrated later. We first have to follow the fate of the three primary 'Kulturkreise' as outlined in Schmidt's sketch of historical development. The three 'Kulturkreise' spread all over the world, overlapped each other in many different ways, and excerted their influence on each other, constantly obliterating the original patterns of culture. Contact thus led to the development of secondary 'Kulturkreise', either matrilineal or patrilineal, but without exogamy. These in turn laid the foundation for the development of tertiary 'Kulturkreise', the oldest higher civilisations of Asia, Africa and America. The system designed by Schmidt is all-inclusive. The detailed description and justification of this immense, all encompassing construct was too much even for Schmidt's unabating energy and good health during the many years of his laborious life. In the twelve volumes of his "Ursprung der Gottesidee" he did not come any further than a discussion of the primeval cultures (Urkulturen) and the 'Kulturkreis' of the primary pastoralists.

It is worth while to dwell for a moment on Schmidt's methods of interpretation. One of his most critical problems was presented by the cultures of the Australian aborigines which somehow or other had to be fitted into the scheme he had designed. They are polygynists and their rules for extramarital sexual intercourse are in flat contradiction with those supposed to characterise primeval culture. Yet, these were not Schmidt's trickiest problems. After all, nature helps to keep polygyny within the strict limits ensuing from equal numbers of the sexes at birth, whereas the Australian rules for extramarital licence clearly refer to established marriage rules. His real headache was the supreme being and its worship including prayer and the sacrifice of first fruits. To that end the eligible Australian gods had to be cleansed from the numerous totemistic and naturalistic traits appertaining to them. This could only be achieved by explaining these traits as traits caused by migrational influences. He does this by assuming that a Tasmanian and an Australian primeval culture were overlaid by Graebner's 'west-papuanische Kulturkreis' with a patrilineal, and his 'ost-papuanische Kulturkreis' with a matrilineal moiety-system respectively. Subtracting later additions and substituting the traits which were lost, he was finally left with a fairly pure supreme being everywhere. The same method sufficed to extract a first fruits sacrifice from the Aranda intichiuma-ceremonies.

The procedure was a challenge. J. J. Fahrenfort in "Het Hoogste Wezen der Primitieven" (1927) flatly denied that the culture heroes and mythical beings of the Australians, the Andamanese, Bushmen, Semang, Sakai and Fuegians, could be called supreme beings. Moreover, he accused Koppers and Gusinde, Schmidt's leading disciples, that they had indulged in tendentious ethnography, and he blamed Schmidt for it. Schmidt replied in a long and trenchant article in Internationales Archiv 29 (1928) entitled "Ein Versuch zur Rettung des Evolutionismus", which in turn inspired Fahrenfort to a counter-attack in a pamphlet bearing the eloquent caption "Wie der Urmonotheismus am Leben erhalten wird" (1930). In those days feelings ran high in the debate around Schmidt, the fighting-spirit or even pugnacity of Schmidt himself strongly encouraging the use of acrimonious expressions. Famous in this respect is the discussion between Schmidt and J. Winthuis, a Roman Catholic missionary who had ventured the opinion that the final aim of ritual was the promotion of bisexuality (in "Das Zweigeschlechterwesen", 1928).

We must return to Fahrenfort's argument. Of course his claim that Schmidt had stretched the data to suit the hypothesis was perfectly justified, but the way he presented it could not possibly convince the partisans of Schmidt's 'Kulturkreislehre'. To that end an exposition of fact could not suffice because his adversaries had their own ways of dealing with facts, derived from the philosophy underlying the 'Kulturkreislehre'. It is this philosophy which should be scrutinised.

The first point for serious criticism is Schmidt's concept of 'Kulturkreis'. A 'Kulturkreis' is not a culture area, or even an attempt at it, in the way Graebner's 'Kulturkreise' had been. The 'Kulturkreis' of Schmidt is an abstract construct of logically more or less correlated culture elements based on a deductive analysis of the concomitants of a dominant type of economy. A culture area, on the other hand, is a spatially coherent group of cultures which have a number of important culture traits in common. Schmidt was well aware of the difference (cf. Handbuch der Methode p.175), but in spite of his keen wit he was too poor a theoretician to note the controversies in which his Kulturkreis-concept had entangled him. In his outline of the origin and initial development of the primary 'Kulturkreise' Schmidt shows himself well aware of the fact that a culture is a coherent whole of correlated culture elements. Once a 'Kulturkreis' has developed, its elements spread freely throughout the world, arbitrarily combining with elements of other 'Kulturkreise'. From that moment on it is no longer a question of either coherence or correlation. In existing cultures the coherence of the 'Kulturkreise' is sadly lacking. To Schmidt culture is an accidental whole of essentially isolated culture elements, equally accidentally acquired in the process of diffusion. Apparently he never considered the possibility that a culture is the expression of a human way of life which has its locus in man. So remote was the need of a critical examination of his concept of culture to his thinking, that he even failed to note that his theory carried him straightaway into the wake of historical materialism.

A second point for reproach is the inexactitude of Schmidt's classifications. The inclusion of a people with such accomplished techniques as the Eskimo in the group of primeval cultures is contrary to logic. His manipulation of the concepts 'Vaterrecht', 'Mutterrecht' and exogamy is based on notions of kinship already obsolete in the early twenties.

A third and more important point for reproof is Schmidt's gross rationalism and his unfounded belief in reason. It is not true that reason leads more or less automatically to the notion of a creator. If reason leads to anything it certainly leads more easily to the negation of each and every thesis concerning matters transcending the observable, than to the idea of a good-natured and kind-hearted creator, a concept at complete variance with the most obtrusive facts of primitive life in which hunger, sickness, lurking dangers and untimely death are common. A theologian may be blamed for ignoring these facts. The problem of theodicy has been a core problem of theology from the very first and no theologian ought to forget this.

We may conclude that Schmidt's cultural history is but a variant of the conjectural history of the evolutionists he despised. The main difference is that the evolutionists based their theories on an analogy with biological evolution, whereas Schmidt used a geological model. Proclaiming the petrifaction of primitive cultures and introducing a method for the stratification of cultural elements, his methodology is as remote from the methods of the discipline of history as that of any of the other historicists mentioned in this chapter. Even Schmidt's claim that his theory — in contrast to the evolutionists' — left scope for the effect of historical accident, must be denied. Historical facts are demonstrated facts, those of Schmidt are hypothesised facts, invented for heuristic purposes. And yet, in spite of all our objections against his theories, Schmidt was a great anthropologist, a man who mobilised a great many fieldworkers and inspired others to comparative studies. If we reject his theories this does not imply that they were of no use. Schmidt's works and those of his followers have certainly contributed substantially to the increase of a body of knowledge which, in combination with archaeological excavations and linguistic studies, may give the necessary support for scientific ethno-historical studies. However, Schmidt's contributions to the science of religion are less than might have been expected, which is a tragedy, because religion was his primary interest. It might well be that this tragedy, as so often is the case, is not undeserved. If Schmidt was interested in religion it was in his own religion, more than in anything else. In his heart of hearts he was an apologist, but an apologist of such stature that he has a right to be contested on exclusively scientific grounds.

VI

Anthropological theory
of religion in France
and the problem of totemism

1. Émile Durkheim (1858-1917)

The study of anthropology in France has been dominated for a long time by Émile Durkheim, a scholar of outstanding merit in the history of social science. His books had an enduring impact on sociological studies; mention should be made of:

"De la Division du Travail social" (1893);
"Les Règles de la Méthode sociologique" (1895);
"Le Suicide" (1897);
"Les Formes élémentaires de la Vie religieuse (Le Système totémique en Australie)" (1912).

Durkheim's oeuvre encompasses a wide span, and a review of his ideas on religion which ignores his other work, necessarily fails to recognise the full scope of the problems which led him to his ultimate standpoint. Durkheim's theoretical approach has its thematical background in the problems examined in "De la Division du Travail social", and its methodological foundation in the "Règles de la Methode", two works which cannot be neglected without running the risk of just missing the point of his theoretical expositions.

Durkheim's basic preoccupation is with the foundations of social solidarity. The origin and nature of the social cohesion which keeps the members of a society united in a common bond, constitutes the central problem of "De la Division du Travail social". In the course of his enquiry he discerns two types of social solidarity. The first is the mechanical solidarity prevailing in primitive society. The members of such a society are characterised by an almost complete similarity of opinion and outlook, which promotes strong feelings of unanimity and togetherness. The second is the organic solidarity of more developed societies in which differentiation and specialisation lead to a state of mutual interdependence through which everyone has to rely on the co-operation of everyone else. This first study of Durkheim is an "effort pour traiter les faits de la vie morale d'après la méthode des sciences positives" (Division du Travail p. XXXVII), a central theme in his unceasing preoccupation with the foundations of human ethics, a preoccupation, endowing his writings with a touch of noble-mindedness which those critics who repudiate his positivistic outlook tend to ignore.

The principles of the sociological method are laid down in the "Règles de la Methode", a small book of less than 150 pages, but a valuable introduction to Durkheim's thinking. It concentrates on the implications of the concept of the social fact: *"Est fait social toute manière de faire, fixée ou non, susceptible d'exercer sur l'individu une contrainte extérieure; ou bien encore, qui est générale dans l'étendue d'une société donnée tout en ayant une existence propre, indépendente de ses manifestations individuelles"* (Règles, p.14). Legal and moral precepts, religious representations and general concepts — including language — are social facts as defined by Durkheim. They exist apart from and independently of the individual; they exert a certain degree of coercion on the individual who cannot escape their influence on his thinking and action. Durkheim does not deny that these concepts also have a place in the individual's own thinking. On the contrary, he simply points out that concepts which are social facts, *a* are shared by a great many individuals at the same time; *b* exist already before the individual's birth and persist after his death; *c* exert a certain measure of coercion on the individual because these concepts are vested with authority, an authority from which the individual cannot quite break away; *d* cannot be explained from the individual as such. The fact that the individual may have internalised the moral concepts of his society, either wholly or up to an extent, does not detract from the coercive nature of these concepts. When an individual accepts a concept or idea of his society (a 'représentation collective') his acceptance cannot possibly change the fact that the idea came to him from outside and that the idea as such was born and developed in and through social intercourse. It is evident that social facts are not simply psychological facts and cannot be accounted for in psychological terms. Social facts should not be treated as ideas either, they are facts, things, in French: 'des choses'[11]. They are subject to social causality, that is to the interplay and interaction of social facts. They cannot be explained from ideas unless the ideas themselves are considered as social facts.

Social facts have a strong emotional impact and this makes it necessary to discard systematically the possibility of prejudice entering into our studies. To that end we need definitions confined to the enumeration of outward characteristics common to all the facts in the relevant category. A good case is Durkheim's definition of crime: "tout acte qui est puni". It is a definition which has important advantages, in spite of the objections which might be raised from the jural point of view. A definition of this kind is evocative of further observation. The question what a punishment is — actually the first to be asked on the basis of this definition — cannot be an-

[11] Durkheim's definition of 'chose' is vague and in the present context even tautological: "Est chose tout ce qui est donnée, tout ce qui s'offre ou, plutôt, s'impose à l'observation" (Règles p.35).

110

swered by forwarding an explanatory definition, such as an act of retaliation, or a pain inflicted for the purpose of the criminal's moral improvement. On the contrary, once we accept that a crime is an act which is punished, we are urged to make systematic observations of all sorts of traceable punishments and find out what it is all about. The definition refers to facts and facts have to be observed and described, that means described in their social setting. Perhaps it is Durkheim's greatest merit that he so strongly emphasised the necessity of strict method and detached, unbiased observation. The concept of social fact is an important contribution to a more objective and above all more relevant description of social reality. Durkheim himself set a good example in his analysis of suicide.

A field of social facts which was of specific interest to Durkheim was that of religion. As early as 1898 he wrote an essay entitled "De la définition des phénomènes religieux" in vol. II of l'Année Sociologique, the annual founded under his leadership one or two years before. In 1902 followed the well known essay "De quelques Formes primitives de Classification", written in collaboration with M. Mauss and published in Année Sociologique VI. The authors gave it the subtitle of "Contribution à l'Étude des Représentations collectives", and that indeed is the essence of the essay's purpose. It is of basic importance for a clear apprehension of Durkheim's philosophy. The authors try to demonstrate that concepts of classification are not the products of formal logical thought, but of the social conditions prevailing in the society concerned. Concepts of classification are social facts, and because they are social facts they have a history of their own. The vestiges of older concepts of classification can still be traced in Greek philosophy. In the far East classificatory concepts prevail which differ from those dominating our thinking, such as *yang* and *yin* among the Chinese.

Really primitive concepts of classification are found amongst the Australians. Simplest among them are those occurring in some of the societies divided into two exogamous moieties. All things of any importance 'belong' to either of these moieties. Among the Wakelburra a sorcerer of the Mollera moiety can only use Mollera things in his magic. When he dies his corpse will be exposed on a platform constructed with the wood of trees belonging to this same moiety. In other parts the system of classification is more complicated because a partition according to clans prevails. An interesting case is that of the Wotjoballuk in southern Australia, where each of the clans is associated with one of the directions of the wind. Thus each clan has its own specific quarter whereas the two encompassing moieties are associated with north and south respectively. Here, then, we find an incipient partition of the universe according to cardinal directions, and this cosmological partition corresponds to the partition of society into component groups.

Other cases are found among the North American Indians. In the ceremonial camp each of the clans has its own specific place allotted to it, and among some of these tribes again we find a combination of clan and cardinal direction. The most elaborate case is that of the Zuñi who are divided into seven: there are six groups of three clans each, whereas the seventh is made up of one single clan. The groups are associated with E., S., W. and N., Zenith, Nadir and Centre respectively, the last being represented by the group of one clan. Each of the regions has its own specific associations: north with power and destruction, east with the sun, magic and religion, etc. Moreover, each of the clans has its own totem, and the various priestly functions within the tribe are associated with the respective clans. The order of the seven groups coincides with the social order observed in tribal meetings, and with the order of the cosmos. The authors point out that this system of classification is a very complicated one and they venture the opinion that it originated from a dual division.

Continuing the argument they point out that divisions of this kind tend to persist independently of the later development of their social substratum. This seems to have been the case in China where we are confronted with a partition into five (the four cardinal directions plus the centre) side by side with a division into eight, which is a reduplication of the partition according to cardinal directions. The combination of the two systems, the 5 and the 8, with other cosmological concepts and divisions lay the foundation for Chinese mantic (divinatory) practice. Classifications of this kind include the most divergent topics: space, the weather, the classification of things, animals and colours, but also mythology and the universe of the deities. They may develop into complete systems of classification and inspire the members of the society to indulge in all sorts of abstract speculation. The conclusion is that the social order has provided the prototype of the classification of the universe.

Up to an extent the introduction of Durkheim's "Les Formes élémentaires de la Vie religieuse" links up with the essay on classification. The author argues that science and philosophy were born from religion, and borrowed their systems of classification and their categories from religious concepts which are the products of the social organisation. This is a rather sweeping statement, suggesting that the rules of logic are the products of the fortuitous development of the social order. This can hardly be what Durkheim had in mind. He states that he simply wishes to let the facts tell their own tale, and that to that end he presents the facts as data derived from nature. Man too is part of nature, and therefore the development of human society is not an accidental one, but a development defined by nature. The system of logic proceeding from such a natural development must be a system relevant to nature. Nature does not err, certainly not in this case, because in logic all the age-long experience of the human race is accumulated (cf. Formes élémentaires p.25). He agrees with the philosophical empiricists on the point that logic is the result of human experience. However, empiricism fails to explain why logic has authority. The compelling and absolute nature of the logical categories is the phenomenon in which Durkheim is interested. The logical categories can derive their authority only from society, because nothing but society can ordain as compellingly as the categories of logic do. Their compelling nature is by definition a specific quality of the social fact.

The emphasis on the compelling nature of the logical categories makes it sufficiently clear that it is misinterpreting Durkheim if we accuse him of reducing the logical categories to an accidental product of an equally accidental social order. On the contrary, there is nothing accidental here because human development is part of the development of nature itself. How foreign the idea of fortuity is to Durkheim's mind is illustrated by his suggestion that the Zuñi partition into seven may have originated from a dual division. Quite another matter, of course, is Durkheim's professed faith in nature. Here he reveals the real foundation of his thinking, a faith which one is free to believe or disbelieve, the weak spot in the armour of every philosophy. We all come to the point where the ground of our philosophy crumbles down and we are left alone on the edge of a fathomless hole filled with nothingness, a hole which has to be covered with the shield of a faith.

Durkheim's naturalistic philosophy led him to yet another important conclusion. If religion is universal, it cannot be based on error as Tylor and Frazer had inferred. Religion must have a function because error never could be so universal and persistent as religion is. Durkheim is, in fact, the founder of functionalism. However, his functionalism differs fairly widely from that of Malinowski, who is more than anyone associated with the term. Calling Durkheim a functionalist is essentially correct, but the caption is confusing and its use cannot be recommended. The basic idea of Durkheim's 'Formes élémentaires' is not functionalism but the remarkable parallelism between the world of the gods and human society: both of them incorporate the highest authority, both of them exert coercive power, they both punish and they both reward. Of both it can be said that they are moral powers, existing at one and the same time in man and beyond him.

Durkheim, as a good methodologist, keeps strictly to his own rules on sociological method and carefully avoids any assimilation of his preconceived ideas on religion with the definition of the phenomenon. The definition is formal, free from every trace of prejudice: "Une religion est un système solidaire de croyances et de pratiques relatives à des choses sacrées, c'est-à-dire séparées, interdites, croyances et pratiques qui unissent en une même communauté morale, appelée Église, tous ceux qui y adhèrent" (Formes élémentaires p.65). Pivotal to the definition is the pair of opposites sacred-profane. The sacred is the interdicted, that which may not be touched, which should be kept strictly separate from the profane. Mixing the profane and the sacred is profanation, sacrilege. However, Durkheim warns against making the opposition an absolute, because man tries to enter into

113

contact with the sacred. But man cannot do so straightaway; he must previously consecrate his person, i.e. he must himself enter into a sacred state. Whoever has thus consecrated his person cannot return to profane life unprepared. Another act is needed, this time one of desacralisation, to permit him to return to the profane state.

The opposition sacred-profane is fundamental and recurs within the sphere of the sacred in the opposition between *fas* and *nefas,* the pure (the holy) and the impure. Consequently, the profane is sometimes associated with the impure without being necessarily identical with it. To a man in the profane state the impure belongs to the sacred, the profane to the category of the indifferent; if he has consecrated himself for a ritual act of sacrifice and thus is in a state of purity, the impure and the profane are both the same for him, impure *and* profane. At the time Durkheim published his 'Formes élémentaires' his followers had already written extensively on the opposition between the sacred and the profane, and before we enter deeper into a discussion of Durkheim's *chef d'oeuvre* it is advisable first to pay attention to the earlier contributions of some of the prominent members of his school.

2. The earlier contributions of the French school of sociologists: Hertz, Hubert, Mauss

An essay wholly dedicated to the opposition of the sacred and the profane is that of Robert Hertz, "La Pré-éminence de la Main droite" (Revue philosophique 34, 1909). Hertz gave his essay the subtitle of 'Étude sur la Polarité religieuse'. The human preference for the right hand side can only be partially explained. The contrast between right and left has been extended into a pair of symbols, applied to a great diversity of oppositional contrasts such as sacred and profane, pure and impure, good and bad, etc. Hertz argues that the origin of oppositional thinking must be sought in the primary opposition of the sacred and the profane. The argument is not convincing but the theme is important; it is a main theme in present day structuralist studies. The essay also proves the importance attached to the opposition of the sacred and the profane by the members of the inner circle of the French school.

That the opposition raises difficult problems is not openly admitted, but these unsolved problems can hardly escape the critical reader of the famous essay written more than ten years earlier by H. Hubert and M. Mauss, "Essai sur la Nature et la Fonction sociale du Sacrifice" (Année Sociologique II, 1898; reprinted in Mélanges d'Histoire des Religions", 1909). The authors oppose the theories forwarded by Tylor and Robertson Smith because they are based on viewpoints arbitrarily chosen. Whoever wishes to draft a theory of sacrifice has to set out with a good description of the facts. For this reason the authors start with an extensive description of Vedic and He-

114

brew sacrifice, because on this subject detailed data are available.

In contrast to a consecration or an anointment which benefits the object of the act, the effect of sacrifice benefits the actor whereas the object is made a victim and destroyed. In the accomplishment of the act three successive stages can be discerned, viz:

1. *The entry.* The sacrificer (the man who brings the sacrifice), the official (the priest) and the sacrifice (the victim) must first be consecrated, i.e. they must be brought into a sacred state of separation and interdiction. The scene of sacrifice also must be consecrated, unless the place of sacrifice is in a temple which has been consecrated before. The sacrifice must be without blemish. If it is a beast the prospective victim is sometimes adorned and bathed; it even happens that it is made drunk. Once the beast has been tethered to or near the altar, it often is held to be so sacred that the sacrificer is no longer allowed even to touch it. Among the Hebrews, after the beast has been tethered, the sacrificer ceremonially lays his hand on the victim, thus giving expression to the bond existing between them. With the Vedic sacrifice it is the priest who performs this act on behalf of the sacrificer.

2. *The sacrifice proper.* In a way the victimisation of the sacrifice is a crime, and the butcher must afterwards purify his person in a manner reminiscent of the penance of a criminal. Sometimes the victim is left to the deity in its entirety, sometimes it is given to the priest, but often the victim, after having been dedicated, is distributed between the priest and the sacrificer. If the sacrificer receives a share this must be consumed inside the precincts and within a certain space of time. Finally it also happens that the victim is chased away instead of being killed (the scapegoat).

3. *The concluding rites (la sortie).* The remains are burned and the scene of sacrifice is cleaned up. Then priest and sacrificer come together and purify themselves by washing their hands, an act serving a dual purpose: on the one hand the purification of the adverse effects of mistakes possibly made in the performance, on the other the laying aside of the sacred state acquired in the course of the ceremonies. The latter motive is evident in the following text, uttered by a Hindu sacrificer after completing a certain act of sacrifice: "O Agni, I paid my vows unto thee, I redeemed my pledge, I again become a man, I descend from the world of the gods to that of men". The holy mass closes with a more or less comparable ritual conclusion. After the cleansing of the chalice and the washing of his hands, the priest pronounces the formula *Ite, missa est.*

The rites of entry are more elaborate than those of conclusion because the performers fear that they might fall short in respect for the sacred. On the other hand they ought to take home at least some measure of sanctity from the performance, and for this reason the rites of desacralisation are necessarily of short duration. Yet, there are also acts of sacrifice which proceed in an order more or less reversed. Such is the case when the sacrificer is already in a sacred state before he enters the ceremonies, for example because he has been contaminated by things impure or by illness, or because he is a consecrated person such as a Nazarene. In that case the rites of entry are omitted or they are reduced to a minimum. From the point of view of formal religion sickness and sin are identical, and for this reason 'sacrifices curatifs' and 'sacrifices expiatoires' can be reduced to a common denominator. Their purpose is the same, viz. the removal of impurity. The scapegoat is ushered into the desert; for the healed leper who has to be pronounced cleansed by the priest, a bird is let loose in the open field. The sacral state of impurity has been transferred to the sacrificial animal. In a case like this the concluding rites are more elaborate. The cured leper has to bring yet a second sacrifice.

Sacrifice serves variegated and even contrary ends; it results in sacralisation and desacralisation, it removes sin and confers holiness. The main point is that the sacrificed object establishes contact between the world of the sacred and that of the profane. The mediator is the victim which is destroyed, and it is destroyed because the sacred is so dangerous that anything contacting it is necessarily annihilated. The victim protects the sacrificer and redeems him. The sacrificer offers a gift but he does not offer his person. The gift, the sacrifice, does it in his place and functions as a mediator. The authors discuss extensively the various ways in which mythology succeeds in turning the victim into a deity. In this context they also pay attention to the theory of Robertson Smith which is rejected as an unproven hypothesis. We need not enter into these discussions. More important are the objections which should be raised against their own theory.

In the first place we note that the observations made by Hubert and Mauss are based on data borrowed from highly developed civilisations with religions which were influenced by the theoretical speculation and meditative thought of a literate priestly class. Under these conditions ritual necessarily becomes more systematised than is the case in less developed societies. The observer attending the performance of a sacrifice in a village on the Indonesian island of Flores would have difficulty in discerning either the rites of entry or those of conclusion; ordinarily he would at best note some incipient forms of them. More important is that the sacredness and the separateness of the performance is by no means as intense and elaborate as suggested by Hubert and Mauss. A fairly easy-going disposition predominates, and more often than once he would be stretching the facts if he tried to point out the mediatory function of the victim. Sometimes these Florenese sacrificers are quite serious, but they certainly do not always take it so gloomily, and the same may be said of the majority of sacrificatory performances in less developed cultures.

In the second place there is the pertinent emphasis on the contrast of the sacred and the profane. It raises the question why people wish to enter into contact with the sacred. Why do they not leave separate what ought to be separate and avoid every contact with it? What is worse, the authors themselves are not consequent. Of the 'rites de sortie' it is said that the sacrificer must take home at least some measure of the sanctity acquired during the rites. This implies that something of the sacred state is supposed to stick to his person, a presentation of fact irreconcilable with the strict separation of the sacred from the profane. It is evident that the authors themselves had an inkling of the problems ensuing from their definition of the sacred as 'séparé et interdit'. In the epilogue added to the re-edition of their essay in "Mélanges d'Histoire des Religions", they return to the subject, but again without making the problem explicit. They argue that their definition of the sacred as 'séparé et interdit' has been borrowed from Robertson Smith. Yet, the sacred is more than only that; the sacred represents the society as a whole, "tout ce qui, pour le groupe et ses membres, qualifie la société". Underlying the notions of separateness, of *fas* and *nefas,* we find those of respect and love, of aversion and fear. The whole social spectre is represented. The explanation is not very helpful; at best it suggests the direction in which a possible solution of the problem should be sought. But even if it is conceded that the sacred represents the society, it is not clear why the sacred should be so absolutely separate. After all, everybody lives in a society. Whence this sharp contrast?

The separateness of the sacred was one of the problems Durkheim had to solve in his "Formes élémentaires", where he too based himself on the opposition of the sacred and the profane. It was not the only problem to which he was confronted by the studies made by his collaborators. Another nasty problem was that of magic. If religion is, as it were, the reflection of society, how and where must the anti-social magic practised by the sorcerer be placed?

Hubert and Mauss had discussed the problem of magic in another essay, entitled "Esquisse d'une Théorie générale de la Magie" (Année Sociologique VII, 1902/03). The essay does not fulfil the promise given in the title. Actually, it excels in description whereas the theory forwarded suffers from a lack of consistency. Caught up in the contrast of religion and magic, the authors try to find a solution for their problem by linking up this contrast with that between the collective and the individual, suggesting that religion is pre-eminently associated with the collectivity and magic with the individual. However, a consequent application of this formula is frustrated by the fact that while the practice of prayer is strongly individualised, its religious character cannot be denied. The authors try to escape the dilemma by defining magic as 'all rites which are not part of an organised cult, and consequently are either individual rites or secret mysteries, with a trend towards the prohibited'. It is not an elegant definition, in its first part sticking to the device of strictly formal circumscription on the basis of external characteristics, while in its second part a vague effort is made towards giving the concept a material content.

The main merit of the essay lies in the description of the phenomenon which gives concrete evidence of the numerous similarities between magic and religion. Like religion the magical act has a sphere of devotion. The medicine-man must be initiated. His acts are meticulously defined. The medicine-man and his client are subject to many prohibitions and prescriptions. The language of magic is the same as the language of religion. Symbols play an important role in this language. The magician repeatedly appeals to the spirits, and magic contributes to the growth of mythology, albeit that myths inspired by magic are rudimentary myths. A conspicuous trait of magic is the unshakable belief in its effect. Another is the important role played by the concept of mana and its equivalents such as physis, brahma, orenda, and so on. Our authors assert that magic is not based on reason but on sentiment. Magic meets certain needs of the individual. In general it may be stated that magic is concerned with the profane life and concrete needs, whereas religion is more especially concentrated on commonly shared ideals of a more abstract nature. The distinction between magic and religion made by our authors is far from satisfactory, and the overall trend of their discussion is to present magic as a by-product of religion. In conclusion we feel justified in stating that, all things considered, Hubert and Mauss offered better arguments in favour of accepting magic as a form of religion than in support of the strict contrast on which they founded their comments.

3. Les formes élémentaires de la vie religieuse

In his 'Formes élémentaires' Durkheim fairly closely associated himself with the views of Hubert and Mauss with regard to magic. Of course he was not blind to the strongly religious character of many magical rites, but the occurrence of magical rites of a profanising nature ultimately convinced him that religion and magic stand in a relationship of pole and counterpole to each other. He succeeded in finding a new and seemingly workable dividing line between the two by the introduction of the concept of church. The church with its priests and community is contrasted to the medicine-man and his clientèle. Representations which are really religious are the property of the community as a whole, whose members are all one because they share the same views with regard to the sacred and the profane. The common faith is expressed in communal rites. With magic the situation is different. Though the belief in magic is widely spread and the relevant representations may be shared more or less universally by all the members of the society, the magic rites are incapable of uniting the people in a common bond. There is not a magic church. In magic the only common bond existent is the one uniting the medicine-man and his client, and that bond is accidental and temporary by nature. Durkheim's definition of magic leaves sufficient room for accepting the religious practice of the individual as true

118

religion. The official religion of the church may prescribe individual religious practice, in which case it is part and parcel of the religious system. Magic is confined to practices defined by the relation medicine-man — client, a relation of a transitory nature. Essentially, Durkheim's definition is very much akin to the one of Hubert and Mauss who described magic as rites which are not part of an organised cult. Actually, Durkheim's definition is an improvement on it, contributing to its applicability. Durkheim must have come to this solution well after the publication of the essay of Hubert and Mauss. In the definition of religion he presented in the article "De la définition des phénomènes religieux" published in Vol II of l'Année Sociologique, the final clause is missing: "croyances et pratiques qui unissent en une même communauté morale, appelée Église, tous ceux qui y adhèrent". The clause is a later addition, apparently inspired by the need to find a solution for the problem of magic.

We will have more to say on Durkheim's views on magic in the next section. Here we have to examine the solution he presented for the other problem mentioned in the preceding section, that of the strict separation of the sacred and the profane. To that end we must first of all give a review of the content of his 'Formes élémentaires' of which, so far, very little has been said. We even hardly mentioned the subtitle of the book, "Le système totémique en Australie". Durkheim chose totemism as his point of departure because it is the prevailing religion of one of the world's most primitive peoples, the Australians. Their social organisation is a clan organisation, and totemism provides each clan with a name as well as an emblem. The analysis of the data available leads to the conclusion that it is not so much the totem itself which is sacred, but the emblem of the totem, as is amply confirmed by the veneration the Australians have for their *churinga*, sacred objects profusely decorated with totem emblems. These churinga, normally stowed away in secret depositories, are the foci of the cult. In these emblems a peculiar, impersonal power is concentrated, which inspires fear and deep respect. This power might be called mana as well as an impersonal clan-god. It is concentrated in the totemic emblem, but the totem, and under certain circumstances the clan members — more specifically the old men — also participate in it. The origin of this belief is explained in the context of the resemblances between a society and a deity. They both help, protect and correct their subjects. The latter behave respectfully towards them and feel themselves under a moral obligation to, and morally united with the deity as well as with the society. The people obey them, and they do so not by coercion but for conscience's sake. In our conscience the power of the collectivity makes itself felt in us; our conscience makes us conscious of our society's claims on us. After an elaborate review of the significance and the power of society, Durkheim proceeds to apply his views to the Australian clan.

Normally the clan lives in diaspora. The clan members roam about in small groups. Sometimes however, they congregate, at one time for a couple of days, then again for months on end. Such a convention is a source of great excitement as is amply corroborated by the wild dances and rites then performed. A reunion has a revitalising effect — it is an event from which power emanates. Under such circumstances people grasp for an emblem symbolising their common union. The emblem is the symbol of the regenerative and vitalising power of their reunion and congregation. Anything may serve as an emblem. Considering the fact that the sacred totem-centres are always located in places where the totem animal or -plant abounds, the clan members apparently selected the obvious, viz. the plant or animal characteristic of the place of reunion. The emblem and the totem make the identity of the clan manifest. Without either name or symbol, the group leads a rather shadowy existence, but with them it is a reality. The power vitalising the members at their gathering, is transferred to the emblem representing the clan. The veneration paid to the object is not the result of error but is based on the experience of a perfectly sound reality, the reality that beyond the individual something exists stronger and greater than his poor self, namely the community. The vitalising effect emanating from the community on the individual is experienced as divine, as mana. It is the mana of the sacred and it is obviously here that the opposition sacred — profane has its origin. The sacred time and the sacred place are the time and place of congregation. After the meeting everybody returns to profane life which, for these people, coincides with the diaspora. The sacred coincides with the contraction of the society, the profane with its dispersal.

In the totem-emblem the people revere the clan, i.e. the society. The veneration of the totem-emblem is a first step on the way to animism and the belief in high gods. The members of the clan participate in the mana of the clan as concentrated in the totem-emblem. This specific relation between the individual and the clan-emblem is confirmed by the fact that either the totem-ancestor who is associated with the emblem, or ancestors of lower rank reincarnate themselves in the children of the clan. Among the Aranda a woman is said to become pregnant at the moment when a germ of such an ancestor enters her womb and announces its presence by the first motion of the foetus. The germ is sometimes thought to have the shape of a minuscule bullroarer (also = churinga). Consequently, a part of the mana of the clan is incarnated in the child at its conception. That part may be called soul but the concept of soul cannot be derived solely from this manifestation of the mana of the clan in the germ of life impregnating the mother. The concept of soul derives its efficacy from the operation of the conscience which time and again reminds the individual of the fact that there is a higher power existing outside himself which is also in him, a higher power which is identical with the society. The immortality of the soul derives from the immortality of the totemic principle, the mana of the clan, which is as immortal as the clan itself. The immortality of the totemic principle is embodied in the founders of the clan, the beings of the *alcheringa* time (the mythical time), who persist forever and ever, whereas the souls of common human beings may be annihilated after a number of reincarnations.

Once the notion of soul has assumed a more concise form, the basis has been laid for the belief in spirits of all sorts. There may be evil spirits among them because there are also evil things in human life and society, and we may expect that these too find their expression in spirit form. This is the origin of the evil spirits of sorcery, but Durkheim does not enter further into this matter since he has excluded magic from the field of religion. He confines himself to the observation that the belief in magic has been developed on the analogy of the belief in religion.

Durkheim pays more attention to the belief in supreme beings. In this context he refers to the initiation rites, because on these occasions not only the clan but the whole tribe gathers, sometimes even more than one tribe. The tribe or tribes include quite a number of clans. In this situation we are no longer confronted with spirits representing a single clan, but with spirits who represent the whole tribe or a number of tribes. These are the spirits who are the founders of the tribal organisation and the initiation rites, the originators also of such things as the bullroarer (often identical with a churinga), the fire and the arms. They are proper culture heroes whose voice is the bullroarer which raises the terrifying noise which keeps the frightened women and children at a distance. These culture heroes symbolise the total human society, and because of this they can be associated with the total universe and thus develop into supreme beings of some sort, the makers of sun and moon and the creators of the human race. Durkheim finds a confirmation of the hypothesis in the fact that some of the Australian supreme beings are associated with certain totem animals from which they apparently take their origin.

In the cult Durkheim distinguishes between negative and positive cult. The negative cult is constituted by the observation of taboos. The negative cult aims at the separation of the sacred and the profane, or at preparing man for entering into contact with the sacred by previous consecration. In his comment he emphasises the identity of the sacred with the collectivity, whereas egoism is associated with the profane (cf. Formes élémentaires pp.452 f.).

The 'culte positif' is constituted by the rites. One of them is the rite of sacrifice. In contradistinction to Hubert and Mauss he follows the explanation of Robertson Smith. The rite of sacrifice takes its origin from the totem-meal, a communion enabling the faithful to participate in the sacred by eating the totem. Apart from its overt effect, i.e. the conscious aim for which the rite is performed, every rite has a real effect of great moral importance. The gathering of the group and the performance of the ceremonies in concerted ritual action intensify the feelings of togetherness and

121

enhance the morale of the group. The real effect of the rites is that the solidarity of the group is strengthened and confirmed.

Special mention should be made of Durkheim's comment on the mortuary rites which previous scholars used to explain as the product of the fear of the spirits of the dead. Erroneously so, Durkheim remarks. If fear had been the motive of the living, death must have corrupted the characters of the bewailed dead relatives very profoundly! An analysis of the data gives evidence that much of the elaborate display of mourning is not spontaneous. The mourning is a demonstration. The community suffered a loss and it is necessary that all concerned show how thoroughly they participate in this distress. Because of their low status the women are more qualified for demonstrating excessive mourning than the men. Consequently, the rites are not the effect of the fear of the spirits of the dead, but the fear of the spirits is the effect of the rites. A second effect of the mortuary rites is their contribution to the belief in an afterlife. The acts of mourning become more meaningful if the dead live on.

4. A critical comment

The French sociologists, and notably Durkheim, made an important contribution to the study of religion, first of all by the attention paid to factual situations and social correlations. The recognition that religious phenomena make part of the total framework of social and cultural conditions necessarily led them to a more considered investigation of details and contexts, above all to a more critical and methodologically stricter approach than is found among earlier students of religion. Of course this does not imply that they immediately reaped the full benefit of this approach. We noted already that neither Durkheim nor Hubert and Mauss managed to break away from the persistent prejudice that there is a fundamental difference between magic and religion. Another point, to be discussed presently, is Durkheim's failure to examine the inner consistency of the notion of totemism. All this, however, does not detract from Durkheim's merits in introducing stricter and more critical methods of investigation.

Another contribution is their partiality for formal definitions based on purely external, observable characteristics. This led to a more penetrating analysis of the formal structure of the phenomena under review. In spite of our objections against the undifferentiated character of the notion of the sacred in their definition, it must be conceded that the study of the opposition between the sacred and the profane has led to some valuable observations such as, inter alia, Hertz's study of the preference for the right hand. Another instance of the advantage derived from purely formal classifications is the tripartition of ritual introduced by Hubert and Mauss in their study of the nature and social function of sacrifice. We will meet with various other cases of tripartition in the course of this chapter, which are important contributions to the preparation of a study of the structure of ritual.

However, there is also a number of points which give occasion to serious objections. One of these was made by Van Gennep, namely that the Australian conditions of life are too specific to afford a reliable basis for the foundation of so universal a phenomenon as religion. We will return to Van Gennep's criticism at the end of this chapter (pp.141 f.). For the present six other points must have our attention, viz.

1 Durkheim's explanation of the origin of totemism and of religion generally;
2 the definition of the sacred and the importance attached to the opposition between the sacred and the profane;
3 the rigid exclusion of psychology from the study of social facts;
4 the monopoly granted to the social category in the genesis of religion;
5 the failure to explain magic as a religious phenomenon; and
6 the insufficient analysis of the concept of totemism.

1. One of the most criticised points in Durkheim's theory is his explanation of the origin of totemism. The argument presented is circular. The clan derives its identity from the emblem which provides the basis for ritual unison. However, the clan is pre existent and its members gather and celebrate well before an emblem has been selected and a proper ritual instituted. Another objection against the theory is the one raised by A. R. Radcliffe-Brown. He denies that in Australian totemism the emblem has the fundamental importance ascribed to it by Durkheim. The sex-, moiety- and section totems have no emblem, "and even for clan totems there are many tribes that do not make representations of their totems" (The sociological Theory of Totemism, 1929, in Structure and Function in primitive Society p.125).

2. The opposition between the sacred and the profane is derived from typically Australian conditions with periods of dispersal and periods of social contraction. This is a very narrow basis for the explanation of a universal phenomenon, all the more so because the Australian conditions are rather exceptional.

We note that the objections raised against the interpretation of the opposition of the sacred and the profane in Hubert and Mauss' study of sacrifice, cannot be held against Durkheim who emphasised that the individual participates in the sacredness of the clan. On this ground it is plausible that the individual tries to enter into a closer relation with the sacred in spite of its separateness. The fact, however, that the individual is desirous of having intercourse with the sacred, is evidence that the sacred is ill-defined by describing it is as 'interdit et séparé'. Essentially, only the impure is 'interdit', whereas the pure, which includes the beneficent and the helpful, is sought for and even consciously sought for. However, the sacred always remains separate, nobody could deny that, and this part of the definition should stand. Consequently, a more correct formula would be "ce qui est séparé et *recherché* ou interdit", separate and sought for or forbidden. Even so the formula is far from satisfactory. The terms 'séparé' and 'interdit' admit the possibility of passive avoidance. The one thing inadmissible vis-à-vis the sacred, whether pure or impure, is to ignore it. The sacred summons man to define his stand. Avoiding the impure is not enough; the faithful are as insistently urged to eschew the unholy and the impure as they are exhorted to partake in the sacred ritual. The sacred calls for action and this urge should be reflected in its definition which should be reformulated as follows: *ce qui est séparé et recherché ou enfui.*

3. The rigid exclusion of psychology from the study of social facts does not make itself felt very keenly in Durkheim's studies of religion because here — in spite of himself — he indulges fairly broadly in observations of a predominantly psychological nature. The disadvantages of his disregard of the fact that the locus of all culture is, after all, in the individual, become more obvious in his theory of social change as expounded in "De la Division du Travail social". Here the growth of the division of social labour is ascribed exclusively to two factors, viz. the increase of the 'densité démografique' and of the 'densité dynamique', social factors surpassing the potential influence of the individual. It is not the place here to enter into a discussion on social change but a short note should be made. The individual who has a new idea certainly is a factor in social change. It is impossible to study change, and to ignore the actions and reactions of the individual. Psychology and in particular social psychology is a branch of science which cannot be brushed aside by the student of culture.

4. A more important point in this context is the monopoly allotted to the social category for the explanation of religious phenomena. As a consequence the cosmological components of myth and ritual must be explained as symbols of social groups. Of course it is possible that social groups identify themselves with symbols borrowed from nature. However, it is decidedly improbable that they do it always, and that they do it in such a way that time and again these symbols together constitute a cosmology which embraces the whole non-human world. A follower of Durkheim might reply that, in such a case, the whole non-human world symbolises the whole human world, and he might add as a proof that the categories of nature implied in the relevant cosmology coincide with the organisation of the symbolised society. The answer misses the point, which is that the specific preference for the use of natural and cosmological symbols still remains unexplained, a preference which is given further emphasis in the dominating trend to involve the cosmic order in its totality. What we wish to object to is that in Durkheim's concept of religion man's dependence on society is monopolised, whereas his dependence on his non-human outer-world is ignored. It is impossible to understand why the periodical renewal of nature

124

(in spring or at the beginning of the rainy season) should not make an equally deep impression on man and raise reactions in him comparable to those during the gathering of the tribe or the clan in the festive season. In short, there is insufficient ground for considering the role of nature in the formation of religious concepts as a mere derivative of the social category.

Going further into the matter we must return to the essay on primitive forms of classification. Do the data forwarded really justify the conclusion that the parallelism between the cosmic order and the social order must be explained from the social order? Is it really the social order which constitutes the categories of the cosmic order or can it be that both orders indiscriminately are based on principles which, though elaborated through social interaction inside the group, derive from more fundamental layers of the human mind? The predominance of dualism in systems of social and cosmic order is more suggestive of a structural peculiarity of the human mind generally than of the accidental result of the division of a society into groups. The case of the Zuñi as presented by Durkheim and Mauss is very suggestive not of the impact of the social organisation on the systems of classification (there are 19 clans) but, on the contrary, of the system of classification on the social order (the clans are rearranged in seven units, six groups of three clans and one, the centre group, of one clan). The basic principle is the division into seven and the social order is adapted to it. Of course, the preference for the number 7 originated in the relevant society, but this does not imply that it derived its origin from the social organisation. Durkheim, who noted that the partition into seven might be derived from a dual division, carefully avoided stretching his argument to its full consequence, but that does not make the argument any better. The effort made by Hertz to explain the dominance of the dual principle in human thought from the opposition between the sacred and the profane (which in turn is derived by Durkheim from the social reactions to the periodicity of the Australian climate) is anything but convincing. Why should the opposition between the sacred and the profane be more fundamental than the one between light and dark, or between male and female? We need not spend many words on it. The anthropologists of France never made an effort to proceed in this direction. On the contrary, Lévi-Strauss, who paid great attention to the various forms of dualism, very explicitly emphasised its significance as a structural principle of the human mind.

5. Durkheim failed to give an operational definition of magic. His argument that there is not a magic church, at the sight of it astoundingly clever, is pure verbalism. More promising was his observation that the magical rites are analogous to religious rites, but it did not lead him to a theory. The problem of magic remained unsolved.

6. Taking totemism as the starting-point for his theory, Durkheim selected a much disputed concept. Two years before the publication of the 'Formes élémentaires' the American anthropologist A. A. Goldenweiser had

launched a devastating attack on the concept of totemism. Although the deficiencies of the concept do not impede Durkheim's use of the concrete data, the critique of Goldenweiser (see below, pp.140 f.) should have prevented Durkheim from reverting to the forms of American Indian totemism for the elucidation of special aspects of Australian totemism, a fact which later incurred the caustic criticism of Van Gennep.

In conclusion we state that there are many reasons for disagreeing with Durkheim. There are at least as many valid reasons not to ignore him. Contested and criticised from many sides, his contributions to the theory of religion are among the most valuable, even where he erred. It still is a stimulating experience to read his works, written in a beautiful and always lucid French.

5. Other contributions of French students of religion

Durkheim's influence has been very strong in France. Among the scholars contributing to the further development of the theory of religion were some of his former students, such as R. Hertz and M. Mauss; others were sympathisers, e.g. Lévy-Bruhl. Again, there were those who combined strong traces of Durkheim's influence with a very critical attitude, like A. van Gennep. Really independent among those whose works are to be discussed in this chapter was Bergson. The present section sets out with a review of an essay written by Hertz; the main part is devoted to Lévy-Bruhl's theory of primitive mentality and the critical comment given on it by H. Bergson.

A more or less forgotten essay until it was translated by Needham, is Hertz's "Contribution à une Étude sur la Représentation collective de la Mort" (Année Sociologique X, 1907). Hertz argues that the community does not accept the death of one of its members. The deceased must live on and persist just like the community does. The mortuary rites are primarily an expression of mourning, but their overt aim is to accompany the dead on their way from the world of the living to that of the dead. The frequent occurrence of a second burial must be placed in this context. When the flesh is consumed the bones are exhumed and cleaned for a second and final interment. The second burial marks the end of the mourning period. The deceased is now really dead, he belongs to the world of the ancestors. Psychologically, the period between the first and the second burial is the period during which the community learns to be resigned to its loss. For the dead it is a period of transition, the time during which they abide their ultimate departure for the land of the dead. The parallels between the mortuary rites and the rites connected with initiation and marriage are obvious. All these rites are connected with transitions from one status to another. This is the reason why the mortuary rites performed for children and old people are far more limited in scope. Young children are supposed to reincarnate quickly after their death; they need not depart to the land of the dead. On

126

the other hand, the old were already in a state in which their demise was expected. The community need not learn to be resigned to their loss; those concerned were already familiar with the idea, and the deceased can depart straight on to the land of the dead.

An interesting feature of the essay is that it is a prelude to Van Gennep's conception of the rites of passage; even the division into three successive phases, first burial, period of transition, and second burial, is already present in an incipient form. Hertz must have been an exceptionally gifted and erudite man. Unfortunately, he was killed in battle at an early age, one of the many victims of the first world war.

In this same section mention should be made of the later work of M. Mauss, more especially of his famous "Essai sur le Don". Because of its singular impact on the concept of structure it will be discussed in chapter IX.

A special place among the French writers on primitive religion must be given to *Lucien Lévy-Bruhl* (1857-1939). He was already professor of philosophy of the Sorbonne when he became interested in anthropology. His first book in this field, "Les Fonctions mentales dans les Sociétés inférieures", was published in 1910. His argument is based on the contrast between 'représentations collectives' and 'représentations individuelles', two concepts which we translate with some hesitation as collective and individual representations; in fact, the similarity in verbal form does not convey an equal similarity of meaning. The dichotomy as such Lévy-Bruhl borrowed from Durkheim who had taught that the formal categories of thought are the products of collective thinking. Durkheim had been very reserved in the elaboration of the idea, but Lévy-Bruhl went a step further and combined differences in 'représentations collectives' with differences in mentality, differences so great that it often is impossible for us to follow the thought of primitive people in their collective representations.

Collective representations are characterised by the following features:
1. they are shared by all the members of the community;
2. they are transmitted from generation to generation;
3. they obtrude themselves on the individual, rousing in him such sentiments as respect, fear and worship of their object. These 'représentations collectives' have the same characteristics as Durkheim's social facts; they exist on their own, independently of the individual, obeying laws which cannot be derived from psychology. They are the products of a belief which should be taken as a social fact. This means that they are part of a social system, and such systems differ from one society to another. From Durkheim, Lévy-Bruhl borrowed the idea that there are different types of societies. Though they have certain traits in common such as the use of language and the presence of a set of traditions, the differences between the various types may be so substantial that Lévy-Bruhl felt justified in comparing them to the distinctions between vertebrates and invertebrates. Con-

sequently, there is ample reason to surmise that these differences go hand in hand with equivalent differences of mentality. To these differences, Lévy-Bruhl devoted his study.

First and foremost Lévy-Bruhl explains that these differences are differences of mentality, not mental differences in the sense of structural differences of the brain, 'l'appareil cérébral'. In western thought representations are of a cognitive nature par excellence. Emotional and motoric elements have been discarded from western thought, whereas these elements make an integrative part of the 'représentations collectives' of primitive people. These emotional and motoric elements have their origin in the conditions prevailing in the situation in which these representations are born. Often they are of a very emotional nature, for example the conditions characterising an initiation ceremony. The emotional atmosphere gives a mystic tinge to the representations which originate under such circumstances. Whereas the people concerned see with the same eyes as we do, their minds are different, not bent towards objectivity, but towards the occult and the mysterious. To them a picture becomes more than simply a picture; veritable life may be attributed to it. The relations between a man and his name or shadow are conceived of as real, i.e. as of a mystic and intrinsic nature. Dreams are not empty but the revelations of a truth of some sort; they refer to real events. The medicine-man sees things which remain hidden to ordinary humans, because he has a knowledge of the mystic relations connecting the one with the other. All this primitive man does not consider to be unnatural or supernatural because the distinction between the natural and the supernatural is utterly unknown to him. To him there is only one universe, one reality, and that reality is mystic by nature.

The author points out that he would be stretching the argument if he averred that these collective representations obey the rules of another system of logic than ours. After all we can learn the languages of these primitive people and understand what they mean. This implies that there is insufficient ground for such a far-fetched conclusion. Yet, we are up against the fact that numerous expert observers of primitive people have argued that it is impossible to understand them fully. In one way or other their thinking differs from ours. We can think a long way along similar lines as they do, and then suddenly we cannot follow them any longer. They perceive a mystic element in the events they experience, and one of the specific peculiarities of their way of thinking is that they repudiate the possibility of chance. The mystic element apprehended in things and events works out in the notion that a kind of mystic participation is connecting anything with everything else. As an example he quotes the story told by a missionary, the Rev. Edelfeldt, about the events connected with the occurrence of an epidemic at Motumotu (Port Moresby). The natives first ascribed the sickness to the missionary's sheep and the sheep was slaughtered to allay their fears. No result forthcoming, they accused his two goats and finally a great portrait of Queen Victoria on the wall of his dining room, a portrait which before had won their admiration (Fonctions mentales pp.71 f.). To satisfy the reader's curiosity we add that the portrait and the goats were more effectively defended than the poor sheep.

The story is a good illustration of the strange and sometimes even baffling forms of causal attribution current in primitive society. If somebody dies from a wound which everybody can observe, notwithstanding the death is ascribed to sorcery. Mystic associations prevail over natural causality. These mystic associations obey a law of their own, a law to which Lévy-Bruhl gave the name of law of participation. The trend towards mystic participation is expressed in concepts such as mana, wakanda, orenda, and so on, which give scope to the mystic connections underlying things and events. The way of thought of primitive man is synthetic, it ignores the *principium contradictionis* and obeys in particular the law of participation. This way of thinking is not a-logic or anti-logic; in many respects it is logical enough. The point where it goes astray is that it ignores the necessity of avoiding contradictions and on this ground he proposes to call this way of thinking *pre-logic*.

There is a close correlation between participating, synthetic thinking on the one hand and social conditions on the other. Humanity did not escape from this erroneous way of thinking before mankind had managed to break away from the total and all-inclusive socialisation proper to the primitive way of life. Here again Durkheim's influence makes itself felt. In his "Division du Travail social", the latter had argued at some length that primitive society is characterised by the absence of individual variation. Any member of the group is like every other member, sharing the same views and opinions. With the growth of culture and the progress of development individual variation sets in, and according to Lévy-Bruhl the increase of individual variation is accompanied by a proportionate decrease of the belief in participation which in the state of total socialisation seemed self-evident. Individual thinking develops progressively and in this process the collective representations are gradually purged of their initial contradictions. However, participating thinking does not disappear entirely; the human heart always aspires after a deeper knowledge than is attainable by pure logic and thus even in our mentality some remnants of prelogic thought persist (Fonctions mentales pp.453 ff.). These remnants play but a small part in our thinking, far smaller than among primitive people. In their individual thinking these primitives think as logically as we do, but collective representations are more numerous and play a far bigger part than among us, and it is exactly these collective representations which are participating, prelogic and mystic.

Lévy-Bruhl's book abounds with a mass of instances presented as proofs and illustrations of primitive mentality as expounded above. Without exception these instances are borrowed from the field of religion. In his later books he did not alter the theory forwarded in "Les Fonctions mentales". "La Mentalité primitive" (1922), "l'Ame primitive" (1927) and "La Mythologie primitive" (1935) present the same theory, demonstrated by new and other instances. Towards the end of his life — he died in 1939 — Lévy-Bruhl began to question the validity of his theory. In his estate a number of exercise-books were found which were edited by M. Leenhardt under the caption "Les Carnets de Lucien Lévy-Bruhl" (1949). As it is not known whether Lévy-Bruhl ever wished for such a publication, it is doubtful whether we have a right to make an appeal to these afterthoughts. What is more, it is not the "Carnets", but "Les Fonctions mentales" which are decisive for Lévy-Bruhl's part in the development of religious theory. In his earlier contributions he broached a problem of great importance and we have to answer the question whether he solved the problem satisfactorily.

It certainly is a great merit that he focussed the attention of the learned world on a fundamental problem of great importance, the solution of which has not become any the easier since Freud exposed numerous analogies of primitive thought with the symbols of the dream and the psychopathologies of neurotics. Another merit of Lévi-Bruhl is that he avoided the fallacy (so often undeservedly imputed to him) of explaining the difference between modern and primitive thought from supposed structural differences in the cerebral apparatus, an explanation repeatedly forwarded on the shakiest grounds. The similarities of primitive thought and the symbolic actions of modern neurotics, if they are an argument at all, certainly are more in favour of structural similarity than of structural differences. However, this question is not in order now; we have to answer the question whether Lévy-Bruhl's solution of the problem is a satisfactory one and this answer is decidedly no. No, for various reasons.

Our first objection must be raised against Lévy-Bruhl's extremely biased selection of the data which he presented as proofs of prelogic thought. All his data are derived from the field of religious thinking. Collective representations relevant to social intercourse, to economical and technical activities, are consistently ignored. Yet, the obligations towards certain kin (e.g. a mother's brother), the rules concerning the exchange of presents on the occasion of a marriage, the technique of growing certain crops or that of canoe-building, are all based on collective representations. What is worse for the theory, these representations invariably are soundly logical but Lévy-Bruhl does not give a thought to them. Evidently, he has seriously underestimated the range of his own concept of collective representations. This implies that he has not presented us with an analysis of primitive thought, but of primitive religion or at least of the way of thinking which is basic to religion. That in this category of thought mysticism prevails can, after all, neither be called a novelty nor unexpected.

In the second place — and this objection is even more serious — the author has not bestowed a sufficient measure of critical reflection on the content of the concepts of collective and individual representations. If he had, he would have stumbled on the fact that the collective is always present in our representations. In a sense, words too are collective representations. The further we penetrate into the problem the clearer it becomes that the contrast between individual and collective representations is void and unoperational. It is a contrast which simply does not exist. We never are, do, or think completely individually nor completely collectively for the simple reason that the collectivity involved is a part of our self, just as we are a part of the collectivity. In this form the problem of the individual and the collectivity is a sham problem and should be discarded resolutely. Nevertheless it is one which kept anthropologists busy for many years until the studies of Sapir, Ruth Benedict, Marg. Mead and R. Linton brought more clarity in our thinking on this point.

Finally we must mention a third objection, the one forwarded by *Henri Bergson* in his book "Les deux Sources de la Morale et de la Religion" (1932), a book which deserves some comment before we return to Lévy-Bruhl.

Bergson's book is a philosophical work, designed to explain the implications of the philosophy of the 'évolution créatrice' and the 'élan vital' on ethics and religion. The book has not been written for anthropologists. Some of them might feel justified in pushing it aside as metaphysical speculation. It would be difficult to blame them for doing so because it is indeed speculation. Yet it is highly intelligent speculation and Bergson's analysis of thinking in a closed society (i.e. in a primitive society) is in every respect worth-while. The author refers to a highly remarkable phenomenon. Man experiences his universe as a universe full of intentions, a universe which holds a claim on him, addressing him with something undefined, urging him to act or to be in some way or another. The experience is strongest in moments of crisis, when events turn up with such an overwhelming force that it is as if they address their victim, delivering a message to him. The English language has a good expression for such frightful events. They are acts of God and they convey a message. The event has an intention, a message concerning the person involved. That is how the event is experienced and, terrifying as the event may be, the apprehended intention is the sole comfort of the victim. The intention gives the incident a meaning. Without the intention the event would be senseless and fatal; through the intention even the most unforeseen calamity acquires something like a human face, which lends the incomprehensible and fateful just that tinge of the intelligible as to enable the victim to apprehend some sort of hidden sense beneath the vacuous and contingent. It encourages him to start a conversation with the event. A perfect example of such a reaction is given in the story which Bergson borrowed from W. James on the latter's experiences during the earthquake which swept San Francisco in 1906. Shortly before he left for

San Francisco a friend warned him that there was a good chance that he might experience an earthquake. When the earthquake shook him awake his first idea was: "By Jove, here's B's old earthquake, after all. And a jolly good one it is, too!" He talked to the earthquake and he forgot to be frightened (Les deux Sources, pp.161 ff.). The story is too long to be retold here (but cf. below, p.229). The main point is that in the conversation with the earthquake the latter lost its terror. Talking to an event is a spontaneous reaction which may occur in any society or culture. Bergson applies the moral of the story to the conditions of early man, a being bereft of instinct, at the mercy of the sole instructions of the intellect bestowed on him but without the proper knowledge to pilot him through the dangerous channels of the events in his universe: "Il se sentirait perdu, si l'effort pour vivre ne projetait aussitôt dans son intelligence, à la place même que cette perception et cette pensée allaient prendre, l'image antagoniste d'une conversion des choses et des événements vers l'homme: bienveillante ou malveillante, une intention de l'entourage le suit partout, comme la lune paraît courir avec lui quand il court" (Les deux Sources p.186). At another place (ibid. p.184) he says: "comme si la nature avait partout des yeux qu'elle tourne vers l'homme".

In a later chapter (below, pp.229 ff.) we have to return more circumstantially to the theme of the man in distress who has the uneasy feeling that a mysterious eye is staring at him, who feels that the event which uprooted his life addresses him with a message of some sort. For the present we confine ourselves to Bergson's commentary on Lévy-Bruhl's interpretation of a fateful accident (Les deux Sources pp.151-156) which he forwards as an introduction to his analysis of chance, "le hasard (comme) . . . une intention qui s'est vidée de son contenu" (ibid. p.155). A man walks on the floor of a ravine during a storm. A piece of rock is detached from the cliff above and falls on his head, killing him. His relatives who saw what happened, ascribe the event to sorcery. To Lévy-Bruhl the case is a perfect illustration of prelogic thought. Bergson, doubting the possibility that collective representations really are incomprehensible to people belonging to another type of society, presents another interpretation of the case. He contests the view that there is anything prelogic in the reaction of the victim's relatives. Do these people deny that there was a gale blowing, that there was a loose rock which fell on the victim's head? Certainly not; they saw it as well as anybody else, but the natural course of the event does not adequately explain that the falling stone hit that particular man. The normal procedure is that rocks fall down without hurting anybody. Why did a falling rock kill a man this time, and not even just any man but their relative? The fact that for once a perfectly natural and not uncommon event causes the death of a man remains unexplained. Had the rock fallen only one second earlier or later, the man would not have been hurt. The event is experienced as if directed by an intention and this intention requires an explanation. Logic requires that causes be equivalent to their consequences. The death of a relative is not explained by a simple conjunction of accidental circumstances.

Bergson introduces a perfectly new element here, an element altogether too often ignored in the theory of religion, viz. the experience of the universe not as a purely neutral field of concurring forces, but as a universe addressing man in one way or another, a universe charged with intentions regarding his person. It is a notion which opens the way to a wholly new approach to the problems of magic and religion. In chapters X and XI the potentialities of this approach shall be submitted to a closer examination.

6. The rites of passage

In the remaining sections of this chapter mention shall be made of the works of Arnold van Gennep, a French anthropologist who initially associated himself fairly closely with Durkheim's school, but who later turned into a sharp critic of the master's main work. The author's independent position affords a welcome opportunity for a somewhat broader discussion of two important issues, the rites of passage including initiation rites (section 6), and the critique of the concept of totemism initiated by Goldenweiser and continued by Van Gennep (section 7).

"Les Rites de Passage" (1909) is Van Gennep's best remembered work. One of the problems discussed in it is that of initiation, a subject which before Van Gennep had been studied by two other authors, a German and an American. It seems advisable first to review their works before we proceed to Van Gennep's "Rites de Passage".

The more important of these studies is the book written by Heinrich Schurtz, "Altersklassen und Männerbünde", a sociological study (1902). The author expresses his intention to make use of ethnographical data for the explanation of certain social phenomena. He concentrates his study on two ubiquitous factors in social life, viz. age and sex. Differences of sex and age play a role in every society. The role of sex differentiation is obvious in the two most important forms of social organisation found in primitive society, viz. the 'Geschlechtsverbände' (more especially the family organisation) and the 'Geselligkeitsverbände' (the greater groups, for example the clans)[12]. In the former the functions of the females dominate, in the latter those of the males.

Intercrossing the sexes are the age groups — children, the adolescent and unmarried young people, and the married adults. Of the three groups the middle one enjoys the greater measure of independence and freedom. Ado-

[12] The terms 'Geschlechtsverbände' and 'Geselligkeitsverbände' are untranslatable, in particular the former. 'Geschlecht' refers equally to sex and to descent. 'Geselligkeit' may be translated as social, but has a connotation of voluntary association.

lescence is a period of sexual licence. The entrance into this stage of life is marked by a feast, a feast which turns into a rite of admission where the young and the adult men are united in a strictly organised sex community of males. Such a strictly organised community of males always goes hand in hand with a strong antagonism between the sexes. Women are excluded from participation in the activities of the male community; their field of interest is that of the family and of the 'Geschlechtsverbände'. Where family life dominates and the influence of the women makes itself felt the male community is in decline. Schurtz extensively discusses men's houses and age classes, institutions marking the independence of a dominant male sex, bent on postponing the contraction of marriage by prolonging the period of sexual licence for the young men. The male communities may develop into dance societies (as among the American Indians), into mysteries (Greece) or simply into a kind of social clubs setting about organising banquets and drinking-bouts. If the male community specialises in sex antagonism and takes to striking terror into women and children, a secret society originates.

Psychologically Schurtz's argument does not delve deep, but his book has two outstanding merits. In the first place it draws attention to an extremely important phenomenon sociologically, viz. the differences of sex and age and the influence of their relative weight on social organisation. In the second place it demonstrates the importance of initiation and secret rites, which until that time had been hardly studied at all. These are merits which cannot, at least not to that degree, be attributed to another book treating a part of the same subject matter, i.e. the book of Hutton Webster, "Primitive Secret Societies" (1908). We confine ourselves to just making mention of it.

Van Gennep approached the subject from quite another angle. Initiation implies a passage from one status to another. Such passages are by no means exceptional. Life abounds with changes of status, such as birth, initiation, betrothal, marriage, pregnancy, becoming a mother or father, and finally death. Such changes of status do not pass unnoticed in society. On the contrary, they are emphasised. In primitive society each status has its own sacral aspect, a peculiarity which has almost completely disappeared in modern society where only the clergy has preserved it. Among primitive people, however, sub-groups such as clan, caste and family all have a clear-cut religious aspect.

The passage from one status to another follows a fixed scheme. There are always three phases, viz. the separation from the old situation, the transition to the new status, and finally the re-admittance into the society in the new status. The successive phases of the passage go combined with rites, the first phase with rites of separation, the second with 'rites de marge' or rites of transition, and the last with rites of absorption. The whole process is demonstrated in rapid succession on the occasion of a festive visit of one

134

tribe to another: outside the village the guests stop short and wait, often dancing till the hosts come out to meet them; then the guests proceed and enter the village in a highly ostentatious way; and finally the fraternisation of hosts and guests follows.

The author describes the three phases of the rites to which a woman is subjected on the occasion of her pregnancy and deliverance, a child at his birth and admittance into the group as a recently born baby (e.g. on the occasion of his name giving). He does the same with regard to the rites of initiation, betrothal, marriage, and burial. Special attention is given by the author to events which normally happen more than once in the course of a life. Such events may be marked by rites of passage when they occur for the first time in the life of the individual. 'Rites of the first time' are performed on occasions such as the first hair-cutting, the appearance of the first tooth, the delivery of the first child, etc.

Important is van Gennep's comment on initiation rites. In his book just mentioned, Webster had included them under the caption of puberty rites. Because the time of performance of the initiation rites often does not coincide at all with the attainment of puberty, Webster had felt forced to denounce such performances as later degenerations. Van Gennep pointed out that Webster had failed to differentiate between physical and social puberty which are two different things. Rites on the occasion of a girl's first menstruation are of frequent occurrence. Yet, social puberty does not coincide with the first menstruation; socially approved sexual intercourse may begin long before as well as long after the first menses. In ancient Rome the marriageable age of girls was 12 years, whereas the French legislation put the age at 16 years and 6 months. The average age of first menstruation does not conform to either of the two. At the beginning of the century it was 14 years and 4 months in France. The fact that we now know that the age of first menstruation is variable (up to a degree), and is earlier to-day than 60 years ago (probably the effect of improved nutrition) does not detract from the value of Van Gennep's argument that there is a difference between the age of puberty and the age of passage from 'le monde asexué vers le monde sexué'.

Among boys the situation is more complicated because the attainment of puberty is less clearly marked. It is a weak argument to explain the many divergencies between the moment of performance of what allegedly are puberty rites, and the age of puberty. Consequently, Van Gennep had to concede that sometimes the relation of so-called puberty-rites to marriage and sexual intercourse is intrinsically absent. The most obvious case is that of circumcision, which in Mohammedan countries is performed at some time between the 7th or 8th day after birth and the age of 12 or 13 years. We note in passing that there are also peoples — but Van Gennep could not know this — where the act of circumcision is performed at a far more advanced age, e.g. among the Galla.

135

Circumcision is one out of various mutilations serving as a mark of distinction indicating a social class[13]. A good illustration of the process of initiation is provided by the circumcision rites among the Australian aborigines where the three phases mentioned above are clearly in evidence. First of all the neophytes are taken away from the group of women and children and kept in seclusion. The period of seclusion is one of instruction. Then follows the second phase, the rite of transition to the new status which is marked by a mutilation, in this case circumcision. The circumcision is the visible token of admittance to the community of (adult) males. Finally the third phase follows, the reintegration into the community at large, a festive occasion for everybody, also for the uninitiated, because they had been told that the boys had to go through dangers of all sorts. On the occasion of their reunion the newly initiated sometimes behave as if they have forgotten their female relatives, or as if they must learn everything anew.

With regard to the marriage rites Van Gennep makes an observation which, at the time, had the merit of relative novelty. The ceremonial resistance of the bride against her removal to the bridegroom's group is, far from being a survival of marriage by capture, a typical case of the emphasis given, in the first phase of a rite of passage, to the fact that a separation takes place.

It is difficult to decide whether the term rite of passage is interpretative and meant as a contribution to the explanation of a certain category of ritual performances, or simply a descriptive term conceived of as a tool for the better classification of phenomena. There is something of both elements in Van Gennep's exposition. His assertion that in primitive society every status has a sacral aspect is undoubtedly an attempt to explain, because it suggests that it is the sacral aspect which is evocative of the initial rite of separation and, the transition completed, of the closing rite of aggregation. However, Van Gennep fails to draw the conclusion and his incipient attempt remains incomplete. The focus of his interest is the classification of the rites, not their explanation and we might well ask why he exerts himself so much to demonstrate that every status has a sacral aspect. Actually, it is a weak point; there is no proof for it. For instance, among the Marind-Anim of South New Guinea successive phases in the growing up of the young child are marked by family feasts; when the child is put into a sitting bag for the first time, taken out from it for the last time, the first decoration with upperarmlets and piercing of the ears for the fixing of earrings,

---

[13] We shall not enter into a discussion of Van Gennep's explanation of circumcision. For a review of modern ideas on this point the reader is referred to Charles Harrington, "Sexual Differentiation in Socialization and some male genital Mutilations", A.A. 70 pp.951-956; Philip Singer and Daniel E. Desole, "The Australian Subincision Ceremony reconsidered", A.A. 69 pp.355-358.

these are all welcome opportunities for a family feast with all the characteristics of a rite of passage (cf. Van Baal, Dema pp.131 ff.) without even a shade of evidence that there is a change in the child's — or the parents' — sacral aspect. The child has not even a sacral aspect at that age. Similarly, the benevolent observer can discern the three phases of a rite of passage also in a modern, perfectly secular marriage ceremony: the hectic weeks preceding the ceremony and the elaborate decoration of the bride, the ceremony at the registry office or in the church, and finally the dinner where the members of the two families and their friends come together with the bridal couple. The successive phases are present, though in a somewhat attenuated form, but there is no question of a sacral status.

While Van Gennep wisely refrained from stressing the explanatory value of his contribution to the classification of rites, other authors have been less reticent. They hastened to give a new name to the rites of passage, viz. *crisis-rites*, thus introducing a decidedly interpretative element. The term suggests that the rite is performed because a crisis must be warded off. Altogether too often such an interpretation turns the order of things upside down. Usually there is not a scrap of evidence of a crisis in the life of the child or the adolescent which could justify the performance of the rite on his behalf. On the contrary, the rite itself produces the crisis and many initiation rites are performed very deliberately for that purpose. A crisis must be provoked in the boy's life in order to turn him into a man. In such cases it is not the crisis which provokes the rite but the rite which provokes the crisis. Similarly, there are also changes of status which are not the cause but the effect of the rite. Thus giving a certain feast may be socially rewarded by a higher title or rank.

There is yet another reason for not using the term crisis-rite as a synonym of rite of passage. There are various rites which are not rites of passage at all, which nevertheless do accompany a crisis, for example rites performed to ward off an epidemic, rites to put an end to a prolonged period of drought, and so on. Some of the rites classified by Norbeck as cyclic rites (cf. his Religion, pp.164 ff.) because they are connected with the progress of the seasons, could for that very reason better be called crisis-rites. They accompany a crisis in nature which is also a crisis in the life of the human community.

Another point is that the equation of initiation rites with puberty rites is highly contestable, even if we follow Van Gennep's interpretation of puberty as social puberty. An initiation rite is intrinsically a revelation. There is a religious secret which must be transmitted to members of a younger generation during the performance of a rite, usually a rite which is to be executed anyway, whether there are neophytes or not. The initiation is necessary in order to admit new members to the company of wardens of the religious secret. The rite is not performed because a number of young men reached the age of puberty, but because the survival of the cult and its secrets must be ensured by the absorption of young initiates. Their initiation may — and fairly often does — coincide with either physical or social puberty but this is not a must. The must is the revelation and transmission of the secret. If in many cases the ritual act is performed well before or a long time after the age of puberty has been attained, the ultimate choice of the age of admittance does not constitute a deviation from the rule but simply another rule, one of the many which are possible. Among the Sukuma of Tanzania initiation takes place long after marriage and coincides with the admittance of the neophyte to the community of the elders. In Central Australia, among the Aranda, initiation is staged in phases and the last phase often is postponed until middle age is approaching. Such an initiation certainly is a rite of passage, because a change of status is involved, but it is not a puberty rite at all.

The real merit of Van Gennep does not lie in his explanation of a certain category of rites, but in his discovery that there is an important category of rites, characterised by a fixed structure of three successive stages, viz. separation, transition and aggregation. All these rites have in common that their performance leads to the acquirement of a new status by those who were the object of the ritual. This is the reason why he stresses the change of status as the ultimate aim of the rites, and it is here that we ought to place a question mark. Van Gennep failed to note (though he must have been aware of it) that a tripartite structure of a ritual is not confined to the rites of passage. Earlier Hubert and Mauss had already demonstrated that a similar structure characterises the rites of sacrifice, and Hertz had found the same to be the case with the mortuary rites among peoples practising a twofold burial. Now the mortuary rites can be classified as another category of rites of passage, but the rites of sacrifice cannot, and this raises the question whether Van Gennep was justified in connecting the tripartite structure with a change of status. There is reason for serious doubt. Van Gennep himself thought it necessary to emphasise the sacral aspect of these statuses. We pointed out that in primitive society not every status has a sacral aspect and that a sacral status is not a necessary concomitant of rites of passage. In spite of the absence of anything resembling a sacral aspect, the ceremonial attending a transition from one status to another may be of the same tripartite structure. In this context we referred to the procedure of a modern marriage ceremony, an example which highlights the similarities on the one hand, whereas there seems to be a difference of degree of intensity on the other. We felt obliged to write that a *benevolent* observer might discern the three stages. There is sound reason to assume that usually the tripartite structure is more pronounced where the sacred character of the proceedings is obvious. This would imply that the tripartite structure is not a characteristic of a ceremony connected with a change of status but of a ritual performance generally. The structure of the rite of sacrifice as described by Hubert and Mauss is an argument in favour of this supposition. Unfortunately, the structure of ritual has not yet been made the object of an encompassing study and the enquiries made thus far suggest that the tripartite scheme, although an important lead for further studies, is just a little too simple for a satisfactory description of the structure of ritual. The analysis made by Stanner (below, p.189) gives evidence that the structure is more complicated. All this does not detract from the merits of the studies of Hubert, Mauss, Hertz and Van Gennep. They are important contributions to the further study of the structure of ritual. However, they all have one and the same weakness, viz. a rather superficial analysis of what is essentially the most varied part of the ritual, the sacrifice proper in Hubert and Mauss and the 'rite de marge' in Van Gennep. A further study of the crucial, central complex of ritual is needed to clarify our notions of its structure.

7. The concept of totemism critically examined by Goldenweiser and Van Gennep

Durkheim had founded his theory of religion on the analysis of Australian totemism. More than any scholar before him he relied on observable facts. He systematically avoided the danger of basing a theory on accidental developments, and he steered clear of the fallacy of presenting totemism as a doctrine. In all this he differed profoundly from earlier and contemporary writers on totemism. Spencer had ascribed the origin of totemism to the imperfections of language (cf. above, p.45). Wilken explained it from metempsychosis, the transmigration of the spirits of the dead into animals (Het Animisme, Verspreide Geschriften III pp.85 ff.). A. C. Haddon suggested that the abundance of a certain animal species in the territory of a clan had led to the adoption of a surname identical with that of the species concerned (Report to the British Association, Belfast 1902). C. Hill-Tout had tried to explain the American form of individual totemism from the custom of acquiring a guardian spirit by prolonged fasting (The Origin of Totemism among the Aborigines of British Columbia, 1902). Frazer, more versatile than ever, presented three different theories in succession of which one, the second, had the merit of being based on a phenomenon of relatively frequent occurrence, namely the clan's performance of specific rites for the increase of the totem. According to this interpretation totemism is a case of magical specialisation by the relevant clans for the benefit of the tribe as a whole (Fortnightly Review 1899; Totemism and Exogamy I pp.89-138).

The problem for all these authors was how to find a suitable explanation for that combination of divergent phenomena which together constitute what they called the totemic complex: the exogamy of the totem clan, the use of the totem as a clan name, the descent from the totem, the taboo against killing or eating the totem, and the religious attitude vis-à-vis the totem. The complex was supposed to be a religious doctrine of world-wide occurrence, just like animism. Even Durkheim had not succeeded in freeing himself from the idea that totemism is, essentially, a more or less uniform complex. He looked upon totemism as the earliest form of religion generally and he used American-Indian data to elucidate Australian facts.

In 1910 *A. A. Goldenweiser* played havoc with current ideas on totemism in an essay called "Totemism, an analytical study" (J.A.F.L. 1910). The essay had originally been written as a doctoral thesis, and the influence of the acute analytical thinking introduced into American anthropology by Boas makes itself felt from the beginning. The question forwarded by Goldenweiser is whether such a thing as totemism really exists. To answer the question he enters into an extensive analysis of totemism as it occurs among the North American Indians and among the Australians. The results of his comparative study are applied to the five main features of the totemic complex mentioned above. The outcome is lethal for the current notion of a totemic complex.

Clan exogamy is not necessarily combined with totemism. Sometimes we find totemism without exogamy. More frequent is the occurrence of clan exogamy without totemism, or clan exogamy combined with only one of the five traits of the totemic complex. The use of the totem as a clan name and the belief in the common descent of the clan members and their totem are far from universal. In American totemism the use of the totem as a clan name is infrequent, and the belief in a common descent of totem-species and clan members is decidedly rare. The taboo on killing or eating the totem is far from universal. Fairly often killing or eating the totem is not forbidden at all. Conversely, there are numerous cases of food taboos which have nothing to do with totemism. A religious attitude vis-à-vis animals, plants and natural objects is by no means rare even where totemism is absent. On the other hand, where totemism occurs the totem as such is rarely an object of religious awe. The emotions felt with regard to the totem vary from complete indifference to direct worship.

Not one of the current traits of totemism is sufficiently universal to permit its use as a characteristic, and the author continues that if the concept of totemism should be used at all, the essence of totemism cannot be found in the sum of the diverse elements constituting the alleged complex, but in the association of the totemic elements with social groups. These social groups need not necessarily be clans; the totemic elements can also be associated with secret societies, independent of the clan organisation as among the Kwakiutl. What remains is that totemism can be defined as "the tendency of definite social units to become associated with objects and symbols of emotional value" or, in a more condensed form, "totemism is the specific socialization of emotional values".

The two definitions give occasion to the objection that the word 'emotional' apparently stands for religion, an interpretation of the religious which invariably leads to confusion. However, in its main purpose, the critique of totemism as a scientific concept, Goldenweiser's analysis was a complete success. It made an end to the fruitless and ill-devised efforts to present totemism as a doctrine. After Goldenweiser, definitions of totemism had to be restricted to a statement on a religious relation of some sort between a group of people and a natural category or object.

Later, in an address delivered in 1917, Goldenweiser returned to the subject, this time not for further criticism of the concept but to defend what had been left of it against Boas, who had averred that "totemism is an artificial, not a natural unit" (The Origin of Totemism, A.A. 18, 1916). In his reply, published under the title "Form and Content in Totemism" (A.A. 20, 1918), Goldenweiser firmly rejected the advisability of banning the term. Totemism is characterised by an attitude versus nature so entirely specific that a special term is needed. In particular clans are often associated with totems. A combination of the two is found more often than can be explained by chance, and Goldenweiser suggests that the combination must be explained by the fact that a clan organisation needs 'some kind of classifyers', in other words, symbols representing the clans. The argument is fairly closely related to that of Durkheim but the two differ in their evaluation of the role of nature. To Durkheim nature is simply a provider of symbols needed for enhancing the identity of the group; to Goldenweiser nature itself inspires religion because it arouses exactly those feelings in man which are typical of religion. According to Goldenweiser, a religious attitude is universal, and he argues that the combination of nature-mystics with a clan organisation offers a proper matrix for the genesis of a totemic complex.

A. van Gennep, in "l'État actuel du Problème totémique" (1920) gives a complete review of all the various theories on totemism which had been advanced up to that year. The critical part of the book is directed first and foremost against Durkheim. Van Gennep blames him for his basic assumption as formulated in the sentence: "La société est à ses membres ce qu'un dieu est à ses fidèles, parcequ'elle a une nature qui lui est propre, différente de notre nature d'individus". In Van Gennep's view the statement is not the result of Durkheim's research but the programme of his approach. To prove its veridity Durkheim's Australian data did not suffice. More than once he was obliged to refer to North American phenomena to clarify the Australian facts. This is more specifically the case in his discussion of the notion of mana, a notion absent in Australia but well-known in the North American continent (orenda, wakanda). Durkheim is forced to prove his thesis by reverting to American data, but that implies that it is impossible to uphold the pretence that his work is based on a description of Australian totemism.

Equally caustic is Van Gennep's criticism of Durkheim's theory of the role of the emblem in totemism. Long before Durkheim, Andrew Lang had already stressed the importance of the totemic emblem. Durkheim's theory is based on exceptional conditions, which are confined to central Australian totemism. The theory turns things upside down by averring that the totem derives its sacred character from the emblem. This implies that totemism could not originate before the group had a name as well as an emblem. However, the group is pre-existent and Van Gennep strongly insists that name and emblem are the outcomes of totemism — the means to visualise the pre-existent ties uniting the totem-mates. If we start with Durkheim from the primacy of the emblem, it is impossible to explain the numerous totemic systems in which the emblem plays either no part at all, or only an insignificant one. Finally, the distribution of totemism throughout the primitive world is extremely haphazard. Its absence among an important number of decidedly primitive peoples remains unexplained.

Our own objections against Durkheim's views have been exposed at some length in section 4 of this chapter and it would take us too far afield to enter into a discussion of the relative importance to be attached to those of Van Gennep, which are not all of the same weight. Instead, we shall pay attention to the points on which he agrees with Durkheim. The first of these is that totemism is a means of strengthening the cohesion and continuity of the group. However, as he was bent on disagreeing with Durkheim, Van Gennep adds that exogamy, initiation, and mystic fraternities tend to have a similar result, a reservation which Durkheim would not have denied. Neither would he have gainsaid Van Gennep's second point, viz. that clans, castes and cosmological systems are as effective means for classification as totemism.

To Van Gennep the main characteristics of totemism are the relation existing between a group and a natural species, and the localisation of the totem to a limited territory. The latter is an interesting point. It is certainly true that everywhere totemism refers to local conditions. Nevertheless, Van Gennep's conclusion is false. It is not true that totem animals are not regarded as totems outside the territory of the relevant totem clan. The one point which can and which in fact he should have made, is that everywhere totemism and totemic myth refer to local conditions and tend to identify the history of the totem and the totemic ancestor with that of a certain locality. If it had been brought up in a more neutral framework, it would have been an important point. One of Van Gennep's conclusions is undoubtedly true. The totemic myth describes the clan territory as its ancestral home; through the totem the clan is locally bound and, by being bound, firmly instituted in nature and natural conditions.

A more important point made by Van Gennep (and one often overlooked by early writers on totemism) is that the clan is not an independent unit but, as an exogamous group, by definition a part of a more encompassing whole, viz. the tribe. Interesting is his remark that totemism by strengthening the solidarity of the members of the clan, may be a threat to the soli-

142

darity of the tribe. In North Central Australia the Arabunna and Gongaru believe that the ancestor, on his reincarnation in a newly born individual, simultaneously changes his sex, moiety and totem. They are simply trying to balance the centrifugal tendencies embodied in clan totemism. Exogamy has a similar and even more positive function. The crucial precept of clan exogamy is not the prohibition to marry within the clan, but the implied injunction to marry with a member of another clan, thus conjugating one clan with the other. The combination of totemism and exogamy is significant; exogamy counterbalances the trend toward isolationism inherent in clan totemism.

Van Gennep expected that his review of the theories of totemism would lead to a renewed discussion. Actually, his book marked the end of the debate. The critique of Goldenweiser had given irrefutable evidence that the traditional concept of totemism had no roots in reality. On this basis discussion was no longer possible. In the works of later authors totemism is no longer presented as a doctrine or as a set of clearly defined concepts, but as a form of expression of the relations between man and nature. New ethnographic descriptions of high quality contributed substantially to a more cautious approach. Special mention must be made in this context of the observations made by Radcliffe-Brown, Elkin, Firth, and more recently by Lévi-Strauss. To those made by Radcliffe-Brown and Lévi-Strauss we shall have to pay attention in later chapters of this book.

VII

The study of symbols;
the works of Freud, Jung and Cassirer

1. Sigmund Freud (1860-1939) and his school

The subconscious is not a term coined by Freud. Before Freud early students of parapsychology already used the concept as a key for explaining various paranormal phenomena. Freud, however, made a really penetrating study of the subconscious and successfully demonstrated its impact on human thought and behaviour. He presented convincing evidence to show that forgetting is not a process ruled by chance. Human beings forget selectively; what they forget and what they remember, i.e. what is held in readiness to be brought back into consciousness, is determined by motivations which are founded in the individual's private history and predilections. An attractive array of instances of how we forget and remember is presented in Freud's essay "Zur Psychopathologie des Alltagslebens" (1901). There are various ways of forgetting. Some contents of our conscious life simply slip away from memory; others, however, and in particular those which are painful or cumbersome, are actively repressed. This does not mean that they disappear altogether; such contents latently persist below the threshold of consciousness from where they may suddenly return, just like events can be remembered which we fancied were long forgotten. Yet, in one respect memories of repressed contents differ from memories passively 'forgotten'; when repressed contents return to memory, they tend to appear in a distorted form, one which disguises the original content in such a way as to make it acceptable to the 'censor' which condemned it to repression; in its distorted form it is let through and allowed to return to consciousness. The distortion may make the old contents altogether unrecognisable.

It is not only unpleasant events which tend to be repressed. Certain lusts too may be repressed, desires which the individual is craving to satisfy but which he does not wish to give in to or even to think of, because he is afraid or ashamed to follow these desires. When these desires are concerned with vital needs — very often sexual needs — any effort to repress them is ineffective, or more correctly, partly ineffective. A strong feeling of deprivation remains and the individual grasps for substitutes to fill the emotional

144

gap. In the more serious cases the feeling leads to the creation of such symbolic acts as Freud came across among his psychiatric patients in fin-de-siècle Vienna. Many of them were well-to-do neurotics, deeply disturbed by sexual problems of all sorts, whilst outwardly they tried as well as they could to conform to the exigencies of the puritan bourgeois ethics of the time. Freud recognised their dreams and disquieting compulsive actions which they could not shake off, as symbols of their secret desires. A good case, expounded in his "Vorlesungen" (pp.272 ff. of the edition in "Gesammelte Werke" XI, 1940) is the one of the girl, the only child of her parents, who could not sleep unless *inter alia* her pillow was put so far from the erect wooden head of the bed that every contact between the pillow and the head of the bed was excluded. Subsequent analysis brought to light that to the girl the pillow symbolised the mother, the wooden head the father. She wished them to be kept apart, i.e. to prevent their sexual congress in order to remain the only child. Of course various other elements played a part as well, but in the present context they can be ignored. What matters is that the girl had repressed her wish to keep her parents separated from each other and that a symbolic act had taken its place, the meaning of which she did not grasp, but which nevertheless was of so much importance to her that she could not sleep without having meticulously separated pillow and head first. As soon as the analysis had taught her the real meaning of the act the symptom disappeared.

Repressed desires, stigmatised by the censor as inadmissible, take all sorts of disguised forms which during his sleep transgress the threshold of consciousness to disturb the sleeper. Dreams abound with symbols of repressed contents and this is what makes them important to the psycho-analyst. They help him to discover the motives which led to the disturbance of which the patient must be cured. In the puritan urban middle class society of Freud's days, among the images obsessing his patients the symbols of repressed sexual desires prevailed, and consequently Freud emphasised the significance of the sexual need which, much to the surprise of his contemporaries, he diagnosed even in the disposition of the young child. He argued that the individual passes successively through an oral and an anal erotic stage before he arrives at the genital stage of maturity. Those people who are physically fully-grown but sexually retarded, are arrested in an earlier stage of development. The numerous taboos connected with sexual life lead to frustrations of all sorts and these in turn to various forms of anxiety, one of the more important among them being castration anxiety. A telling example is the variety of stories concerning women with a vagina dentata. Freud found a rich treasury of stories and symbols in the works of anthropologists. Primitive myth and religion apparently abounded with cases of symbolic acts and representations strongly resembling the symptoms produced by his patients. It seemed to Freud that anthropology could afford the necessary data for an all-inclusive evolutionist theory explaining his own observations and fitting them into a wider framework of theoretical thought.

Freud condensed his studies in this field in four essays which appeared in 1912 and 1913 in the first two volumes of 'Imago', the psycho-analytical quarterly he had set up. The essays were collected afterwards in his book "Totem und Tabu" to which he gave the significant subtitle "Einige Übereinstimmungen im Seelenleben der Wilden und der Neurotiker". The ethnographic data worked up in the essays he had borrowed from Frazer, Robertson Smith, Tylor, Lang, Reinach, and a number of other authors belonging to the evolutionist school of thought.

In the first essay Freud discusses the 'Inzest-scheu'. The strong aversion to incest occurring everywhere suggests that the aversion is not the product of a natural dislike but the outcome of a repressed desire. The prevailing attitude of extreme touchiness is symptomatic of rules based on repressed desires; and indeed, we find ample evidence that the aversion towards incest is counteracted by a strong desire towards it. During the first stage of a child's life the sexual drive is focussed on the mother. Later the sexual desire may be transferred to another person as its object, a transfer which sometimes has an intermittent stage during which the sister is the desired object. Even if successfully transferred, the incestuous desire never disappears completely. Hence, all sorts of measures must be taken in situations in which there is a risk that things may take a bad turn. A typical case is that of the relationship between son-in-law and mother-in-law. Mother-in-law-avoidance is an extraordinarily widely spread institution and there is a sound reason for it. To the son-in-law the mother-in-law is a mother substitute as well as a substitute for his wife. To the mother-in-law the relationship is hardly less tempting. Identifying herself with her daughter she is capable of strong incestuous desires vis-à-vis her son-in-law. Hence the two must be kept apart by strict taboo regulations.

A decisive step forward is made in the second essay, "Das Tabu und die Ambivalenz der Gefühlsregungen". Psycho-analytic research has revealed that underlying a taboo there is always a forbidden act which is the object of a strong, subconscious desire. Sufferers of compulsive neurosis develop taboos of all sorts. Time and again these seemingly unmotivated, self-imposed prohibitions are found to originate from 'Berührungsangst', primarily fear of auto-erotic fingering, the source of a strictly forbidden satisfaction. To compensate for the loss of the forbidden satisfaction the patient takes to a surrogate in which both the original lust and the prohibition can be recognised. The taboos produced by neurotics are characterised by their ambivalence.

The same ambivalence can be observed in the taboos of primitive people. A king is honoured as well as hated. He is envied by his subjects who make him the object of an intricate ceremonial which bestows great honour on him, but at the same time makes it all but impossible for him to enjoy a

146

human way of life. Similarly, the beloved and honoured dead are also hated beings to whom all sorts of mischief are ascribed. The dead are feared because during their lifetime they were hated and beloved at the same time.

In the third essay "Animismus, Magie und Allmacht der Gedanken", the evolutionist Freud takes precedence. He starts with a description of the 'omnipotence of thought' in psycho-pathological praxis. Neurotic patients sometimes pretend that they only need to think a thing, for example the crashing of a precious vase, and it happens. In the course of a successful treatment the patient occasionally confesses how he lent a hand to chance to keep up the fancy of almighty thought. More important is that this way of thinking is magical. Magicians coerce the course of events. In the magical thinking of neurotics the ego takes precedence. Such patients still live in the puerile stage of narcissism in which the sexual desire selects the ego as its object. Omnipotence of thought is one of its symptoms. Magical thought is, in fact, the oldest form of human thinking. It is older than animism which originates when people become aware of the contradictions implied in magic and set out to project part of their own desires and wilfulness on to the spirits of the dead. Animism, however, does not lead to the abolition of magic. The two occur together and Freud combines the two stages of religious evolution under the caption of the animistic stage, the stage in which man ascribes omnipotence to himself. The next stage is the religious one in which omnipotence is attributed to the gods. The animistic stage coincides with the narcissistic phase of the development of the individual, whereas the religious stage concurs with the phase in which the individual, turning away from the ego and from narcissism, makes the parents the object of his sexual desires. The final stage is the scientific one which has its complement in maturity when the individual, adjusting himself to reality, turns to the outer world as the object of his desires.

The theory is completed in the final essay, "Die Infantile Wiederkehr des Totemismus". The author returns to the study of taboos, specifically the taboos connected with totemism, viz. exogamy and the prohibition to kill or harm the totem. The origin of the two taboos must be found in the primeval horde, from which the sons are expelled at the age of puberty. Because their respect for their father is deep enough, they submit and allow themselves to be thrown out. Yet, as well as admiring and respecting the father, they also hate him. They even refer to him with the name of an animal. Finally, the rebellious sons unite and agree among themselves to kill the father. They are not satisfied with killing him; in an effort to achieve complete identification they even eat him. Disenchantment follows; the complete identification with the father miscarries because, to that end, each of the sons should possess all the father's wives, an obvious impossibility. The killing is a failure and — as always — repentence follows in the wake of failure. The affectionate feelings for the venerated father (which have always been present) now get the upperhand and 'in nachträglicher Gehorsam' the rebellious sons decide to abstain from possessing the father's coveted women. They institute the rule of exogamy. They even go further. The animal whose name they had used to symbolise the hated father is tabooed and from now on venerated and respected as a totem. This is the origin of the two main taboos of totemism. Unfortunately, success is again incomplete. Periodically, the pride of the sons renews itself and their hatred against the father returns, because whatever else changes, the ambivalence of the sons' feelings vis-à-vis their father does not. When that happens the father is killed once again, this time in the shape of the totem animal which is subsequently eaten, an act aimed at renewed identification with the father.

The patricide and subsequent patrophagy of primeval time constitute the original sin of the human race. Every now and then feelings of guilt incite renewed religious activity. Everywhere the god-father has assumed the shape of the human father, and everywhere the Oedipus-situation has involved the son in the never ending conflict with the father whom he hates and admires. Having tried in vain to identify himself with the father by eating him, the son subsequently strives for propitiation by doing penance in repentance. In the Christian religion a complete propitiation is realised because the son (the murderer) pays a perfect penance by allowing himself to be killed. Yet, even this is a failure; through his perfect penance the son becomes identical with the father. He becomes God next to the father and the son-religion takes the place of the father-religion. Building on the suggestion implicit in Robertson Smith's conception of sacrifice as a transformation of the totem-meal, Freud explains the Christian communion as a repetition of the propitiating death of the son, and a renewed repudiation of the father.

Freud was deeply convinced that religion is an illusion. Yet, he was emotionally involved and he did not bother about concealing the feelings of hostility roused in him by religious notions. The attack on Christian belief made in his "Totem und Tabu" was a rude one in the eyes of his contemporaries. Towards the end of his life he launched another attack in his book "Moses and Monotheism" (New York, 1939). Based on historical nonsense, the theory offered might conveniently be shelved as an old man's ramblings. However, the tragic circumstances under which the book was written raises it to the rare level of a *document humain*, the brilliant Jewish atheist in the agony of his expatriation and approaching death maintaining his firm repudiation of religion as an illusion and yet implicitly suggesting that there is a grain of truth in the reproach that the Jewish nation once killed God; they killed the father twice because they also killed Moses.

The theory presented need not be discussed. The main value of "Moses and Monotheism" is its unveiled exposition of the dogmatism which in the course of time had taken possession of Freud and his followers. The theory that ideas are innate and hereditary is openly admitted: "the archaic heri-

148

tage of mankind includes not only dispositions, but also ideational contents, memory traces of the experience of former generations" (Moses, p.157). Once we accept that the Oedipus-complex is genetically transmitted, it becomes possible to explain the long latency period which sometimes separates the first symptoms of a neurosis from the traumatic experience which is recognised as the cause of the process. If hereditary even those cases of neurosis which cannot be ascribed to a traumatic experience, can now be explained by a latent Oedipus-complex. That the supposition that ideational contents are genetically transmitted is in conflict with current scientific opinion, gives Freud no reason to revise his opinion. On the contrary, he is perfectly intransigent; also on other points. A striking case is the following: "I have often been vehemently reproached for not changing my opinions in later editions of my book [Totem and Taboo], since more recent ethnologists have without exception discarded Robertson Smith's theories and have in part replaced them by others which differ extensively. I would reply them that these alleged advances in science are well known to me. Yet I have not been convinced either of their correctness or of Robertson Smith's errors ... Above all, however, I am not an ethnologist, but a psychoanalyst. It was my good right to select from ethnological data what would serve me for my analytic work. The writings of the highly gifted Robertson Smith provided me with valuable points of contact with the psychological material of analysis and suggestions for the use of it. . ." (Moses, pp.207 f.). The argument is, of course, untenable, all the more so because what he borrowed from Robertson Smith were not data but theories.

An old man of 79 should not be blamed for his dogmatism. However, we may blame his followers for it; they were even more dogmatic than the master. An outstanding case is that of *Geza Roheim*, a Hungarian psychoanalyst who did anthropological fieldwork in Australia, resulting in a couple of books which are also of ethnographic interest, viz. "Australian Totemism" (1925) and "The Eternal Ones of the Dream" (1945). Roheim's more intimate acquaintance with ethnographic fact does not result in a more realistic approach in his theoretical work, at least not in his main work, "Animism, Magic, and the Divine King" (1930). We might call it a psycho-analytic version of "The Golden Bough". The motif underlying religious behaviour is castration anxiety, a very fundamental complex which has its ultimate origin in the fission of the cell, the primeval catastrophe to which all life owes its origin. Without even for a moment disclaiming allegiance to Freud's theory of the human horde (Father of the Primal Horde is always reverently printed with the initial letters in honorific capitals), Roheim tries to penetrate deeper into the proto-anthropoic history of *homo sapiens* than the master did. Following Ferenczi, he hypothesises a kind of organism already differentiated into males and females, the males of which have not yet developed a genital apparatus ejaculating spermatozoa into the female organ. In this phase of evolution the sexual act results in the separation of the male genital organ from the body and its incorporation in the female organ. When in a later phase the sperma and no longer the penis is left behind in the female body, the concomitance of the sexual act with castration anxiety remains. This complex which *homo sapiens* inherited from his distant proto-anthropoic forebears, still plays an important part in neurotic disease and in primitive forms of magic and religion. Savages are afraid to cut off their hair or finger-nails. These are penis symbols and contain elements of the soul. For this reason they are privileged tools for making black magic. The fear of magic is essentially castration anxiety. There is more to it than only this. At death the soul is thought to leave the corpse in the guise of a penis symbol such as a snake or a bird. Death too is a case of castration, and a final one. Fortunately, the subconscious succeeds in disguising the unbearable in a more acceptable attire. The human soul, the exponent of immortality, is a concept which originates from the notion of sperma. Thus death is turned into a coitus or a marriage. The bridge to be crossed by the soul on its way to the realm of the dead is a penis, the soul the sperma, and the realm of the dead itself a womb in which the soul meets with its ultimate destiny. The soul enters into heaven just like sperma enters the womb. The king is the phallus par excellence; he is the Lord of the Primal Horde who marries his sister, who is surrounded with numerous wives and concubines, and who must finally be killed by his son. In this vein the author continues for hundreds of pages of oracular language, turning with his magic wand everything he touches into penis symbols and castration complexes. We need not dwell long on Roheim's theories. It is evident that Roheim lost the path of science and exchanged it for that of myth, scientific myth perhaps, but little better than the primitive myths he tried to explain by it. This is what happens when a theory — and a great and daring theory actually — is turned into dogma.

One of the first to come into conflict with the dogmatism of psycho-analysis was *B. Malinowski*. In two articles published in Psyche (1924) he had argued that on the Trobriand Islands, where matrilineal descent is combined with patrilocal (more accurately: viri-avunculocal) marriage, the development of an Oedipus-complex is impossible. The Trobriand father is a good friend and a helper, whereas the mother's brother exerts authority. Accordingly we do not find any tensions in the relationship between father and son, but they are evident in that between mother's brother and sister's son. The mother's brother's role is the same as that of the authoritarian father in a patriarchal society; the sister's son is his heir and successor. Malinowski had also pointed out that he had not come across the slightest indication of incestuous inclinations of sons towards their mothers. On the other hand incestuous leanings towards sisters were evident. In spite of the strict rule of sister-avoidance cases of brother-sister incest were not wholly unknown and the inclination towards sister incest was confirmed by dreams which had been told him.

A retort did not hold off for long. In the International Journal of Psycho-Analysis of 1925, E. Jones argued that Malinowski's lack of interest in the genetic aspect of the Oedipus-complex had led him to misjudge the actual situation. The occurrence of an Oedipus-complex among the Trobriand people is evident, but the role of the primordial father has been distributed between two persons, viz. the kind and helpful father and the moralising and authoritative mother's brother. Similarly the sister must be recognised as a substitute for the mother.

The answer was not of the kind that appeals to a social anthropologist raised in the tradition that cultural facts should as far as possible be explained from cultural conditions. Malinowski replied, not in an article, but in a complete book, "Sex and Repression in savage Society" (1927).

It is evident that he had been angered by the dogmatic attitude of the Freudians. He first directs his wrath against Freud's statement that the primordial patricide had been "the memorable, criminal act with which... began social organisation, moral restriction and religion". Malinowski's rejoinder that thus, by a collective patricide, the ape has attained culture and become man (Sex and Repression p.163), has the merit of being sharp-witted, but essentially it is as loose a statement as the one made by Freud. It is impossible to say anything sensible on the origin of culture without referring to the origin of language. (In parentheses it must be added that very little sensible can be said on the origin of language either and that, consequently, all assertions of this kind are highly speculative).

Even so, it gave Malinowski a good start for a lengthy argument on the differences between culture and instinct. Man is not guided by instinct. Even the instinct of gregariousness is a myth. The simpler the culture the less extensive the need for co-operation between individuals. Food-gatherers, although by no means solitary in their way of life, can do most of their work alone. "Human sociality increases with culture, while if it had been mere gregariousness it should decrease or, at least, remain constant (ibid. p.191).

Human activities must be learned. The human family differs profoundly from its animal counterpart, the family of apes. Among the latter courtship begins with a change in the conditions of the female genital, a change which has a compelling effect on the males in her vicinity. The female will chose one of the males after a fight has taken place between them. The partner who is accepted will stay with the female all along the period of pregnancy and lactation. Every species has its own invariable type of behaviour. Humans are completely different. There is neither a necessity to copulate nor a mating-season. This freedom makes the institution of certain rules of behaviour a necessity, but these rules are neither compulsory nor general. They differ from one group to another, and the one thing they have in common is that sanctions are included to ensure that the rules will be obeyed. The stress exerted by these rules may result in repression of some sort. The relations between father and son are a case in point. A father's role in a non-matrilineal society being always a combination of loving care and austere authority, maladjustments on the side of the son easily ensue.

Malinowski's argument has its weak points. His description of the behaviour of apes is incorrect and belied by fact, at least as far as anthropoid apes are concerned. Nevertheless, his emphasis on the non-instinctive nature of human behaviour is an important contribution. It has a strong foundation in the wide variety of cultural behaviour. Instincts are prefigurated behaviour patterns, which are conspicuously absent among humans. Human behaviour is characterised by a liberal measure of plasticity, and Malinowski, carefully avoiding the pitfall of denying the impact of genetic factors, strongly emphasises the plasticity of innate endowment. Nature and culture merge, and its effect is a considerable variability of behaviour within a framework strongly favouring recurrent attitudes of paternal and maternal care. Malinowski's objection to Freud is that the latter's theory credits human heredity with a greater measure of specificity than is warranted by human behaviour, the forms of which strongly depend upon environmental and social conditions. In between we note the emergence of the contrast of nature and culture which was destined to play such an important role in Lévi-Strauss' thought.

We must, at last, return to Freud and the theory he presented. First and foremost the fact should be recognised that Freud did far more than presenting a theory. He enriched the science of man with a method which disclosed vast and hitherto unexplored realms of the human mind. It is necessary to keep this in mind all the time that we discuss his theory of totemism and taboo, and finally turn to an evaluation of his contribution to the theory of religion.

It is easy to criticise the theoretical framework of Freud's "Totem und Tabu". The legendary primeval horde is, without doubt, its weakest point. It is a concept long rendered obsolete. Equally improbable is the story of the repentant sons. Why should they repent? We might also ask, why should they be angry with their father? They were free to go where they wished and, each of them, free to kidnap a female whenever an opportunity presented itself. When all is said and done, the myth of the 'Father of the Primal Horde' is at best a romantic story of low probability.

The consequences drawn from the events ascribed to the final days of horde-life are equally open to question as is the theory of the primeval horde itself. Why should a simple case of patricide followed by an act of patrophagy result in a modification of the genes pattern, charging subsequent generations with the nuisance of an Oedipus-complex? Once we take the heredity of the complex for granted, we are up against an even

152

more difficult problem. If the Oedipus-complex constitutes part of our biological heritage, we must explain why some people do not show any signs of being possessed by it, and not even some people, but a fair majority. Freud's explanation of aberrant behaviour turns the normal into a problem.

A third objection and again a serious one, is that Freud's theory has a male bias. The women stand aside. They had no part in the acts of patricide and patrophagy. If there was a change in the genes pattern it must have taken place in the males. The same holds true if we should wish to subscribe to the castration theory. It is only males who are involved. Of course, it is possible that a change in the genes pattern of the males accounts for the difference between our forebears and us, but from whatever angle we look at it, it is a weak theory which excludes females and concentrates on males. It certainly suffers from a lack of elegance.

Finally, there is the prominent part admitted to totemism in the early history of mankind, a hypothesis which at the time Freud published his essays on "Totem und Tabu", had already been disproved by Goldenweiser's analysis.

Evidently there is every reason for questioning the necessity of going far back into human history to explain the frequency of the occurrence of a father complex and of the deep impact it has on neurotic phenomena and religious representations. The father complex is characterised by two major components, confidence and admiration on the one hand, hatred combined with fear of punishment on the other. Situations provocative of ambivalent feelings of this kind are extremely numerous in human relations. They may be prevalent in the attitude of the servant versus his master, of the student with respect to his teacher, of one spouse vis-à-vis the other, of the trespasser with regard to the ruling authorities, of the sinner who fears the wrath of his gods. Among all institutionalised human relations the most general and at the same time the most provocative of conflicts of this kind, is that between a father and his son. It is the father's role to help his son and to admonish him, to be kind to him and to punish him, to be a refuge and an exacting authority, and to be all in one. What is more, the ambivalence of this relationship is experienced early in the life of each and every individual. It makes part of his very earliest memories. The ambivalent father-image is the most obvious and most natural symbol for the never ending series of ambivalent situations and feelings every human being has to pass through in the course of his life.

Is this all we have to say on Freud and his work? Most certainly not. Discarding his explanations does not imply that we fail to recognise the importance of his discoveries and his methods for penetrating deeper into the underlying motives of human thought and action. Freud's contribution to the knowledge of man cannot easily be over-estimated. He opened our eyes to the ambivalence of human aspirations and evaluations, to the distortion in the subconscious of the memories of our repressed experiences and wishes, to the significance of symbols and to the similarities between the symbols of dream and neurosis and those of magic and religion. What counts is the facts he discovered, the depths of the human mind he disclosed. The refutation of his theories should be combined with a recognition of their value as an instrument which helped him to pursue his discoveries by offering a first and preliminary framework for ordering his facts as well as his thoughts. And facts will stand forever.

2. C. G. Jung (1875-1961)

Jung, a psychiatrist at Zürich, was a younger contemporary of Freud. Initially closely collaborating with Freud, Jung later dissociated himself from him, *inter alia* in regard to Freud's rather extreme emphasis on the sexual. Jung's preoccupation with anthropological data coincides with Freud's studies in this field. His "Wandlungen und Symbole der Libido" appeared in 1912, later to be re-edited under the title of "Symbole der Wandlung" (quotations in the present text from the 4th ed. of 1952). Unfortunately, Jung is often obscure in his writings. Recommended introductions to his writings are his book "Die Beziehungen zwischen dem Ich und dem Unbewussten" (1928) and the one written by Dr. Jolande Jacobi, "Die Psychologie von C. G. Jung" (1939). The present author feels obliged to make the proviso that his presentation of Jung's theories is necessarily nothing more than his own, fallible interpretation.

In the human psyche Jung discerns three layers: the conscious, the personal unconscious (which in part can be identified with the subconscious), and the collective unconscious. The personal unconscious includes first of all everything the individual can immediately make available in the form of memories, and secondly everything which, either wholly or partly forgotten, slumbers in the depths of the subconscious together with such ideational contents as have been actively repressed and distorted. On the point of repression and its effects there is no difference between Freud and Jung. The lowest layer is the collective unconscious, a confusing term because it has very little to do with what we usually call collectivity. It comprises all the hereditary dispositions and talents of the individual together with the hereditary traces of the experiences of the species which the latter acquired in the course of its evolution. Jung denies that these traces can be equated with ideational contents. They refer to "eine angeborene Disposition zu parallellen Vorstellungsbildern, bezw. universelle identische Strukturen der Psyche" (Symbole der Wandlung p.260). These structures of the unconscious he calls archetypes, and he compares them, not to ideational contents, but to the biological concept of behaviour patterns. What he means are instinctive reaction patterns, and these patterns must be strictly differentiated from the archetypal images which are called forth by these patterns when the latter are stimulated into action by the total situation of the psyche.

154

The stimulated patterns act upon the personal unconscious, provoking the propagation of such archetypal images as those which emerge into the conscious through dreams and visions. There is a close interaction between the conscious and the unconscious. When in his conscious life the individual becomes entangled in an inner conflict which is not solved but repressed, a reaction of the unconscious follows. The same happens when a person violates his own natural disposition by continuous, lop-sided activity, e.g. by incessant engagement in intellectual activity. The unconscious reacts and the emergence of archetypal images is a warning that something is going wrong.

The cause of a psychical disturbance need not necessarily be a frustration of the sexual impulse. The term 'libido' which in this context is relevant, has in Jung's writings a more encompassing content than in those of Freud from whom Jung borrowed the term. To Jung the libido is the total mental energy of the individual, energy "welcher sich irgend einem Gebiete, der Macht, dem Hunger, dem Hass, der Sexualität, der Religion u.s.w. mitteilen kann, ohne dass es je ein spezifischer Trieb wäre" (ibid. pp.225 f.). The libido arouses the reactions of the unconscious which, as the custodian of the condensed experience of the human race, calls forth the symbols which urge the individual to come to order. The individual experiences the activity of these symbols as the action of powers from outside the self and superior to it, and in this respect the individual is not mistaken. These symbols have normative value; they symbolise a reality which transcends the individual because they emanate from the unconscious, the guardian of the traces of the total genetic prehistory of his race.

The unconscious is stratified; the traces of more recent experiences lie on top. They arouse the archetypal images of a more recent age, the symbols of the father and the mother. The older and deeper layers are less easily stimulated and the symbols emanating from their reactions are of a vaguer nature than those which are the product of the higher and younger levels. Often the images of the dream refer to a far, bygone past. Freud's conclusion that, consequently, the thinking of the dream must be equated with infantile thinking, is rejected. The images of the past appearing in dreams are images and symbols once produced by mature individuals, even though these were individuals still equipped with gills (ibid. p.37). The collective unconscious bears the traces of man's proto-anthropoic past.

However, the anthropoic past too left its traces in the collective unconscious. "Auf einer frühern und tiefern Stufe seelischer Entwicklung, wo es noch unmöglich ist, einen Unterschied zwischen semitischer, hamitischer und mongolischer Mentalität aufzufinden, haben alle Menschenrassen eine gemeinsame Kollektivpsyche. Aber mit dem Einsetzen von Rassendifferenzierung entstehen auch wesentliche Unterschiede in der Kollektivpsyche [the collective unconscious]. Aus diesem Grunde können wir den Geist fremder Rassen nicht in globo in unsere Mentalität übersetzen, ohne letztere empfindlich zu schädigen" (Beziehungen p.54, footnote 1). We must conclude then, that Jung assumes a structural difference between our mind and that of primitive man. The latter, he notes, lives more than we do in a state of "Unbewusztheit und daher der Ununterschiedlichkeit, von Lévy-Bruhl als 'participation mystique' bezeichnet". In other words, primitive people are really primitives. In Jung's thinking the development of the human psyche proceeds from a state of low consciousness to one of increasingly higher consciousness. Evidently, he places the so-called primitives in a lower phase of evolution than modern man. The structural differences hypothesised as characteristic of the collective unconscious of the one and the other respectively, confirm that this indeed is his opinion.

The conclusion is a serious one with important consequences, far more important than is realised by most of Jung's admirers and followers. Whoever assumes that there is a structural difference between the brain of primitive people and that of modern man of the kind and magnitude as suggested by Jung, has to give up the expectation that primitive people are capable of progressive cultural development up to a level comparable to that of Western civilisation. It is a conclusion which is politically unacceptable and, fortunately, belied by fact. Jung's argument is the immediate consequence of his hypothesis that dreams and the way of thinking peculiar to dreams, reveal regressive states of mind, characteristic of earlier phases of evolution. Once he set out to borrow data from exotic and primitive religions to elucidate the archetypal symbols of dreams, visions and neurosis, the inevitable conclusion was that in these religions we are dealing with phenomena belonging to an earlier phase of evolution; from the very beginning a built-in conclusion.

The similarities between the products of primitive religious thought on the one hand and the symbols of dreams and those produced by neurotics and sufferers of schizophrenia on the other, are interesting as well as disquieting problems. Jung contributed substantially to our knowledge of these similarities. We cannot fully discuss the problem here, but one observation must be made, viz. that these similarities can also be advanced as an argument confirming the essential conformity of the mind of primitive man and that of his modern contemporaries. If we discard the assumption that dreams and the products of psychopathic thought are symptoms of a regressive state of mental evolution, we regain the freedom to start with a new approach.

At one place at least Jung himself presents us with an important clue to a more satisfactory solution of the problem. One of the most intricate difficulties obstructing the explanation of specific symbols is their polyvalence. The snake, for instance, is found to symbolise alternately a penis, eternal life, evil, threatening death and human passion. The polyvalence of symbols did not escape Jung's attention and he pointed out that symbols do not refer to any clearly defined matter, but are ambivalent expressions which may have more than one meaning at a time. "They refer to matters hard to define, i.e., to matters which are only partly known" (Symbole der Wandlung p.205). Their meaning can only be defined on the basis of an extensive knowledge of the patient's inner life, i.e. after laboriously collecting and analysing his dreams. We note that what is true of the patient and his dreams, is also true of myth and symbol in primitive culture. Their meaning can only be fathomed after a comprehensive, analytic study of the relevant culture as a whole. This, however, is what Jung never did and what psychologists generally are negligent of, much to the detriment of their interpretations.

3. Man the symboliser

The symbols analysed by psycho-analysts are symbols of a special kind, all belonging to a few well defined categories out of a great variety of different sorts of symbols. Man expresses himself in symbols. For a proper understanding of the meaning of any specific kind of symbols it is imperative to consider its nature and distinctive traits within the framework of an overall review of symbols generally. To that end we turn to the work of *Ernst Cassirer* (1874-1945), the neo-Kantian philosopher who pointed out that man always expresses himself in symbols, and that language, science, art and myth have their own systems of symbols. He expounded these views in the three volumes of his "Philosophie der symbolischen Formen". The first volume, "Die Sprache", appeared in 1923; the second "Das mytische Denken" in 1925, and the third, "Phänomenologie der Erkenntniss", in 1929[14]. Many years later (in 1944) he gave a short introduction to his philosophy in "An Essay on Man".

The philosophy of symbolic forms is, in essence, a study of the cultural process of the growth and development of human knowledge. Its basic problem is one of epistemology, that of the intrinsic truth in knowledge, and of the progress of the refinement and extent of knowledge throughout the course of the development of culture. Knowledge is not the result of pure sensory impressions on the human mind, but emanates from the combination of sensory impressions with concepts produced by the mind. In Cassirer's philosophy knowledge is a creative act of the mind, and the same is the case with art and language. They have in common that in all of them the mind expresses itself in symbols, a category of signs which should be clearly differentiated from signals. Signals are operative within a given context. Detached from the context a signal is meaningless. A green light alongside a road means that the way is clear for the approaching car-driver. Placed in the centre of a cornfield it is senseless. The referee's blow on his

[14] An English translation has been edited by Yale Univ. Press (1953), reprinted in 1957. The first volume has a very enlightening introduction, written by Ch. W. Hendel.

157

whistle is a signal to the footballers to stop their play. It is pointless without players. Symbols are different. The system of symbols called language enables a speaker to discuss the referee's blow on his whistle some two or three days afterwards at a hundred miles' distance from the football-ground. Signals belong to a context, symbols refer to it. This holds true of all symbols, those of dream and neurosis as well as those of language. They all refer to something and that something need not be present or obvious. It may be something far off or long ago as well as nearby or present; it may also be something carefully hidden and kept secret as in the case of the symbols of neurosis.

A symbol may be anything. It may be an act like that of the neurotic girl who separated her pillow from the wooden head of her bed (above, p.145). A painter makes use of pictorial symbols to convey how he saw his object. The composer in a piece of music expresses his mood by means of musical symbols. A word is a symbol, and the combination of word-symbols in a sentence may refer to anything imaginable. The faculties of language to refer, are practically unlimited. Everything can be the object of the symbolising activity called language. Language enables man to refer to all and everything. It is man's most important and fundamental talent.

Cassirer illustrates his point with a well-chosen and really illuminating case, the story of Helen Keller (Essay on Man, pp.53 ff.). She was a blind and deaf-mute little girl of about six when her teacher taught her a few 'words' by spelling them out in the palm of her hand. This went on for some time when one morning, shortly after she had learned the sign for water, Helen and her teacher were in the pumphouse where the teacher pumped fresh water out over her hands. Helen asked the sign for water by touching the hand of the teacher. When it was spelled in her hand, she seemed startled. "She dropped the mug and stood as one transfixed. A new light came into her face. She spelled 'water' several times. Then she dropped on the ground and asked for its name and pointed to the pump and the trellis and suddenly turning round she asked for my name. . . .. All the way back to the house she was highly excited, and learned the name of every object she touched, so that in a few hours she had added thirty new words to her vocabulary". From this day onwards her behaviour changed significantly. She made a steady progress. She learned to speak, and afterwards she even went to the university where she successfully pursued her studies. The story is well-known and we shall not dwell on its dramatic aspects. The really significant point is her sudden discovery that everything has a name and that a name is of universal applicability (ibid. p.54). The mastering of language opened to her closed mind, impenetrable by sight or sound, a new and significant world. From this moment she was able to lead a really meaningful life.

A special kind of language is that of mathematics and of the natural sciences generally. It is characteristic of Cassirer's early training and outlook that in volume I of his Symbolic Forms he first of all turns to these specific symbols, beginning with an elaborate exposition of the theory of signs and the function of mathematical symbols as developed by Heinrich Hertz. The physicist, studying the necessary connections in natural phenomena, must turn away from the world of sensory impressions. He operates with "concepts of space and time, of mass and force, of material point and energy, of the atom or the ether [which are] free 'fictions'. Cognition devises them in order to dominate the world of sensory experience and survey it as a world ordered by law, but nothing in the sensory data themselves immediately corresponds to them, yet although there is no such correspondence — and perhaps precisely 'because' there is none — the conceptual world of physics is entirely self-contained. Each particular concept, each special fiction and sign is like the articulated 'word' of a 'language' meaningful in itself and ordered according to fixed rules" (Symbolic Forms I p. 85). The development of natural science goes hand in hand with an increasing refinement of its system of signs, signs which ought to be called symbols. The development of this system of symbols reflects the growth and development of culture. The philosophy of symbolic forms is primarily a philosophy of culture, of its growth and of its development.

At this point we must take leave from Cassirer's argument (we shall return to it later) in order to follow up a lead suggested to us by his work, and concerned with the classification of symbols into categories. Cassirer divides them according to subject matter into symbols of science, language, art, and religion. We prefer another approach, one suggested by his differentiation between mathematical and linguistic symbols. An important difference between the two ensues from the fact that mathematical symbols (and the same is true of the symbols used in physics, mechanics and chemistry) are lucid, precise and always unequivocal. They are well-defined, excluding the possibility of misunderstanding. Finally, they are also international and 'translingual', unaffected by the influence of any particular language. If we compare these symbols to other forms of symbolic expression it is possible to arrange them in a scale of diminishing degrees of licidity and precision.

High up in the scale are the mathematical symbols whereas those of language are somewhere in the middle. Words often have a broad range of connotations. A language has homonyms and synonyms among its word symbols. Language may be clear and lucid but can also be vague or confusing. Linguistic symbols can be anything; they are not necessarily unequivocal like mathematical symbols. Language can be used in a way which keeps us guessing.

At the bottom of the scale we find the symbols of dream, myth and neurosis. They stand for something, but we do not know exactly for what. Jung was certainly right when he stated that these symbols "refer to matters hard to define, i.e. to matters which are only partly known" (above, p.157). Often they bear the clear traces of a conflict between opposing motivations, or of the effort to avoid an inner conflict by repressing the memory of disturbing thoughts or events. Others again are expressive of the perturbing effect of stirring experiences which the individual fails to express in adequate terms because he is incapable of sizing up their quintessence. It may also be that the individual is physically incapable of controlling the course of his thoughts, as happens when he is dreaming. On waking up, his efforts to give verbal shape to his dreaming experience result in an inevitably vague and contradictory account of events rapidly effacing themselves in a complete void.

Our effort to classify symbols according to their lucidity is based on the assumption that man is a being who expresses himself, an assumption derived from Cassirer's philosophy of language. In language "content and expression become what they are only in their interpenetration; the signification they acquire through their relation to one another is not outwardly added to their being; it is this signification which constitutes their being. Here we have to do not with a mediated product but with that fundamental synthesis from which language as a whole arises and by which all its parts... are held together. And not only the... language of words, but even the 'mimetic' expression of an inner process shows... that the process does not in itself form a finished, closed-off sphere, out of which consciousness emerges only accidentally, as it were for the purpose of conventional communication to others, but that this seeming externalisation is an essential factor in its own formation. In this sense the modern psychology of language was right in assigning the problems of language to the general psychology of expressive movements" (Symbolic Forms I pp.178 f.).

Unfortunately, Cassirer did not consequently follow this line of his thinking in his philosophy of mythical thought. Here he allowed himself to be led astray by evolutionist theories on myth and magic which belittle primitive man's capacity of reason. He finally arrived at the conclusion that the tendency to confuse the names of things with the things themselves, leads primitive man to the erroneous concepts of magic. Although later, in his Essay on Man, other notions about magic and myth are added, the influence of evolutionist speculation on his reflections on myth and magic is too important to permit us to accept Cassirer as a guide through the labyrinth of primitive thought. The assertion that myth is a symbolic expression "of a fundamental and indelible 'solidarity of life' that bridges over the multiplicity and variety of simple forms" (Essay on Man p.109) is, without doubt, a meaningful and helpful comment on the essential features of myth; but it lacks the support of a general theory which avoids the fallacy of ascribing fundamental errors to the reason of primitive man. If what Cassirer says about language as a means of expression is true, it must be applicable also to the products of mythical and magical thinking. In other words, myth and magic must be the expressions of a state of mind in which vague and

160

perhaps contrary notions compete. We should discover these notions and try to find out what the experiences are on which they are based. In a later chapter we will make an effort to that end; for the present we must return to the assumption that man is a being expressing himself.

The assumption seems self-evident; self-expression is a characteristic not only of human beings but of animals as well. It is a simple truth known to everybody who ever had a dog. Yet, it is not as self-evident as all that, although there is much to confirm it. The fact that human beings are able to hide their feelings cannot be forwarded as an argument to deny that self-expression is a must; whilst dissimulating man still expresses himself, trying to pose as the one he wishes to seem. Moreover, simulation is difficult; practically no one fully succeeds in covering up his inner person. There are always others who see through the mask of the simulant. In one way or another he betrays himself. He expresses his efforts at concealment through his uneasiness or evasiveness. Lying is also technically difficult. The present author acquired some experience of its technique during the years spent as a prisoner in a Japanese camp. If caught in a forbidden activity (as were most of the activities useful or attractive to prisoners) it was never difficult to fabricate a story; the trouble was to remember its details exactly when re-examined, and to stick to them without venturing to amend or correct the improbabilities of the first rendering of the invented story. All this goes to confirm that expression is natural to man. We might even call it an innate need[15], common to all mankind. And this is exactly where the problem arises; 'homo exprimens' is singularly curtailed.

If it is true that expression is an inner necessity we may expect its satisfaction to be as easily within reach as the satisfaction of the need for bodily exercise. Actually, it is not. The adequate expression of the self is subject to serious limitations. It is never complete and often even defective. Individual differences in power of expression are great and variegated. Some people express themselves more easily and better than others. We all know scholars, respected as clear and capable thinkers by their fellows, who fail when they must put their ideas in writing. Others again fail when they must deliver a speech or make a simple toast. In art the limitations are even more striking. Some people are incapable of composing even a simple poem. More stringent still are the limitations set to pictorial and musical expression. In part the limitations are technical and can be overcome by training. For another part, however, they are of a psychological or even existential nature. No one really wishes to express himself completely. The mere possibility of complete self-expression is, in fact, a horrifying idea. Complete self-expression means complete self-revelation, the loss of being a self, of

[15] The word 'need' as used here and in the following pages refers to an existential, inner necessity, not to what also could be termed a 'want'.

161

having anything of one's own. It implies a nakedness far beyond that of the nudist. It is the nakedness which is really shameful. At the bottom of one's heart there is a deep need for concealment counteracting the need for expression; the self must be protected.

Artists have more powerful means of expression than ordinary people and a quotation from a novel may help to give shape to the effect of the competition between expression and concealment in human behaviour. "And no one ever really knows anyone else. There is always a part which remains secret and hidden, concealed in the deepest part of the soul. No husband ever knows his wife... and no wife ever really knows her husband. There is always something just beyond that remains aloof and untouched, mysterious and undiscernable because we ourselves do not know just what it is. Sometimes it is shameful, sometimes it is too fine, too precious ever to reveal. It is quite beyond revelation even if we chose to reveal it" (from Louis Bromfield, The green Bay-tree, pp.143 f. of the pocket ed.).

Expression is never complete or perfect; there is always something just beyond. The necessity to express is counteracted by the necessity to conceal, and the result is that expression is always imperfect and inadequate. In other words, expression is not simply a human need, it is also a difficult task, a problem which must be solved anew each time. This is an important point; it implies that successful cases of more or less adequate expression necessarily acquire the value of models. *Homo exprimens*, hampered in his efforts to express himself, is out for models which he borrows as a means of giving shape to his experience in appropriate symbolic form. The need for models for expression is an experience common to everybody. It is most pressingly felt by people trying to speak or write in an other language than their mother-tongue, but even those using their own vernacular frequently find themselves groping for a word or a better expression to convey their thoughts, i.e. to convey them in such a way as to meet their need to express themselves without detracting from the competing need to conceal certain things. Models are mediators, means for expression within the limits set by the need for concealment. Therefore they are the proper vehicles for inter-human communication which, without them, would be impossible. Actually, the severe restrictions vexing the power of expression have a definite function in the socialisation of symbols. If the individual were capable of boundless, genuine expression, a system of fixed, interpersonally applied symbols as that of language, would be impossible.

The difficulties incumbent on expression fully justify our efforts to arrange various categories of symbols in a scale of higher and lower lucidity. We realise that our scale is crude and incomplete. Pictorial and musical symbols have been left out, although in theoretical treatises on painting and music, lucidity is a term of fairly wide application. We also refrained from trying to make more subtle distinctions than just three different grades of

162

lucidity. For our present purpose they suffice. We note that the highest degree of lucidity is attached to the symbols used in scientific occupations which are devoid of human interest, the lowest to those connected with strong emotions and contradictory psychological conditions. Another point of interest is that lucidity seems to be inversely proportional to genuineness. The symbols of mathematics are the result of age-long international co-operation and conscious agreement; their use is subject to strict rules which are mandatory. Language too is the result of social interaction, but the linguistic rules incumbent on the speaker or writer leave him a great freedom of choice of words and forms; he can have his own style and develop a highly personal way of expressing himself through language symbols. Finally, far more genuine are the symbols produced by dreamers and neurotics. They give the impression of being strictly original reflections of highly personal experiences. Yet, much of that originality can be explained from the fact that they are expressions of a state of mind deviating from the normative patterns of cultural behaviour. In so far as these experiences are given linguistic expression, all the rules of language are incumbent on the person concerned. He has greater freedom in his choice of symbolic acts or ways of pictorial expression, but we may be sure that even the neurotic and the dreamer are, in some way or another, hampered in their freedom of expression. The neurotic phenomena and those dreams which are of interest to the psycho-analyst are the outcome of contradictory or, as the case may be, chaotic states of mind, in which competing motives severely restrict the possibility of expressing any of them adequately. The neurotic is necessarily as much in need of models for the expression of his experiences as the sane. Perhaps some similar restriction limits the freedom of the dreamer but it is contradictory to say that he is in need of anything. The one point which can be made is that current models may have played a role in his dream.

In conclusion we may state that the genuineness of the expression given to their experiences by dreamers and neurotics is not really confirmed. We can only confirm that the experiences on which these expressions are based deviate from the prevailing cultural pattern, and that for this reason the relevant expressions deviate accordingly. In so far as deviation is a symptom of genuineness they may be called genuine, but it would be erroneous to ascribe to these expressions perfect spontaneity. Any impulse towards spontaneity is always held in check by an impulse towards concealment. The recurrent appearance of a restricted number of apparently favoured symbols such as father, snake, and bird, give substance to the assumption that there is as urgent a want of models for the expression of experiences of a confused and emotional nature, as there is for that of experiences of a more neutral character. The problem is whether these preferences are the result of social or genetic causes. The father-symbol is a rather clear case of a symbol of social origin. The father-son relationship is the most widespread case of a relationship in which loving care and harsh authority, admiration and hatred compete with each other. We do not need to call on the mythology of the Oedipus-complex to explain its universality. It is different with the snake symbol. Snakes are rare in Western Europe, and yet most people are extremely afraid of them. Why does an infant of less than two years old, educated by a pair of considerate parents, shriek for fright when for the first time in her life she sees an earthworm emerge from the soil? Explanations range from archetypal images produced by the collective unconscious to purely natural reactions to an uncommon event. We need not decide between them, but it cannot be denied that some images are more generally impressive than others. A disposition favouring the preferential use of certain images as symbols appears to be fairly general and it would speak of dogmatism if we tried to explain these preferences from social causes exclusively. After all, social life too has its roots in the innate dispositions of the individual.

The really important point is that man is hampered in his freedom of expression and therefore largely dependent upon the availability of models. The limitations set to man's inventiveness are apparent from the restricted variability of the symbolism dominating in dreams, neurosis and even mythology. Although a serious effort to make an inventory would undoubtedly reveal a far greater richness of symbolic means than is commonly accepted, this richness is not unlimited. A striking fact is the preference for certain themes. As far as neurosis and myth are concerned this relative paucity cannot surprise us. They are concerned with states of mind in which vague and competing motives are at war. Here the difficulties of adequate expression are greater than in any other case. The frequent borrowing of mythical themes and the multifarious use made of a single plot are, in fact, nothing strange. They are welcome models to give shape to contents of the mind which are highly refractory to adequate expression.

164

VIII

Religion
in anthropological theory after 1920

Until the end of the second decade of the present century religion was a subject of focal interest to anthropologists. They belonged to a generation taught to respect the traditional forms of religion, and many of them felt personally committed to the scientific problems presented by the rapidly increasing knowledge of foreign and more especially of primitive religions. The anthropologists of subsequent generations are less vitally concerned about religion. They are more keenly interested in the social aspects of culture and they have acquired a new field of intriguing studies in the problems of culture change and development. The weal and woe of a society as a going concern is the main focus of their studies. The growing awareness of the valuable contributions anthropologists can make in the fields of native administration and social and economic development concurs with an aversion to the strongly speculative nature of the theories of origin designed by a succession of evolutionist theorists, and, simultaneously, with a continued decline of the impact of religious belief on western civilisation itself.

Under these circumstances anthropologists more and more turn away from the problems of the historical and psychological origin of religion to concentrate on the possible contributions of religion to social life and human welfare. The main interest is that of the description of religion in its cultural (including its social) context. The religious phenomena are included among the values and ideas which, in their entirety, constitute the cultural matrix of a society. The effect of religious belief on social life gains in importance, whereas the study of its origin and foundations in the human condition tends to be neglected. Even the historicists of a later period pay more attention to the descriptive aspects of religious phenomena than to the ultimate problems of their presumed history. While our knowledge of religious facts increases rapidly, the study of the fundamental problem, the belief in a reality which cannot be verified empirically, is on the wane. In the present chapter we discuss successively the functionalist approach, the studies of the German historical schools, the turn given to the ideas of the phenomenological school by M. Eliade, and the contributions made by the American students of cultural personality to the solution of the problem of the relations between the individual and his society. The next chapter is devoted to the structuralist approach of religious studies.

1. Functionalism

The term functionalism is associated primarily with the names of two prominent British anthropologists, viz. *Bronislaw K. Malinowski* (1884-1942) and *A. R. Radcliffe-Brown* (1881-1955). Each of them had his own ideas on the content of the notion of function which had been introduced into anthropological thinking by Durkheim. Of the two, Radcliffe-Brown was closer to the teachings of the French sociologist than Malinowski whose preference for the psychological argument does not fit in very well with the 'Règles de la Méthode sociologique'. Radcliffe-Brown defines the function of any recurrent activity as the part which it plays in the social life as a whole, and concentrates on its contribution to the maintenance of the structural continuity of the whole (Structure and Function p.180), whereas Malinowski's concept of function vacillates between "the part played by any factor of a culture within the general scheme" (Introduction to Hogbin, Law and Order in Polynesia p.XVII) and the ability of any cultural institution to serve the vital needs of the community and its members (cf. A scientific Theory of Culture, 1944). Usually these vital needs are more emphasised by him than the relations of the relevant institution with the other constituent parts of the cultural whole. The utilitarian aspect often ranks prior to that of structural cohesion. Because Malinowski is the more prolific writer of the two, certainly with regard to religious subjects, the discussion of his contributions should precede those of Radcliffe-Brown. The more important among the former's studies in religion are the two-volume monograph "Coral Gardens and their Magic" (1935; a description of Trobriand agriculture and agricultural rites) and the collection of essays "Magic, Science and Religion" edited by Redfield (1948).

The essay "Magic, Science and Religion" from which the collection edited by Redfield took its name, dates back to 1925. Much of the argument the author derives from his fieldwork in the Trobriand Islands. The islanders are perfect agriculturalists and expert builders of canoes, well aware if a work is well executed or bungled by a technical error. Nevertheless, magic is extensively applied. In spite of thirty years of missionary influence and European administration, and notwithstanding a century of recurrent contacts with white traders, not a single garden has ever been laid out without concomitant execution of the incumbent rites (Magic, p.28). The ritual does not detract in the least from the performers' dedication to technical perfection. "Experience has taught [the native]... that in spite of all his forethought and beyond all his effort there are agencies and forces which one year bestow unwanted and unearned benefit of fertility, making everything run smooth and well, rain and sun appear at the right moment,

166

noxious insects remain in abeyance, the harvest yield a super-abundant crop; and another year the same agencies bring ill luck and bad chance, pursue him from beginning till end and thwart all his most strenuous efforts and his bestfounded knowledge. To control these influences and these only he employs magic" (Magic pp.28 f.). In "Coral Gardens and their Magic" (I pp.75,76) he points out that the technical and the magical aspects are well discerned. "The two ways , the way of magic and the way of garden work, *megawa la heda* and *begula la heda*, are inseparable. They are never confused, nor is one of them ever allowed to supersede the other. The natives will never try to clean the soil by magic, to erect a fence or yam support by a rite. . .". Yet, in spite of their technical knowledge, magic is indispensable: "magic aims at forestalling unaccountable mishaps and procuring undeserved good luck" (ibid. p.77).

Malinowski's description of the magical procedure in the Trobriands is of wide application and the main points related here can be confidently generalised. They constitute a substantial contribution to our knowledge of the magical ritual. In his further comment Malinowski avoids stressing the contrast between magic and religion without giving up the difference between them. They both belong to the realm of the sacred, a category which he does not trouble to define but which in his train of thought is best identified with the supernatural. Magic is a specific act for concrete and definite ends, whereas religion is of a vaguer and more abstract nature, "a body of self-contained acts being themselves the fulfilment of their purpose" (Magic p.88). The definition is anything but satisfactory and in vain the author tries to give his definition of religion a more definite content. He refers to the fact that religion has no such simple technique as magic, that it is more complex and refers to a whole supernatural world of faith. Its ultimate function is found in the value of belief and ritual for human well-being (ibid.). The exposition remains vague and elusive. Even the appeal made by the author to native testimony to give substance to his differentiation between magic and religion, does not suffice to confirm the suggestion that magic and religion are essentially distinct. "The native can always state the end of the magical rite, but he will say of a religious ceremony that it is done because such is the usage, or because it has been ordained, or he will narrate an explanatory myth" (ibid. p.38). The statement only proves that some rites have a concrete end whereas others have not; it does not say that the natives themselves see those directed toward a concrete end as pertaining to a category distinct from the others.

The function of religious ritual is discussed in the section devoted to "the creative acts of religion". Initiation ceremonies are presented as "a ritual and dramatic expression of the supreme power and value of tradition in primitive societies; they also serve to impress this power and value upon the minds of each generation, and they are at the same time an extremely efficient means of transmitting tribal lore, of insuring continuity in tradition and of maintaining tribal cohesion" (ibid p.40). It is all well said, except that it is pure rhetoric, one of those passages Leach must have had in mind when he wrote: "Malinowski on Culture in general is often a platitudinous bore" (in Firth, Man and Culture p.119). The problem is not how the value of tradition and tribal lore are demonstrated and transmitted, but how people could ever believe these to be true and effective. It is a problem which the author ignores, just as he passes over the curious fact that the core of every initiation is the revelation of a secret which is sacred truth to the faithful, but altogether too often an inscrutable puzzle to the observer. Although Malinowski does not say so with so many words, he suggests that to the natives the blissful effect of the rite on their minds is sufficient proof of its truth. The influence of William James' pragmatism, brought out by Leach in his study 'The epistemological background to Malinowski's empirism' (Firth, op. cit. pp.121 ff.), is as evident here as it is in the theory of totemism, presented under the caption "Man's selective Interest in Nature" in this same essay "Magic, Science and Religion" (pp. 44 ff.).

He argues that some species of animals (and plants) inspire the native with more genuine interest than others, for example because they constitute important foods or because they are more dangerous than others, and so on. The wish to control these species induces the belief that some people have a special power over them. This belief in turn leads to certain activities, "the most obvious being a prohibition to kill and to eat; on the other hand it endows man with the supernatural faculty of contributing ritually to the abundance of the species" (ibid. p.46).

More satisfactory is the discussion of mortuary rites. He stresses the ambiguity of the emotions evoked by death. Fear and anxiety concur with genuine love and compassion. Unfortunately, when elaborating on the theme rhetoric again takes the upper hand: "the savage is intensely afraid of death... He does not want to realize it as an end, he cannot face the idea of complete cessation, of annihilation. The idea of spirit and of spiritual existence is near at hand, furnished by such experiences as are discovered and described by Tylor. Grasping at it, man reaches the comforting belief in spiritual continuity and in the life after death" (ibid. pp.50 f.). The comment rapidly proceeds to a solemn chorale: "Religion saves man from a surrender to death and destruction, and in doing this it merely makes use of the observations of dreams, shadows and visions" (ibid. p.51). The unescapable conclusion that it is all wishful thinking is drowned in a symphony of panegyrics singing the praise of the functions of ritual and belief. Initiation rites sacralise tradition, the agricultural rites "bring man into communion with providence, with the beneficent forces of plenty", totemism "standardizes man's practical, useful attitude of selective interest towards his surroundings" (ibid. p.52) and in the mortuary rites "religion counteracts the centrifugal forces of fear, dismay, demoralization and provides the most powerful means of reintegration of the group's shaken solidarity and of the re-establishment of its morale" (ibid. p.53). The reader might feel inclined to stop for a hymn.

Equally shallow is Malinowski's 'explanation' of magic which can be characterised as an improvisation on a theme by Marett. To the mind of the actor, inspired by passion and emotion, the imitative act subjectively acquires the value of the real action "to which emotion would, if not impeded, naturally have led" (ibid. p.80). "Obsessed by the idea of the desired end, he sees it and feels it. His organism reproduces the acts suggested by the anticipation of hope, dictated by the emotion so strongly felt" (ibid. p.79). And a few pages later on: "a strong emotional experience... leaves a very deep conviction of its reality, as if of some practical and positive achievement; as if of something done by a power revealed to man" (ibid. p.81).

The merits of the essay are not in the eloquence of its author but in the description of the facts observed. Especially in the field of magic Malinowski's observations are really valuable. In "Coral Gardens and their Magic" he gave an elaborate description of the agricultural rites of the Trobriand Islanders which highlighted the fundamental importance of the magical formula for the act as a whole. Again, Malinowski's effort to explain the effect of the magical rite is the weakest part of the work. He very properly started from his observation that the magical formula is extremely important. It inspired him in the second volume of the work to 'An ethnographic Theory of Language'. Here he argues that words are not merely means of communication, but parts of an activity and themselves equivalent to action. Whoever wishes to understand the function of words should observe people co-operating in the execution of a common task, such as building a house. Here words are not used to transmit ideas but to co-ordinate the various activities and to ensure that the various acts and movements are carried into effect at the right moment. Words are "a verbal act by which a specific force is set loose", a thesis which he tries to give more substance by referring to the effect of such signs as an S.O.S., or of the stammered words of an infant. We are told that "human beings will bank everything, risk their lives and substance, undertake a war or embark on a perilous expedition, because a few words have been uttered. The words may be the silly speech of a modern 'leader' or prime minister, or a sacramental formula, an indiscreet remark wounding 'national honour', or an ultimatum. But in each case words are equally powerful and fateful causes of action" (Coral Gardens II p.53). All the time the author laboriously misses the mark. Of course words have an effect provided they are heard and interpreted by other human beings. In magic we are confronted with words which have an effect without being heard or interpreted; usually the words are not even addressed to human beings. The ethnographic theory of language does not explain much; even the theory of language as such suffers from serious shortcomings, such as its failure to discern between symbols and signals. The real importance of the word derives from the fact that it is a symbol, enabling the speaker and the hearer to be engaged with things absent. In Malinowski's case of the house builders words are used as mere signals. Actually, they are superfluous; a small collection of slightly variegated cries would suffice to meet the exigencies of the situation.

Finally mention must be made of another famous essay, also re-published in Redfield's edition of "Magic, Science and Religion", viz. "Myth in primitive Psychology" (1926). The critical reader of to-day will have no difficulty in appreciating this highly praised eulogy of myth as another proof of the author's versatility in English prose. He even will be willing to agree with the author's conclusion that "the function of any myth, briefly, is to strengthen tradition and to endow it with a greater value and prestige by tracing it back to a higher, better, more supernatural reality of initial events" (Magic p. 146). However, all this does not make us any the wiser when we wish to understand why people prefer such abstruse stories to endow their tradition with greater value and more prestige.

In conclusion we state that Malinowski's direct contributions to the theory of religion are modest. His merits are that he introduced new standards in description, and that he opened the eyes of anthropologists to the intrinsic interconnection of all social facts within their cultural context. This makes it impossible to deal with religious phenomena as a field apart from other cultural institutions. In Malinowski's case the interconnection of all phenomena within the cultural whole is no longer a matter of philosophy but a well demonstrated reality, inviting fieldworkers and theorists alike to pay more considered attention to the cultural setting of the religious phenomena than to the general principles conducive to their puzzling forms.

Malinowski's influence on the study of primitive religions must be characterised as ambiguous. It is to his credit that he set high standards in description and that he inspired a number of young fieldworkers to make extensive and really penetrating studies of the religious belief and practice of the peoples among whom they made their investigations. Outstanding among them are the studies made by Raymond Firth and E. E. Evans-Pritchard. In "The Work of the Gods in Tikopia" (2vols, 1940) and the essays collected in "Tikopia Ritual and Belief" (1967) the former gave a comprehensive description of a Polynesian religion which is of specific value for theoretical studies because it enters into so many details which are of peculiar interest to the theorist. Evans-Pritchard made a valuable contribution to our knowledge of witchcraft, magic and divination in his "Witchcraft, Oracles and Magic among the Azande" (1937). He also gave a very interesting description of a primitive religion centering around the belief in a high god in his "Nuer Religion" (1956), a study unfortunately distorted by the author's dogmatic standpoint that a description of magical practices should not be included in a description of religion. Many other authors should be mentioned besides. For our knowledge of Australian religions we

are indebted to W. Lloyd Warner ("A black civilization", 1937), A. P. Elkin, C. and R. Berndt, W. E. H. Stanner and M. J. Meggitt. Many more
names should be mentioned for the African and American fields, but then
there is little sense in compiling a list of book titles.

We have also to consider the adverse effect of the example set by Malinowski. He introduced what has been captioned facet-ethnography, the
description of selected facets of a culture. The method has great advantages
as far as composition and readability are concerned. Descriptions focussing
on a central problem are more absorbing than those given to the task of
presenting all the data collected. From a more formal point of view, however, the latter method is preferable and the history of ethnography since
1930 has amply justified the claims of the formalists who are more interested in the dry facts than in the form of their presentation, however much
they may appreciate the attractive style of the well-written monograph.
During a period in which current research is focussed on problems of social
structure and culture change, it is only natural that religious phenomena are
studied not for their own sake but as a factor in the total field of social
forces connected with the main theme of the research plan. It is, however, a
highly unsatisfactory situation that the many data which do not appear to
be relevant within the chosen context, have to await publication until such
a context presents itself. Time and again the publication of fieldnotes
concerning the religious aspects of a culture has to be postponed because
they do not fit in the scheme of the author's monograph devoted to problems of greater actuality. Consequently, many data remain unpublished
or, if published, are scattered over numerous papers which are sometimes
difficult to get at. The poor prospects for comprehensive publication of
the religious data combined with a diminished interest in this aspect of culture generally, necessarily has an adverse effect on the study of religious
data in their cultural context; religion is a rather neglected field in modern
anthropology. Nobody doubts its function but few are prepared to study it.

Malinowski's use of the term function oscillated between a pragmatic utili-
tarianism and a formal recognition of a multiplicity of correlations within
the context of a cultural whole. Radcliffe-Brown, more deeply influenced
by Durkheim's thinking than most of his British contemporaries, never lost
sight of the close interconnection of function and cultural whole. If religion
has a function it is one within the cultural whole. Without being primarily
interested in religious problems, Radcliffe-Brown made a few interesting
contributions to the theory of religion which may be characterised as variations on a Durkheimian theme, even though in some respects his ideas on
Australian totemism — and on totemism in general — differ widely from
those of the French master.

The more important function of religion is that it expresses a sense of
dependence in a twofold aspect. On the one hand it implies confidence in

the powers ruling life and events, on the other the human subject feels morally obliged to fulfil his social and religious duties. Through religion man is part of a moral system, which induces him to obey the society's rules and customs, assuring him that he in turn may rely on the assistance of the powers on which his well-being depends (cf. the essay "Religion and Society" in Structure and Function pp.153-177).

Religion does not merely give expression to the meaning which man's relations with his fellow-men have to him; it also reflects his experience with nature. Australian totemism is a specific form of expression of the relations between man and nature. Durkheim's theory that totemism derives its origin from the totemic emblem must be rejected. The role of the totemic emblem is geographically rather narrowly limited, and the emphasis on its impact ignores the all-important fact that not a single case of clan-totemism stands by itself. A clan is always part of a more encompassing group, the tribe, and the clan's specific connection with a species or any other restricted department of nature invariably goes accompanied with more cases of similar connections relating other clans with other departments of nature. What is more important still is that ritual relations between man and nature are of very general occurrence and by no means confined to totemism. "Any object or event which has important effects upon the well-being (material or spiritual) of a society, or anything which stands for or represents any such object or event, tends to become an object of the ritual attitude" (The sociological theory of totemism (1929); Structure and Function p.129). Typical cases of non-totemistic peoples cherishing ritual relations with natural species are those of the Eskimo and the Andaman Islanders who treat all the more important animals and plants as sacred to every member of the society. "Such a ritual relation of man to nature is universal in hunting societies. . ... When the society becomes differentiated into segmentary groups such as clans, a process of ritual specialization takes place" (ibid. pp.126 f.). The totem becoming a symbol of the clan expresses the solidarity of the clan members but, being part of nature and existing side by side with other totems, it is not only an expression of the clan's individuality and its differentiation and opposition between clan and clan, but also a symbol of "the wider unity and solidarity of the whole totemic society... [which], through its segments, stands in a ritual relation to nature as a whole" (ibid. pp.128 f.). The correlation between nature and society implies that "the natural order enters into and becomes part of the social order. The seasonal changes that control the rhythm of social life, the animals and plants that are used for food or other purposes, these enter into and become an essential part of the social life, the social order" (ibid. p.130). This socialisation of nature is not specific to totemism; it is a general feature of religion, expressing man's dependence on nature and society alike.

It would be incorrect to conclude that Radcliffe-Brown recognises the contemplation of nature and natural events as a primary source of religion.

172

Man's relation to nature is only part of his experience. He exists as a member of a society and his social conditions determine his connections with nature. Consequently, the ritual value attributed to nature is by and large a matter of social conditions. In his essay "Taboo" (1939; Structure and Function pp.133-152) he points out that taboos are not the effect of natural conditions but the expression of the fact that the tabooed person is not occupying a normal position in the social life. A taboo on certain kinds of food cannot be explained by the dangers involved in eating them. They have been turned into ritual objects and because they are ritual objects they cannot be eaten straightaway. "It seems very unlikely that an Andaman Islander would think that it is dangerous to eat dugong or pork or turtle meat if it were not for the evidence of a specific body of ritual the ostensible purpose of which is to protect him from those dangers" (ibid. p.149).

Throughout the problem of the foundation of religion in the human condition remains untouched. The point of interest is its role in human society as a means of consolidating the solidarity of the group, and the position of the individual in a universe which must be understood as a moral order ensuring the individual's well-being as long as he stays within it. Radcliffe-Brown's views on the structural aspects of this order will be considered in section 2 of the next chapter.

2. *Historicism and the phenomenological school of thought*

The historical school of Father Schnidt maintained its fairly prominent position in German anthropology until about 1940. In 1938, however, a first attack on Schmidt's 'Kulturkreise' was launched from within, viz. in a book by Father Fritz Bornemann s.v.d., "Die Urkultur in der historischen Ethnologie" (St. Gabrieler Studien VI, 1938). He criticised Schmidt's concept of 'Kulturkreise' and argued that Graebner's concept of 'culture areas' was more realistic and consequently more satisfactory. The preference for a concept of 'Kulturkreis' more akin to the American one of culture area rapidly gained support. Schmidt's death in 1954 brought the end to the 'Kulturkreislehre' which he had so valiantly defended for almost half a century. However, the abandonment of the 'Kulturkreislehre' in its classical form did not imply the renunciation of the belief in 'Kulturschichten'. This cherished child of historicism remained on stage in the German speaking theatre. Its most prominent promotor was the influential leader of the Frobenius-Institut in Frankfurt, professor A. E. Jensen.

Jensen, who did fieldwork in Indonesia (Seran) and in Ethiopia, summarised his ideas on primitive religion in his book "Mythos und Kult bei den Naturvölkern" (1951) to which he gave the sub-title "Religionswissenschaftliche Betrachtungen". His ideas are in many respects original; it is impossible just to classify them, though the influences of the historical

173

school and the phenomenologists are undeniable. Jensen's problem is primitive religion, not religion in general. Religion belongs "zum wahren Mensch-sein". Jensen strongly denies that religion serves any specific purpose. The essence of religion is neither in salvation nor in ethical perfection. Expressions of interest in salvation and salute are signs of a degenerative development; even in primitive society ethical ideas do not need a religious foundation. "Die primäre religiös-sittliche Forderung in den naturvölkerischen Religionen bindet vielmehr den Menschen sich stets des göttlichen Ursprungs der Welt und der Teilhaberschaft des Menschen am Göttlichen bewuszt zu sein. Deshalb ist die echteste Form religiösen Verhaltens das Bewusztmachen und das Lebendig-Erhalten eines besonderen 'Wissens' vom Wesen der Wirklichkeit. Ihm dienen die Riten und Zeremonien" (Mythos und Kult p.101). "Frommes Handeln ist also in erster Linie eine Besinnungs-Tat. Unfromm und ohne religiöse Sittlichkeit ist derjenige, der nicht das besondere 'Wissen' hat und der nicht bereit ist, sich darauf zu besinnen" (ibid. p.102).

In other words, true religion is the inner realisation of a religious truth. This realisation of divine action and revelation is not a mean thing. It must be taken seriously. Religious ideas derive their origin from creative intuitions, from stirring experiences which only really creative men are able to express in a communicable form, in myths which are the vehicles of their visionary intuitions of the true essence of reality. Unfortunately, successive generations rarely succeed in keeping alive the stirring experience which in the first phase of expression inspired those who participated in the internalisation of the newly discovered truth concerning the essence of reality. Instead of revitalising and re-experiencing the original visionary cognition by renewed reflection on divine action and truth, they try to appropriate this knowledge for their own salvation or even for material gain. The phase of creative expression has given way to that of application and falling-off. It is the phase generally prevailing among primitive peoples. Their expressions of religious truth have their origin in a remote past, long before the origin of higher civilisation: "Sie treten uns zwar heute in sehr erstarrten Formen entgegen... aber sie waren zu der Zeit ihrer Entstehung zweifellos gewaltige geistige Schöpfungen der Menschheit" (ibid. p.4).

One of the merits of the book is that the reader is not left in uncertainty about the author's real stand. It is the old misconception of fossilised primitive cultures which are petrifactions of the past. In this particular case the emphasis on the fact that at one time these fossilised cultures of to-day were fully alive, is combined with a highly objectionable concept of culture. Cultures are presented as either in a phase of expression (Ausdruck) or of application (Anwendung) and falling-off (Ablauf). However, a culture, any culture, is always expression, the expression of a human way of life. On the top of all this the introduction of the notion of creativity is a step backward into the twilight of romanticism. It is easy enough to write feelingly one page after another about the stirring emotions and impressive visions of the great creative spirits of the past, but with the dearth of great and really epoch-making ideas the present cannot be but a poor reflection of the glorious past. Jensen does not belittle the consequences. In such a situation magic prevails, and the appropriation of the fossilised forms of great ideas for the furtherance of private ends drives out true religion. The fervent appeal of the author for appreciation of the human values of primitive religion and recognition of the greatness of its original conceptions by making use of a 'verstehende' approach, leads in the end to the discouraging consequence that the actual state of primitive religion is one of the most deplorable rigidity. The 'Überschwenglichkeit' of the picture drawn of past glory is but the poor cloak of the author's condescending disesteem of the allegedly degenerated present.

One of the great religious ideas developed in a very remote past is the *dema*-concept, a term introduced by Jensen to identify gods and mythical heroes who found a tragic end. From their remains the principal food-crops originated or such important animals as pigs. Often the dema is also the god of the netherworld. The departure of the dema and the coming into being of the food-crops marks the end of the mythical era. The descendents of the departed dema and his fellow-gods are ordinary human beings, feeding themselves on the crops produced by the dema, and bound to commemorate in the cult the decisive event of the dema's passing away. The relevant acts are sacrifice, cannibalism and headhunting, often combined with initiation-ceremonies. The acts are characterised as killing rituals, the essence of the rite being the commemoration of the dema's violent death as handed down in myth. As the repository of the great creative ideas of the past, myth has a decisive influence on all the forms of social and religious life. Cult and social organisation are founded in myth. The author is so perfectly sure of the accuracy of his hypothesis that he is not for a moment perturbed by the disquieting fact that in some cases rituals of violence occur without an explanatory dema-myth. In such cases the explanatory myth is simply lost (cf. Mythos und Kult pp.60 and 216). He even feels justified in adding that he is well aware of the hypothetical character of his explanation but that the same holds true of the explanations based on various pre-animistic theories: "*Aber das sind die sogenannten Zauber Erklärungen im gleichen Umfang*" (ibid. p.60). It is a rather surprising argument, but he thinks it convincing enough to have it printed in spacing.

The dema-concept as presented by Jensen is a very encompassing one, comprising the ancestral dream-time beings of the Australians as well as culture heroes and vegetation gods all over the world. The author associates its origin with the 'alt-pflanzerische Kultur', the culture of palaeo-cultivators, but he does not satisfactorily explain the presence of dema-gods among the Australians and the Eskimo. The term dema he borrowed from the Marind-anim of South New Guinea where dema is the term used for the ancestors of the totem-clans, and for characterising extraordinary phenomena of an apparently supernatural character. Its application as a generic term in the wide sense given to it by Jensen seems hardly warranted. Dema is a typical Marind-anim term and its use to indicate the gods and culture heroes of other peoples can only add to confusion. Besides, only a few of the Marind-anim dema answer Jensen's terms of reference.

In the preceding paragraphs we have tried to summarise the main points of Jensen's theory. We refrained from discussing his expositions about the Lord of Animals. Much had to be left out as immaterial to its central argument, viz. the relegation of religious belief to the stirring experiences of a small number of creative men who in a remote past gave shape to their visionary intuitions in myths which successive generations since have re-enacted in ritual in pious commemoration, re-vitalised in acts of violence, and altogether too often misapplied for magical purposes. The theory re-introduces the false conception that primitive societies and their religions are the fossilised relics of the past. It ignores the solid fact that in every culture man gives expression to his ways of life and to the inner stirrings of his being. The concept of religion presented by Jensen is of the ideal-typical kind, borrowed from a romantic philosophy placing the highest value on creativity, stirring experiences and unlimited devotion. It is a philosophy of religion which blesses not the poor in spirit but the rich. Actually, the demands made upon the pious are unanswerable. In his ritual the faithful must re-vitalise the rite's original meaning. What is a ritual's original meaning? In the case of the mass, is it the death of Christ (necessarily unique), or should the faithful go further back to the sacrifice of the easter lamb or to the expiatory sacrifice in the temple? Apart from all this, the most serious objection which must be raised against Jensen is that he has no respect for facts. A poet has a right to invent myths, not a scientist.

Jensen's influence in Germany has been deep and important. The culture-morphological school is his creation. He continued the old historicist traditions and in this context he strongly promoted culture-layer studies of New Guinea and Melanesia, an unpromising activity anyhow at a time when linguistic data were insufficiently available. He also introduced the notion of 'Schöpfungskraft'. The late Carl Schmitz applied it in his monograph on the natives of the Wantoat valley, where he used it in the astonishing form of 'Partikelchen Schöpfungskraft', suggesting that this was what the poor natives hoped to acquire by their ritual (Beiträge zur Ethnographie des Wantoat Tales p.149). The concept thus applied is closely akin to Kruyt's conception of soul-substance. Though we have reason to surmise that Schmitz, who was a brilliant scholar, later changed his views, the term 'Schöpfungskraft' still plays a part in German anthropology. Much to my surprise I found in a review of my book 'Déma' the term déma translated *inter alia* as a 'schöpferische Eigenschaft', and a liberal use made of such terms as 'Schöpfungsvorgänge' and 'Schöpfungsgeschehen', although it is clear in the book that the idea of creation, 'Schöpfung', is blatantly absent from Marind-anim religious thought (cf. F. Jachmann in ZfE 92 pp.305 ff.).

Mircea Eliade is another scholar whose works bear the traces of the influences of phenomenologists and historicists. He is the author of an important and widely read study on shamanism (Le Chamanisme, 1951). His special field is the history of religion, more than that of general anthropology. Among his numerous works mention should first of all be made of his "Traité d'Histoire des Religions" (1948), translated into English under the title "Patterns in comparative Religion" (1958). Another important book, more or less a sequel to the former, is "Images et Symboles" (1952).

To Eliade religion is a matter of course. In his religion man is confronted with the sacred and the eternal. He meets with the sacred in the things which surround him. Discovering the sacred in these things they become *hierophanies*, revelations of the sacred which point to a reality exceeding the things which disclosed it. Ultimately each hierophany is essentially a figuration, an image or reprint of the mystery of reincarnation, referring to God, to the sacred, without being sacred itself. Each hierophany represents in fact an abortive attempt to disclose the mystery of the encounter between God and man.

Primitive people are more aware of these hierophanies than humans participating in our modern, profanised world, in which the symbolic patterns of the past persist only in the emaciated shape of romantic themes, such as the Paradise myth in the South Sea novel. These symbolic patterns are not wholly fortuitously chosen. Although their meaning is often ambiguous and polyvalent, definite preferences are apparent as is well demonstrated by the frequent occurrence of certain privileged patterns in combination with a very restricted number of possible meanings. The sky, for example, symbolises transcendence, power or immutability; the sun is correlated with kingship, initiation and social stratification; the moon is a symbol of the human life, of change and repetition, associated with dual oppositions, fertility and periodic regeneration; water, in turn, is a symbol of semen, purification, and connected with fertility and the notion of the water of life. In this vein he discusses one symbol after another, presenting numerous data, unfortunately without analysing any of them exhaustively. His comments are interesting, often even illuminating, but they are never conclusive. They always return to the point of departure, the fact that things refer to a higher reality. They are signs signalising another reality than that of the visible world.

Personally, I can appreciate the notion that our universe refers in its details to another and higher reality which gives meaning and sense to a discouragingly bleak every-day, phenomenal world. Yet, a philosophy of life, however necessary and edifying in itself, does not make science, even not science of religion. The difficulty with Eliade's books is that there is too much in them of sublime tenderness and too little of cold analysis. The merits of his work are also its essential weakness.

3. *Anthropological Theory in the United States*

American anthropologists never played a dominating part in religious anthropology. Nor did they in the period under discussion now, but the American contributions to anthropological theory during these years are important enough to devote a special section to them because of their impact on the problem of the interrelation of culture and religion. The main focus of these studies is the relation between the individual and his society, a problem which involves the relations between psychology and sociology. Durkheim showed psychology the door because social facts can only be explained from social factors. Nevertheless, a society is hardly as concrete a reality as the individual and his behaviour. Consequently, the relations between the individual and his society remained a moot problem until American anthropologists, well trained by Boas in analytical observation and mistrust of generalisations, succeeded in clarifying the situation by enquiring into the effects of education and early conditioning upon what can be defined as the culturally privileged attitude. The first step in this direction was Margaret Mead's research in Samoa where she studied the problems of adolescents in adapting themselves to the requirements of their culture. Her "Coming of Age in Samoa" (1928) was an eye-opener and in his foreword to his student's first field-study the master of American anthropology, Franz Boas, aptly stated that it confirmed "the suspicion long held by anthropologists, that much of what we ascribe to human nature is no more than a reaction to the restraints put upon us by our civilization". A few years later Margaret Mead published another study on youth problems, viz. "Growing up in New Guinea" (1930).

The theoretical implications of education and early conditioning were outlined briefly and lucidly in two articles written by Edward Sapir (1884-1939), viz. "Cultural Anthropology and Psychiatry" (1932), and "The Emergence of the Concept of Personality in a Study of Cultures" (1934). In the first of these articles he argues that many descriptions of cultures tend to deteriorate into systematic enumerations of the socially inherited behaviour patterns abstracted from the behaviour of the majority of the group's members. Such descriptions are inadequate. They ignore the individual and convey the misapprehension that the locus of a culture is the society. However, when all is said and done, society is a theoretical construct and the real locus of a culture must be sought for in the interaction of specific individuals and in the meaning consciously or unconsciously attached to this interaction by each individual personally. Each and every individual is literally a representative of his culture. "The true psychological locus of *a*

culture is *the individual* or a *specifically enumerated list* of individuals"
(Selected Writings pp.517 f.). The concept of individual applied here is not
that of a simple biological unit, but "that total world of form, meaning and
implication of symbolic behaviour which a given individual partly knows
and directs, partly intuits and yields to, partly is ignorant of and swayed
by". With this very concise definition of what actually is the definition of a
cultural personality, Sapir laid a foundation for the argument of his second
article where he advocates the desirability of combining cultural with psychological and linguistic studies. Cultural patterns must be converted to the
life situation from which they have been abstracted just like, reversely, psychological information must be placed in the social matrix of the personalities under observation. The further we penetrate into a culture, the more
such a culture takes the shape of a 'personality organization' (ibid. p.594).
Therefore we must pay specific attention to the growth and formation of
the individual's personality in a culture. There is nothing mysterious about
the concept of personality; it is "a distinctive configuration of experience
which always tends to form a psychologically significant unit and which, as
it accretes more and more symbols to itself, creates finally that cultural mi-
crocosm of which official "culture" is little more than a metaphorically and
mechanically expanded copy" (ibid. p.595). The first ten years of a child's
life are its culturally formative years and great care should be paid to the
observation of the process of growing up.

In the same year 1934 Ruth Benedict paid an important contribution to
the study of cultural personality with her book "Patterns of Culture". Cultural personality soon developed into a major topic in American anthropology. Ralph Linton gave it a place in "The Study of Man" (1936) and col-
laborated with the psychologist Abram Kardiner as a contributor to the
latter's book "The Individual and his Society; the Psychodynamics of primitive social Organization" (1939). In 1947 Linton published a special study
entitled "The cultural Background of Personality". In the meantime
new contributions to the study of the correlations between personality and
culture had been made by, *inter alia,* G. Bateson ("Naven", 1936) and G.
Bateson and M. Mead, "Balinese Character" (1942). They need not be discussed here. The main point is that personality and culture can no longer be
seen as contrasting entities. In his book "Cooperation in Change" (1963)
Ward H. Goodenough, following up the line of thought first formulated by
Sapir, based his analysis of the concept of culture on that of the private
culture of the individual, a notion more or less identical with that of personality.

The important contributions psychology can make to the knowledge of
other cultures is no longer a matter of controversy. In fact, the concept of
culture and that of personality have much in common. The definition of
each is a matter of endless diversity and discussion. C. S. Hall and G. Lindzey, the authors of "Theories of Personality" (1957), doubt whether any

179

adequate definition of personality is possible. Similar doubts are fostered by anthropologists with regard to the concept of culture. Both terms have to encompass so much in a single word that they lose in content and weight with the constant growth of the body of information. In the concept of personality, cross-culturally applied, we are not only confronted with interpersonal differences of innate talents or emotional behaviour, but also with differences in knowledge, fundamental and technical attitudes, systems of classification and basic notions, and we are made aware that a personality is like an iceberg; nine tenths of its contents remain under the water. Personality studies present difficulties similar to those of culture studies; they are of a comparable order.

A good illustration of the affinity between personality and culture was given by Ruth Benedict in "Patterns of Culture". Following a discussion of style and style periods in European history she gives a description of three different cultures, the Zuñi of Arizona, the Kwakiutl on the coast of British Columbia, and the Dobu of the d'Entrecasteaux Islands near the far eastern end of New Guinea. Each of these cultures has its privileged personality type, the result of education and early conditioning, and each of these cultures is characterised by an integrated pattern of fundamental concepts and attitudes. Among the Zuñi mutual tolerance and complaisance prevail, the Kwakiutl are characterised by personal rivalry, defiance and strife, and the Dobu are ridden by distrust, fear of sorcery and group egoism. The persistence of these attitudes is promoted by the prevailing conditions of social life and educational practices. They are a guarantee of perpetuity and of the further development of dominant trends. The author tries to bring some order in the multitude of possible patterns by distinguishing between Apollonian and Dionysian types of culture, a distinction which is neither convincing nor very useful, the less so because she feels obliged to admit that other cultures are characterised by a lack of integration. Considerations of this kind distract from the main point, the correlation between personality structure and culture. It is quite plausible that what at first sight presents itself as a lack of integration is, after all, the integration of contrasting modes of behaviour. Neither a culture nor a personality organisation are necessarily characterised by harmony of motivations. Moreover, diversification and specialisation are very real possibilities which must be taken into account. On this point Ruth Benedict herself shows the way when she draws attention to the circumstance that a culture may offer specific opportunities for characters deviating from the privileged type. The berdache institution among North American Indians is a case in point. It gives a culturally recognised opportunity for self-realisation to individuals who fail to live up to the heroic ideals of the dominating warriors. Tolerance vis-à-vis deviating personalities is common enough in primitive societies. Even Dobu society is not exclusively intolerant. One of the natives was always friendly and had no terror of the dark. His fellow villagers thought him a silly aberrant, yet he was accepted as such. More differentiated cultures naturally offer more divergent opportunities.

The main point is that the culture in which a man grows up offers him the opportunity for self-realisation through his education and conditioning. He grows up under circumstances promoting his participation in cultural life. Still, there is a broad margin of possible variation and even of deviance. Variation and deviation are hardly less important than cultural conformity; they are a constant source of culture change and renewal. The classification of cultures into certain types tends to obscure the variety of cultures between them, as well as the extreme complexity of each culture in itself. In one way or another cultural life reflects the broad spectrum of motives and attitudes of its participating individuals and every effort to characterise a culture by a sketch of its salient features tends to obscure the variability of the competing and sometimes even contrasting motivations of its participants. It is a pitfall from which Ruth Benedict's characterisations of three cultures have not escaped. They are too straightforward, almost too rectilinear, and as such a misjudgement of the complexity and inner contrarieties proper to any culture. The same objections must be raised against another effort to make a typology, the one made by Margaret Mead in "Sex and Temperament in three primitive Societies", a book which appeared in 1935, a year after "Patterns of Culture". The analysis of a culture is an arduous and time consuming task, not a matter of the rapid condensing of a restricted amount of information.

All this does not detract from the basic value of these studies, viz. the recognition and clarification of the relations between culture and human personality, and the restoration of the connections between psychological and sociological studies. Without paying any immediate contribution to the theory of religion, the impact of these studies on it is evident. If it is true that religion reflects man's inner stirrings, then the ways and means of cultural conditioning necessarily have a far reaching effect on religious forms and expressions.

IX

Structure and structuralism

1. The concept of structure

The use of the term structure is subject to much controversy in the social sciences. Actually, it is a confusing term even in daily usage. Sometimes the word is used as a somewhat emphatic synonym of organisation, whereas on other occasions organisation and structure are opposed to each other as concepts conveying clearly divergent meanings. Further we find that, as a noun, structure is used in two different ways, viz. either to indicate a certain quality, as in the statement 'the structure of the family', or to refer to an object, a thing, as in the title of a famous book, "The elementary Structures of Kinship". In scientific usage the battle runs between two mutually exclusive views, the one claiming that the structure of an institution is part of its objective reality, open to observation, the other that it is a hidden power, a latent rational system present in the observed institution. The former might be called a horizontal notion of structure, the latter a vertical because it wishes to penetrate into the depth, whereas the horizontal concept confines itself to the observation of the ordered arrangement of parts (Nadel) or a set of relations amongst unit entities (Radcliffe-Brown).

The present author's sympathy is on the side of the vertical concept as championed by Lévi-Strauss. Yet, he has certain preferences of his own, and for this reason it seems useful first to give the author's opinion on how the term structure should be applied. To that end we must return to the difference between structure and organisation which we referred to in passing. It is not a small difference. "An organization is created, a structure is found, discovered. An organization is the result of conscious, purposeful action and it can be modified or liquidated by such action. A structure may change, but it is a change which occurs independently of purposeful action. Purposive action may be implied, but it is not a necessary condition. An organization is man-made, the product of organizers, whereas a structure is simply there: a cohesion or configuration which is the result of something emanating from the constituent parts of the structure themselves" (Van Baal in Anniversary Contributions, 1970, pp.21 f.). The difference between

182

the two is that the one results from purposeful action, the other from inner cohesion.

Unfortunately, it is not as simple as all this. It is possible to speak about the structure of an organisation. What is worse, when an organisation is lacking in structure the organisation is bound to disintegrate and to collapse. An organisation cannot thrive without the inner cohesion called structure. The point is that in organisations we are dealing with human beings who are always structuring, as has been conclusively demonstrated by Gestalt-psychology in its analysis of perception. It is little wonder then that the terms organisation and structure are often confused, even to the extent that the term structure is sometimes selected to designate the better and more enduring kind of organisation. We shall avoid this usage. It is incompatible with the vertical notion of structure to which we referred above. Instead, we shall dwell for a while on a case of structure which is generally accepted as paradigmatic, the gift, as described by M. Mauss in his "Essai sur le Don" (1924). It may help us better to understand the implications of the term structure.

"Essay sur le Don" was written long before the term structure had become a bone of contention among sociologists and anthropologists. The author does not discuss the term structure. If he used the word at all it is not given special emphasis. He simply wrote his essay as a study in — as the subtitle says — "Forme et Raison de l'Échange dans les Sociétés inférieures". It is a sociological study but, even if there had not been a dispute on structure and structuralism, we still should have had to devote a special section to it, because of the important role played by gift-giving ceremonies in ritual, and of the impact of the gift on form and content of sacrifice.

The gift is characterised by a number of universal and highly interesting obligations. Everywhere there are situations carrying with them an obligation to give. The gift should always be reciprocated and the return gift should be of equal or slightly higher value than the initial gift. Giving lends prestige to the giver and receiving a gift humiliates the beneficiary who is unable to render a return-gift. Gift-giving can be turned into a weapon in the competition between antagonistic groups. Famous is the case of the Kwakiutl 'potlatch'. The ceremony is initiated by one party challenging its adversary to perform a potlatch. After due preparations there follows a huge exchange, often including a deliberate destruction of valuable goods. It lasts until one party has nothing left to reciprocate the gifts of the other. The winning party glorifies, the defeated one loses its prestige and social status.

The rules of the gift are compelling. Among the Maori certain valuable objects exchanged in gift-giving ceremonies are said to have a *hau*, a kind of mana which forces the recipient to offer a return-gift in due course. If he fails to do so, he will certainly fall ill and die. However, we should not insist on these more dramatic cases. The normal function of the gift is to keep up friendly relations. Gifts are exchanged between friends. They serve as an introduction to the establishment of new relationships, such as a partnership in trade or ritual, or on the occasion of a marriage. Gifts given to maintain peaceful relations are free from unnecessary boasting, and the return gift, which is never lacking, will be of more or less equal value. Even when competing villages organise gift-giving ceremonies with each other, in which one is the winner and the other the loser, the winning party usually takes care not to win a second time, lest relations become strained by injured feelings. Most important of all, gift-giving occurs among all peoples. Even modern society has its occasions when bringing a gift is obligatory. Nobody goes empty-handed to a marriage party or a Christmas celebration. The return gift belonging to a marriage gift is only seemingly lacking. It is an extended return, awaiting the giver's own marriage. A gift which is not returned is a fee; it is possible only between parties of different status, and for this reason fees are unpopular in modern society. A fee is often described as a free gift. Erroneously so, because the recipient is expected to render services in turn. Actually, there are no free gifts. Even those between lovers are not really free; their purport is to cement the common bond. The rules of the gift are as strictly binding on modern westerners as they are on an American Indian or a Maori. A case in point are gambling-debts. They cannot be claimed by legal procedure because gambling is unprotected by law. Nevertheless, these debts are usually paid more quickly and honestly than the bills of the grocery and the butcher. The gambler who does not pay his debts soon becomes an outcast.

With his study of the gift Marcel Mauss has opened our eyes to the compelling nature of an act which at first sight seems to be completely voluntary. One of the most outstanding examples of the compelling power of the gift is that of the reactions aroused by international technical aid. More than any nation the United States has experienced that aid given on a large scale inspires strong feelings of discomfort among the beneficiaries. Aid is a gift and a gift humiliates the recipient who cannot help feeling so even if he asked for it. The situation cannot be undone by speaking of international co-operation instead of technical aid. Words cannot alter material conditions; it is the gift-configuration which prevails and produces its inescapable effect. In other words, it is the structure of the gift which displays its power.

In the ordinary exchange of gifts the binding effect dominates. In his comment on the gift Lévi-Strauss points out that the exchange of gifts is spontaneously established between young children who are finding out how to hold their own and yet to get on with each other: giving means asserting oneself, receiving a gift implies recognition and partnership (Structures élémentaires de la Parenté, rev. ed., pp.99-102). The essence of the gift is that the agreed transfer of a valuable from one individual to another changes

184

the two into partners, and adds a new quality to the value transferred (ibid. p.98).

In conclusion we state that what we call structure has to do with an innate necessity, an inescapable effect proper to the configuration, in the present case to the gift. We shall not try to find out where this necessity has its roots; it is sufficient to state that it must stem from human nature or from the human condition. The universality of the concomitant features of the gift does not leave any room for doubt in this respect. Structure thus conceived is not equivalent to an ordered arrangement of parts, open to direct observation. It is the innate necessity which through its coercive power defines the pattern of recurrent action. In other words, structure is the form in which social law presents itself in standard configurations of human activity. It has to be found out through progressive analysis which of necessity leads the student to problems connected with the fundamental workings of the human mind.

2. The beginnings of structuralism

The "Essay sur le Don" has laid the basis for modern structuralism. The strict and universal pattern of the gift highlights a regularity which must have its basis in human nature. Nevertheless, Mauss did not formulate a general theory to this purport; he was a discoverer out to disclose system in human action, just as he had done before in collaboration with Durkheim in their common study of systems of classification (see above, pp.111 f.). The scholars who had been influenced by Durkheim's thinking might occasionally use the term structure, in general they preferred the word system. It is certainly not a synonym of structure; its meaning is more restricted. These scholars were not prepared to take the leap from the phenomena of culture straight to the foundations of human nature, and the one among them who did introduce the term structure — Radcliffe-Brown — did not think of going that far and strictly kept to the facts of given reality. These scholars simply were alive to two things: first of all, that culture is not a haphazard collection of unrelated items but a well-knit system of mutually related phenomena, and secondly that the study of culture must in the long run bring us closer to the fundamentals of human nature.

One of these was *J. P. B. de Josselin de Jong* (1886-1964), professor of anthropology at Leiden. He had come to anthropology through linguistics and he was deeply convinced that the systematic integration characteristic of language was a cultural trait which could not be limited to the linguistic aspect of culture, but must be a property of any culture. He did not use the term structure; he preferred to speak of the system of a culture. In his thinking he came very near to Lévi-Strauss whose "Structures élémentaires de la Parenté" he welcomed as a major achievement in anthropology (cf. his essay "Lévi-Strauss's Theory on Kinship and Marriage", 1952). The congeniality between the two becomes apparent in De Josselin de Jong's lifelong interest in the implications of dualism. It had been the subject matter of his doctoral thesis, "De Waarderingsonderscheiding van 'levend' en 'levenloos' in het Indogermaansch vergeleken met hetzelfde verschijnsel in enkele Algonkin-talen" (1913). He always returned to dualism, most of all in his teaching, but also in his scarce publications, two of which must be mentioned here. The first is his lecture on the origin of the divine trickster ("De oorsprong van den goddelijken Bedrieger"), delivered to the Royal Academy of the Netherlands in 1929, more or less in answer to Kristensen's paper on the same subject submitted to the Academy in 1928. Following Kristensen (an outstanding authority on Mediterranean religions), De Josselin de Jong first of all turns to Hermes. He is a typical trickster who is the herald and messenger of the gods and a benefactor of mankind, as well as a libidinous adventurer, a cunning impostor, and the clown among the gods. He keeps up relations with the powers of life and death, the gods of upper- and underworld, and, with Aphrodite, he makes part of a primeval androgynous deity. American and Melanesian mythology abound with characters of a comparable nature. They all have a dual aspect, spending good and evil things. Sometimes they are represented as two brothers, the one a benefactor, the other a deceiver or a fool. Basically, the two constitute a unit, just like the two opposing and often antagonistic moieties of the tribe belong together as the two parts of the all comprehensive whole. Or, in the author's own words: "where the available information is not altogether too scanty it appears that a dual grouping conceived as a grouping of opposites, is basic or at the very least inherent to every human order" (Oorsprong goddelijken Bedrieger p.6).

In 1935 De Josselin de Jong returned to this theme ("De Maleische Archipel als ethnologisch Studieveld"). Studies made by his students Duyvendak and Van Wouden had demonstrated the wide spread of the matrilateral cross-cousin marriage in the Indonesian Archipelago, and elucidated the implications of this type of preferential marriage for the social structure. One of these implications is that there is always a tripartite grouping, every exogamous group being affiliated with at least two other similar groups, one of bride-givers which as such is superior, and one of bride-takers which as such is inferior to the middle group. This position of every group as a middle group between a superior and an inferior one is reflected in the religious conception of the earth as a middle world between an upper- and an underworld. The duality and its unity, the division in two which is also one in three, are clearly brought forward. The affinity with Durkheim is evident in the interlacing of the social and the religious aspects, that with Lévi-Strauss in the emphasis on dualism. The latter would later elaborate on the theme in his essay "Les organisations dualistes existent-t-elles?" (cf. below, pp.193 f.).

De Josselin de Jong never cared to explain his views in elaborate studies or to put them in a philosophical context. He disliked philosophical treatises and preferred the strictly methodical exposition of fact. He held the view that our knowledge does not suffice to construct an all-embracing theory of culture. Yet, he was in sympathy with any enquiry into the cohesion of the various aspects of culture and he strongly stimulated analytical studies of culture which clarified the innate interconnections of seemingly incoherent cultural phenomena. Of his students G. W. Locher concentrated on the dialectics of dualism and oneness in his thesis "The Serpent in Kwakiutl Religion" (1932). He argued that the divine is conceived as both dualistic and monistic at the same time. The snake, the symbol of divine power, is primarily associated with the underworld, the chthonic aspect of the universe. Nevertheless, the snake is also associated with the upperworld as, reversely, the representatives of the latter, the birds, are also connected with the underworld. Locher supported his argument with data borrowed from various other parts of the world, such as ancient Egypt, but he refrained from entering into a more penetrating analysis of the concomitant social structures.

The study of a case of interaction between social structure and religious representations is the outstanding merit of another Leiden dissertation, viz. the late G. J. Held's "The Mahabharata" (1935) in which he described the central theme of the epos as a huge potlatch. Held's analysis of the social structure of the old Indian society is so well-known to readers of 'Les Structures élémentaires' that further comment on this study is superfluous.

Radcliffe-Brown's affinities to structuralism have already been mentioned briefly in the preceding section of the present chapter. Earlier we discussed his contributions to functionalism. In many respects he stands farther away from the structuralist approach than Mauss and De Josselin de Jong. Yet, the faith that in some way or another a culture is a coherent whole could not fail to influence his thinking and toward the end of his life he made a noteworthy contribution to structural thought in his essay "The comparative Method in social Anthropology" (1951; Method in Social Anthropology p.108). Here he draws attention to the same problem as the one raised by De Josselin de Jong, but he comes to it from a completely different angle. He points out that among the Haida, eagle and raven are antagonists; they are the totemic symbols of the two competing moieties. According to a myth the eagle kept fresh water in a basket which the raven stole. Flying away with the heavy basket the raven spilled water from it which formed the lakes and the rivers. At the same time "salmon made their way into the streams and now furnish food for men". A rather similar myth is found among various tribes in Australia where the antagonists are eaglehawk and crow. Here again the eagle owns the water which the crow steals and spills. There are many other pairs of mythical antagonists in Australian folklore, very often birds but sometimes quadrupeds as well. They are always associated with groups: moieties, the sexes, clans and so on. The comparative method leads to the discovery of some widely spread phenomena which, in turn, raise the problem of totemism. He refuses to enter deeply into it because here his problem is not that of totemism but why "such pairs as eagle-hawk and crow, eagle and raven, coyote and wild cat are chosen as representing the moieties of a dual division" (Method in Social Anthropology p.114). However, in passing he makes two noteworthy observations on totemism which should not be overlooked. Lévi-Strauss later referred extensively to them. First of all Radcliffe-Brown states that in totemism we are up against two problems. "One is the problem of the way in which in a particular society the relation of human beings to natural species is represented, and as a contribution to this problem I have offered an analysis of the non-totemic Andaman Islanders. The other is the problem of how social groups come to be identified by connection with some emblem, symbol, or object having symbolic or emblemic reference. A nation identified by its flag, a family identified by its coat of arms, a particular congregation of a church identified by its relation to a particular saint, a clan identified by its relation to a totemic species; these are all so many examples of a single class of phenomena for which we have to look for a general theory" (ibid. pp.113 f.).

After this digression he returns to a further study of his problem, the symbols of dual division. In a way these symbols are opposites but they are not merely opposites. There is also something they have in common. Eagle-hawk and crow are both meat-eaters and this is how the Australians see themselves. The difference is that the hawk is a hunter chasing life prey and the crow a thief, feeding on carrion and garbage. Other pairs of symbols such as the owl and the nightjar have other things in common. They both operate at night and during the day hide out in hollow trees. They symbolise an opposition which separates as well as unites, and "the more correct description would be to say that the kind of structure with which we are concerned is one of the union of opposites" (ibid. p.123). It is a description which also suits a description of the relationship between the two moieties or between the sexes. Dualism is a widespread phenomenon and by no means restricted to the simple social structures of primitive tribes. A case of the same type is that of the opposition of *yang* and *yin* in ancient China where one yang (e.g. day) and one yin (e.g. night) make a unified unity of time. Although Radcliffe-Brown is well aware that thinking in opposites is a universal feature of human thinking (ibid. p.118) he does not enter into further speculation on the human mind but returns to the subject matter of his lecture, the expectation that the comparative method "will provide us with knowledge of the laws of social development" (ibid. p.129).

An independent and stimulating contribution to the study of structure is W. E. H. Stanner's monograph of Murinbata religion, published in Oceania (vols. 30-33) under the title of "On Aboriginal Religion". One of the points of interest is the parallelism between the procedure of sacrifice and that followed in initiation. Sacrifice and initiation have in common that they are concerned with human operations on things, including persons. The study being primarily of a descriptive nature we shall not try here to discuss the various theoretical implications of Stanner's often somewhat cryptically posited views. An exception must be made for one point. By concentrating the attention not on the formal procedure but on its consequences for its object, he arrives at another and slightly more complicated scheme of operations than Hubert and Mauss and after them Van Gennep. The tripartition of the French authors is substituted by one into four phases by a division of the central phase into two, in itself a strong point because the central phase is the really decisive one. In another respect Stanner's explanation of the structural parallelism of sacrifice and initiation is not fully satisfactory. After all, the object of sacrifice is destroyed, whereas the object of initiation is promoted, a difference which Hubert and Maus showed they were well aware of when they pointed out that the procedure of a sacrifice is exactly the reverse of that of an anointment. In the latter the action is to the benefit of the object, in the former the object is made a victim (above, p.115).

3. Claude Lévi-Strauss. Introduction

In section 1 of this chapter we called structure the innate necessity which through its coercive power defines the pattern of recurrent action. Lévi-Strauss might remark: not only of recurrent action. To him the ultimate source of structure is the unconscious, which is the last determinant of human action. The study of structure aims at discovering the hidden rules of human thought and behaviour, rules of a kind similar to the linguistic rules of grammar and phonology, unconscious to the speaker and yet meticulously obeyed.

The oeuvre of Lévi-Strauss is characterised by the combination of an impressive command of broad anthropological knowledge with a profusion of acute dialectical philosophy and artistic refinement. Anthropologists, united in recognising the author's professional competence, often feel exasperated by his dialectics which take them far afield to problem-areas where they no longer feel sure of their ground. For this reason we shall pay specific attention to some of those peculiarities in his way of thought which more than others give difficulties to the student of anthropology. This course inevitably leads to a rather critical approach of our author's presentation of theory, a criticism which should not be misunderstood. Its real aim is to encourage the student to read Lévi-Strauss, and to assist him in overcoming the difficulties and ambiguities which he has to face. To that end we take as our guide the critical introduction to structuralism written by Yvan Simonis, "Claude Lévi-Strauss, ou la 'Passion de l'Inceste'" (1968; to be quoted as Simonis).

Simonis points to the sources from which Lévi-Strauss derived his inspiration: Freud, Marx, and the study of geology. Psycho-analysis and geology have in common that they try to explain the visible and perceptible from an invisible rationale under its surface, a pursuit again found in Marxism which refuses to accept that social science could be based on a study of events. The three disciplines are one in their search for the rational behind the world of sensorial perception. The problem of knowledge is the discovery of a kind of super-rationalism capable of integrating the perceptible into the rational (Simonis, p.15).

In the field of anthropology Lévi-Strauss was influenced by the works of M. Mauss and E. Durkheim. Simonis gives special attention to the differences between Lévi-Strauss' thinking and that of Durkheim (Ch. III). In our opinion the basic relationship between the two is more important. Durkheim had founded his epistemology on the firm conviction that nature cannot err and that man is part of nature (above, pp.112 f.). Lévi-Strauss holds a similar view: "La connaissance... consiste dans une sélection des aspects *vrais*, c'est-à-dire ceux qui coïncident avec les propriétés de ma pensée. Non point comme le prétendaient les néo-kantiens, parce que celle-ci exerce sur les choses une inévitable contrainte, mais bien plutôt parce que ma pensée est elle-même un objet. Étant 'de ce monde', elle participe de la même nature que lui" (Tristes Tropiques p.43; quoted from Simonis p.16). Confidence in and solidarity with nature are thematic in structuralism. Taking its departure from the contrast between nature and culture, between the conscious and the unconscious (the theme of the introductory chapter of the 'Structures élémentaires'), the final argument returns to nature and to the unconscious as the ultimate foundation and rationale of culture and the conscious, reducing the latter to a function of nature or — what often amounts to the same — of the unconscious. The true determinants of culture and the conscious must be found in nature and the unconscious. By reducing the conscious to the unconscious, and culture to nature, the philosophy of Lévi-Strauss tends to obliterate the contrast on which it is founded and repeatedly falls into an ambiguity of which Simonis exclaims: "Le 'naturel' en Culture est porteur des explications. Ambiguïté permanente — et normale dans l'oeuvre de Lévi-Strauss — de cette explication" (Simonis p.78).

Ambiguity indeed, but an ambiguity which finds support in reality. No one can deny that humanity, culture, the human spirit, are founded in nature and subject to its laws. With infallible certainty Lévi-Strauss takes his position. The contents of speech are conscious, but the form, the phonological structure and the infrastructure of language generally, are unconscious. In language the conscious and the unconscious are inextricably interwoven. Structural linguistics are paradigmatic for Lévi-Strauss' methods of analysis

190

which he applies first of all to the structures of kinship. The analogies between language and kinship are aptly formulated and diagnosed. Both are means of communication, language by the exchange of words, kinship by the exchange of women between groups of men. Human society begins when women are recognised as signs which can be exchanged, just like words are signs which are exchanged. The origins of language and of the incest taboo are co-terminous. They could not be otherwise; both are products of the human mind, the structure of which is the ultimate aim of his investigations.

We shall not dwell on the more speculative aspects of his philosophy; here we must first consider the procedure followed in the analysis of kinship forwarded in 'Les Structures élémentaires de la Parenté, Lévi-Strauss' first and epoch making effort to unfold the impact of structure on human institutions (1949; quotations are taken from the revised edition of 1967). The incest taboo is his point of departure. Incest taboos differ in content from one nation to another, but each and every nation has a set of regulations marking intimate connections between certain persons of different sex as incestuous. Even where marriage to a sister is allowed, as is the case in a number of royal families, we still find rules prohibiting sexual intercourse with other kin. The prohibition of incest is a universal, but the content of the prohibition differs from one people to another. Universals refer to nature and the fact that the prohibition of incest is a universal implies that the taboo belongs to the order of nature. Nevertheless, incest occurs, and the relevant taboos differ from place to place. The taboos are culturally defined. In the incest taboo nature and culture are inextricably intertwined. Incest taboos cannot be explained from a natural disinclination to mate with closely related persons. An explanation of this kind is belied by fact. A renewed analysis is called for which leads to the discovery of three mental structures, viz. "l'Exigence de la Règle comme Règle; la notion de réciprocité considerée comme la forme la plus immédiate sous laquelle puisse être intégrée l'opposition de moi et d'autrui; enfin, le caractère synthétique du Don, c'est-à-dire le fait que le transfert consenti d'une valeur d'un individu à un autre change ceux-ci en partenaires, et ajoute une qualité nouvelle à la valeur transférée" (Structures élémentaires p.98). The three structures mentioned inevitably lead to a system dictating the exchange of women between men, in its elementary form the exchange of sisters belonging to different family groups by their brothers.

The structures concerned are discernable even in the behaviour of infants. Referring to observations made by Susan Isaacs among a group of infants, Lévi-Strauss points out that every child has to solve the problem of how to get on with the other children of the group. It does not take the child a long time to find out the significance of rules for his own position in the interaction of the group. At an early stage the child discovers the necessity of reciprocity. Susan Isaacs also noted the spontaneous development of

191

a pattern of exchange of gifts among the children of her group. Each child will in time act as a giver. As a spender he has power because he has a place and a function in the interaction of the group. At the same time another child is a receiver of gifts, not powerful but recognised as a member of the group because he is taken into account. Giving and receiving are the signs of group membership and recognition; it is not the gift itself which is important, but the recognition of partnership signified by the gift. Participation is a matter of primary importance to all the members of the group. These observations are valuable because the participants of the group have as yet very little been socialised. The current rules of social conduct have not yet been internalised, and consequently these children have a wider freedom of choice for their patterns of action than older children whose patterns of behaviour have already been stabilised to a greater extent. It is the same in social behaviour as in language. Once the child has mastered his mother tongue his potentiality for learning other languages is limited by the internalisation of a certain phonemic system which is only partly compatible with another one (cf. Structures élémentaires Ch. VII). We note in passing that this reference to child behaviour is of a very different nature than Tylor's identification of primitive mentality with that of children. The point of interest to us is that the case forwarded by Lévi-Strauss as an illustration of the three structures observed in the analysis of the rules of kinship, raises a question, viz. how unconscious is the unconscious?

The question should be explained. To Lévi-Strauss structures are concerned with what is universal in human behaviour; they belong to the order of nature and thus to the unconscious. Culture originates with the exchange of linguistic symbols and women by men. The structures controlling the exchange systems necessarily pre-exist, they must belong to nature, i.e. to the unconscious. But do we need to make an appeal to the unconscious to explain the universality of the three structures mentioned, the recognition of rules, the acceptance of reciprocity and the synthetic character of the gift? Obviously, Lévi-Strauss refers them to the unconscious. He explicitly calls reciprocity the form "sous laquelle puisse être intégrée l'opposition de moi et d'autrui", thus giving precedence to formal reciprocity. It is a legitimate question to ask whether the statement should not be reversed and reciprocity be recognised as the inescapable outcome of the opposition of the self and the other. Similar questions could be raised with regard to the other two structures.

The answer is yes as well as no. It is yes in so far as the economy of reasoning forbids attributing to the unconscious what can legitimately be explained from the conscious and the directly observable, in the present case from the human condition. However, it is also no and even rather strictly no, because the conscious cannot be separated from the unconscious. It would be foolish to deny the impact of nature and the unconscious on man's conscious behaviour. If we object against the over-accentuation of the role of the unconscious as apparent from the author's inclination wholly to include the three 'structures' in the order of nature, we fully agree with him when, in the course of his argument, he explains that at the roots of reciprocity, exchange, and marriage is the tendency of man to think in oppositions, a tendency which cannot be explained from any other factor but must be recognised as the point of departure of every effort at explanation (ibid. p.158; cf. Simonis p.64).

It is not our task here to investigate the problems of the interrelations between the respective contributions of the conscious and the unconscious to the forms of culture. We only have to review some of the main lines of Lévi-Strauss' philosophy. One of these is his concern with the human tendency to think in opposites. The outcome of this fundamental trend as reflected in the widespread occurrence of dualistic forms of organisation necessarily arrested the attention of Lévi-Strauss. A penetrating analysis of a highly intriguing aspect of these systems is given in his essay "Les organisations dualistes existent-t-elles?" (Antropologie structurale Ch. VIII). The problem here discussed is that of the combination of dual and triadic systems, a phenomenon singled out some twenty years earlier by J. P. B. de Josselin de Jong (above, p.186) for whom the present essay was written in honour of his 70th anniversary (Bijdragen 1956; Anthropologie Structurale p.147). Lévi-Strauss demonstrates that diadic and triadic systems repeatedly go hand in hand, illustrating his point with a few well-chosen cases of a dual division concentrically arranged. The best known instance is that of Omarakana village as described by Malinowski; in the centre of the village are the houses of the chief, the dancing place and the lodges of the bachelors, surrounded by a circle of yam-houses. Then follows concentrically a broad alley with the family-houses on the outside. The dual arrangement is essentially triadic; the opposition between the centre where the raw food is stored and cooking is forbidden, and the periphery where food is cooked in the family houses, evokes as a third party the alley separating them. The concentric arrangement combines the diadic with the triadic. Without becoming purely triadic, it nevertheless differs profoundly from a symmetric arrangement consisting of two equal halves, such as the camp arrangement of some American Indian tribes mentioned by Durkheim and Mauss in their essay on primitive forms of classification. In the subsequent discussion Lévi-Strauss argues that fully symmetric systems are rare. Often one of the halves is superior to the other, making the symmetry incomplete, or one of the moieties is again divided into two, making the system diadic and triadic at the same time. Dual systems are not as simple as they are often supposed to be. In one and the same society systems of symmetric and of concentric, of diadic and triadic divisions may exist side by side. It is evident that the term dualism must not be applied as a mere catchword. The dualistic tendency is of a structural nature; it gives shape to the arrangement of social relations in ever new forms without depleting itself in

193

any of them in particular. Any form of dualistic arrangement resulting from this tendency evokes new oppositions and new arrangements, i.e. complications upsetting the dualism. The content of social reality cannot be comprised in a simple formula. It is a gross misinterpretation of structuralism to believe that structure produces pure and simple forms of social organisation. Structures are founding forces, stimulating the emergence of new forms. The title of the essay, 'Do dualistic organisations exist?', raises a legitimate question because every form of organisation necessarily fathers another one. A purely dualistic organisation, conceptually the most simple as well as the most probable form of organisation, actually is a marginal and improbable form. The realisation of the dualistic principle necessarily leads to ever new complications. If it were different we would have to admit the possibility of the obviously incompatible, viz. that the structural tendency to think in opposites has solidified in its self-realisation.

The source of action is the unconscious, a category presenting serious difficulties to scientific thought because it is by definition empty. Lévi-Strauss describes its function as follows: "l'inconscient est toujours vide; ou, plus exactement, il est aussi étranger aux images que l'estomac aux aliments qui le traversent. Organe d'une fonction spécifique, *il se borne à imposer des lois structurales, qui épuisent sa réalité*, à des éléments inarticulés qui proviennent d'ailleurs: pulsions, émotions, représentations, souvenirs. On pourrait donc dire que le subconscient est le lexique individuel où chacun de nous accumule le vocabulaire de son histoire personnelle, mais que ce vocabulaire n'acquiert de signification, pour nous-mêmes et pour les autres, que dans la mesure où l'inconscient l'organise suivant ses lois, et en fait ainsi un discours" (Anthropologie Structurale pp.224 f.; italics ours).

The passage just quoted makes the position clear; in the words of Simonis, the author says precisely what we wished to know (Simonis p.85). The structural laws exhaust the reality of the unconscious. The unconscious is the law because it has no content of its own. It is the law which organises the raw materials of experience and memory, a law also which is common to all humans and thus makes communication possible, organising experience and expression along the same lines in all individuals. Its most important function is that it calls forth symbolic activity, the fundamental characteristic of the human mind. Symbolic thought lays the foundation of all cultural and social life. "Pas de social, ni de culturel, sans pensée symbolique" states Simonis in his résumé of the position taken by Lévi-Strauss, and a few lines further down he adds: "Autrement dit, le symbolique ne jaillit pas de l'état de société, c'est l'apparition de la pensée symbolique qui 'rend la vie sociale à la fois possible et nécessaire'" (Simonis, p.82). Through the symbolic, the social and the cultural refer to the unconscious. The position thus defined necessarily leads to a methodology which borrows its principles from structural linguistics, the discipline which focussed its analytical studies on the unconscious aspects of language.

One of the important methodological tools Lévi-Strauss borrowed from structural linguistics is the opposition of the signifying and the signified, 'le signifiant et le signifié'. The signified is the concept, the signifying the acoustic image applied to signify the signified. Together the signifying and the signified constitute the linguistic sign. In the French word 'soeur' the acoustic image s - ö - r is the signifying, the concept of sister the signified, the word 'soeur' a sign (cf. Simonis, p.160).

So far the the meaning of the signifying and the signified is clear enough. The two belong together, united in the sign. However, the close complementarity characterising the connections between the signifying and the signified in linguistics, is lacking when these same terms are used by Lévi-Strauss in the context of his reflections on mana and magic, reflections which belong to the field of epistemology, far more than to that of linguistics. In the following statement, taken from his analysis of mana, the distance between the signifying and the signified is optimal: "l'homme dispose dès son origine d'une intégralité de signifiant dont il est fort embarassé pour faire l'allocation à un signifié, donné comme tel sans être pour autant connu" (Introduction à l'Oeuvre de Marcel Mauss, in Sociologie et Anthropologie par M. Mauss, p.XLIX). Here man is depicted as a signifier who is at a loss because he has a plethora of signifying at his disposal but not an address where or an object on which to bestow it.

Lévi-Strauss bases this presentation of the situation on a theory of origin. When in the course of evolution language made its appearance, it must have happened all of a sudden. The birth of symbolism meant a transition from a stage "où rien n'avait un sens, à un où tout en possédait" (ibid. p.XLVIII). The appearance of language is a sudden event, a matter of discontinuity, in contradistinction to knowledge, which is a matter of continuous growth. Knowledge slowly develops in a situation in which man is confronted with a universe which signifies something to him, but in which that something has no exact content, at least partly so. This undefined signifying is described by Lévi-Strauss as a 'signifiant flottant', a 'floating signifying', the volume of which is gradually reduced ('sponged down') by knowledge without ever being fully effaced.

It is probably not superfluous to note that in this context the term signifying does not stand for an acoustic image as in linguistics, but for a sense perception evoking a human reaction. One of these reactions, and a very necessary reaction in fact, is to give it a name. Every language has words for things poorly understood, for values of undetermined signification. By way of example Lévi-Strauss mentions the word 'oomph', used in American slang to indicate a quality not precisely definable, attributed to certain women. One of the terms covering the poorly understood and the indeterminate, is mana, with its equivalents in American Indian and various other languages. Lévi-Strauss (ibid. pp.XLI - LII) does not deny that mana can

195

sometimes be circumscribed as a mysterious or secret force; he simply points out that the specific significance attributable to the term in certain circumstances is necessarily of lesser importance than the fact that the term belongs to that wider category of words which are the conscious expression of a semantic function "dont le rôle est de permettre à la pensée symbolique de s'excercer malgré la contradiction qui lui est propre" (ibid. pp.XLIX,L). Expressions of this kind are stopgaps which fill a vacuum. They have a symbolic zero-value; they mark the need of a symbolic content without defining it.

Lévi-Strauss is interested in the category of words which have a borderline function in symbolic expression, not in the specific content these words may have. He warns explicitly against the danger of setting too much store on native explanations of the mana-concept. (In parentheses we note that the counsel is a dubious one; "setting too much store on native explanations" cannot be more dangerous than ignoring them). The main point to Lévi-Strauss is the zero-value of the concept, marking the borderline case which must have been of such frequent occurrence in the situation created by the sudden appearance of language. At that moment the whole universe set out to signify, but knowledge was still lacking. Elaborating on this theme he argues that the two categories, the signifying and the signified, originated at the same moment as two blocks which are each other's complement. From the beginning the two blocks are there, and expanding knowledge has the function of combining certain aspects of the signifying with certain aspects of the signified, a process which proceeds but slowly. In this continuous process words like mana must be placed, words expressing the incertitude and hesitation characteristic of a lack of knowledge.

Before we return to the mana-concept we must point out that we are up against a remarkable, not to say surprising presentation of fact. The term signifying is sometimes used of the universe which signifies something to man, and then again of man who disposes of a plethora of signifying which must be bestowed on the universe which is signified. The terminology is confusing, as confusing as is the suggestion that with language a block of signifying originated simultaneously with a block of signified which are each other's complements: "les deux catégories du signifiant et du signifié se sont constituées simultanément et solidairement, comme deux blocs complémentaires" (ibid. p.XLVII). We may well put a question-mark here. We are far away from the immediate complementarity of the signifying and the signified characterising the linguistic sign, far away also from the spontaneity marking their conjunction in Cassirer's philosophy. The disjunction of the signifying and the signified is thematic in Lévi-Strauss' thinking on situations characterised by a lack of knowledge, the situations in which he places his comments on magic and mana. An interesting statement in this respect is the one made in "Le Sorcier et sa Magie": "En présence d'un uni-

vers qu'elle est avide de comprendre, mais dont elle ne parvient pas à do-
miner les méchanismes, la pensée normale demande toujours leur sens aux
choses, qui le refusent; au contraire la pensée dite pathologique déborde
d'interprétations et de résonnances affectives, dont elle est toujours prête à
surcharger une réalité autrement déficitaire... Empruntant le language des
linguistes, nous dirons que la pensée normale souffre toujours d'un déficit
de signifié, tandis que la pensée dite pathologique (au moins dans certaines
de ses manifestations) dispose d'une pléthore de signifiant" (Anthropologie
Structurale pp.199 f.).

The repeated shifts of the use of the terms signifying and signified from
their linguistic to their epistemological sense and back again, are confusing,
not because they are the results of confused thinking, but because we hold
the view that in linguistics the signifying and the signified are characterised
by their conjunction in the linguistic sign, in epistemology by their disjunction in the act of knowledge. Lévi-Strauss does not recognise the opposition
between linguistic and epistemological as absolute. In his view the two must
ultimately coincide, the signifying and the signified must be reunited. "The
emergence of symbolic thought has thrown man out of nature, the emergence of humanity is a measure of expulsion. Scientific knowledge must
mend the 'tear' by rejoining the signifying and the signified. Scientific
knowledge will sponge off the mana", the vague concepts taking the place
of knowledge in an earlier stage (Simonis p.106). Lévi-Strauss expresses his
expectations as follows: "Le travail de péréquation du signifiant par rap-
port au signifié a été poursuivi de façon plus méthodique et plus rigoureuse à
partir de la naissance, et dans les limites de l'expansion, de la science mo-
derne. Mais, partout ailleurs, et constamment encore chez nous-mêmes... se
maintient une situation fondamentale et qui relève de la condition humaine,
à savoir que l'homme dispose d'une intégration de signifiant dont il est fort
embarassé pour faire l'allocation à un signifié, donné comme tel sans être
pour autant connu" (Introduction à M. Mauss pp.XLVIII f.; Simonis, loc.
cit. ftn.57).

Throughout, the nostalgia for the restoration of the primeval unity of before the birth of symbolic thought persits. Magic is one of the means serving this purpose. We find this clearly expressed in the 'Introduction à M.
Mauss': "Toutes les opérations magiques reposent sur la restauration d'une
unité, non pas perdue, (car rien n'est jamais perdu) mais inconsciente, ou
moins complètement consciente que ces opérations elles-mêmes" (p.XLVII).
In this respect magic, exchange, and dialogue serve a common aim, that of
communication (ibid. p.XLVI). There is little with which we could agree
more, but we cannot agree with Lévi-Strauss' point of departure, the reduc-
tion of the rupture brought about by the emergence of symbolising to a
problem of knowledge. Symbols and knowledge cannot bridge the gap
which they created. There is an existential problem here which cannot be

solved by the increase of knowledge. We shall return to this in the next chapter.

After this digression we must revert to the mana-concept. It is a good example of Lévi-Strauss' refusal to treat religious phenomena as phenomena constituting a separate category, apart from that of knowledge. To him mana is primarily a word indicating a zero-value, referring to something undefined, something not yet known and not understood. We also note that Lévi-Strauss warned explicitly against paying too much attention to the content of the concept in native philosophy. The point of interest to him is the most general aspect of the concept in which mana presents itself as a word belonging to a special category of undefined thought. His ultimate aim is to study the effect of the unconscious. Yet, had he paid more attention to the conscious aspects of mana he might have arrived at another conclusion. He then might have noted that mana, although referring to something not exactly known, is often ascribed to things and persons which are perfectly well known. Of the various cases of belief in mana mentioned in the course of the preceding chapters, the content given to the concept of mana by Lévi-Strauss is confirmed only once, namely in the case of the fish of a kind never seen before, which was returned to the river because it was manitou, mana (above, p.68). It is not confirmed in that of the mana of the chief whom everybody knows or in that of the stone which has mana for yams, or for all the contents of the West African *nkisi* (above, pp.64 ff., 80). These objects are all perfectly well-known and yet something uncanny, mana, is ascribed to them. It is attributed to them and we are fully justified in asking why it is attributed, since it is applied only to these objects and not to others of the same kind. Apparently, the native 'sees' something in them. The questions why and what he 'sees' are not merely legitimate but compelling. They cannot be brushed aside as the products of a probably misleading native philosophy, it is exactly this philosophy which begs the question. The mana is not inherent in stones and claws generally, but in these specific ones for reasons which obviously are not caused by a lack of knowledge concerning these objects, but by an act of attribution based on knowledge.

The objections we have against Lévi-Strauss' approach of the mana-concept cannot be raised against his studies of magic. Here he goes into great detail and the result is two magnificent essays which are of great interest to us, viz. "Le Sorcier et sa Magie", and "l'Efficacité symbolique", both reprinted in Anthropologie Structurale. In the first he examines the belief in magic and sorcery. There are always three parties, the patient, the public and the medicine-man. The belief of the patient is manifest. He knows that he is bewitched, he feels ill, and if the medicine-man declares that his ailment is incurable he will as probably die, as he will recover when the medicine-man gives hope by performing the appropriate ritual. The belief of the public is as evidently manifest. They bewail the victim even before he is

198

dead, thus precipitating his death. The symptoms of his ailment are of the same nature as those of shock caused by bombardments or accidents. The terror exerted by the belief in the efficacy of magic is as devastating to the organism as that caused by the fright of imminent physical danger.

Finally there is the belief of the medicine-man himself. He is the only one of the three parties concerned whose belief is subject to doubt. He combines his ritual activities with légerdemain and tricks but does that make him an impostor? There may be sceptics among these medicine-men and Lévi-Strauss offers his readers a fascinating instance of such a marginal character in the story of Quesalid, described by Boas. Quesalid mistrusts all medicine-men. He wishes to expose their deceit and to that end he serves an apprenticeship with an expert medicine-man. When he is called upon to cure a patient himself, he finds to his amazement that his treatment is effective. Quesalid becomes a medicine-man of great renown. He remains a sceptic with regard to the magic of other medicine-men but he firmly believes in the efficacy of his own methods. The analysis of his contests with competing medicine-men gives evidence that the belief of the public, i.e. the group, is of basic importance to any successful performance of magic.

The point is brought home from another angle in the second essay, "l'Efficacité symbolique". It gives a detailed account of the ritual performed to assist a woman in labour when the child fails to come down. The ritual acts out a myth which itself is a symbolic account of an impregnation followed by a successful birth. The amazing effect of the ritual is that it works; it removes the psycho-somatic obstacles and the child comes down. The procedure followed in the shamanistic treatment of a patient has its analogies in psycho-analysis, but the analogies are reversed. During the shamanistic séance the patient is passive and the medicine-man produces a myth. In psycho-analytic treatment the doctor is passive and the patient produces a myth. The myth produced by the patient under psycho-analytic treatment is the myth of his personal past, the myth produced by the medicine-man belongs to the mythical past of the community concerned. The difference between the two kinds of myth is inevitable. Our mechanised society has no other locus for a mythical past than somewhere in the private history of the individual. There is no place for myth in the history of the society, the locus of myth in a primitive community. The locus of the myth being reversed, the order of the process is necessarily reversed too. The result is the same, the curing of the patient's psycho-somatic ailment. The parallel reaches even further. The shaman is the counterpart of the psychopathic patient. Both are abnormal in this sense that they brim over with signifying, and Lévi-Strauss continues with the reflections on normal and pathological thought which we discussed above (pp.196 f.). The analysis elucidates the social function of the shaman as well as the significance which the group's faith in the shaman's power has for a successful treatment. The ailment is a matter which normal thought cannot understand and the group

199

invites the shaman, the psychopath, to invest his affective richness of signifying which otherwise has no point of application.

In his explanations of the magical act and its efficacy Lévi-Strauss returns to the line of thought followed in his analysis of mana. It is the formal characteristics which arrest his attention, the act of signifying, the profusion of signification attributed, not the specific content of the signified.
In the present case the analysis led to important results, viz. the demonstration of the analogies between shamanistic and psycho-analytic treatment of
patients. Nevertheless, we doubt whether the problems presented by shamanism and magic can be solved by simply presenting the shaman as a psychopath 'débordant de signifiant'. More attention should be paid to the specific content of that signifying, in other words to the elucidation of the part
of culture in the process. It seems probable that then we might discover
that, first of all, the shaman is not a psychopath, and subsequently, that the
analogies of shamanistic and psycho-analytic treatment are a more important contribution to the study of psycho-analysis than to our knowledge of
religion. In other words, we agree that the investigation of structures is important but we insist that in the investigation equal attention should be
paid to the analysis of conscious contents. In the course of the next section
we will have occasion to substantiate our reservations when the structures
of myth are discussed.

4. Lévi-Strauss on classification and myth

The central problem to Lévi-Strauss is the structure of the human mind.
How does it work and what are the laws directing its activities and controlling its functions? Rules are the products of culture, laws are the immutable forms imposed by the unconscious (empty itself) on the workings of
the mind. It is inevitable that Lévi-Strauss focusses his attention on the unconscious. In his efforts to discover its laws, he necessarily turns to linguistics for support. The contents of speech are conscious but its form is not.
Unconsciously the speaker obeys the laws of grammar and phonology.
These laws have been studied by linguists. Yet, language is only one of the
aspects of the human mind and the study of these other aspects, notably
those belonging to the domains of social life and culture, necessarily leads to
the problem of the 'grammar' of human thought in culture. A privileged
field for the study of this 'grammar' is that of those phenomena of culture
which cannot possibly be derived from the activities of conscious deliberation. This does not mean that these phenomena could be characterised as
irrational. On the contrary, rationality is the fundamental property of nature itself. The aspects concerned are those in which spontaneity prevails
and rationalisation, if present at all, bears all the marks of a secondary justification of preconceived ideas. Inviting cases are those of the systems of
classification and of myth, and it is to the investigation of these aspects of

culture that Lévi-Strauss shifted his activities after the completion of his 'Structures élémentaires de la Parenté'.

First of all he turned to the study of classification. The results were laid down in two separate books which both appeared in 1962, viz. 'Le Totémisme aujourd'hui' and 'La Pensée sauvage'. The former, translated by Needham in 1963 and used for references in the present work, is devoted to a specific pattern of classification, that of nature in its relations to mankind. The author points out that the confusion with regard to the concept of totemism is caused by the failure of successive students to put the totemic phenomena in a proper logical context, that of a set of relations between man and nature. "The term totemism covers relations, posed ideologically, between two series, one *natural,* the other *cultural.* The natural series comprises on the one hand *categories,* on the other *particulars;* the cultural series comprises *groups* and *persons*" (Totemism p.16). There are four ways of associating the terms:

	1	2	3	4
NATURE	Category	Category	Particular	Particular
CULTURE	Group	Person	Person	Group

The error consistently committed by all students of totemism is that they confined the use of the term totemism to the cases number 1 (group totemism) and 2 (individual totemism). They failed to note that the particular-person and the particular-group combination should have been included in the same category. As an example of the third combination he refers to "Mota, in the Banks Islands, where a child is thought to be the incarnation of an animal or plant found or eaten by the mother when she first became aware that she was pregnant... The group-particular combination is attested from Polynesia and Africa, where certain animals... are objects of social protection and veneration" (ibid. p.17).

Having successfully clarified the position of totemism as a relational concept, Lévi-Strauss turns to the nature of this relation. He contests that it is one of identity, connecting a group of people with a natural category by ascribing them similar or even identical properties. Of course he does not deny that cases of identification of totemite and totem do occur, but he considers them to be the incipient developments of a caste system. It is not the identity of group and category which is important but the difference between one totem and another, a difference which runs parallel to the difference between the relevant groups. Referring to Radcliffe-Brown who had pointed out that sex- and moiety-totems symbolise a difference in a context of similarity (cf. above, p.188), he argues that not the similarities and identities are important, but the differences. The differences (or contrasts) between the totems are identical with the respective differences (or contrasts) between the groups. Totemism is a system of identical differences, using differences between natural categories to symbolise differences between social groups. The idea has been presented in a schematised form in 'La Pensée sauvage' (p.152):

NATURE : categ. 1 $(\neq)$ categ. 2 $(\neq)$ categ. 3 $(\neq)$ – – – – – – categ. n
CULTURE: group 1 $(\neq)$ group 2 $(\neq)$ group 3 $(\neq)$ – – – – – – group n

When the relations between group and category become so close that the relations between the group and its totem become more important than the differences between one group and another and those between one category and another, the clan system changes into a caste system. As soon as the clan is conceived as identical with its totem, the differences between one clan and another are no longer differences of a similar nature as those between categories, i.e. differences between entities belonging to one and the same order. They become differences which ascribe a different nature to the members of one cultural group and to those of another; in other words, the differences between the groups become so important that the exchange of women between groups is made impossible because the women of one group differ in nature from those of all others and are no longer interchangeable between groups. A caste system develops which can be systematised as follows (ibid. p.155):

| NATURE | category 1 | category 2 | category 3 | category n |
| CULTURE | group 1 | group 2 | group 3 | group n |

The logic of the argument seems imperative. Nevertheless, it is void; it ignores the function of the 'context of similarity' which plays such an important role in the initial part of his theory. What is worse, the ethnographic literature makes mention of many instances of totemism recognising a certain degree of identity of totem and totemite, and nevertheless the number of caste systems is extraordinarily small. The point is that the assertions of native informants, claiming that a clan member is identical with his totem, have always been mistaken for assertions that an identity *in re* was assumed, whereas all the informant had in mind was a functional identity in ritual, based on a specific relation of a religious nature. The Marind-anim are a case in point; they claim a sometimes fairly close similarity between totem and clan member, but the analysis of their cultural institutions gives irrefutable evidence that the differences between members of different clans are not differences *in re*, but differences in ritual function and supernatural relations (Van Baal, Dema pp.958 ff.). The Marind-anim have a system of exogamous clans and the notion of castes is foreign to them. Moreover, the assumption that totemism is primarily a system of differences between groups, parallelling one of differences between categories, is wellnigh inapplicable in cases of multiple totemism. As soon as each clan has more than one totem there is no longer a clear system of differences between categories. The assumption is particularly contestable in the case of the Southern Massim where each clan has for its totems a bird, a snake, a fish and a plant (cf. above, p.47).

The fundamental weakness of Lévi-Strauss' hypothesis is that he based his argument on moiety- and sex-totemism, i.e. on cases of dual division in which a binary opposition is inherent. His model of differences between categories and clans is an elaboration on the model of a dual division. Consequently, categories and groups are arranged in a lineal order in which 3 follows 2 and precedes 4. However, this is not the order in which clans are related to each other. Each clan has relations with every other clan, and these relations can only be schematised by means of the model of an n-sided regular polygon with all the possible diagonals drawn in. Each clan keeps up relations with (n-1) other clans and these relations can only be expressed by identifying clan and totem. Lévi-Strauss' linear model mistakenly restricts the number of relations to two only (cf. Van Baal, Bijdragen 121 p.150).

Another objection which should be raised against Lévi-Strauss' model of totemism is the arrangement of categories and groups under the captions of nature and culture. The relevant opposition is not one of the order of nature to the order of culture which, in Lévi-Strauss' thinking, is one of the order of the unconscious to that of the conscious. It is an opposition of the order of nature to the order of man, of the non-human to the human, correlating the non-human with the human. The dominating dichotomy is that of man and his environment, not that of culture and nature. The introduction of the latter is confusing, substituting concepts borrowed from analytical philosophy for the categories of expressions of vital experiences. Nature, as conceptualised in totemism, is as thoroughly culture as culture itself. The natural categories discerned are cultural categories, products of human classification, a classification opposing the human to the non-human.

Quite another thing is the human effort at classification itself. Totemism is only one of its multifarious forms, which Lévi-Strauss examines in 'La Pensée sauvage'. We shall not dwell for long on those forms of classification, nor on the extreme variability of systems of classification. Lévi-Strauss very successfully demonstrates the identity of the logical principles and procedures applied in these systems, no matter whether these systems derive from primitive cultures or from modern efforts at scientific taxonomy. Human beings are always classifying; even name-giving and the use of proper names in daily parlance appear on analysis to be based on principles of classification. Classifying is an innate necessity; people must organise their experiences and observations into some sort of order lest thought is lost in chaos. From the structural point of view, classification is another proof of "l'exigence de la Règle comme Règle", one of the three structural forms disclosed by the study of the structures of kinship. A closer study of the native knowledge of nature reveals the presence of a real "science du concret", a science of the tangible which, without being overtly or purposively systematised, is all the same a body of systematically ordered knowledge.

And yet, in spite of the structural homogeneity of primitive and modern thought, there is a difference. There must be one; otherwise it would be impossible to explain the stagnation of progress following the neolithic age, which was a period of immense discoveries and decisive developments. The difference which does exist is particularly apparent in myth and ritual, but Lévi-Strauss does not call on any forms of primitive religion to define the nature of this difference. On the contrary, he turns to a phenomenon of frequent occurrence in modern society, that of the 'bricoleur'. 'La pénsée sauvage', 'savage thought'[16] is not specific to 'savages'. It is found among ourselves as well, and the example of the 'bricoleur' serves the double purpose of elucidating a particular way of thought and of manifesting its universality. The point is that there are two distinct modes of scientific thought. The two modes do not belong to unequal stages of the development of the human mind; they occur side by side and represent two divergent, strategic levels from which scientific knowledge directs its attacks on nature, the one quite close to immediate perception and imagination, the other more at a distance (Pensée sauvage pp.24 f.). The former is the strategic level of the 'bricoleur', the latter of the engineer.

We must first of all elucidate the term 'bricoleur'. Unfortunately, the term is untranslatable. The amateur and 'do it yourself' man come pretty near to it, but they do not really express what is typical of the 'bricoleur' as we all know him in each and every part of the modern world, the active constructor of new things by using old odds and ends, the man who dissects his worn-out alarm-clock and carefully stows away its parts, because each of them may serve a purpose. Our 'bricoleur' has quite a collection of parts: they constitute his 'treasure' and he consults this treasure every time he has some design in mind. All these parts can serve various purposes and anything he constructs with them bears the traces of the past on the one hand, of the limitations set by the fortuitous composition of his store of parts on the other. The engineer constructs or orders the parts according to the design he has made, the 'bricoleur' makes his design according to the parts he has in store. The point stressed by Lévi-Strauss is that, to the 'bricoleur', the parts constituting his treasure have a meaning, referring alternately to their past use and to their potential future appliance. They are not just parts, they are also means loaded with potential 'destinations' of all sorts. In other words, these parts are to him things halfway between percept (just parts) and concept (potential means to a future end). In this respect they function as signs, and we are explicitly reminded of the fact that in linguistics a sign

[16] But also *viola tricolor*, popularly known by the names of pansy, hearts-ease and love-in-idleness!

is the combination of an (acoustic) image and a concept (ibid. p.28). The activities of the 'bricoleur' are on the side of the sign, those of the engineer on that of the concept. The concept aims at making reality transparent, whereas the sign adds a stratum of humanity to reality (ibid. p.30).

The introduction of the opposition between sign and concept leads to similar difficulties in regard to the distinction between the signifying and the signified as those discussed on p.197. The author refers to the meaning of the term sign in linguistics. However, in language concepts are incorporated in signs, i.e. in word symbols; one cannot just oppose the concept to its proper sign. The sign-concept used by Lévi-Strauss to signify the activities of the bricoleur, is of another order; it does not belong to the linguistic order but to that of objects. The objects constituting the treasure of the bricoleur are not words, but objects which 'signify' their past usage and potential future destination. The emphasis on the meaning of the term sign in linguistics tends to reduce the distance separating the concept from the sign; concept and sign are presented as different points on one and the same axis, which need not be at a great distance from each other. The presentation fits the idea that we are dealing with two modes of thought which represent divergent strategic levels for the acquisition of scientific knowledge. They serve a common purpose, and in the discussion of the two modes of thought all the emphasis is on the dialectics of their formal differences, whereas very little attention is paid to that difference in content of the two sign-concepts, the linguistic and the bricoleur's, which he himself very aptly formulated when he wrote that the sign (and this time the bricoleur's sign) "accepte, et même exige, qu'une certaine épaisseur d'humanité soit incorporée à cette réalité. Selon l'expression rigoreuse et difficilement traduisible de Peirce: "It addresses somebody" " (ibid. p.30; cf. supra p.204).

The fact that signs and symbols as applied in myth and ritual have an affective component, is duly recognised (Pensée sauvage p.50) but its effect is minimised. Referring to a zoologist's touching description of the human countenance of a dolphin, the author concludes: "Mais, si la taxonomie et l'amitié tendre peuvent faire bon ménage dans la conscience du zoologiste, il n'y a pas lieu d'invoquer des principes séparés, pour expliquer la rencontre de ces deux attitudes dans la pensée des peuples dits primitifs" (ibid. p.53). The logic of the two attitudes is identical, but the materials are different. Those belonging to the attitude of the bricoleur have something in common with a kaleidoscope; the different pieces are of all sorts, just like the parts in the bricoleur's treasure are of all sorts (ibid. p.49). The fragments brought together in myth are of divergent origin, carrying divergent associations, a diversity which is the cause of the apparent contingence of the bricoleur-type of logic. We shall return to this later when we discuss the study of myth; for the moment we simply note that again we are diverted from a study of conscious contents to one of forms which must disclose to us the workings of the unconscious.

205

It is certainly not so that this study of forms is unrewarding. The reader is confronted with an amazing wealth of information on the ordered body of knowledge available in primitive cultures. The order of classification may be surprising from the point of view of our system of classification, it is always a logical order, inspired by the bricoleur's attitude to whom things signify something. The fundamental fact is the signification attributed to nature and its specific phenomena. It has a twofold effect; on the one hand it leads to the humanisation of the laws of nature, and on the other to the naturalisation of human activities. The two are interdependent and inseparable. It is impossible that man ever could "peupler la nature de volontés comparables à la sienne, sans prêter à ses désirs certains attributs de cette nature en laquelle il se reconnaissait" (ibid. pp.291 f.). Considerations of this kind lead the author to the conclusion that religion and magic are inseparable, religion consisting of the humanisation of the laws of nature, and magic of the naturalisation of human activities (ibid. pp.292 f.).

We shall not dwell on the intrinsic value of this distinction between religion and magic. In our opinion it is too clever and too casual to be of any use. We return to Lévi-Strauss who continues his argument with a very lucid demonstration of the incompatibility of sacrifice and totemism. The two belong to very different systems of classification. Although the argument is interesting as well as cogent, we must refrain from discussing it, because it would lead us too far astray, far away from the questions which are aroused by Lévi-Strauss' presentation of the 'bricoleur'-concept. We wish to know why these different peoples so often adopt the attitude of the bricoleur, irrespective of the question whether they are participants in totemic rituals or pious performers of sacrificial acts. Why do they indulge in "une dévorante ambition symbolique" (ibid. p.291), attributing a significance to the phenomena of nature which by far exceeds the limitations of natural conditions? A statement such as the following one, necessarily raises further questions: "La pensée sauvage ne distingue pas le moment de l'observation et celui de l'interprétation, pas plus qu'on n'enregistre... les signes émis par un interlocuteur pour chercher ensuite à comprendre: il parle et l'émission sensible apporte avec elle sa signification" (ibid, pp. 294 f.). The problem is why is significance attributed to the object of the observation. This attribution does not result from the observer's critical interrogation of the object, it is a visionary's reaction, the projection of an act of recognition of some human element. And how does the projection acquire such a sense of reality that its result is embraced as an expedient to further interpretation? The question should be made more specific: why is the projection accepted in one case and rejected in the other? Even among the most primitive people the attributive mode of thinking goes hand in hand with the scientific. The attitude of the bricoleur and that of the engineer exist side by side in each and every individual. There must be a reason that the individual at one moment adopts the one attitude, and then again the other.

206

Although the two attitudes occur side by side in every culture, it is evident that the bricoleur's attitude is more important in the technically less developed cultures. We feel inclined to surmise that there must be a correlation between the approach of the bricoleur and an apparent lack of scientific knowledge. The body of knowledge available in primitive society may be more comprehensive than is often thought, it was certainly not the intention of Lévi-Strauss to deny its relative poverty. Actually, the metaphor of the bricoleur suggests poverty. He must make do with odds and ends, derived from the remains of his well-worn possessions because he cannot afford to buy the really adequate materials. The native suffering from a lack of knowledge is in a similar position. However, at this point the relevance of the metaphor breaks down. The poor bricoleur of modern society who makes do with old odds and ends acts as a sensible man: he takes the only possible way leading to the fulfilment of his desire. It is different with the native who adopts the bricoleur's attitude when confronted with a lack of knowledge. Instead of projecting significance into the objects of his search, he should try to acquire more adequate knowledge by interrogating them, i.e. by adopting the engineer's attitude. Although the bricoleur's attitude does not exclude the possibility of acquiring more and adequate knowledge, the progress made along this way is slow, much slower than if he had accepted the engineer's attitude. Again we must ask why, the more certainly so because every individual adopts one of the two attitudes in turn, and we should know why he now prefers the one and then again the other.

Lévi-Strauss does not even try to give an answer. The implicit correlation between lack of knowledge (poverty) and the bricoleur's attitude is not submitted to further questioning. His preoccupation is with the unconscious components of structure. Nevertheless, the questions raised are legitimate and we shall return to them when we have finished the discussion of Lévi-Strauss' study of myth.

The foundation of structure in the unconscious leads almost of necessity to the study of myth. Of all products of the human mind, myth is the most fantastic, the least ruled by reason or conscious deliberation, and the nearest to the motions of the unconscious. Whereas the structures of kinship may in part be co-determined by extraneous causes, in particular by the exigencies of the institutionalised forms of social life, myth stands apart from the necessities of daily practice. Myth is a product of spontaneous creation and if its apparent freedom and arbitrariness can be shown to be subject to laws operating at a deeper level, the conclusion is inescapable "que si l'esprit humain apparaît déterminé jusque dans ses mythes, alors *a fortiori* il doit l'être partout" (Le Cru et le Cuit p.18).

The rules incumbent on myth must be of a nature comparable to the laws of language. They remain unconscious to the speaker or 'raconteur'; if in the course of his exposition he consciously tried to apply the relevant laws of grammer and phonology, he would immediately lose the thread of his story. That story, if a myth, has a structure, a superstructure superimposed on the structures of language. The object of the enquiry is to define the nature of this superstructure, a task which Lévi-Strauss concisely formulates as follows: "Nous ne prétendons donc pas montrer comment les hommes pensent dans les mythes, mais comment les mythes se pensent dans les hommes, et à leur insu" (ibid. p.20). *À leur insu,* outside their knowledge, that means that the object of the investigation is not the conscious content of the myth as such, but the unconscious rules followed in its structure. The myth-producing process must be disclosed by the systematic comparison of transpositions in mutually related myths and in this context the bold expression must be understood that, up to an extent, "les mythes se pensent entre eux" (ibid.). In fact, the expression is not as risky as it seems to be, because a myth has no author, at least not one who is known.

Lévi-Strauss describes his method in an essay of 1955, republished in "Anthropologie Structurale" under the caption "La Structure des Mythes". Each myth must be dissected in its elements, i.e. in short phrases consisting of a subject and a predicate, in other words a relation. These elements are combined in small 'packets' of cohesive relations. These 'packets' are the gross units which must be compared with the gross units of all the different variants of the dissected myth, and subsequently with those derived from the dissection of all the other myths considered to belong to the same family of myths. The various combinations of the gross units, the frequency of their occurrence, the shifts and inversions noted in the occurrence of various combinations, are now open to examination. To that end the use of a computer is a necessity, because the number of the gross units and their possible combinations rapidly multiplies when the number of the examined myths increases. The examination discloses what happens to the various combinations of gross units when a myth or a mythical motive is transferred from one group of people to another, when the message conveyed by the myth is altered or a change takes place in the composition of the *dramatis personae* of the plot. Taking the myths of Oedipus and his lineage as an example, he demonstrates that in the various transmutations of the myth a certain order prevails, although it is an order which is refractory to formulation in more general terms. The kind of order can best be demonstrated by means of another example given in this early essay, the comparison of the European tale of Cinderella and its American Indian counterpart, the story of Ashboy. The two stories convey the same message, the acquisition of fortune by a poor adolescent through the intervention of a supernatural agency. The two stories are each other's completely inverted parallels, and in this case there is no indication of a historical connection. However, the parallelism suggests that if one term is changed, all the other terms follow suit:

	Cinderella	*Ashboy*
sex	female	male
family relations	has a stepmother	is an orphan
appearance	a nice girl in dirty clothes	a forbidding appearance
social situation	nobody loves her	crossed in love
change by supernatural aid	receives a magnificent attire	acquires an attractive appearance

The conclusive force of these examples is weak of course, and in the "Mythologiques" Lévi-Strauss makes an effort at a comprehensive demonstration of the structural regularities in the transpositions of mythical themes. So far three volumes have appeared, "Le Cru et le Cuit" (1964), "Du Miel aux Cendres" (1967) and "l'Origine des Manières de Table" (1968). The author leads the reader from one myth to another through a gradually enlarging universe of ever new transformations of old themes. In the first two volumes he concentrates on South American mythology without limiting himself exclusively to this area. Sometimes the mythology of the Old World is drawn into consideration as well. In the third volume the field is extended to North American mythology and we must await where the next one will lead us to. It is impossible to give a review of this remarkable work, a monument of competence and professional craftsmanship on the one hand; of the evasive and enigmatic character of myth and mythological systems on the other. The work is primarily a reconnaissance in a vast and thorny field where the view is obstructed at every step. Actually, it raises more problems than it solves, and the author is well aware of it. One of these problems is the extremely wide spread of astronomic constellations and the myths connected with them. The parallels demonstrated in the relevant section of "Le Cru et le Cuit" (l'Astronomie bien tempérée) are baffling, and even more baffling are the inversions of the functions of the various characters in opposing hemispheres.

The inversions are, in fact, the one and only phenomenon which can be subsumed under a general rule which I, reluctantly, reformulate as follows: if, from one myth to another, the plot remains the same and the component actors change, the message is inverted. The formula as given by Lévi-Strauss is more general but also more evasive: Quand on passe d'un mythe à l'autre, *l'armature* (un ensemble de propriétés qui restent invariantes dans deux ou plusieurs mythes) se maintient, *le code* (le système des fonctions assignées par chaque mythe à ces propriétés) se transforme, et *le message* (le contenu d'un mythe particulier) s'inverse (Le Cru p. 205). I shall not try to translate this; instead I take the example given on pp.320/21 (Le Cru) and relate it in a very condensed form. We are dealing with two myths, the one of two old men who pull down the nest of an eagle (a carnivore), the other of a man and his wife's young brother who pull down the nest of a parrot (a fructivore). In both cases the one who climbs the tree (an old man and the young brother-in-law respectively) is left by his companion when he has reached the top of the tree, without being able to descend. The old man is set free by an eagle, the young man by a jaguar. The story of the old men concludes with the explanation of the origin of the different colours of birds (a natural asset), that of the two brothers-in-law with that of fire and the roasting of food (a cultural asset). The plot (pulling down nests on top of a tree where the nestler is left helpless) is the same, but the personnel (two old agemates and two brothers-in-law of different age, nests of a carnivore and of a fructivore respectively) changes, and the message is inverted (from nature to culture or inversely).

In other respects the data are evasive, so evasive that Lévi-Strauss decided that he had to construct the composition of his work on the model of a complicated musical composition. Hereto however, Lévi-Strauss was motivated by other reasons besides; a little while ago the reader's attention was directed to the structure of the tales of Cinderella and Ashboy. The nearest parallel to this case of parallel inversion is that of the inversion of a musical theme. To Lévi-Strauss the equation is essential. He points out that music and myth have much in common. They have a specific connection with time: every myth refers to a mythical past irreversibly gone by, and yet reciting a myth brings the past to new life again and confirms its eternal presence; in music time is irrevocably diachronic and irreversible, and yet listening to music conveys an experience of timelessness in which the progress of time has been immobilised. "Tout se passe comme si la musique et la mythologie n'avaient besoin du temps que pour lui infliger un démenti. L'une et l'autre sont, en effet, des machines à supprimer le temps" (Le Cru p.24).

Music and myth have a mysterious power over man. Reciting a myth is often accompanied by music and chant, evoking rhythmic corporeal reactions. The rhythmic corporeal movements provoked by music are too well known to need comment. The mythical material of a society is a selection of a limited number of events from a theoretically unlimited series of historical or quasi-historical occurrences; a society's musical material is a selection of tones, a gamut, taken from a theoretically equally unlimited series of physically realisable tones. Myth and music both affect the listener emotionally and strongly stir his feelings. Everybody is capable of experiencing their effect. Nevertheless, a myth has no known author and only very few people are able to compose a piece of music. The pertinent similarity of myth and music is not in the production or in the performance, but in listening. When listening to a myth or to music man receives a message about himself: "la musique se vit en moi, je m'écoute à travers elle. Le mythe et l'oeuvre musicale apparaissent ainsi comme des chefs d'orchestre dont les auditeurs sont les silencieux exécutants... La musique et la mythologie confrontent l'homme à des objets virtuels dont l'ombre seule est actuelle, à des approximations conscientes... de vérités inéluctablement inconscientes et qui leur sont consécutives" (Le Cru pp.25,26).

At this point we must end our attempts to synthesise the main points of Lévi-Strauss' ideas on myth. It is a point at which we may well ask where Lévi-Strauss has taken us to. Simonis gives a definite answer to this question: to a philosophy of aesthetics, not a philosophy of science. Listening to music as a 'silencieux exécutant', Lévi-Strauss again turns to the unconscious. "La musique réalise le renversement de perspective que poursuit le structuralisme et cette réussite est sa supériorité sur le langage" (Simonis p.297).

The text quoted from Lévi-Strauss is a remarkable one; the statement "des objets virtuels dont l'ombre seule est actuelle.... approximations conscientes.... de vérités inéluctablement inconscientes", could as well be used as the point of departure for a philosophy of religion as for one of aesthetics. Simonis uses the text as proof of a passion for the unconscious, for the return to silence. We would prefer to put it differently. Here, music has been substituted for religion, in the expectation that it will yield the peace to the soul which in St. Matthew (11:20) is promised to the meek and the lowly in heart. It must be noted that while music can have a religious function, religion and music are not interchangeable. They move in opposite directions; in religion man is in search of a foundation for his own unfoundedness; in music he takes off in a flight which carries him up from his ground where sooner or later he must return. The difference can be summarised, but not in every language. It can in German as it can in Dutch, but for reasons of courtesy I will use German: the former is "eine grundsuchende Ungegrundheit", the latter "eine grundfliehende Grundgebundenheit".

These diversions in dialectics do not bring us much further. We must return to myth and to the amazing regularities reported by Lévi-Strauss, in particular to his statement that, if the 'armature' does not change, but the 'code' does, the message is inverted. Is this really a model of an unconscious structure? I doubt it, and I doubt it very sincerely. Inversion is one of the more obvious means of giving expression to the fact that there is a difference in identity. The Marind-anim consciously make use of inversion in their mythology and ritual to express a combination of similarity and difference, identity and contrast (cf. Van Baal, Dema pp.320, 665 and 926 f.). Actually, it is difficult to imagine a simpler method of indicating that something out-of-the-ordinary plays a part than by inverting the ordinary. Inversion is a means of indicating the extra-normal which is attached to or hidden behind the normal, because it draws the attention to the deviance without conceptualising its nature. This is an important point because in religion we are always dealing with notions which can hardly be conceptualised. Notions referring to a reality which cannot be verified are by their nature refractory to conceptualisation. Signs, symbols must take the place of concepts. Inversion is such a sign, and the mere possibility that it can be applied consciously leads us back to a question raised earlier in this chapter, viz. how unconscious is the unconscious? How unconscious *inter alia* are the laws of grammar and phonology?

There is every reason for raising the question in this context, that of the transmutations taking place in the form and content of a myth in the process of its diffusion. Why is a myth borrowed? Lévi-Strauss does not try to answer this question, because he is too much interested in the unconscious components of the process to pay much attention to its conscious aspects. Yet, the question is legitimate. The fact that many mythical themes are widespread and that in many cases their diffusion is clearly a matter of borrowing, has important consequences, the most obvious among them being that the spontaneity of myth apparently is subject to severe limitations. It is a curious coincidence that the answer to our question why myths are borrowed can be borrowed from Lévi-Strauss himself. The metaphor of the bricoleur is a very enlightening one. Primitive man is, indeed, a bricoleur. Hampered by a lack of knowledge for understanding the proper workings of his universe, he eagerly accepts any new means which he deems fit to clarify his situation. This is exactly what a myth does; however abstruse, a myth gives a solution to a problem. The bricoleur has to make do with whatever comes to his hands and this is what primitive man does with mythical themes which happen to come his way. This is most pertinently true of myths and representations concerning astronomical constellations. Three years of emprisonment in the tropics have brought home to me what the night means to primitive man; when there is a moon, everything is all right but half the time there is only the starlit sky. That sky is a challenging problem. The multitude of stars constitutes an utterly unstructured whole, calling for some sort of order which nobody can give except the expert who knows the constellations. How utterly arbitrary most of these constellations were to me, a few of them excepted such as the Southern Cross, Orion, or the Pleiades. And yet, how rewarding that somebody knows his way in this challenging chaos of stars, and brings order in this confusing multitude. Order means sense, even if this sense is nonsense. It is always better than no sense at all.

Of course, this observation does not solve the challenging problems of the homologies of astronomical constellations so pertinently singled out by Lévi-Strauss. The purport of this observation lies elsewhere, viz. in the part which should be admitted to conscious deliberation in any study of myth and ritual. Turning away from conscious motivation to unconscious structures, Lévi-Strauss over-emphasises the part of the unconscious and neglects the contributions of culture and conscious life. Actually, the notion of the unconscious is a dangerous notion which ought to be tabooed. As a reification of the laws governing man's spiritual life, the notion of the unconscious necessarily leads to mystifications. It did so with Jung, up to an extent it does so to-day even with Lévi-Strauss. Of course there are laws regulating the activities and expressions of the human mind. Why should we reify them by calling them the unconscious instead of just trying to find out what these laws are by tracking down the regularities? The unconscious is rather an unmanageable metaphor. It is a nothing, because — by definition — it has no content. A quest for structure can only be a quest for law. To the end of this quest we still are groping our way. 'Les Règles de la Méthode structuraliste' are yet unwritten; for the time being we must make do with examples, some of which — notably among those given by Lévi-Strauss — have paradigmatic value. We still are at the beginning of a long line of research and there is little certainty on the road to be followed. The one thing we know for certain, and which after all my previous criticism should be emphasised, is that as Simonis said in the first line of his book: you cannot study Lévi-Strauss without being transformed. You need not agree but you do not escape untouched.

One of those who did not escape untouched is Edm. Leach. His recent book, "Lévi-Strauss" (1970), is a noteworthy and stimulating contribution to the study of myth. An anthropologist who tried to keep aloof from structuralism is V. W. Turner. Yet, there is more substantial proof of Lévi-Strauss' influence in Turner's "The ritual Process" (1969) than does appear from the book's sub-title, "Structure and Anti-structure." Equally evident is Lévi-Strauss' influence in Mary Douglas' stimulating book "Purity and Danger" (1966).

Our final question must be what structuralism has contributed to the study of religion. The answer is necessarily ambiguous. It contributed little in so far as it neglected the problem by confining itself to the study of religious phenomena as cases of the formal categories created by the structures of the human mind. Yet, it contributed substantially to our understanding by demonstrating the structured nature of the workings of the mind, and by pointing out that a man's universe is a signifying universe, signifying to its signifyer. We are thrown back on the problem of man.

213

X

The human foundations of religion

1. *The major characteristics of religion*

Many anthropologists acknowledge that little progress has been made in anthropological theory of religion during the last fifty years. A few years ago Geertz complained that it is in a state of stagnation (A.S.A. Monographs nr.3 p.1). Actually, every student of anthropology is aware of it. If he asks for more information about religion and religious motivations, he is invariably referred to theories and sources of half a century ago, always with the reminder that he should read them critically because on many points these theories are open to question. And yet, we may ask whether it is fair to put it that way. We are much better informed on the variety of religious forms than fifty years ago. We have learned to keep our distance from bold theoretical concepts and daring explanations, and we have arrived at a certain degree of consensus on many topics. It is worth while to make a modest effort to enumerate some of the most significant points.

A major trend in studies of religion is the abandonment of attempts to explain religion from transitory historical incidents and circumstances. There is full agreement to-day on the deep truth of De Brosses' statement that it is not in eventualities but in man himself that man must be studied (cf. above, p.13). It would be wrong to conclude from the fact that the statement is 200 years old, that we have made no progress at all. De Brosses, who formulated the principle, was unable to apply it. He was the first to indulge in historical speculations of a dubious kind. Even Tylor who a hundred years later quoted De Brosses' statement as a motto on the front page of his "Primitive Culture", did not manage to steer clear of the charybdis of conjectural history. Modern students of religion are better placed to give content to the adagium. Relying on a vastly increased knowledge of man, they may profoundly differ in their opinions of the value of religion, its importance and its origin, yet they are one in accepting that it has its foundation in the human mind or condition.

Another point on which there is fairly general agreement is that religious representations tend to be concerned with the society at large as well as with the surrounding universe. Cosmological concepts in particular are predominantly of a religious nature. Even where clear cosmological concepts are poorly developed or absent, we still find scattered references to diverse parts of the universe in the prevalent religious concepts or symbols. The apparent lack of systematisation of these references does not imply that an interest in the universe is absent. On the contrary, the facts give sufficient ground for the conclusion that, to a greater or lesser extent, a people's religion is always interconnected with its total (i.e. social and physical) universe.

When we turn to the actual forms of religion, we note that those most general are the belief in spirits and souls, and the tendency to represent the manifestations of the supernatural in a personified form. We find them wherever there is religion. The belief in an impersonal supernatural power — mana, magic — is not a belief which stands apart from the belief in spiritual and personal beings. Mana is rather a term for the power of these personified manifestations of the supernatural than a belief in some independent and blind power floating in or over the universe. The often highly pragmatic nature of mana (cf. above, p.66) is a serious warning against substantialising it as a metaphysical entity. Mana is in all those personal beings who together animate the universe, many of them leading a shady existence, whereas others have developed into clearly defined characters, well known through myth and oral tradition. Mana is a concept, taken from religious systems abounding with personal supernatural beings; the concept should not be divorced from this context.

An interesting point is that mana may also be the property of human beings. However, not of everyone; it is only the selected few who have mana. It is different with the soul. Practically everywhere human beings are supposed to have a soul. All religions, Buddhism included, concur in ascribing to man a soul, a life-principle or whatever it may be called, but anyhow something which survives its owner's death. A man or woman need not have mana, but a soul of some sort they have. In other words, there is something in man which essentially, or at least ultimately, belongs to the realm of the supernatural. This supernatural something in man need not be activated during his lifetime, but it certainly is at his death. By the simple (but decisive) fact of dying, man enters the realm of the supernatural and he enters it through something which is in him or part of him — at any rate something inseparably his own.

The ultimate connection with the supernatural substantiated by the soul-concept stands in sharp contrast to the experience of the supernatural as the quite other, *das Ganz Andere,* the sacred which is usually defined as the separate and forbidden. In our comment on this definition of the sacred we pointed out that it should be reformulated as "ce qui est séparé et recherché ou enfui" (above, p.124).

Actually, the fact that the soul-concept creates a direct connection be-

215

tween man and the separate sacred had already been noted by Durkheim (ibid. pp.119 and 124), but he did not pay attention to the conceptual contradiction it implied. The important point to him was that man's direct participation in the sacred provides an explanation of his concern for it, a concern which would be inexplicable if the sacred were only separate and forbidden. However, once it has been conceded that there is something in man which belongs to the realm of the sacred, the separateness of the sacred is seriously affected. How can what is part of one's innermost being be separate as well? And yet it is undeniable that everything sacred is separate; the religious experience and behaviour of all peoples confirm that the sacred must be approached with the greatest circumspection and awe. The sacred is different and dangerous, it belongs to a wholly different order and it is taboo. Nevertheless it must be sought and revered. The separateness and forbidding nature of the sacred are evident; we simply have to accept this as a fact. The contradiction is unsoluble; in spite of its forbidding sublimity there is also something sacred in man, giving him access to what is separate and forbidden.

Man's participation in the sacred is not only a matter of the belief in a soul. It is manifest too in his surprising knowledge of the hidden powers ruling his universe, the powers whom he addresses and influences by word and action in the numerous rites called magic, the simple rites performed with a concrete end in view. To a certain extent this knowledge is the privilege of the few who cultivate and increase it by fasting, dreaming and shamanistic exercise, activities which bring them into immediate contact with these powers. Through personal contact man receives their advice and acquires knowledge of their will. The means applied are not restricted to dream and vision; prayer, divination, trance and inspiration should be mentioned as being of equal importance. Here again the personification of the representations of the sacred must be emphasised. The sacred is encountered in a personal form. It is also a personal form by which man addresses these powers. Quite apart from the question whether or not magic is based on a concept of supernatural power, the study of the spells accompanying the magical act gives convincing evidence that the powers conjured or invoked are represented either in a personal form, or as the personifications of a something, or at the very least as if the something were a person. The object of the act is addressed, and addressing the object means that the object is placed in an interpersonal context. The personification need not go far, it need not be developed into more accomplished forms, but a tinge of personification is the inescapable effect of the simple act of addressing.

The tendency towards personification implies a tendency towards the humanisation of the representations of the sacred. Although the result may be frightening, nevertheless the fact that the personified sacred can be addressed makes the power more human; contact is evidently possible if not preconceived. Religious acts are practically always accompanied by some

216

forms of address: to put it in a more homely way, man always talks with the manifestations of the supernatural. It is a well-known fact which cannot easily be contested; yet it was rarely given the attention it deserves. To mention only one thing (we will have to revert to it later), the trend to converse with the manifestations of the supernatural implies not only a humanisation of the supernatural but, through it, a shortening of the distance which separates man from the sacred. Again we find that the sacred is not as perfectly separate as the definition says. There is an ineluctable tendency to overcome the separation, as ineluctable apparently as the tendency to maintain or even to enlarge the distance. From whatever angle we look at it, we are always thrown back on contradictions similar to those highlighted by the act of sacrifice, a communion, but a communion by means of a substitute which is made a victim.

These contradictions are not restricted to the notion of the sacred and the relations between man and the sacred; they are also characteristic of the manifestations of the sacred themselves. All the personifications of the supernatural are janus-faced, again a phenomenon which is well-known, but one rarely remembered outside a psycho-analytic context. Gods and spirits are one in that they can both help and harm, be good and bad, kind and angry, and all this either at the same time or alternately.

This duplicity is veiled because some of the gods (and spirits) are conceived of as predominantly kind and helpful, others as mainly harmful and bad. Yet, there is not one who is not dangerous, and among the dangerous even the most vicious may at times be inclined to be helpful. This dualism is so fundamental a characteristic of the gods that even a consequent categorisation of the gods into a dual opposition of good and bad cannot deprive them of their innate duality. In Christian theology we are confronted with the contrast between God's love and God's wrath, and the fear of the latter cannot be reduced without degrading the former to indifference. The contrast between the two is more important then the one between God and Satan, seemingly one of the absolute good and the absolute evil, but in fact a pertinent contradiction theologically. God and Satan are not equals; God alone is omnipotent and Satan is the subordinate. His mere existence immediately raises the problem of theodicy, usually solved by interpreting the divine permission to let Satan have his way as an opportunity for the manifestation of the magnitude of God's loving mercy in Christ. The solution leads us back to the contrast between divine love and wrath. Under these circumstances it is small wonder that theology did not make much of Satan. It is quite different with popular belief of former times which took delight in depicting his tricks and wiles. It is of specific interest that in these stories Satan is not really as bad and black as he is painted; though the price is high, those who prefer the temporal pleasures of sin to the bliss of eternal life can come to terms with him.

217

Any effort to explain the problems religion presents to our understanding shall have to take into account the contradictions mentioned in the preceding pages. They are fundamental, inherent in the religious forms and representations in all their major apparitions. In fact, the contradictory character of religion does not come as a surprise. We defined religion as all explicit and implicit notions and ideas, accepted as true, which relate to a reality which cannot be verified empirically (above, p.3). Commenting on it (ibid. pp.4 f.) we drew attention to the absurdity of religion. The contradictory nature of its various forms corroborates the absurdity of the belief in an unverifiable reality, a belief altogether too universal to be called abnormal, and too deviant to neglect its challenge. If we wish to explain the problems of religion, even such thorny problems as the belief in the efficacy of magic and in the truth of such unbelievable stories as those presented by myth, we shall have to forget, at least temporarily, the problems for *the* problem: the foundation of a belief in an unverifiable reality. Any effort to explain religion by starting from some specific form is necessarily void. Our primary problem is the fact of religion, i.e. the belief in an unverifiable reality, not the specific forms of religion which vary from one culture to another. Of course, the variations are important too, and the belief in the efficacy of magic and witchcraft certainly calls for an explanation, but the explanation of specific phenomena should never be divorced from that of the founding phenomenon, i.e. the more or less universal belief in the existence and influence of a reality which cannot be verified empirically. The European missionary who opposes the religious representations of his potential converts, shares with them the belief in such a non-verifiable reality. This is the point which must have primacy.

Concentrating our attention on the most general characteristic of religion it is important to know whether this characteristic is of universal occurrence, in other words whether religion is a universal. Since Tylor most anthropologists have accepted the universality of religion as a fact. Religion is a phenomenon found in every culture and society and as long as we define a universal as a cultural element recurring in every culture, religion must be called a universal. Nevertheless, the evidence presented by Western civilisation raises doubts as to the adequacy of this definition of a universal. In every modern country the number of individuals repudiating every form of religion is rapidly increasing. In the communist countries the practice of religion is discouraged or even condemned, and apparently with considerable success — even though it has not led to the disappearance of religion. The allegation that stressing circumstances may cause freethinkers to relapse into some form or other of religious practice, is a weak argument for refuting the obvious truth that a great many people manage to live without indulging in any form of religion.

We might call irreligiosity a characteristic of modern civilisation, but the statement is somewhat dubious in the light of the fact that a few primitive

218

cultures are known in which the role of religion is a fairly modest one. Hans Fischer described such a group (a Kukukuku community in the Territory of Papua) in his book "Negwa" (1968). The people concerned certainly are not irreligious and the same holds true of other similar communities, but all the same the way of life of these societies confirms that even on a low level of cultural development religious practice and belief (so-called magic included) need not always have the importance which is usually ascribed to them. Moreover, freethinkers are to be found in various preliterate societies; in the course of this book we came across the cases of Quesalid (above, p.199) and of the village aberrant of Dobu (ibid. p.180). The missionary Alb. C. Kruyt makes mention of a freethinking chief among the Toradja (Van Heiden tot Christen pp.45 f., 86).

All the evidence tends to confirm that religion is a very general phenomenom, but that it really is a universal seems disputable to us. Of course, the universality of religion could be maintained by changing our definition, for example by calling religion all that pertains to notions or concepts of ultimate reality. We would lose more than we win that way. By extending the concept we definitely sacrifice the recognition of a clearly and operationally defined category of human action for a broad philosophical concept which by its intellectuality obliterates all the specificity of the religious. In other words, the wider definition safeguards the universal applicability of a term by forsaking its content. The study of religion is poorly served by such a procedure.

As it is dubious whether religion, taken in its proper sense, really is a universal, any direct relation between religion and a hereditary feature of the human race should be excluded. Yet, religion is an extremely widespread phenomenon. Religious groups and beliefs are found in every society, including those where religious manifestations are disapproved of or forbidden by the ruling authorities. Religion is found on every level of cultural development, and everywhere its more prominent features are characterised by ambivalence and contradictions. All things considered there is every reason for supposing that there is a link between the contradictory nature of the more prominent manifestations of religion and some basic contradiction or ambiguity in the human condition, i.e. in the existential conditions of human life generally. We must make an enquiry into these conditions.

2. The fundamental contradiction of the human condition

The distinctive feature of the human race is the faculty of man to express and store his experiences by means of symbols. The symbols materialise, substantiate as it were, his experiences and give them a more enduring form. Symbols make these experiences transferable; every individual can communicate them to others, thus reproducing his experiences in a sharply defined form. The remarkable story of Helen Keller (above, p.158) is a good illustration of the immense significance of the fact that everything has a name, that everything can be symbolised. Through language man has acquired a firm grip on reality; he can memorise, communicate and discuss his experiences at any time and place, regardless of the situation in which the experiences were made. Symbols make experiences 'translatable'. They can be reproduced. This implies that these experiences are also reified, at least up to an extent. They have a tangible form which turns them into objects of consideration and discussion. When the symbols are written down the object-character becomes even more prominent. A word can be changed or the word-order modified; we ponder on the use of a particular word. However, in principle the same is the case with the spoken word; by putting the symbols into writing we only enhance that specific object-character of the word-symbol which is already present in the spoken word. The word objectifies the experience. To a being able to reify his experiences in symbols, reality acquires a new dimension. It is no longer restricted to the immediacy of the actual experience; the experience, i.e. the experienced reality, can be taken along in the shape of symbols to be made the object of memory, speech, discussion, analysis and thought where and whenever the symboliser wills.

There are always these two, the symbol and the symboliser, i.e. the symbolising subject who deals with his symbols, the symbolised reality, as objects. The opposition of subject and object is the primary result of symbolising. The two poles of the opposition are incongruous. The objects are infinitely numerous, ever alternating with each other in unabated succession; the subject is always the same, ever identical with himself in uninterrupted perpetuity. The subject is unique and timeless, the object one out of many and temporal. The symbolising subject's experience of himself is that of a self, totally different from his world, the world of objects. Everything symbolised turns automatically into an object, an object of speech or thought, of action or discussion, but always object and other than the self. The opposition between the self and the other is not restricted to the interaction between humans; it is fundamental to every form of human experience.

Reflection on the uniqueness of the subject and the otherness of his world leads to the traumatic discovery that the self stands alone in his uniqueness and timelessness, separated from the world of objects by an unbridgeable gap. The subject recognises himself as the lonely observer on the bank of the stream of events speeding oceanwards one or two yards below his feet. Or he sees himself as the man at the assembly-belt which slowly carries onwards, taking with it the result of his activity, a result which he shall never see again. The subject is really lonely; nobody has or can have access to his unique experience of himself as different from and opposed to his world of objects, his universe. Even when conditions are reversed and the subject considers his death, the effacing of his identity in and by an inexorable, permanent world, the opposition remains. He still is his own self, which is always identical with itself, and in this identity of a timelessness of a wholly different order than that of the permanency and perpetuity of his world.

However, the individual is not only a subject. He is also part and parcel of his universe. He interacts with his universe and he knows quite well that he is part of it. He does not need the confirmation of others that he is part on the ground that they observe him as part of their own universe. Actually, such affirmation is not important and even misleading because, if he only were part in the observation of others, he would be part as the object of the observation of others. Instead, he is part in his own right, through his interaction with his universe. The fact is so fundamental that it cannot possibly escape anyone's notice. Man is so much part of his universe that he can justifiably be described as its product. Human existence depends on a very specific combination of ecological conditions with a very narrow allowance of variation. Temperature and the composition of the air must conform to highly specific requirements. Without a variety of minerals including water no form of life is possible. At every step the law of gravitation reminds us that we belong to our world. We cannot escape from the earth and the few who made an excursion to the moon did so by means of extremely complicated machinery of which every detail confirmed man's utter dependence on earthly conditions. There can be no doubt about the fact that man in general, and every individual in particular, is part of his universe. Individuals exist only as parts, participating in the life of their universe. Participating is a must; even the most obstinate individualist plays a part in his universe, whether he wills or not. The reality of the universe of which every man constitutes a part flatly contradicts the justifiability of the loneliness and utter unrelatedness which follow from his symbolising activity. Yet, as a subject everyone is unique and separate. The individual may discover all the arguments confirming that he really is and makes part of his universe, but the thinking of these arguments is a process in which the awareness of the otherness of his universe increases with the acuity of his thinking. Thinking, and in particular analytic thinking is not an act of participation but of detachment and dissociation, a process affirming the distance between the subject and his world, between the self and the other. Reflecting on his universe the subject is not one with his world (the terms world and universe are used as synonyms) but more than his world, judging it, thinking about it: a timeless entity viewing the transitory and passing.

In the loftiness of his aloofness the subject is a non-entity. Experiencing himself as timeless he knows that he is mortal; judging his world he knows he is nothing without it. The unrelated, isolated subject is senseless and meaningless, a space-traveller who missed his target and faces nothingness. Psychologically the withdrawal of the subject from his universe is negatively valued and rejected as alienation, estrangement and loneliness. On the other hand, in neoplatonic and medieval mysticism full participation with one's universe is associated with supernatural joy, bliss, the *summum bonum.* Full participation is the unattainable ideal, the state of alienation an ever lurking danger. There is no way back to paradise for he who ate from the tree of knowledge.

So far we have emphasised the alienating effect resulting from man's symbolising action. The effect may be called forth by misfortune and ill-luck, but its full realisation is a matter of reflecting, of pondering upon one's fate. Reflection is a dangerous activity. "In jeder Reflexion als solcher, in aller rationalen Einstellung liegt eine Tendenz zur Auslösung, Relativie-rung dessen, worüber reflektiert wird" says Jaspers, supporting his state-ment with a selection of quotations taken from Hegel which are all one in admonishing against the disintegrating power of rational reflection (Jas-pers, Psychologie der Weltanschauungen pp.287 f.). Why exactly is reflec-tion so dangerous? Reflection is an inner process, and in this process sym-bols need not necessarily take the clear and fairly rigid forms which they have in spoken language. If our analysis were exact we should expect alien-ation to obtrude strongest where the symbolising activity is at its best, viz. in a discussion. This is not what happens, and there is a sound reason for it. In the first place, reflection is an act of introversion in which the subject addresses his own self. Turning his back to the world he can hardly expect to discover his partnership with his world. And in the second place, sym-bolising is a means of expression. This is an aspect of language of which we were reminded by Cassirer (above, p.160). Expression is not an act per-formed in a void, certainly not in the case of a discussion. What is true of expression during a discussion is true of every form of expression: when expressing himself man acts in a universe, of which he is part and of whose action the component parts take notice. Symbolising his experience in words man acts as part of his universe, projecting himself towards his universe, communicating his experience to it, and evoking its reactions. Symbolising is not merely an act of objectifying, it is also one of communication. The position is dialectical through and through. The means of communication at man's disposal are also the cause of his alienation; the source of his estrange-ment is also the highroad to interhuman contact and participation. We must refer here to what we wrote in section 3 of Ch. VII: "Expression is never complete or perfect; there is always something just beyond. The necessity to express is counteracted by the necessity to conceal" (above, p.162).

The question arises whether it really is the pursuit of concealment which hampers communication, or the impossibility for the subject of giving up being a subject, another than others. Giving up being a subject is not a real possibility. Although we say of some people that they throw themselves away or that they make themselves dirt-cheap, these objects of our censure did not for a moment stop acting as subjects. What is described as a loss of subjectivity is in effect primarily a loss of meaningful participation. The slaves of drugs and passion have this in common with the slaves of political or economic systems of exploitation, that they never become objects or slaves in every respect; they all have their secret thoughts which they keep to themselves.

Really giving up being a subject would mean giving up having secret thoughts. The one way to this end is perfect openness, permitting everyone to see through all the corners of one's inner life by publicly turning oneself inside out, an utter impossibility because nobody ever managed to penetrate into the core of his own inner life; the known self always being the object of the knowing self, the real subject perennially retires from observation, even from observation by the self, let alone by others. The other way (equally impossible) is that of giving up symbolising, a return to silence or, in Lévi-Strauss' terms, to the unconscious. The way nearest to it is that of mystic unification, the surrender of the soul to his God, to the One, to the universe, usually described as a process in which the soul, merging with the Other, is depleted of its subjectivity. Although there is no doubt that the experience affects the individual to the core of his heart, we may well doubt the correctness of an interpretation which stresses the individual's depletion of subjectivity. The positive aspect, that of an experience of oneness and participation, seems to us more important than the negative aspect of depletion. It is a state of mind consciously pursued by the subject and the experience itself is destined to remain a highly personal one of a strictly subjective nature, later remembered with gratitude as a temporary state of grace and election, a comfort for the subject in periods when he is forlorn. Unfortunately, the experience is short-lived and because of its extreme subjectivity its veridity (the depletion of the subject) is open to doubt.

The positive and concrete form of communication is the integration which is the result of interaction, of acting in concert with others by the exchange of words and ideas, of values and services. The subject must be a subject among other subjects, respecting them in their individuality, accepting them as other subjects, just as in reciprocity he is himself respected and accepted in his individuality by them. Communication is exchange in concert. In "Les Structures de la Parenté" Lévi-Strauss has made a penetrating study of the implications of exchange, and his summary formulation of the three mental structures on which he has based his analysis of kinship ends with a definition of the synthetic character of the gift which has revelatory significance: "Le transfert consenti d'une valeur d'un individu à un autre change ceux-ci en partenaires, et ajoute une qualité nouvelle à la valeur transférée" (Structures élémentaires p.98). The exchange changes the participants into partners. They act together and their combined action involves the mutual recognition of their partnership, i.e. of being part of the greater whole, of the group. The certainty of being a part is found in communication, in concerted harmonious action, in every form of togetherness and reciprocity which affirms that the partaking individual belongs to it. The exchange of words and values is the most obvious means of establishing communication and of expressing and confirming partnership. The question is, how far does it reach, to what extent has it the power to ensure the individual that he is a part of his universe?

Communication is limited by three different factors. The first of these we have already met with, viz. the limited possibilities of expression. Expression is curtailed by what we called a need for concealment, a term which now seems unsatisfactory to us. Communication and partnership are based on reciprocity and exchange, combined with the recognition of the other as other in his own right. This implies the recognition of each of the partners as a self, as a subject who holds his own. No subject is supposed to give up being a subject, nobody can even give it up without becoming valueless in terms of interaction. Instead of a need for concealment we had better speak of an imperative need for self-containment. The subject cannot be anything but subject. The self must be maintained in its uniqueness; there is a private sphere which the individual must protect from intrusion. He cannot be perfectly open; socially not, because he would say the most terrible things; and personally not, because he would give up the shelter protecting his state as a subject, an observer and judge of his universe in his own right. The need for self-containment hampers him in his self-expression; some things he will consciously keep for himself, others again are beyond expression because his basic experiences are too vague and contradictory and his need for self-containment prevents him from making a serious effort to clarify. The result was cogently formulated by Louis Bromfield: "no one ever really knows anyone else. There is always a part which remains secret and hidden, concealed in the deepest part of the soul. No husband ever knows his wife. . ., and no wife ever really knows her husband. There is always something just beyond that remains aloof and untouched, mysterious and undiscernable. . ." (cf. above, p.162). In the deepest part of his soul everyone is lonely; that deepest part is excluded from communication. Man is doomed to be a subject. He must always keep something behind: his inalienable self.

The second limiting factor is the society. Communication is possible between individuals but how should one communicate with his society at large, i.e. how should one experience the reality of his partnership in society, feel oneself absorbed in his community, an active, appreciated, functioning and meaningful part? In Western society a public meeting, a demonstration, an active role in a successful political action are opportunities for realising this, but how often has a simple citizen an opportunity to participate? The society as such is intangible and in its elusiveness an intellectual construct. Yet in human experience that construct is a solid reality. It is the they, the capitalists, the government of popular complaint, the elusive power apprehended behind the dull round of every-day work, the social system condemned by revolutionaries. In Western Europe there has never been a time like ours, in which everyone is so well cared for by his society; from the cradle to the grave he is object of welfare activities. Neither has there ever been a time in which the existing social system was condemned so harshly and unrestrictedly as to-day by a generation which grew up in a period of unprecedented prosperity. Why? One look at a twenty storey block of apartment buildings suffices to explain what is wrong. There they all are, everyone in his own apartment identical with all the other ones, each having his meals in the same corner, his bed-room on the same side, all alike and all isolated, the one from the other, each in his own cell in the shiny honeycomb. Our social welfare has been depersonalised. In the social machinery it is not the person who counts but the function. The people fulfilling the functions are interchangeable, not the functions. The huge exchange of values and services of our social fabric has lost the power of the gift to change the interactors into partners because the actors are no longer individuals, but functionaries. I am aware that I am exaggerating. Unfortunately, others are not, namely those who more than I feel themselves the victims of the dehumanising aspects of modern development. How to come to grips with one's own society is an extremely thorny problem which leads to the creation of bogeys of all sorts (except the supernatural?).

Of course society at large has always been a problem to the individual. Friendly communication with the members of the small in-group does not shield a person from the experience of feeling himself a poor outsider in his dealings with the larger, more comprehensive group. Nevertheless it is essential for him to be accepted as a partner, and to find this partnership confirmed in forms of concerted action and intercommunication. He needs the inner awareness of belonging. Where, and how shall he find it? He cannot realise it by talking to everyone else. There are too many others. He is in need of symbols which confirm his partnership and confirm it not only intellectually, but emotionally as well, that is in that part of his inner life which because of its inexpressibility is not accessible to direct intercommunication.

The third limiting factor is of a somewhat comparable nature. A man's universe consists of more than only his fellow-men. Hunters and gatherers in particular are even more directly dependent upon Nature[17] than they are on their fellow-men. Of course, the hunting area is familiar since early youth and every tree and water-hole is well-known. The Australian aborigines know where to look for wallabies or sizable wild yams, but they are not always sure that they will find them. There are periods of plenty when all goes well and the world in which they live is mild and friendly, a good and homely world and a source of delight. But Nature is fickle, and man's command over it is minimal. Nature is far less a potential object of man's activities than an alternately indulgent and resistant power. There are no means of communication with this power. Yet, scarcity and failure are 'felt' as acts of hostility, abundance and prosperity as signs of grace. The

[17] Here and in the next section written with a capital N to forestall ambiguities.

225

gatherer's existence is a perilous one, utterly dependent upon the 'whims' of Nature, a Nature which he cannot see through. Its rules of seasonal succession and its periodical changes of dearth and plenty are as well known to him as its irregular deviations from the normal pattern, but the causes producing these phenomena are as far beyond him as the means to obviate the consequences of unforeseen misfortunes. The gatherer is at the mercy of a whimsical world, and he knows it. He cannot come to grips with its uncertainties; the natural world is more 'other', more different than the world of his fellow-men. Yet, he belongs to that world and he is aware of it because that natural world is his 'familiar' home. He lives in it, he enjoys its bounties, but at times it can be so inimical to him as to let him go hungry, fall a prey to incident or sickness. His care and his shrewdness are of no avail if fate is against him. His world then turns into a discouraging world to which he has no access.

The conclusion must be that man, in each and every respect part of his world, is reiteratively exposed to the experience that he does not belong to it. He is other than his world, a subject who among subjects like himself is incapable of communicating with them beyond a certain limit, a limit just excluding his most intimate stirrings. His relations with his society at large are even more dubious, evoking the awareness of being an outsider who does not count, who is valued at best for his functional merits but not for his person. The non-human world is altogether incommunicable; though sometimes generous it is also resistant, tricky and forbidding. There is little trouble when all goes well but prosperity rarely lasts long. Man's self-consciousness again and again reminds him of his otherness, his separateness from a world to which he belongs but which defies his efforts to get along with it. Observing his universe with detachment, the one thing he invariably discovers in times of misfortune or stress, is the meaninglessness of his existence, a lonely life curtailed in its relations with its fellow-men, barred from the blessings of Nature. Yet, this same lonely creature is too thoroughly part of his universe not to go on trying to find ways and means to convert this theoretical truth into an experience of real partnership. After all, he *is* a part and functioning as a part implies that his life has a meaning. He must find the means of communication.

It is evident that man has found these means in religion. The characteristics of religion summarised in the previous section answer the needs and the problems enumerated here. The cosmological implications of the supernatural and the personifications of its manifestations offer the desired opportunity to communicate with the universe as a whole. Again, the predominant role of the spoken word in the various forms of religious practice confirms that there is a need for communication with that world. The fact that the sacred, though strictly separate, is also in one form or another in man himself, reflects man's basic condition: though a part of his world he experiences that world as strictly separate, whereas he intuits that this cannot be

226

true. The double-faced gods faithfully reflect man's experience and expectations of his world which lures and repulses, promises and refuses, spends and takes away. That the gods are far off and inaccessible, and nevertheless so close at hand that they can be approached by man, is a statement which can be applied with equal right to man's universe. The basic contradictions of the human condition are reflected in religion. The problem is how man could so firmly believe in the significance of its symbols. The fact that the creation of a supernatural world answers a need has long been recognised, but a useful function is never a guarantee for credibility. To presume that primitive man is so much more credulous than we are, would be an act of credulity on our part.

3. Conflict, misfortune and comfort

Man is a part of his universe and a subject opposing it. All his acting is acting in his universe and he must, and usually does act as a part of it, but the inner experience called forth by his conscious activities is one which discloses separation, distance and otherness. Reason and observation confirm that he is a part of his universe, but the experience associated with acts of reason and observation is one of separateness and contrariety. Yet, the inner awareness of being a part is a necessary concomitant of a meaningful life; in its perfection such an awareness is a state of bliss, ardently pursued and rarely achieved. Actually, such perfection is incompatible with the individual's activity as a subject. Human happiness can exist only as a compromise. It is the compromise which is pursued and it usually is realisable too, provided the individual's universe does not act too overtly in a manner conducive to the activation of the individual's awareness that he is but a lonely other, a subject who will always be a stranger in his world. Conflict, misfortune and resistance are the occasions which call the individual's partnership and place in his universe in question. How does the individual react to these situations? His self-interest leads him to minimise the intensity of his excited feelings of frustration which otherwise might turn misfortune into disaster. What are the individual's techniques — if any — to prevent the emergence of feelings of estrangement and being ostracised? We are not primarily interested here in religious concepts or philosophical considerations, but in spontaneous reactions common to everyday life and experience, in the most simple, the most general and uncomplicated reactions to situations which are potentially conducive to the emergence of feelings of estrangement.

The modern intellectual's tinkering with technical tasks which are foreign to his daily routine, offers an interesting field for observation. Trying in vain to extract a rusty nail from an oak beam, he complains that he is 'turned down' by the darned thing which 'wills' not as he wills. Trying to start his motorcar after a rainy night he becomes angry when the engine 'refuses' to ignite. Eventually he will state that 'she' won't go, adding a few adjectives of the kind which he would have used to describe his neighbour's young son if the boy had kicked a football through his front window. The personalisations called forth by the 'unwillingness' of his car are mild when compared with those elicited from his lips by a collision in the dark with an open door or window.

Addressing a lifeless object is not always a matter of wrath or dismay. It is done in a more friendly mood as well. When a heavy table must be pushed aside, we may say, 'come along boy'. In 1945, at the time Djakarta was in revolt, we called a stengun a boy. We all indulge in personalisations and talk to the objects of our exertion. When questioned we are ready to explain that we do not mean anything in particular by it. Of course we do not, but the fact itself certainly has a meaning. The curious devices of personalisation are the involuntary expression of how we feel about it, and that is that we 'feel' resistance as something directed against us personally, and the source of the resistance as something acting like a person, provoking us to address it as such. The act of addressing has a singular effect, certainly if it is more than an expression of pure dismay. By addressing the object the refractory thing is humanised, and our talking is an unfinished, rudimentary form of communication with the object of our exertion. Even the angry address which expresses our dismay has a communicatory aspect. Addressing is in itself an act of personification, even if it is done in anger. The personalisation of the object of our wrath humanises it. If we fail to realise our wishes as regards the object, we at least can 'tell' it what we think of its refusal to comply. The object, originally a cold denier of our wishes and of our natural relations with it, is turned into an object to 'whom' we communicate our feelings. Our 'relations' with the object are decidedly unfriendly, but there are relations, not the unrelatedness which is fundamental to estrangement.

Talking with objects assumes the most elaborate forms in our dealings with domestic animals. We are prone to humanising animals and they get their full share. They are given names, the members of the family talk to them, and they are quite sure that the animals understand them. Within certain limits they are not mistaken; the animal reacts differently to kind words and angry ones. Nevertheless, there is a lot of nonsense in our conversations with animals; the point of interest is that this nonsense has a comforting effect.

That a beast has a will and intentions is evident, but our interpretations tend to be grossly exaggerated. We ascribe intentions not only to animals but also to events, very often to events with a frustrating effect. The notion of adverse intentions is almost irrepressible when the train or the bus takes off strictly in time on the one occasion that we, always punctual, were retarded and for once arrived at the stop less than half a minute over time. We cannot help 'feeling' it as a case of intentional badgering. Some

228

people are quicker than others to ascribe intentions to events. I remember a kind old lady, a neighbour, whom I met just after a thunderstorm, inspecting a huge branch torn from an old beech which stood at the edge of the wood opposite our houses. "What a blessing that no one stood under it", she said. Actually, I had never seen anyone standing there, but 'feeling' that I had to respect her feelings, I meekly agreed.

Nevertheless, the sensation that an event has an intention or carries a meaning can be extremely impressive. We came across a few cases of this kind in our discussion of Bergson's analysis of the event with human significance as an event loaded with intentionality. One of these was that of William James talking at length with the earthquake which destroyed San Francisco in 1906 (above, p.132). The full text of James' comment on his reaction is of interest here:

"First, I personified the earthquake as a permanent individual entity. It was *the* earthquake of my friend B's augury, which had been lying low and holding itself back during all the intervening months, in order, on that lustrous April morning, to invade my room, and energize the more intensely and triumphantly. It came, moreover, directly to *me*. It stole in behind my back, and once inside the room, had me all to itself, and could manifest itself convincingly. Animus and intent were never more present in any human action, nor did any human activity ever more definitely point back to a living agent as its source and origin.

All whom I consulted on the point agreed as to this feature in their experience. "It expressed intention", "It was vicious", "It was bent on destruction", "It wanted to show its power", or what not. To me, it wanted simply to manifest the full meaning of its *name*. But what was this "It"? To some, apparently, a vague demonic power; to me an individualized being, B's earthquake, namely "(William James, Memories and Studies pp.212 f.; Bergson, Les deux Sources, pp.161 f.).

Bergson's comment is too partial to his philosophy of the *élan vital* to be of much help. What is important is the facts, the personalisation of the experience and its interpretation in terms of an intention, a personal will. The facts are not exceptional. On the contrary, we all feel that events which have a decisive impact on the course of our lives, 'address' us, have 'something to say to us'. The Monday morning newspaper reporting that the weekend traffic resulted in sixteen fatal casualties only elicits the comment from us that the figure adversely affects the mean figure of traffic accidents. However, if our own child is among them, our comment is quite different. Why, for all things, did we let the child go? Why had he to be there on that fatal moment? Why? Some people say: why should this happen to the poor child, so young, so unfortunate? There are also parents who complain: why should this befall me? It does not matter so much what anyone says. What matters is that they feel addressed, as if some power had intentionally staged the casualty. There are non-religious parents who afterwards mend their ways and go to church; there are churchgoing people who also mend their ways and stay at home. The reactions are wholly different but both are one in the conviction that they received a message.

Events, in particular fateful events, carry a message. The Dutch language has the expression, literally, 'disasters from higher hand'. English is more outspoken and calls them 'acts of God', and that is exactly how believers and unbelievers feel: an affliction sent by a superior power, the believers rationalising it as an admonition, and the unbelievers as a sign of unreasonable wilfulness. In the main they agree; they have been addressed and they know it. The contingence of the fateful accident is rejected. Any form of contingency is unacceptable to man; it is a denial of meaning, that is of being placed in a context, the repudiation of the subject as a part who takes part.

We should not dwell too long on these dramatic aspects lest it be presumed that personalisations and apprehensions of intentionality are phenomena specifically connected with exceptional or stressing situations. We should not forget that the sun shines bright, that the dark clouds have a silver lining, and that yesterday we listened to the singing of the wind in the pine-trees. The good too has its personalisations. Personalisation is not a disease of language but the reflection of our personal experience. There is not a single language which does not 'suffer' from this irrepressible leaning towards personalisation; even apparently purely descriptive terms such as capitalism, the political system, socialism etc. are not always used as objective, emotionally neutral references. In political speeches of a propagandist nature these scientific concepts sometimes come to life as bogeys, assuming the shape of threatening demons. The conclusion must be that underneath our conscious thought, speech, and actions we are involved in a vague, subdued, evasive, but all the same never ending dialogue with our universe. We treat it as if it were just 'a tiny little bit' human and sometimes (not often) we feel addressed by it. These feelings are most marked in our experience of Nature, but they are not less real in our dealings with social powers or technical implements. Consciously we try to act in a matter of fact way, but on the margin of the subconscious reverberate the tones of a vague dialogue, effacing the sharp contours of otherness which, if not retouched, might reveal our separation from our universe in all its austerity. We experience the dialogue as an 'as if', but the 'as if' serves an important function, that of the humanisation of our situation.

The universe of preliterate people differs in many ways from that of modern man. The former are utterly dependent on a not very reliable Nature. They live in the midst of a wholly unadulterated Nature. It is impossible to realise what this means to them without discussing first what Nature means to us. It is something radically different, although in a way we are exactly as dependent upon Nature as they.

To modern man Nature is the field for the self-realisation of humanity in incessant concerted action. To the individual, however, access to Nature's resources is to a very modest extent a matter of his own activity in the material world. The modern worker does not act alone like a hunter or gatherer; he is a member of a gang of labourers, acting in concert with other gangs as small sub-divisions in an extremely intricate pattern of collaboration by the division of labour through specialisation and diversification. This organisation enables modern man to realise his claims on Nature's riches to an unprecedented extent. For the individual this realisation is not a matter of direct confrontation with his natural surroundings, but of adept manipulation of his social relations. Nature's resources have been socialised and the economic relations between man and Nature have been diverted to the social organisation of interhuman relations, turning the social organisation into a power which, when diagnosed as 'the System', assumes a shape comparable to what Nature must be to our 'primitive contemporaries'. In parentheses we note that the latter's experience of Nature need not be as oppressive as that of Kafka's heroes with 'the system'. However that be, in our society the direct confrontation between man and Nature has been reduced mainly to two fields, viz. that of recreation in the open air, and that of the scientific investigation of infinite space, the infinitesimal, and the basic laws of nature.

The free Nature of recreation is an emasculated Nature. To the tourist who enters upon the premises of Nature, well catered for with provisions and conveniences, Nature can show only its pleasurable and comforting aspects. The visitor calling on Nature in order to enjoy peace and silence, beauty and harmony, readily finds what he came for. The terms on which the meeting with Nature are arranged, are carefully prepared and the conditions laid out. As soon as peace or silence becomes oppressive, the visitor is free to leave or to switch on a transistor radio. The Nature of recreation is a discovery made as recently as the 17th century; this Nature is not a human condition but a human achievement in developing Nature's friendly and comforting aspects by isolating them from its menacing and refractory ones. These friendly aspects have the reassuring effect that they make the visitor feel himself at home, incorporated in a harmonious atmosphere. Here he can really feel himself a part of his natural world.

The few occasions on which modern man is confronted with Nature's relentless power are those of a catastrophe such as an earthquake, a hurricane or a volcanic eruption. However, the catastrophe does not find him unprepared like fifty years ago. He is warned in time that something is going to happen, and after it has happened all the world co-operates to undo the adverse effects of the 'act of God', the churches, ironically enough, taking a large share in the operations.

Of all people it is only the scientist who knows Nature in its primeval inaccessibility and unruliness. The Nature of infinite space, of the puzzling intricacies of the infinitesimal, and of the secrets of life and energy is still its own unaltered self: forbidding, secretive and of overpowering majesty, rewarding the exertions of ever new generations of inquisitive students with the awareness of the fathomless depth of their ignorance of ultimate reality, yet forcing them to try for provisional answers. *Ignoramus et ignorabimus;* science invariably is the training-school of humility as it has always been.

How different are the relations of primitive people with Nature! Their way of life is one of incessant direct contact with Nature. They have their full share of its bounties and they enjoy its pleasurable aspects as intensely as anyone. At the same time, however, they are often in peril of their lives. Death takes a heavy toll from people who depend on the gifts of an untamed Nature for their livelihood. After some twenty thousand years of uninterrupted occupation of their continent, the Australian aborigines numbered no more than about 300.000 people at the time they had the misfortune of being discovered. Fairly powerless against sickness, the death-rate is inordinately high among such people, and only a few live on to old age. We need not indulge in fancies about the dangerous life of early pleistocene man in a world overrun with savage animals. The life of the Australian hunter of more recent years was poor enough. He was insufficiently protected against cold and rain, an easy prey of severe colds. If the rains were late or fell out of season the growth of seeds, bulbs and roots was impeded, and the crops harvested by the gatherer were poor. Hunger was always imminent, and they had no baker or supply store round the corner. The family of the hunter or fisherman who had a day of ill luck, had on that day neither meat nor fish to enrich the poor meal of vegetables collected by the women.

Social relations were not very reassuring either. Within the small in-group a man could feel at ease and protected by group-solidarity, but his relations with members of other groups and his position in the society at large were a matter of recurrent tensions and incertitude. Always in danger of being crossed and frustrated by Nature or society, his life abounded with occasions for feeling ostracised. Misfortune more often than not was a matter of life and death.

What should a man do who lives in such circumstances? He is certainly in more need of reassurance than anyone. Living on the verge of feeling ostracised, he badly needs confirmation of the fact that he belongs to his universe, that he is part of and a partner in his non-human and human world. What shall his reactions be? We need not immediately think of religious reactions; moreover, they are our problem. There are other means of affirming the experience of togetherness and communication. More often than once, I have been standing in the dark, for hours on end watching the dances of the members of a hill-tribe in South New Guinea or of those of the mountaineers of the Bird's Head in the North. In ordinary life the tensions between the participating groups were numerous and serious. Here they were all together, working themselves up in a frenzy. As far as I could ascertain there was nothing religious in what they were doing; they were just behaving like madmen, each in exactly the same way as the other, acting out a kind of togetherness which was not of a common order but of the 'in-spite-of-everything-type'. I have never seen anything more surprising than their abandonment to the dance, their oblivion of everything else. Each time I was struck by a quaint touch of extravaganza and constraint. Means of this kind necessarily have a short-lived effect unless they put the seal on some successful reconciliation of the participants, a reconciliation, however, which need not last.

We must return to ordinary life. We may be sure that these people feel more than we do the need of communication with their physical universe, simply because it plays such an all-encompassing role in their life. Moreover, it is more forbidding. It is a universe more urgently in need of being humanised than ours, and reactions conducive to the personalisation of experienced resistance must accordingly be stronger among them. More often than we, they are in situations which tend to arouse the sensation of an innate intentionality, more frequently also they are faced with events which convey the impression of addressing them. Their life is unprotected, and events befalling them easily carry a threat of imminent death or serious misfortune. How will they react? The sensation of intentionality of course is one of the 'as if' type, but what are they going to do with it? Can they reject it as easily as we do as the fruit of imagination? Above all, let us remember that in spite of our rejection of these sensations, we still indulge in irrepressible habits of personifying expression. We too experience a 'will' in the activities of our universe; but our situation is different. We are reasonably well informed and we know where to find the means necessary for overcoming a difficulty or for meeting the exigencies of a situation. The resources of the Australian aborigine and the Papuan horticulturalist are restricted, and they are poorly informed in comparison. They do not doubt that everything has a cause, but they have only the vaguest notions about the effective cause of sickness or health, rain or sunshine, a good crop and a poor one, and the means of obviating the risks are correspondingly limited.

We should be careful not to dramatise the situation. Theirs is a difficult life but it is viable. Moreover, primitive people are not ignorant. They know their surroundings perfectly well. If in consequence of unfavourable weather conditions one kind of vegetables or animals is scarce, the same weather may favour the proliferation of another species; when there is scarcity in one place they may know another where it is better. When all goes wrong there are always substitute foods, less palatable of course and as a rule of low nutritional value, but usually sufficient to keep them alive. The Papuan horticulturalist has similar safeguards if his gardens fail him. He knows how to make do. Although scarcity may result in an increased mortality-rate, the community as such survives. These people should not be

233

underestimated; they are adequate, often even perfect gardeners, carefully selecting the soil-type, applying accomplished techniques and making effective provisions for protection. Rain and sunshine, however, sometimes deviate from the expected pattern. And nobody knows where the blight and the rust, the locust and the plant-louse and all the other pests come from which one year destroy half of their crop and in other years, for no known reason at all, stay away. The danger is not always immediate. Their difficulty is in the incessant uncertainty. There are too many surprises, most of these disagreeable. They can never be sure.

Under these circumstances the apprehension of an intention or a hidden message is not as insignificant as it is to us, who always have plenty of information and fairly reliable forecasts near at hand. With his lack of information on more remote causes the apprehension of hidden intentionality is to the primitive gardener or hunter one of the few clues at his disposal. Why should he immediately reject it as fancy? He never had the training in critical and systematic thinking which begins at school. No one told him to distrust observations which are not measurable. We are always ready to make the warning that appearances are deceptive; from his point of view the poor gatherer may reply with equal right that appearances are the primary data of proper observation.

Actually, there is a profound reason for his reluctance to reject his apprehensions as fancy. Primitive man's life is embedded in silence. It is not the kind of silence we look forward to, the silence glorified in lyrics. Our silence is the silence of the tamed Nature of recreation, a silence which we can seek, flee from or disturb at will. The silence of the primitive world is different. That silence rules; it is a silence which is practically always present day and night. It is 'heard' at all times, and it is one of the basic conditions of primitive man's life. The trouble with silence is that it 'speaks'. All real silence is speaking silence, activating peace and happiness, but also the solicitudes, the apprehensions and anxieties which lie at the bottom of the heart. Such a silence has a strong grip on people living on the outskirts of the jungle. It covers their existence like a wet blanket. They dislike it; a man rarely goes out alone. They love company to break the regime of silence. Of course they are never quite successful because the silence is always there, making them hear things which are not really there, because they are the things of their own hearts. Left alone with their apprehensions, the apprehension of hidden intentions necessarily becomes a strong one.

Yet another circumstance contributes towards intensifying this effect. These people have not been trained from early youth to be always active. Our education is very effective in this respect. Parents stand ready with toys at the baby's cradle. The child must learn how to play and very early in life he is taught to pile up his blocks. Children must do something and they have internalised the habit of doing already before they are five years old. Everyone who has ever travelled with children on a freighter has had the experience that after half a day, when the novelty has worn off, the children start complaining: 'mummy, what shall I do now'. Children raised in another type of society never complain that they have nothing to do. They have learned to relax, to sit down without doing or thinking anything in particular. These people, young and old, can relax for hours. However, sitting down without concentrating on anything in particular, is exactly the attitude most favourable to paranormal experience. In that state of mind the conscious is more than otherwise open to contents obtruding from the subconscious. Sitting down and relaxing, when nothing breaks the silence except the occasional cry of a bird, apprehensions — and vague ideational contents generally — easily assume more concrete forms than ever happens among people who are actively engaged. Our final conclusion must be that primitive conditions intensify the prevailing trend to 'translate' experience in personifying terms, and encourage their interpretation in conformity with apprehensions of intentionality.

As the cultural and ecological conditions are conducive to dreams and visions, the question arises whether there is any kind of dreams and visions which may be expected to arrest the attention more specifically than any other category. We shall not try to answer the question by the way of empirical research because relevant data are scarce and haphazard. We must stick to the basic fact: that of a way of life dependent on Nature's generosity and whims. Under such circumstances we must expect dreams and visions symbolic of the uncertainty inspired by a universe which is at one time mild and generous, then again forbidding and unreliable. The symbols of uncertainty will take precedence because they are the expressions of experiences of vital importance, concerned with questions of life and death, of plenty or famine. Dreams which give shape to the apprehended intentionality of the universe must appear to be more significant than any others. Such dreams necessarily abound with symbols which are personifications. Frightening as these personifications often are, as personifications they also have a human aspect, offering exactly that opportunity for communication which is so sadly lacking in the experience of misfortune or resistance. One cannot expect otherwise. As products of the subconscious they reflect the hopes of the dreamer as well as his fears. The reifications of apprehended intentionality allow for the need for talking to the difficulty, the nasty surprise, the disquieting disappointment. They detract from the austere contingency of the events and set the closed door of their forbidding inscrutability ajar. The mystery thus disclosed is not immediately of practical convenience, but it enables a dialogue of some sort, permitting the frustrated subject a faint hope that he is not fully let down but still in communication with his universe. Visions which give scope to the humanisation of the experienced contingencies of life must be welcome to people badly lacking objective information, who feel[18] ostracised by their universe. When the experience of contigency is strongly felt, the vision (or dream, as the case may be) is the one ray of hope.

Another important point is that visions and dreams are communicable. Those symbolising apprehended intentions even call for communication; because they are the direct products of a need for communication which was obstructed and impeded, such symbols invariably have a social component. Moreover, the personifications of apprehensions of intentionality refer to experiences common to all, because they are the results of situations which do not vary widely between one individual and another. The actual experiences of estrangement are too vague and above all too personal to be communicable. They belong to the private sphere of the subject; the intentionality of the universe is felt deepest when the individual is curtailed in his being a part and feels that he is thrown back on the loneliness of his subjectivity. He cannot easily speak of his loneliness, but when his experience has assumed the symbolic form derived from dream or vision, communication need no longer be censored. The vague experience has now acquired a tangible and definable shape, apart from the individual's subjectivity, yet sufficiently recognisable as the reflection of the inner meaning of a not uncommon experience to call forth a response in others who went through similar experiences. It meets all the requirements to become a model in the sense of our previous comment on expression and concealment (above, p. 162). As a model it has the semblance of objective reality which alone can shield the subject's most private stirrings whilst it is used as a means for communication. The members of the community are all in the same situation; they share a common fate and the sensation of being ostracised by certain developments in Nature or in the society at large, are common to most of them. A dream or vision reflecting frustrating (and sometimes encouraging) conditions common to all, and impressive enough to incite the dreamer or visionary to communicate its contents to others, necessarily elicits a response of recognition or at the very least of thoughtful consideration among his fellow men. A positive response is extremely important. To the individual, who by himself is unable to communicate his most private stirrings, the response signifies that he is not alone in his vague but disquieting feelings of discomfort. In the symbolised forms of his vision they call forth an echo among his fellow men.

Not every dream or vision will elicit positive reactions. The dream or vision must be meaningful, i.e. it must fulfil three basic conditions. First, it must give shape to the experienced whimsicality and wilfulness of the universe and express its menace, power and otherness, as well as its potential richness or generosity. Secondly, the beings of dream and vision must be

[18] The term 'feeling' here as elsewhere has the meaning of a vague and badly conceptualised ideational content.

236

prepared (under certain conditions, as the case may be) to grant the favours so badly needed by the members of the community. Finally, these beings must give an opportunity for communication. A vision meeting all these requirements gives shape to human fear and disappointment on the one hand, to man's hopes and expectations on the other, and for the individual it is a confirmation that in spite of his adverse experiences he is really a communicating part of his universe, because he is a partner in its innermost secrets, because he has been told by a revelation what is hidden to the uninitiated and the ignorant.

The verification of the vision or dream by the community is of essential significance. The reactions of the listeners determine its value and trustworthiness as more than a mere dream or hallucination. The purport of the dream and the vision is the communication between man and his universe. This cannot be an individual affair. It is the one available opportunity for sharing one's more intimate stirrings with others, to communicate on a higher level than that of daily problems and events. Discussing the experience means discussing the model of an experience of emotional value. Keeping this all for oneself would be a denial of its proper source, the need for vital communication as a part and partner in one's non-human and human universe. Its origin dictates that it be made communal.

It dictates even more. Something must be done with the vision. It is not and cannot be a piece of information duly to be noted and laid aside. It is a means for communication, a way out of isolation and ostracism, an offer which must be grasped with both hands. The vision must be acted upon; it elicits the rite, the act of communication.

Communication can be realised by various means: by a dialogue, by a gift, i.e. an act of exchange, and by identification. The dialogue implies prayer and the use of sacred formulas, the gift sacrifice, the identification the staging of the vision in ritual. They confer on the participants the certainty that all is well between themselves and their universe, because knowing its hidden shape and truth, and approaching these secret powers in the prescribed way, they know that they are 'in', taken up as parts in the essence of their universe. The communal action of the rite confirms that related feelings and ideas stir the hearts of all the participants. In the celebration they are one among themselves and one with their universe.

The revelation of the vision is always the revelation of a hidden truth. The 'open' truth is the experience of being ostracised, of a closed universe to which the individual is an outsider, isolated, meaningless, superfluous. The vision sets the door ajar, it opens the way to penetrate into the depth of its essence which announced itself in the apprehended intention, the message overheard in the fateful event. The apprehension must be clarified, the message deciphered. The medicine-man, the shaman and the prophet are the ones who work on the task. They are not like ordinary people; they court the solitude where the voices of the hidden world ring louder and are better overheard than in the company of men. The late Verschueren told me about a medicine-man, highly esteemed by his fellow-villagers, who one night made a social call on him. They were talking pleasantly when suddenly, in mid-sentence, he broke off. He rose, walked to the door and without a word he disappeared into the dark of the night. Three days later he returned to his home. No one, not even one of his housemates, has ever learned what he did during these three days and nights (Van Baal, Dema p.886). He was simply one of those intent on listening to the secret voices which can only be heard in solitude.

Thus far we have considered the existential opposition between being a subject and being a part mainly from its negative side, the sensation of abysmal contradiction evoked by experiences of conflict and misfortune. A state of dysphoria is more conducive to the conscious realisation of the contrast than one of euphoria. Yet it is the latter which is aspired to, and the medicine-men and shamans would be sorry masochists if their efforts did not exactly aim at overcoming the conflict and the reconstitution of a state of harmony. Human experience is not exclusively an experience of misfortune and conflict; life does have its periods of prosperity and its hours of harmonious togetherness. Earlier in this section the reader was reminded of the day on which the sun shone bright, when he listened to the singing of the wind in the pine-trees. At times Nature, even a Nature of paramount power and wilfulness, can be kind and comforting, and the reassured soul sings: "He maketh me to lie down in green pastures; he leadeth me beside the still waters" (Ps 23 : 2). The society at large is not always like Hobbes' Leviathan either; there are festive days on which conflicts rest and parties convene to celebrate in dancing and singing. The state of euphoria is not an empty dream; the experience of it is common enough even though it does not bear analytical reflection very well. The reflection on conflict and misfortune necessarily calls forth a recollection of harmony and well-being. We cannot consider the one without remembering the other, and a study of the effect of the oppositional duality of the human condition which concentrates on conflict and misfortune would be unduly biased. Being a subject as well as being a part, means that both ends must be realised; the subject must act as a part in his universe and realise that he is one. The contrast must be overcome, the gap must be bridged, and experiences of comforting harmony are duly noted. The Australian native loves his desert land and the Eskimo feels at home in his icy surroundings. Studies of myth and ritual give abundant evidence that the spirit world of these people is not simply or exclusively a frightening one, but has its comforting and reassuring aspects as well. There is hardly a better illustration of this comforting aspect than Willidjungo's account of his calling to become a medicine-man as communicated by W. Lloyd Warner (A black Civilization, pp.212-214). It follows here by courtesy of the publishers in a slightly condensed form:

One day when Willidjungo was a mature man having several wives and children he was out in the bush looking for wild honeybees' nests. After a time he decided to return home. On his way back to camp he felt a pain in his right leg near the hip. He knew afterwards that the familiars which he later acquired had given it to him. His leg became very stiff and stayed that way for over a week. During this time he lay in the camp and covered himself with paper bark to keep warm. One of Willidjungo's wives slept by him. The two familiars, who were a little boy and girl, started talking to him underneath the paper bark. They talked in a rhythmic chant: "Dul dul dul — ter ter ter".

Said Willidjungo, "the sound was like a small frog out in the lilies".

Willidjungo woke up his wife. "You better sleep among the women tonight", he said. His wife left their hut and went over to her mother's and father's. She was very frightened of these two spirits. The two continued talking. They went back into the bush and Willidjungo followed them.

"I kept listening to that noise they were making. I listened but I did not look, and followed them. The two things came back to camp and I came with them. They sat down by my fire and talked. When it was night and dark those two spirits flew in the tops of the trees. They had the sound of a quail flying. They sat on the top of my head and on my shoulders. They had white feathers, but I did not know that at that time. I could only feel them on my head".

Morning came. Willidjungo went out to look for food and to fish. The spirits left and did not come back until the afternoon. "They did not come back for me then but I went out to look for them. I saw them out in the bush then for the first time. Their bodies looked like jabirus. Their eyes looked like your glasses. Their face and stomach looked like a man and their legs looked the same way. They had big stomachs like children. Their arms were like wings and had little feathers on them. Their wings had big feathers. They were standing on a tree. I took my spearthrower. I put the hooked end under my arms and put sweat on it. I took it out then to reach for those two spirits. I caught them and put them under my arms. I held them in my hands like you would a small bird when you catch a wild one. They left me before I came back to camp. Before they left they said to me, 'You have a wife. It is better that you go back by yourself'."

Willidjungo said, "Oh, no. I don't want to do that". He then said to them, "what are your names?"

"We are two na-ri (familiars). Don't you try to cure people yet. If people are sick you let them alone and tell some other doctor to try to cure them".

"Then I came back to camp. Dorng's daughter was sick. I did nothing but look at her. She had a big hole in her chest. It had cracked open. I kept on looking. One of the old doctors tried to fix her but he couldn't do anything, but I didn't do anything. Afterwards I took the flesh and put it together and she became better rightaway the first time I tried. I made her well when she was half dead. Those two spirits talked to me then. They said, 'The first time you have tried you have done a good job. The next time anyone is sick you treat them. That is your work. We gave this to you and it will help you, but there are some things you cannot do. You must not go in the salt water and get covered with it. You must go along near the shore. If you go down under the salt water, we two will be dead'.

If I should dive in the ocean these spirits would die. These two spirits come around at night, usually in the middle of the night. Yesterday I carried a kangaroo on my shoulder and pressed hard on my armpits. I hurt one of my familiars, and I am sore under my arm. Last night the little one that was not hurt left me and went into the bush to look for another spirit. The other followed him. The sick one said, 'My master is sick now like me. You come and we will fix him'.

The well one took something out of the sick one and they came back. They found something hard in my chest and took it out.

When I was getting these spirits I went around very quietly and said nothing. I did not smoke very much. I only ate vegetable food and stayed in one place. I made an old doctor my friend. I fed him and gave him tobacco. One of the spirits left him and came with me".

239

Amburro, one of the old doctors of the western clans, watched Willidjungo's behaviour very carefully. Finally he said, "He is a true doctor all right. He has some things sitting on his shoulder". Many people were sceptical about it at first, but they were convinced: Willidjungo disappeared into the bush one night, and when he came back they heard the clicking sound, a kind of beating against his shoulders. Everyone said, "He has those children there". From that time on everyone believed that he was a medicine man.

Willidjungo's universe is a world of optimal intimacy and familiarity to its inmates. A man able to associate with his universe as fully as Willidjungo, is really 'in'; he lives in full communication. Willidjungo's way of thinking can be characterised as *ascriptive*. He ascribes a hidden meaning to the phenomena of his universe, we might as well say another side to his world. The bearers of this hidden meaning are his partners in communication, showing him the things as they really are, i.e. as they are at the inside or other side which is hidden to the eye of the layman and to that of the blundering colleague who failed to observe the wound in the woman's chest. Willidjungo is able to talk with his universe. The latter has its exigencies and there are things which are taboo to our medicine-man, but there is a great reward in meeting these exigencies, viz. that of a great intimacy with the surrounding world, based upon a secret knowledge of its inner stirrings. It is a kind of knowledge which is of small value to us. Yet, this poor knowledge gives Willidjungo's way of life a touch of human warmth and inner peace unknown to the modern pragmatist. In spite of his poverty Willidjungo is well cared for; as a subject he is a part of his world because he lives in full communication with his universe.

The present chapter has dealt with the human origins of religion, i.e. with its foundation in the human condition. It does not aim at reconstructing the history of the development of religious thought and institutions, but at disclosing the sources of its incessant rebirth in human minds. The data available are insufficient for a reconstruction of the past. The primitive religions of the present are not really primitive at all. They are as much the result of an age-long history as the so-called historic religions. The three points which can be made with reasonable certainty are the following. First, that man everywhere has been engaged in ascriptive activity, seeking visions, taking note of his dreams, attent to the voices whispering a message from his universe. Secondly, that he has been trying to increase his knowledge of the hidden world by the exchange of experiences, revelations and myths, because the exchange of these ideas and concepts is an act of communication and a fulfilment of their initial purport. And finally, that everywhere men have been elaborating on the scarce knowledge of the hidden world they had, trying to work up the available data into a meaningful and communicable whole which gives shape to their inner experience of their universe. Lévi-Strauss' description of the bricoleur is appropriate here. Surrounded by data which to his ascriptive mentality are supposed to be potentially meaningful, 'primitive' man is out for clues which may help him to increase his knowledge and improve the communicability of his universe. The result of the continuous additions made to the treasure of traditional lore by new visions, recent dreams and occasional borrowings from other peoples, is a really wonderful world, alternately frightening and kind, forbidding and comforting, but always open to communication to those who are prepared to pay the price.

As an after-thought on the basic significance of communication and its correlations with the category of the personal (so important in religious representations) I may add the following. Communication between individuals implies the recognition of the other as a partner, the acceptance of the subject as a part. This can be demonstrated by making a comparison between gift-giving and trade. Each of the two activities is concerned with the exchange of goods between persons, but only one of them is an act of communication. The exchange of goods does not in itself suffice to explain the binding effect of the gift. There is something in gift-exchange which is absent in trade. The former has not, as in trade, its aim and foundation in the need for the goods exchanged, but in the relations between the parties concerned. In the gift the goods exchanged are means to an end, the acceptance of the other as a partner. In a trade transaction the relations between the 'partner' are exhausted with the completion of the act of exchange; in gift-giving the relations begin with the completion of the act or are strengthened by it. Consequently, the meaning or intention of the gift, the communication between subjects, makes part of its structure. The goods are only means. It is nowhere clearer than in a holocaust, where the means are destroyed on behalf of its effect, the personal relation. The question arises to what extent a certain degree of personalisation of relations is a basic condition for the effectuation of the individual's communication with his universe. The question cannot be answered without further research. Yet, it has to be raised, as the answer might have an important impact on modern man's quest for religious reorientation.

XI

Symbols for communication

1. Introduction

Religion is a system of symbols by which man communicates with his universe. In the course of our argument we equated these symbols with models mediating between the individual's conflicting needs for self-expression and self-containment. Giving concrete, objective shape to the unspeakable, the model acts like a shield, protecting the individual's most intimate stirrings (of which it is a modified expression) from direct exposure. The model is operational within the framework of interhuman relations and unites believers in a common experience, without requiring them to enter into a direct, mutual exchange of highly intimate ideational contents. The interhuman communication is realised by the communication between the individuals and their common model of ritual action.

We also touched upon the problem of the credibility of religious symbols. We pointed out how and why certain symbols are accepted as veritable revelations of a hidden truth and thus as vehicles for ritual action. However, we did so in rather general terms, without going into specific questions. The various forms of ritual action were merely mentioned in passing. Yet, the credibility of religious symbols and the ritual action involved are always questions of the credibility of specific symbols and rites. Therefore, we must now proceed to a somewhat closer examination of a few specific forms of religion in which the credibility of the symbols and symbolic activities is a crucial problem: religious forms such as the magical rite and the belief in its efficacy, and the belief in the persistence of souls and in the power of the ancestors. Another problem deserving more attention is that of the role of speculative thought and conscious deliberation in the growth and development of religious systems.

The discussion of these topics shall not be presented in the form of a purely theoretical treatise but as a commentary based in part on our exposé in the preceding chapter, in part on data borrowed from two specific religions. As the intention is not to prove a theory but only to test the viewpoint developed in the course of this work on its heuristic value, it did not seem advisable to make broad comparative studies. They would lead us too far afield, because the only comparative study which really makes sense is one of previously analysed religious systems as consistent wholes, a task of too wide a compass to be undertaken here. Our present purpose is of a more modest nature, namely that of formulating a few suggestions for a better explanation of a small number of puzzling phenomena, suggestions which follow from our theory and might be of use in future studies.

As all religious phenomena have to be studied within the context of the religious system of which they are part, we shall set out with a short résumé of the main characteristics of the two religions selected as a background to our comments. These résumés have been borrowed from analytic studies previously undertaken. The first of these is concerned with a totemistic religion with a strong preference for ritual activity and an elaborate system of magic, namely that of the Marind-anim of South New Guinea. The second is a typically animistic religion with sacrifice, prayer and divination as its main forms of worship, i.e. the religion of the Ngad'a of Flores, one of the eastern Lesser Sunda Islands in Indonesia. The two religious systems are widely different in almost every respect. In our subsequent discussions we shall not narrowly limit ourselves to the problems specifically mentioned, nor desist from comparison with data from other cultures whenever it seem proper to do so. Ultimately our perigrinations through facts and theories should lead us back to the fact basic to all religion, the quest for a non-verifiable reality allowing the human subject to communicate with his universe.

a. The Marind-anim[19]

Marind-anim is the name used by a considerable number of autonomous territorial groups to describe themselves. They occupy a vast area of the lowlands of South New Guinea, stretching all along the coast from the southern entrance to Strait Marianne south-eastward to 15 miles beyond Merauke. Inland they occupy the greater part of the hinterland from the western coastal area up to the headwaters of the Bian and Kumbe rivers. The division into territorial communities is transected by a division into genealogical groups, patrilineal totem clans which are subdivided into subclans, ramifying into sub-subclans and local lineages. The clans are grouped in moieties, each moiety with two phratries. The phratries are exogamous as are all the other genealogical groups of lower order; the moieties are exogamous in part of the district but not everywhere. In each territorial group the four phratries are represented by subclans or sub-subclans belonging to one or more clans of each; in other words, the social structure is fundamentally the same everywhere and corresponds with the structure of Marind-anim society as a whole. There is no organisation covering the whole tribe,

---

[19] For a description and analysis of their culture cf. Van Baal, Dema (1966). *Anim* (sing.: *anem*) means people, men.

each territorial community being a fully autonomous group. However, a certain degree of tribal identity is recognised. Headhunting is not directed against other Marind-anim communities but against other tribes, and is often performed by various territorial groups in common. In the performance of ritual we also find a certain degree of co-operation or at least of co-ordination. Ritually, the Marind-anim can be divided into three main groups; the Mayo-Marind who have their ritual centre at Buti in the vicinity of Merauke, the Imo-Marind who have a comparable centre at Sangasee, a big village west of the mouth of the Bian, and the Marind of the upper-Bian who have their own ritual, less elaborate and based on concepts vaguely related to those dominant among Mayo- and Imo-Marind.

The most interesting ritual in this context is the mayo, but before we describe its more prominent traits, we must deal with Marind-anim totemism. Each clan has several totems and one or more associated activities which are said to belong to that clan. They all derive from the clan ancestors who made or produced the totems, or simply were identical with them, and instituted the associated activities and customs. These totem-ancestors, the *déma*, retired after they had completed their task, but they are still able to manifest themselves. Déma is a word not only used for totem-ancestors; it can also be used adjectivally, for example for a dangerous boar or a strange looking bird. They are said to be a déma-boar or -bird, something aweful or supernatural being attributed to them. A déma can also manifest himself during a ritual performance or by means of a vision. The déma are still nearby as is apparent when a myth is narrated. A good raconteur tells the myth with such a vivid directness that it is as if he were relating something which happened only yesterday. To Marind-anim ideas the mythical era is not primarily a concept of time, but of the hidden side of reality, the time-difference merely indicating the distance separating the phenomenal world from its hidden foundations.

The mythical heroes or déma are the ancestors of the various clans. Even those déma who according to myth never had offspring, are all the same looked upon as ancestors by the members of their clans. Déma and clan members belong together, just as the clan and its totems belong together. The clans and totems combined constitute the total society as well as the total universe. Since practically everything which has any use or importance is associated with one or other of the clans, the result is a comprehensive classificatory system in which society and physical universe are organised in strict parallelism.

The system is based on a number of recurring contrasts, the most important of which are: southeast versus northwest or, more precisely, southeast monsoon versus northwest monsoon, a contrast which has the connotation of dry and festive season versus wet season with sickness and mosquitoes; coast versus interior, correlated with that between coconuts on dry ground versus sago-palms in swamps; dry versus wet; land versus water; day versus night; male versus female; homosexual versus heterosexual in which homosexual is associated with male and the good way of life, and heterosexual with female, danger and warfare. The contrasts enumerated coincide with those between the two moieties of which the first, the *Geb-zé*, is associated with southeast monsoon, sun and moon, fire, beach, coconut, dry land, peaceful animals, the male sex and homosexuality. The Geb-zé are leaders of the mayo- (and of the imo-) ritual and the homosexual Sosom-rites. The other moiety, that of the *Sami-rek*, is associated with northwest monsoon, water, swamp, sago, night, copulating, headhunting, sorcery and aggressive animals. They are the leaders of the headhunt which follows the performance of the mayo-ritual (as it does that of the imo-ritual and the initiation rites of the upper-Bian people), and they are also the leaders of the feast celebrating a successful headhunt, a feast which gives occasion to very elaborate performances and enactments of mythical events.

The relations between the two moieties are complementary. They are each other's helpers, the Sami-rek assisting the Geb-zé in the performance of the mayo- (and imo-) ritual, the Geb-zé aiding the Sami-rek in the performance of the headhunt and concluding feast. Consequently we find that a moiety is not only associated with traits and totems typical of that particular moiety, but that each of them is also — dialectically as it were — connected with aspects typical of the other. The duality of the whole is reflected in each of the halves, sometimes by déma who have many of the traits typical of a déma belonging to the other moiety, at other times by bestowing attributes on a déma which seemingly should be more properly associated with a déma of the opposite half. A typical case of the second possibility is that of the sago-déma *Wokabu*. As a sago-déma he is one of the main heroes of the Sami-rek moiety. Wokabu is also connected with feasts. Sago makes part of the festive dish and feasts are the responsibility of the Sami-rek. So far there is nothing strange. However, feasts are celebrated on the beach or at least on dry land and sandy ground. It is the Geb-zé who offer a place for the feast because they are the 'owners' of the beach. Offering a place for the celebration is part of the complementary relations between the two moieties. When the initiation-rites of the mayo take place, the rites (of which the Geb-zé are the leaders) are performed inland. It may be a coconut-grove (again associated with the Geb-zé) but the place is called *timan*, i.e. inland, interior, and as such associated with the Sami-rek. Wokabu's association with feasts is expressed in myth by attributing to him numerous relations with the marine fauna on the sandy beach, and by his role as originator of coconut-oil, a product derived from one of the main totems of the Geb-zé. Coconut-oil is the most important ingredient for body-paint and adornment as required for a festive occasion, and thus a Sami-rek déma has to be the first to prepare it.

Another case of duality is that of *Geb*. He is a giant who is all the dry land and whose cut-off head is the sun. A cut-off head is also the coconut, the most important totem of the Geb-zé. However, Geb is also the moon, a somewhat astonishing fact because in these parts sun and moon are more often associated with contrasting moieties. Moreover, from the mythology as a whole we may conclude that the moon has rather strong relations with the Sami-rek moiety. More interesting still are the dialectics of the myths dealing with Geb as sun and moon. As the sun, Geb is a red-skinned man living in the far west of the territory near the place where the sun descends at nightfall through a hole underground and passes to the east where it emerges at sunrise. Geb, in the far west, kidnapped boys with a red skin like himself. Found out by the men, the women persuade the men to kill him. They cut off his head which goes underground to the place of sunrise. Geb as the moon, however, is a boy whose body is white because it is covered with acorn-shell. He lives in the far east (in the area of sunrise) and here it is the women who find him. Unfortunately, the men capture him, they clean his body and sodomise him, whereupon Geb, after having produced the banana (a typical moon-symbol), climbs up to the sky and changes into the moon.

The case is related at some length because the intelligent contrasting displayed in the two myths raises some doubts with regard to the thesis that "les mythes se pensent dans les hommes, et à leur insu" (above, p.208). We shall return to this point at a later stage. We must first pay attention to the mayo-ritual and its mythological foundation.

Two myths are of interest here, the first the one of the origin of man, the other the central myth of the mayo. The former can be summarised as follows. Once upon a time the déma made a great feast underground near Sangasé (the imo-centre; according to others near the place known as the area of sunset). After the feast the déma went eastward, travelling underground. Near Kondo (a place associated with sunrise) they came near the surface. A dog dug a hole which filled with water in which a number of catfish-like beings appeared. Resembling a catfish is more or less the same as saying that they were like bullroarers (Cf. Van Baal, Déma pp.204 f., 485-487, 552). A stork (the initiates of the mayo and imo are called storks) pecked them out of the water, but was chased away by the fire-déma (according to other sources by Aramemb, one of the leading characters of the mayo) who shaped their legs and arms, etc. After being properly shaped the newly born people went westward, populating the country. The first to go was also the first man to die (ibid. pp.209-211 jo. 269 ff.).

The second myth states that a mayo was held in the eastern part of the country and that Waba, the coconut-déma who is also identified with the sun (ibid. p.239), was among the initiates. He had brought his wife, Betel-woman, the sister of the crocodile-déma, a Sami-rek. She ran away and Waba followed her until he found her in the far west. He saw her enter a hut and at nightfall he followed her into the hut. He copulated with her but could not free himself from the act. The pair had to be carried east-

246

ward on a litter and it is explicitly stated that they were covered with mats. On their return to the mayo-place they were put down in a hut where they lay in copulation until (apparently after many days) Aramemb succeeded in disengaging Waba by turning him over and over. Flames flared up from the woman's vulva; the friction had sparked off the fire, thus causing its origin. Simultaneously, she gave birth to a cassowary (the bird of the fire-clan) and a stork (the symbol of the initiate). All sorts of events followed which cannot be discussed here without entering into their symbolic meaning. The point of interest to us is that the myth is primarily a sun-myth but also a more elaborate version of the myth of the origin of man. Waba and Betel-Woman, carried under the cover of mats — certainly not for decency's sake — are like the déma who travelled underground. The stork (initiate) is born in fire just like the new men in the first myth are shaped by the fire-déma. The life of man is like the life of the sun; born in the east, they go westward to copulate and die.

Yet, the mayo is far more than a mere ritual of the sun and the rebirth of the sun to power during the east monsoon. The mayo is at the beginning of everything. There is not a single myth on the origin of the mayo; on the contrary, every myth of origin sets out with a mayo celebration. The mayo is simply there, the matrix of every new development. A mayo initiation takes place in a specially enclosed area outside the village. The novices, covered by a shapeless cape of leaves, are carried into the enclosure by a functionary called Mayo-Mother. They have to behave as ignorames who have everything to learn during a process lasting many months in succession. The myths of origin of all the various foods and customs are told and enacted by initiates belonging to the relevant clans, then the food — forbidden since the day of entering into the mayo-place — may be tried or the custom or the technique practised. The rite adds a meaning to the relevant food or custom, a meaning which it does not have for the uninitiated, and which for the people concerned is important enough to stage scene after scene (cf. Van Baal, Déma p.544). The scene of the flight of Betel-Woman takes place only a few days after the beginning of the rites. Then there is a pause until the pair's return is enacted in symbolic form after which the instruction of the novices is recontinued for months on end until the day that the scene of the birth of fire and stork can be brought to the stage, a scene symbolising the completion of the initiation.

Some time after the initiation a headhunt is organised which carries the participants far into foreign territory. In former times the Marind even haunted the banks of the Fly-river. The return of the war-party is an occasion for a new celebration, sometimes elaborate enough to justify a year of preparation. A Marind-anim feast is something really spectacular, requiring very extensive preparations. The feast following a successful headhunt is a perfect opportunity for the performance of a *déma-wir*, a déma-performance, i.e. the enactment of a great number of myths by the members of the respective clans, every performer necessarily being a member of the clan of the déma who is personified. The déma-wir is a re-enactment of the mythical history, a dramatic representation of the inner meaning of the universe. Instead of a great déma-wir a small one may be staged, followed by a dance in which the men appear in their most magnificent attire, an attire which transforms them into the equals of the elaborately adorned déma-performers. Clan-membership is of importance in ritual performances of all sorts. The formulas used in magic, the private rites performed for specific pragmatic purposes, can only be performed by members of the relevant clan. A member of the coconut-clan must perform the rite propitious for the growth of the coconut, one of the sago-clan must act when sago has been planted, and so on. Although allowances are made to accommodate cases of pressing needs, the system as a whole requires the ritual co-operation of the members of all clans, or at least of all phratries, in order to ensure a ritual accompaniment to all the divergent aspects of every-day life.

One specific aspect has so far scarcely been touched upon, that of death and the dead. In the religious system the cult of the dead stands more or less aside, an epiphenomenon isolated from the cult proper. Up to an extent this is true, at least among the Mayo-Marind where the ceremonies held in honour of the dead stand apart from the cycle of ceremonies constituted by the consecutive celebration of initiation, headhunt (a richly ceremonious affair in itself) and final feast. It would be wrong to conclude that the cult of the dead is of minor importance. The ceremonies held in honour of a man or woman who died in the prime of life are numerous and elaborate. After it is painted the corpse is interred in a carefully prepared grave. A few days later the men meet at nightfall to sing *yarut,* the dirge, a very elaborate series of songs describing the journey of the dead from east to west. The singing lasts from early at night until dawn. Then the grave is reopened, the corpse (already in a state of putrefaction) washed and inspected in order to find out whether there are signs indicating that death has been caused by sorcery, signs calling for consecutive divination to discover the culprit. Before the grave is closed again a new ceremony takes place, a small déma-wir (déma-performance). Performers representing totems of the four phratries parade alongside the grave. At the end of the ceremony a taboo is laid on the coconut-groves of the deceased.

A few days later the women celebrate a ceremony. Conducted by a young woman dressed up to represent the Mayo-Mother, they go out in procession to visit the places frequented by the deceased during his life-time. At these places they sit down for a while, scattering some food and betel-nuts for the deceased when they leave. This second ceremony is the women's farewell-ceremony, just as the former was the one of the men. Shortly afterwards the *yamu* is held, the great meal for the dead. The night preceding the meal is again devoted to the singing of yarut. The meal itself is an occasion for food-exchange on a fairly large scale. About a year later another, smaller meal is held. Now the signs of mourning are discarded and the taboos on the coconuts lifted, the latter a ceremony which may call for the participation of a few men representing the relevant déma. Yet another ceremony takes place on this occasion. The bones of the deceased are exhumed and painted red after which they are re-interred. A hardwood stick is planted to indicate the place of the grave. Usually there are more graves nearby and later, perhaps many years later, an elaborate pig-feast will be celebrated on the spot. The blood of the pigs, dripping down on the sand, is a last farewell to the deceased. At the end of the feast the hardwood sticks are pulled up and the graves are permitted to fall into oblivion (Van Baal, Dema Ch.XIII, sect. 1 and 2, and p.846).

The dead are supposed to attend these festive occasions. For some time following the occurrence of a death many people are nervous, afraid to go out at night and ready to ascribe any noise or unexpected rustling of the leaves to the presence of the dead. The dead are associated with the night. They do not act as protectors of the living, nor do they watch over the growth of the crops. Assistance of this kind is a matter for the performance of minor rites usually described under the caption of magic. They will be discussed in the next section. The spirits of the dead do not play a role in any of these rites. In daily life their one and only function — if it can be called a function at all — is that of frightening people who are walking about during the night. The connections between the spirits of the dead and the déma are tenuous. There is a certain degree of likeness between déma and spirits; they all belong to the realm of supernatural beings, but the spirits of the dead are hardly functional in ritual. The cult of the dead is primarily one of commemoration, not a cult for the furtherance of the private ends of the performers. It is different in the case of the Imo-Marind among whom actors representing the dead participate in the cycle of central rites, whereas the Marind of the upper-Bian use one and the same term for déma and for spirits of the dead. However, space is limited and we cannot include the rites of these groups in our résumé. For the same reason we must abstain from a description of the homosexual Sosom-ritual and of the many implications of headhunting. We shall confine ourselves to a short commentary on phallic symbolism. This symbolism is tied up with the basic theme of Marind-anim myth and ritual, that of the conflict between the sexes, of the proud homosexual caught in copulation. Claiming that all fertility comes from the sperma produced by the males, the males nevertheless have to submit to the women. In the secret rituals of mayo and imo the Mayo-Woman and the Imo-Woman are the leading characters. The dialectics ensuing from this central theme are as interesting as they are complicated and culturally specific.

The *bangu*-rite of the imo is a dramatisation of the first part of the myth of Waba and Betel-Woman. On a moonless night two performers dance at

249

the bottom of a pit, impersonating the two déma. The pit is surrounded by a number of big shields which have a small hole in the centre into which an arrow-head has been inserted. The shields symbolise Betel-Woman with Waba, the phallus (the arrow-head) pinned in the shield. At the end of the dance the performers throw off their paraphernalia, climb out of the pit into which the shields are thrown to be buried with the garments of the dancers. Waba and Betel-Woman are sent off on their journey underground to the east. The point of interest is that the shields with the arrow-heads are called *pahui*. A pahui, however, is the ceremonial spear and club of the headhunters, a weapon with a long shaft which is inserted through the hole in a flat stone disc which is also a club-head. Actually, it is spear and club combined. The pahui is the headhunter's weapon, i.e. the ceremonial weapon of the males who set out on the warpath after the final ceremony, when Waba is rescued from the act of copulation. The ceremonial spear is a long phallus (according to one of the myths a penis of such enormous length that its owner had to bear it over his shoulder) and this spear is inserted in a very small vulva, the stone disc. The superiority of the male member is as evident here as the preponderance of the woman is in the case of the big shield with the small arrow-head, a penis symbol of minuscule proportions. The dialectics are more complicated than that; the triumphant headhunter is associated with the female moiety, with crocodile, boar, night and north-west monsoon, whereas the overpowered male, the arrow-head caught in the shield (the woman), symbolises the representative of the sun, the member of the leading moiety, the proud homosexual associated with east-monsoon and daylight. The symbolism is altogether too sophisticated to explain it as a pure product of the subconscious. We even have evidence of conscious word-play in this context. The name of the déma with the long penis (pahui) is Diwa. The pahui is a spear but also a club with a disc-shaped stone-head (vulva). Diwa has a counterpart in the opposite moiety by the name of Dáwi. Dáwi is a headhunter like Diwa, setting out after a mayo-initiation. In contradistinction to Diwa he carries a club with an egg-shaped stone head, a male symbol. As if afraid that we should fail to note the complementarity of Diwa and Dawi, Diwa has Yugil as an alias, and Dawi has a clan-brother called Yagil (Van Baal, Déma pp.758, 763).

b. *The Ngad'a of Flores*[20]

The Ngad'a are a mountain people living in the southern part of central Flores, one of the lesser Sunda Islands in Indonesia. They are cultivators of

[20] The description presented here is the abstract of a study published in Van Baal, "Over Wegen en Drijfveren" pp.166-218 (1947). This study is based on an analysis of articles written by Father P. Arndt s.v.d. in Anthropos vols. 24, 26, 27, 31 and 32, and of a fairly voluminous collection of Ngad'a myths which Father A. Mommersteeg had brought with him to the prisoners' camp in which we awaited the end of world-war II. We studied these myths together. F. Mommersteeg's knowledge of the language and customs of the Ngad'a were an immense help and I derived great profit from his comments.

rice, maize and tubers. Although irrigated rice-fields are — or were — unknown in the area, the Ngad's are herders of water-buffaloes which are an important article of wealth. The people live in villages, each one out of several belonging to one or other of the seven chiefdoms which together constitute the Ngad'a princedom, ruled by the radja of Badjawa. Our knowledge of the overall structure of the princedom and of the social structure generally is limited. According to Arndt there are seven main clans, four of them associated with rain-giving wells in the upperworld, and three with water-receiving wells on the earth. The clans are subdivided into subclans but exact information is lacking. We do not know whether the partition into seven main clans is connected with that into chiefdoms. We think it fairly improbable because this would imply that the clans are localised. Since the preferred form of marriage is with a mother's brother's daughter, men who wish to marry outside the clan might have a long way to go to seek a bride.

Another point of interest is the partition into classes. There are nobles, commoners and slaves. Again, our information is limited. It seems probable that nobility is a matter of primogeniture and not of membership of a particular clan. We note, however, that the noble class is associated with the sun, that of the commoners with the moon. We should be careful not to pay too much attention to this distinction because in Ngad'a religion the moon-symbol is of far greater importance than the sun.

Ngad'a villages are built on the mountain slopes and they derive their orientation from the opposition uphill-downhill. Consequently, they all follow the same pattern of village-outlay, namely a number of successive terraces, one above the other with uphill, 'the head of the village', the houses of the nobility and the sacred sacrificial poles which are the property of the chiefs of local subclans. The houses of the commoners are lined alongside the terraces which lead to the 'head of the village'. The lower part is called 'the tail of the village'. Some villages are occupied by only one subclan and consequently have only one sacrificial pole, but in the larger villages there are more.

The spirit-world of the Ngad'a is based on a cosmogony which distinguishes three worlds: the upperworld where *Déva*, the supreme being resides, the earth inhabited by mankind, and the underworld which is the abode of *Nitu*, a female deity. Déva is said to be the creator of everything, also of Nitu, but the notions concerning the process of creation are rather confused. Originally there was only the ocean having in its centre a very small island, an egg or an isolated mountain. Here Déva made the first human beings. According to another myth the first male descended from heaven whereas the first female was born from the earth. At first they were very small but they rapidly grew, and along with them the earth increased in size. Originally the earth was liquid and soft; when Déva gave the sun and the fire the earth became solid.

Déva watches the conduct of the people on earth, rewarding the virtuous with prosperity and wealth, and punishing those who do wrong. He decides when people shall die and he sends rain and sunshine. In all this Déva is a typical supreme being. However, the situation is far more complicated. There is not one Déva but there are thousands of déva who have been created by the great Déva and are called his children. These déva are found everywhere, in particular on hilltops and in the upperworld. In addition, every village, every house, and even every human being has his particular déva who watches him and if necessary reports to the great Déva. Often it is linguistically impossible to decide whether the déva mentioned is the great one or one of his numerous manifestations. The effect is confusing or, more correctly, gives evidence that déva is a confusing concept which should not be identified unreservedly with the concept of a supreme being.

There are additional reasons for caution. Although invisible, Déva manifests himself in dreams as an old man of high stature with a long white beard, luminous and covered with a golden mantle, adorned with ivory bracelets. There is something of a personalisation of the moon about Déva, the great one. The same is the case, and even more explicitly so, with his secondary manifestations who have all sorts or adventures of the kind the mythical heroes have, who are often vague personalisations of the moon. Next to the veiled references to the moon apparent in the exploits of the secondary déva and in those of the mythical heroes, consideration should be given to the relations between déva, man and water-buffalo. Several of the lower déva are intimately connected with buffaloes. One of them even adopted the shape of a buffalo. Déva herds the people on earth just like men herd their buffaloes. The buffaloes tended by men are the souls of déva; the buffaloes herded by the déva are the souls of human beings. When the people on earth slaughter a buffalo they kill a déva; when the déva in heaven kill a buffalo they slaughter a human being. The text should not be interpreted as proof of the thesis that human beings are capable of killing the déva but as an indication of the very close association of déva and buffalo. The buffalo is the sacrificial animal par excellence, and for great ceremonial occasions not just any buffalo will do, but only the old, long-horned animal.

The long flat horns of an old buffalo are a typical moon-symbol, a projection of the sickle of the waning moon. The sacrificial pole in the village has two arms on top of the pole and these arms are called its horns. The sickle of the waning moon is the symbol of approaching death. A text noted by Arndt says: "when the new moon appears just above the western horizon he is like an infant, but the full moon is like a mature man. When he has become small again the moon resembles an old man, and when at new moon he disappears he is like the dead" (Arndt, Anthropos 24, p.843).

The most obvious characteristic of Déva's relations with the moon is their evasiveness. It is nowhere said that the moon is a symbol of Déva, that Déva has specific relations with the moon or uses the moon as an ornament. Nevertheless, a relation of some sort obtrudes time and again, and to an even higher degree the same is the case with the mythical heroes. They are a strange lot, many of them travelling from west to east like the moon which is first seen on the western sky as the new moon, and every day stands a little bit more to the east at nightfall until the full moon, when the moon rises on the eastern horizon at the hour of sunset. It is impossible to give a review of the relevant myths. The recurrent themes are those of two quarrelling brothers, one of whom leaves the country and afterwards returns with wealth; the pregnant woman who lives in a cave or in a forest and gives birth to a son who matures in a fortnight; the cock who brings riches and palmwine; the golden mat, the golden pillow and the gold dust which are stolen, etc. A good case is that of *Ulu*, a word meaning head but also used by the Sun as a term of abuse for the Moon. Ulu quarrels with his older brother. He becomes very small, as small as a coconut. He flies to Sumba where he is well-cared for. After he has been covered with *waru*-leaves (the waru is a tree bearing big yellow flowers) he regains his old stature in ten days. In gratitude he teaches his benefactors the art of fire-making, who in turn reward him with gold. After some time Ulu returns to Flores and makes peace with his brother. His riches, however, are coveted by *D'ake*, the giant. He calls his thirty partisans and when the moon is waning D'ake attacks the village of Ulu and robs him of his riches. Arndt is undoubtedly right when he associates D'ake with the dark moon which swallows the waning moon. Nevertheless, it is not so that D'ake can be identified with the dark moon. All that can be said is that this story (like that of Ulu) could be applied to the moon.

The same applies to another typical story, that of the wife who is captured by a witch. The leading character is *Lado Manu* (Sir Cock) who comes from Sumbawa (west of Flores) to find himself a wife. He finds one in Flores and marries her. During her pregnancy she is captured by a witch who gouges out her eyes and keeps her enclosed in a cave. The witch takes her clothes and ornaments, thus impersonates the poor wife, and Lado Manu fails to notice the difference. In the meantime the real wife gives birth to a son, Prince Sina, who reaches manhood in half a month. He meets his father and the deceit is discovered. The witch is killed, the mother returns and some time afterwards Prince Sina becomes the owner of a cock which has magical power; the cock restores the mother's eyesight and enables Prince Sina to create a complete village with houses, people and buffaloes, a village which still exists. The assumption that Prince Sina (who grew up in half a month) is identical with the waxing moon, and his mother (conquered by the dark moon, the witch) with the old moon, is confirmed by an alternative reading in which the father is called Star, father's brother Moon and the woman herself *Lélu*, i.e. cotton. Cotton is closely connected with the moon. During the annual *reba*-celebration, a feast taking place either at

253

the new or at the full moon, the Ngad'a prepare a comb with thirteen teeth. On every subsequent new moon one of the teeth is wrapped up in cotton. The comb is a symbol of the waxing moon. Witches are said to be extremely afraid of combs; it is the only effective weapon which can scare them off.

The connections of the leading characters of the myth with the moon are fairly evident. Nevertheless, there is not one of them who really is the moon or is explicitly identified with one of its phases. It is the same in the case of other myths which cannot possibly be related here, not only because there are too many of them, but mainly because the traits in them which refer to the moon are often of such subtlety that it would take pages of elaborate analysis to elucidate the connection. However that be, in 59 out of the 103 myths of the collection, elements which are typical for a moon-myth could be traced, but there is not one which really is a myth of the moon. The real content of these stories is that the mythological heroes are pictured as people who have something in common with the moon, something more than ordinary human beings who resemble the moon only in the respect that their lives are temporary like that of the moon and characterised by a period of waxing followed by one of waning. Another important point is that many of these mythical beings are ancestors, still venerated as clan-ancestors, who gave their names to the sacrificial poles and other sacred places in the various villages. A few of these ancestors are of specific importance because they taught the Ngad'a people certain things. This is especially so in the case of the mythical sisters *Vidjo* and *Vadjo* who taught them how to celebrate the *reba* and how to take care of a newly born baby. Such myths are exceptions; the great majority of these myths are just stories which derive their interest mainly from the fact that they refer, with greater or lesser lucidity, to the moon.

Before we turn to the sacred places in the village and the spirits inhabiting them a few words must be said of Déva's counterpart, Nitu, the goddess of the underworld. On ceremonial occasions, i.e. when sacrifices are made, she is usually invoked along with Déva and, although lesser than him, her name is mentioned first in the recurring formula Nitu-Déva, Mothers and Fathers, etc.[21] Nitu is associated with death and underworld. She is the Black Mother who allots a place to each newcomer to the country of the dead, the underworld, where she also takes care of them. In one text it is said that whereas Déva is very wise, Nitu is perfectly ignorant (Arndt, Anthropos 24 p.826).

Just as Déva is surrounded by lesser déva, so Nitu has thousands of nitu who live with her in the underworld or manifest themselves to human beings either as snakes or beautifully adorned women. The dead too are called nitu. They live in the underworld in the same way as on earth, eating

[21] It is possible that the precedence given to the Mothers must be associated with the fact that the guests of honour usually are the bridegivers who are maternal relatives. Without further research the question must remain undecided.

254

grass-seeds for rice and tending porcupines, rats and cats instead of buffa-loes, pigs and goats. In general nitu are malicious, a somewhat curious state-ment which should be more specifically applied to nitu manifesting them-selves near water-wells and rivers, and not to the multifarious nitu who live in the village where they are worshipped as ancestors.

Next to déva and nitu there are two other kinds of spirits. In the first place the *no'a*, a kind of slightly malicious déva who live in black rain-clouds and take tribute from the live-stock. In the second place there are the *ngebu*, a benevolent kind of nitu who can be further specified as ngebu of the house and the small live-stock, ngebu of the village and ngebu of the fields.

So far we have dealt only with spirits in general. Everything becomes more specific as soon as we enter the village where each subclan (if there is more than one) has its sacrificial pole dedicated to the founding ancestor. Behind the pole stands a *menhir*, which is the sanctuary of the clanfather's father. Halfway down the village is the shrine of the clanmother, a house which has a hearth which is only used on certain ceremonial occasions. Fi-nally, there is a small shrine on the roof of one of the houses which is dedi-cated to the clanfather's mother. Clanmother's mother and -father have their shrines in the palm-wine grove outside the village, not at all an unim-portant place because the palm-wine grove is a centre of social life. An in-teresting detail in this context is that the shrine dedicated to the clan-mother's mother, a small but elegantly adorned house, used to be the place for the performance of the now obsolete circumcision ceremony.

A second category of places of religious interest within the village are the graves. The dead are buried within the village compound. Some of them are given stone monuments; others again are entombed in the stone walls under the houses of the clan-leaders or simply commemorated by three small stones representing a fireplace. The only people buried outside the village are the victims of a violent death. The Ngad'a are surrounded by their dead who on festive occasions receive their share of the various offerings prima-rily presented to Nitu, Déva and the more important ancestors worshipped in the special shrines dedicated to them.

Another place where the ancestors and the dead generally are supposed to reside is the stone walls separating the ascending terraces. Here they live to-gether with the ngebu of the village. The people say that for the dead these walls are as important as in war-time the outer wall of the village is for the living.

Yet, the spirits of the dead are not only outside the houses, they are also within. Every house has its digging-stick, its palm-wine bowl and a little basket to be used during the reba-celebration. Each of these is given the name of a deceased relative who is supposed to have his abode in it, and each of them receives his share when a sacrifice takes place. In addition, there are the golden ornaments of the family which bear the names of ancestors who are worshipped through prayer and sacrifice. Then again there are the hearth and one of the three hearth-stones. They too are dedicated to a specific ancestor. The Ngad'a is surrounded by spirits. When he leaves his village he runs the risk of meeting nitu at the well where he draws water; when he visits his rice-field he knows that there are ngebu living in the low stone walls protecting the field; apart from all this he has his house-déva and his private déva. He is beset by spirits wherever he goes and it is worth noting that it is not the spirits who reside in the village, but some categories of spirits who live outside the village that he is afraid of. In the village are the ancestors, the déva, and the ngebu, and on the ricefield or the field where he planted his tubers he is surrounded by the benevolent ngebu who have their abode in the stone walls encircling the field.

The Ngad'a regularly communicate with these spirits. Every time an animal of the live stock is killed, whether a buffalo, a pig, a goat or a hen, the spirits are invoked and they receive their share. It is a minimal share because the Ngad'a are well aware that the spirits do not really eat. Nevertheless, homage is paid to them, and their assistance is invoked, whatever the occasion. It may be that visitors have come to negotiate a marriage, that a man recently dead must be commemorated, or a sacrifice is brought because somebody has to fulfil a vow after recovering from illness, the ancestors are always remembered and requested to give their protection and aid to the living.

We shall not try to describe the ceremonial feasts of the Ngad'a. The most impressive feasts are those connected with the installation of a new sacrificial pole, the outward symbol of the establishment of a new, independent subclan. On such an occasion scores of buffaloes are killed. Impressive too are the great sacrifices brought in commemoration of a deceased noble. Compared with feasts of this kind the annual reba is an extremely simple affair, primarily connected with family relations. Yet it is worth while to pay some attention to it.

A month before the reba a preliminary celebration takes place. A sacrifice of tubers is brought to the shrine of the clanmother's father, an indication that the group of bride-givers is implied. A month later the feast begins, preceded by the singing of songs which all have the words 'Oh Moon' as a refrain. Sacrifices are brought to various shrines followed by dancing and concluding with the same songs as before, but now the refrain refers to the tubers. The next day the nearby villages are visited, according to Arndt to ensure peaceful relations, a statement which undoubtedly is correct but probably not exact. The ceremony at the shrine of the clan-ancestor's bride-giver suggests that the primary aim of these visits is to pay tribute to the bride-givers. When the visits are completed everybody goes home to offer new sacrifices that same night. On this occasion each family father recites a very lengthy text, inviting the ancestors to come from Sina and Java, and describing their journey to Flores. When he is finished the door is opened to let the spirits of the dead enter. A quarter of an hour later the door is closed again, and divination follows in order to find out whether during the coming year a boy or a girl shall be born. Then a meal is served, during which eating alternates with singing.

An interesting point is the invitation to the spirits to enter the house. It is not an uncommon feature in Ngad'a ritual. On the contrary, in every sacrificial formula the request returns in one form or another. These formulas usually begin with the invocation: Oh Nitu-Déva, Mothers and Fathers, followed by the names of a series of mythical ancestors. Then follows the specific request for which the sacrifice is brought, invariably associated with one for health, prosperity and a long life, alternating with invitations such as the following: "come thee down to sit on our necks, to stay on our shoulders". Another favourite clause is the request to be as a wall encircling and enclosing the worshippers. If the Ngad'a is beset by spirits on all sides, it is because he wishes it to be so, because he experiences their presence as a protection.

A very widespread practice is that of divination. A popular technique is that of using a piece of bamboo which has three knots. When put in the fire the bamboo explodes at one end first. Previous to this a hen is tied to a stick planted in the hearth. The hen is called a buffalo and the stick a sacrificial pole. If divination is applied because one of the inmates of the house is seriously ill, the bamboo is requested to give an unmistakable sign whether the patient will die or not. One side of the bamboo is for death, the other for life. The bamboo is then put in the fire. If an unfavourable answer is given, the procedure is continued. The bamboo is now requested to give evidence if the patient has stolen or has committed any other sin. It is a lengthy procedure, including requests for counsel about what should be done to redeem the error committed, for information as to who among the ancestors may be willing to give assistance to the patient, and so on. Finally the hen is slaughtered and the meat offered to the ancestors.

The sacrifice is purely symbolic; we might call it a case of pious deceit. However, deception does not play a role here. If the patient recovers a real sacrifice will be brought. If a buffalo has been promised, a real buffalo will be killed and in this case not an old but a young one, apparently because it is connected with continuous life. The real point of interest in the procedure is that this technique of divination is actually a protracted process of negotiation with the spirits. They are consulted about what to do and at the same time requested to give their assistance.

The faith in the effect of the procedure, however, is limited. Arndt gives an elaborate description of the divinatory activities preceding a war raid, and he tells us that his informant finally added: "In spite of the numerous bamboos which have been exploded and the many questions which have been asked, nevertheless some people will be conquered or captured". A good medicine-man warns the warriors not to ask him whether they will

257

return from the raid or not. "On many occasions the words of the medicine-man come true, on others not. Yet, we must obey his words, otherwise disaster will certainly befall us" (Anthr. 26, pp.719 f.). We conclude that divination does not guarantee success but that it is a means of escaping with a minimum of damage.

Dreams can be important as omina. Bad dreams, presaging disaster, lead to various kinds of sacrifice to ward off the danger. Sacrifice is the obvious means for contact with the supernatural, and we hear very little of the use of magical formulas or magical rites. Most of the few cases mentioned by Arndt are connected with sacrifice. Nevertheless, it is by no means impossible that there are more instances of the use of magical formulas than those cited by observers of Ngad'a life. It is a well-known fact that it is extremely difficult to acquire information about the simple formulas used in the course of the daily routine, for example while cooking. However, this need not bother us here. The focus of Ngad'a religious thought lies elsewhere: in the communication with the gods and spirits by means of prayer and sacrifice, in the symbiosis of men and spirits. The spirits are always there, participating in the life of the people and receiving their equitable share of every festive dish.

2. *The belief in the efficacy of the magic rite. Spell and Prayer*

The belief in the efficacy of magic is one of the thorny problems of religious anthropology. Anthropological literature abounds with baffling stories. A good collection of perplexing cases is that presented in R. M. Berndt's articles on "Wuradjeri Magic and 'Clever Men'" (Oceania 1947). One of the minor features related is that of 'sinking' quartz crystals into the bodies of the initiates. More interesting is the report that medicine-men climb up trees by producing a mysterious cord from their scrotum which goes upward by itself, after which the medicine-man follows in reversed position (his feet up and his head down) until he has reached the top of the tree where he settles in a nest. The informants claim that they were present. Unfortunately, it all happened many years ago and it is impossible to collect additional information.

W. Lloyd Warner was better situated when he made his enquiries into the techniques of the sorcerers of Arnhem Land. A few of the most absorbing pages of "A black Civilization" are those in which a sorcerer describes how he killed his victims (pp.198 ff.). He first stunned his victim by hitting him or her on the head. Then he opened the body by cutting a hole permitting him to insert his hand to take away the heart and the lungs. He then put thistles and dry grass in their place and carefully closed the wound which healed without leaving a trace, whereupon he sent the victim home telling him that he was going to die in two or three days, as he actually did. The stories enter into the most gruesome details; every phase of the process

258

is described realistically to such an exent, that the listener can only think of a cruel murder in cold blood. In a way it is, because the victim, made aware that a spell has been cast over him, dies. The victim does not doubt the efficacy of the ritual any less than the sorcerer and dies under symptoms of shock. Yet, what really happened even Lloyd Warner was unable to discover.

Fortunately, we are better informed on Marind-anim sorcery where almost identical techniques are applied, or more correctly, where stories are told which are of a similar kind as those reported by Warner. The stories are of a most impressive realism. Although already fairly well informed of the ins and outs of Marind-anim culture at the time I served at Merauke as a young controleur, i.e. as an assistant district officer and magistrate combined, I nevertheless committed here one of the biggest blunders an anthropologist can make. A man was brought to court who admitted that in cooperation with his helpers he had killed a young man by inserting a pointed stick between his spread-out legs and driving it right away upward as far as the victim's throat. The procedure was depicted with such a convincing realism that I never doubted a moment that it was real murder in cold blood, until some thirty years later, discussing the case with my old friend Verschueren, the latter quietly remarked: "have you never thought of sorcery? It sounds like it". Of course it was sorcery; it could not have been anything else.

Among the Marind-anim sorcery is certainly an anti-social act unless it is performed to kill somebody who is considered to be an enemy of the community, for example because he revealed the secret of the ritual to an outsider. Whether performed for private or for communal ends, sorcery is always a ritual act, based on myth and mythically associated with one of the clans. We have no evidence that the performers must be members of that clan; in fact it is hardly probable. We do know, however, that there are always several working in concert and that their leader must be a medicine-man, an important datum, because the initiation to which a medicine-man is submitted marks him out as a man who has very special relations with the hidden world. His initiation is a protracted ordeal. Cadaverous fluid is blown into his eyes; he has to inhale it through his nose by means of a hollow reed; he has to eat a sago-dish soaked in cadaverous fluid. Not every candidate can take the treatment. Those who do are changed men, and of course they are. They have gone as far as anyone can to intrude into the world of death and decay, the world at the back of things. Yet, in all this there is nothing specific. There are numerous societies where the medicine-man and the shaman have to submit to really atrocious ordeals. There are telling examples of it in Australian, Asian and American ethnography. The candidates go to the verge of the bearable, to the ends of endurance, submerge into the products of death and decay, balancing on the very edge of humanity at the point where the other world, the world of the reverse, of the other side, is presumed to begin.

A second point is that he formulas used by the sorcerers, contain references to myth. Although the references are comparatively few, they are unmistakable, at least one of the names used by the performers to describe themselves being a name derived from myth (Van Baal, Dema pp.905 f.). The performance is not an act which stands apart from ordinary religious practice but refers to it, just as the religious system itself refers to sorcery. It has a place in the socio-religious system by its association with one particular clan, a place defined by the classificatory system.

Finally, the act is a symbolic act. This is, of course, what everybody had guessed, but Verschueren found out what really happens. After due preparations the party of sorcerers sets out during the night, taking their various ingredients with them. When they come closer to the victim's house they stop and the leader puts a charm on a magical instrument *(tang):* "Suddenly the *tang* has vanished. It is said to have gone off to fetch the victim. Shortly afterwards the leader pretends that the victim has arrived. He gives a few beats on the ground with his club, then takes a bamboo knife and makes some movements as of cutting. After that, blood... which has been brought in the bladder of [an] animal... is poured out into the bamboo-tubes containing the water and the sperma. The blood is the victim's blood, which the assailants now drink. Sometimes they also eat of his flesh symbolized by a young coconut mixed with sperma. The leader then pronounces a second formula, upon which the victim is believed to wake up and return to his house, where he will die within a couple of days. The party see to it that some token is left on the spot, so that people may know what has happened during the night" etc. (ibid. p.907).

Hardly less interesting is that one and the same expression is used for the rapidly worsening condition of a victim of sorcery as for the cause of death by old age, viz. *mui baren*, the flesh has been consumed. What at old age is a long process of wear and tear is effectuated in two days by means of a symbolic consumption of the flesh (ibid. p.909). However, not by symbolic consumption alone. The presence of a medicine-man, the knowledge of the secret formula and the reference to myth are as essential to the act as the symbolic action. In common concert they constitute what to the performers, the victim, and the community at large is the essence of reality, a reality which is so true that they only speak of it in terms borrowed from physical reality. Apparently they feel that any reference to the symbolic nature of the procedure would detract from the fact that the so-called symbolic act is actually the essence of the process.

The complicated dialectics ensuing from the tension between the visible reality and a symbolic reality which is essentially more real than the visible one, were brought home to me when on a bright morning in 1937 I interviewed a Marind-anim medicine-man. He showed me the stone which he

260

had produced from his sick son's belly by means of massage. He told me that he was kneading his son's belly when all of a sudden he held that stone in his hand which had come out of the belly. What is more, soon afterwards the boy recovered. As even the smallest pebble in this alluvial part of the country has been imported, it was altogether too evident that he had brought the stone with him to conjure it up at the right moment, and this is what I pointed out to him and to the numerous bystanders. But all in vain; even after an hour of remonstrating and questioning everyone present stuck to the medicine-man's story with genuine sincerity. The stone had come out of the boy's belly. The symbolic act is a real act, as real as the hole in the woman's chest which only Willidjungo saw (above, p.239).

The problem is how they can believe the symbol to be more true than the tangible fact, the image more real than its prototype. How can they prefer the shadow of the thing to the thing itself, the imitative act to the real one? It is at this point that a closer study of the magic formulas may shed some light. After all, to the people concerned the formula is the well-nigh inseparable constituent of every magic act, the indispensable and effective core of the action. Whence does it derive this mysterious and yet universal power?

Strangely enough, the formulas accompanying the ritual act often pass unnoticed. Informants tend to be unwilling to communicate them, and as the texts are often obscure their collection presents itself as a rather unrewarding occupation for the ethnographer. Consequently, we are rather under-informed as far as magical formulas are concerned. Fortunately, the ethnographic literature on the Marind-anim is an exception. Wirz collected some sixty odd formulas, some of them probably incomplete, but on the whole sufficient to give us a clearer notion of their purport. Eighteen of these formulas refer to the déma or to myth and a few of them could more appropriately be called prayers. As to the formulas in general, the most outstanding feature is the names. The names are the heart and core of the matter, at least to the Marind-anim, whether it be names of déma or names of unknown origin. The Marind-anim are always keen on collecting information on secret names, and it is worth while going more deeply into this by analysing a few formulas using names which cannot be derived from mythology or from any other known source of secret knowledge. The relevant formulas describe the object of the rite in a very peculiar manner.

Planting a banana-shoot the planter addresses the shoot with the following words: "Gomat-oar! on this spot thou shalt bend". The hunter, goading his dogs to catch a wallaby, addresses them as follows: "Kékus-teeth! Bite into Saparim-coconut" (ibid. pp.875 and 871). The Gomat-oar of the first formula refers to the future banana-leaf. It is not called a leaf but it is named after something resembling the banana-leaf, viz. an oar. As if this were not enough, it is called a Gomat-oar. Nobody knows who or what Gomat is; presumably it is a personal name, but one of an utterly unknown person. The same procedure is followed in the second formula. The coconut is a reference to the flesh of the wallaby, tender like that of a young coconut. The name Saparim cannot be explained, it is added on, just like Kékus is added on as a personal name to the teeth, in this case the dog's teeth. The personal name, the name of an unknown person, adds a new quality to the teeth, as it does to the coconut and the oar, viz. that of being associated with something personal of unknown origin. In other words, the object of the simple rite is represented as more than it really is: the banana-leaf refers to an oar, and a very specific one, a Gomat-oar; the flesh of the wallaby to a coconut and again not to every coconut but to 'the' Saparim-coconut. Superimposed is a reference to a totally different object which because of its specific qualities shares a certain likeness with the object of the rite, and this symbol of the object is further qualified as an image belonging to a mysterious personality. The additions add unknown qualities to the object, they refer to things unsuspected by the layman which nevertheless are proper to the object. Nobody would know that a banana-leaf is also a Gomat-oar, if he had not been told so. The leaf is more than it seems to be, and the formula describes the mysterious surplus of the leaf. Similarly, the formula for goading a dog describes the mysterious surplus concealed in a dog's teeth and the flesh of the wallaby she is going to catch. The Marind-anim are well aware of this. They classify the formula of the magic rite as *kuma meen*, speech which is *kuma,* i.e. secret and hidden, that which is at the bottom of a thing, in figurative speech also the female genital.

The statement that the formula describes the mysterious surplus of the object can be further specified. It describes the hidden side, the *kuma*-aspect of the object in the situation of fulfilment of the operator's wish. The formula states that this *kuma*-aspect, i.e. all that is unforeseeable, refractory and arbitrary in the object, complies or is going to comply with the performer's desire. The personified *kuma,* the Gomat-oar, the Kékus-teeth, the Saparim-coconut, are going to act accordingly.

In spite of all that has been said against it, have we to admit that casting a spell is a compelling act anyhow? And the opposite of a prayer? If a prayer really were what some scholars pretend it to be, namely a declaration of resignation and pious abandonment, the champions of the contrast between spell and prayer could not be gainsaid. However, their notion of prayer is not the kind preached in the gospel, where the believers are exhorted to ask in good faith for the fulfilment of all their needs whatsoever. "Ask, and it shall be given you; seek, and ye shall find; knock, and it shall be opened unto you;. . .. Or what man is there of you, whom if his son ask bread, will he give him a stone?. . ..If ye then, being evil, know how to give good gifts unto your children, how much more shall your Father which is in heaven give good things to them that ask him" (St. Matthew 7:7-11). "And whatsoever ye shall ask in my name, that will I do. . .. If ye shall ask any thing in my name, I will do it" (St. John 14:13,14). An important point is good faith: "He that believeth on me, the works that I do shall he do also; and greater works than these shall he do" says Jesus (St. John 14:12). And elsewhere: "If ye have faith as a grain of mustard seed, ye shall say unto this mountain, Remove hence to yonder place; and it shall remove; and nothing shall be impossible unto you" (St. Matthew 17:20). In good Christian tradition there is more to prayer than abandonment and sheer resignation. After this digression we may return to the analysis of our formulas.

The formula (spell) takes it origin from the discourse between man and his universe, in the case of a particular formula a discourse concerning a certain object and the fulfilment of a desire. In this discourse man feels addressed or singled out by his universe, and he endeavours to address it in turn, trying to discover the kind of address to which his universe will be willing to answer, that is, willing to show itself communicable. The formula he finally discovers in answer to his quest is not really man's discovery but a gift, a revelation bestowed on him by his universe. The formula is the outcome of an act of communication in which man's universe reveals to him the secret of how it should be addressed in this or that circumstance, a secret which is at the same time a revelation of its hidden essence in that particular field, in Marind-anim terms its *kuma* in the state of wish-fulfilment. Such a formula is not consciously man-made but comes to him as a gift received in a dream or vision as by an act of grace. The formula is necessarily an effective formula or spell because it is the answer to man's need to overcome the source of a certain type of anxiety which, whenever aroused, threatens to plunge him into feelings of being ostracised. This particular anxiety must be taken from him by a formula which spells success for him, a formula which really works. The formula is the answer to man's call for help. It is at the same time a call for communication and partnership. Togetherness and partnership of the individual with his universe do not exist independently from his success in life as a hunter or gardener. Lack of success necessarily ousts him from the certainty of being part of his universe. When man cries for help he means effective help which alone is the verification of true communication and partnership of subject and universe. The need for help and that for communication cannot be separated from each other; they belong as much together as the call and the answer, the need and its fulfilment.

Is there then no difference at all between spell and prayer? Of course there are differences but we should guard against overstressing their impact and precision. The two concepts overlap on all sides. Spells are usually directed towards concrete, pragmatic ends. The same can be said of many prayers and if in this respect there is a difference it can only be that a prayer may serve wider, more universal ends than a spell generally does. Spells often are accompanied by symbolic acts. However, a prayer is said kneeling, with the hands clasped and the eyes closed. The prayer can also be accompanied by a sacrifice. Spell and prayer are both ritual acts and parts

263

of rituals. If there is a difference between the two, it is this that the ritual acts accompanying a spell are more often imitative acts symbolising the rite's pragmatic purpose, whereas those connected with praying are preferably of the kind which expresses notions of respect and worship. It is a vague difference, linked up with another, namely that the personalities addressed in the spell are usually closely connected with the object of the rite, whereas those addressed in prayer are more often mediators ruling from a great distance over man and the object of his wishes alike.

The great variety of forms of spells and prayers makes it difficult to extract from this amazing mass of never absolute differences a hard and fast rule which can be made operational as a mark of distinction between the two. Therefore we might try yet another way, taking our point of departure in the fact that both spell and prayer are based on the firm faith that the word will be heard and the call answered. The spell is a gift of the gods and, if properly applied, it works. Though the same is essentially the case with prayer there is a slight difference. In prayer we have the role of the mediator to think of, the divinity to whom the prayer is sent up. Although the faithful knows that he can rely on it that his god will answer his prayer, there is the possibility that in a specific case the god will think better of it and answer in a way diverging from the one the worshipper had hoped for or expected. There is a degree of latitude between the prayer and its fulfilment which is wider than in the case of the spell. The spell does not allow for doubt that the rite could be ineffective, whereas the prayer does. Religious belief is more absolute, more unconditional in the case of the spell and the magic rite than in that of prayer, for some students an embarassing conclusion perhaps but all the same an inescapable one.

The conclusion is of interest in connection with the dispute on the coercive character of the spell in which prayer tends to be presented as the shining example of humble piety and true faith. The kind of prayer thus presented is an ideal-typical concept, one emptied of every concrete, so-called selfish end, in which of the traditional content of prayer no more than four or five items have been spared: the confession of guilt, the prayer for remission and redemption, the 'pouring out' of the soul crowned by a 'Thy will be done', and a doxology. It is the kind of prayer suiting the needs of modern Christians who for obvious reasons no longer believe in divine interference in the affairs of this world, in other words the kind of prayer allowing for a really considerable amount of doubt. We cannot use this ethnocentric concept of prayer in the anthropological science of religion. The reality as observed by anthropologists is that to the people concerned neither spell nor prayer are man-made devices but divine gifts, products of revelation which may and must be used as means to ends. If the belief that the use of these means is a guarantee for success is co-terminous with coercion, then the one is as coercive as the other, only with this difference that prayer permits a variable allowance for doubt with regard to the result, which is lacking in spell. The degree of variability of the allowance for doubt is defined by the degree to which success in life is conceived of as a token of divine favour, to which it is inversely proportional.

We can at last return to our point of departure, the solid belief in magic as demonstrated by the description of a symbolic act of sorcery as an act of real murder. The effect of the symbolic act cannot be doubted without calling the whole worldview into doubt, a view based upon the belief that man can penetrate into the secrets of his universe, secrets which are identical with its hidden other side. For this reason the symbolic performance of the sorcerers necessarily is the true essence of a terribly real process. Speaking of it in other terms than those derived from real, pragmatic action would be a misrepresentation of its purport and essential nature. The performer would be mocking both himself and the impact of his deed if he presented it in terms of its outward form. The observable action is only its shell: what the performer really did is what he says he did. He does not for a moment doubt its truth. More often than once repenting sorcerers confessed to the priests of the mission that they were guilty of murder, describing their action in the same realistic terms as those here reported.

And yet, this acme of blind faith is at the same time a clear symptom of the strain exerted by the logic of the magic rite. The logic is a compelling one. Once the identification of spell and hidden essence of reality has been accepted, belief in the efficacy of the rite is a must. One cannot doubt it without doubting the whole worldview, the communicability of the universe as revealed by the symbols of its apprehended intentions. The necessity to believe makes it necessary to repress every doubt with regard to the credibility of the magic rite, a repression which betrays itself in certain overtones. One of these is the refusal to describe the act in other terms than those of the pragmatic action for which the rite is a substitute. It is by no means the only one. The formula must be combined with symbolic acts and the performers must be specially qualified to pronounce the spell. Either they must be members of the proper clan, or medicine-men who acquired entrance to the hidden inner world by submitting themselves to a cruel process of special initiation.

These devices to strengthen the effect of the rite are in fact limitations on the effect of the spell which only works under certain conditions, and it is interesting to note that among the most important of these conditions is the presence of certain pre-established personal relations between the performer and the object of his rite. They must belong to the same clan. The apparent automatism of the ritual procedure is restricted by personal relations which refer directly to the need for communication which is the foundation of the ritual. It is not a trait of minor importance. Among the Australian tribes the specification of such personal relations has, just as among the Marind-anim, led to an elaborate system of ritual specialisation by clans. The classificatory system resulting from it combines the total fabric of the physical universe with that of the society at large.

This systematisation leads us to an aspect of the magic rites which we have thus far ignored. In our discussions we have more than once presented the case of magic rites and of ritual generally as that of more or less spontaneous reactions inspired by visionary experiences. Undoubtedly some rites originated that way; we have a number of good examples in modern cargo-cults. Here however we are dealing with magic rites making part of elaborate religious systems which are the outcome of an age-long development and integration of cultural institutions, a development which has led to a highly perfected pattern of distribution of ritual functions. It is difficult to reconcile such a systematisation with the notion of spontaneity.

There are other reasons besides urging us not to over-emphasise the role of spontaneous action in the genesis of ritual, certainly not as far as magic rites are concerned. The foundation of the religious complex in the existential conflict between being a subject and being a part stresses the importance of the total, comprehensive aspect of the relations between the subject and his universe. The scores of transitory wants and anxieties connected with magic rites are of another, a lower order. That an individual's temporary concern about the growth of his newly planted banana-shoots, or lack of aggressivity of his dog could lead to a spontaneous origination of ritual action, seems far-fetched to say the least. Instead, these rites should be seen as elaborations and variations on a central theme, that of a universe teeming with intentionality, a universe inviting communication and interaction with its secret powers.

It is this central theme which is the incessant source of inspiration for medicine-men and shamans who indulge in mystic speculation. We came across such a functionary among the Marind-anim, a man who unexpectedly retired to the solitude of the savannah to listen to the voices of the hidden world which can only be heard in silence (above, p.238). We do not know whether he brought a message home on that occasion; we only know for certain that it is the medicine-men who are the innovators of ritual. Their innovations usually are of minor importance; actually, they could not be anything else because they originate within the existing cultural pattern and must be accommodated to it. However, these innovations keep the system alive and adapted to the needs of the community.

A closer inspection of some of the magic rites gives support to our view that they are elaborations on a central theme. The magic rite for the prosperous growth of a banana-shoot is a typical case of a rite which cannot possibly be the fruit of privation or anxiety. On the contrary; there is not the slightest reason for a Marind-anem to worry about the growth of the banana-shoot he planted. Bananas are not a difficult crop and the thing will grow anyhow. He does not need a rite for its well being. However, the banana is an important symbol in ritual and myth, an important totem and moon-symbol originated by Geb. One cannot just plant bananas without caring about their mythical and religious impact. What counts is the individual's communication with his universe, and in that universe the banana has an important place. The ritual act on its behalf is only one out of a multitude of specific acts, each of small importance by itself, but in their totality constituting a system of continuous communication between man and his universe.

The Marind-anim highly appreciate these 'means of communication'. They appreciate them so much that they constantly try to increase their knowledge of these rites and formulas. They try to acquire new ones when visiting other villages or receiving guests from elsewhere. We noted already that they are extremely interested in secret names which may be implemented in rites and formulas. Such formulas and names are exchanged between friends, sometimes even with members of foreign tribes, a procedure not wholly consistent with secrecy. Actually, the secrecy observed is primarily an act of recognition by the people concerned that they are dealing with knowledge of the hidden essence of reality which by its very nature must be respected as a kind of knowledge meant for insiders only. It must be handled with the same respectful care as displayed in the personal contacts with the beings to whom the relevant knowledge refers. Far from a fossilised whole the body of religious (that is also magic) knowledge is a living, ever developing body of knowledge and symbols serving man's communication with his universe.

3. The animistic complex. The belief in the persistence of the soul and the power of the dead

Tylor's definition of religion as the belief in spiritual beings who derive their origin from the belief in persistent souls, was a stroke of genius. Later research has amply demonstrated that there is not a single religious concept as widely spread as the belief in persistent souls. Religions which attribute little power or influence to the spirits of the recently dead nevertheless put great store on the role of ancestors, i.e. on dead who passed away long ago. Ancestors are the leading characters of myth and ritual not only in the religion of the Marind-anim but in those of the Australian tribes as well. Formally at least, the belief in ancestors who still make their power felt, presupposes the belief in the persistence of the soul. Where does this belief come from? Why do and how can people believe — and believe so universally — that the living persist after death? And secondly, how can people attribute to the dead a power over nature which they did not have during their lifetime? The problem can be put more pointedly: how can men and women who became the victims of the wilful and wayward powers ruling the universe, after having been victimised be enlisted in this same category of wilful powers? Or: how can people who died because they failed to manipulate the forces of nature to their own profit, become rulers of nature by virtue of their death?

The problem is complicated by the fact that ancestors are extremely convenient symbols for communication with the powers of the universe. The fact that they are dead symbolises their otherness, their seniority the authority admitted to them, and the family relation a certain willingness to enter into communication. The perfect suitability of the ancestor-concept for the fulfilment of its role in religion opens the road to the fallacy of mistaking its functional suitability for an explanation.

First of all we have to consider the problem of the persistence of the soul. The current explanations of this belief do not carry conviction, the one offered by Tylor least of all. It is one thing to set store on dreams as potential revelations of hidden truth, it is another to believe that a deceased still lives on because somebody dreamt of him. Tylor's theory of the primitive philosopher who constructed the belief in souls by carefully combining the facts of life, death and dream, is a weak one. Philosophy is never the reliable and unshakable basis for belief which belief is for philosophy.

The argument forwarded by Preusz, viz. the impossibility for the individual of imagining his own death, is hardly more convincing. Preusz himself pointed out that various tribes believe in an aftermath which does not last longer than survival is supposed to be bearable (above, p.92). Apparently the individual *is* capable of imagining his own death. Far worse for the theory — and for any theory presented thus far — is the belief in a dual or plural soul. In Truk the natives believe that the deceased live on in two different forms, one tricky and dangerous, one inclined to beneficence and succour. Goodenough explains the belief as a projection of the ambivalent feelings harboured by every Trukese with regard to his parents, a consequence of the negligence characteristic of child treatment in this culture (Cooperation in Change, pp.132-140, in particular pp.137-140).

The belief in a dual or multiple soul is not confined to Truk. It has been reported among many peoples and places but it was never paid much attention to in anthropological theory. The belief is so utterly inconsistent with what reason is to us, that it cannot possibly fit in with any general theory. However, it is worth while to give more specific attention to Goodenough's explanation. His point of departure is not what people think about their own fate after death, but what they think can be expected of a recently deceased relative. He reverses the position from which the approach to the problem is made, namely from one's own death to the death of the other. The approach from the position of ego is typical for western civilisation. Its way of thought is defined by the Christian tradition in which death involves a judgement, a judgement which no one can stand. In this tradition death is an ever flowing source of unabating concern: "For we are consumed by thine anger, and by thy wrath are we troubled. Thou hast set our inequities before thee, our secret sins in the light of thy countenance" (Ps.

268

90:7 f.). The association of the notion of death with that of final judgement has greatly intensified the terror inspired by death. Under such conditions thinking on death necessarily implies thinking on ego's own fate.

The situation is different when the concept of death is not combined with that of judgement, when the expectations with regard to life after death are vague and modest, and when, most important of all, no action of ego can be of any influence on his fate in the aftermath. Under such circumstances it is senseless to indulge in reflections upon one's own death. Of course, death is a misfortune, but the only sensible thing to pay attention to is how to postpone it. Somebody may occasionally worry about what will happen to his soul after death, but it cannot possibly be a major preoccupation in a whole people's way of thought. The ethnographic information available confirms this view. When the living worry about souls it is not about their own souls but about the souls of those who preceded them into death, and their real concern is not primarily whether these souls are happy or unhappy, but what these souls are likely to do to the living, whether they will be vindictive or benevolent, ready to help or to badger them. Typical of this pragmatic attitude is the lack of precision in the Ngad'a representations of the dead. They abide in the village but also in the underworld.

Consequently, any effort to acquire a better understanding of the motives underlying the belief in the persistence of souls should begin with an analysis of the impact which the death of a man or woman has on his or her surviving relatives. The facts are simple. A man has just stopped breathing. There he lies stretched out in the hut, a corpse, confronting his relatives who used to share the hut with him, with the necessity of making a decision. Something must be done with the corpse.

We shall not try to make an inventory of all things which can possibly be done with a corpse. Instead, we wish to point out what can *not* be done with it; namely, it cannot be ignored and it cannot be thrown away like dirt, even though dirt it is. This most logical procedure cannot be followed because the corpse is more than only a corpse; it is the dead father, husband and friend. One cannot deal with a deceased relative as with an annoying piece of filth. The deceased was 'one of us', a long-time partner in 'our life'. The surviving relatives are 'bereft' by his departure. No one can ignore this fact without intimating that the deceased relative meant little to him. Ignoring the bereavement implies the denial of true partnership. The neglectful mourner places himself outside the community. The denial of the partnership of the deceased relative has yet another consequence: it calls the negligent mourner's own partnership in the group in question because his negligence denies the emotional value of partnership, of being part of a group. It is an action which adversely affects the existential need of being a part.

Something must be done by the members of the group to express their feelings of distress and attachment. The emaciated body must be washed and adorned, the deceased himself must be bewailed. The loss must be given form by stating its depth and extent in clear and unambiguous words. They praise his abilities, they pity themselves before him and reproach him for his untimely departure. The presence of the corpse, lying outstretched in the midst of the group of wailers, irresistibly provokes them to address their words to him as if he were present and well aware of what is going on. He is still with them and one of them, as if he were alive.

As if he were alive... the situation is suggestive but everyone can see that he is not alive. Moreover, the situation does not last long. Presently he will be carried off to be laid to rest. An as-if situation is never a sufficient basis for interpreting it as real, unless the situation can be conceived of as a sign, a token, that there is more to it than is apparent to the eyes. And this indeed is actually the case. In primitive society hardly anyone lives on until old age. Death practically always comes as untimely, contingent and unreasonable, a blow to the frightened bystanders. They feel addressed by the event. The intentionality of the universe hardly ever makes itself more keenly felt than on the occasion of an untimely death. The obtrusive notion of a mysterious power hovering over the minds of the mourners, changes the corpse into a manifestation of otherness, emanating mystery because the deceased is at one and the same time himself and not himself, more than he was and less than it.

The situation is of the kind in which any otherwise unimportant event can contribute substantially to the feeling that some mysterious power is manifesting itself. Does this suffice to explain the origin of the notion of soul? Does the experience of a mysterious power manifesting itself necessarily lead to the interpretation that it is really the deceased who is manifesting himself? The assumption seems a rash one to us: it is a very specific interpretation of a highly undefined experience which could equally well be attributed to the cause of the death, as to its victim, or to something wholly unknowable. A specification, attributing certain manifestations to the deceased and, in general, to any specific cause, presupposes a matrix from which the specific must derive its significance. In other words, the emergence of the notion of soul presupposes a worldview which ascribes intentionality to the universe, an intentionality manifesting itself in personified beings existing independently of souls. Tylor's thesis that the spirits ruling the universe have been modelled in imitation of the soul-concept is a random guess, because it can be inverted. The statement that the soul-concept has been modelled after that of spiritual beings, stands an equal chance of being true. The formulation of the dilemma is just a little bit too acute, too precise for accepting it as a fully satisfactory point of departure for a discussion of the origin of the soul-concept. These concepts are the results of an age-long development, which began with notions and images very inadequately conceptualised. It would be stretching the argument to contend that the notion of soul could not develop before a complete spirit-world had

270

originated. A limited degree of simultaneity seems probable, on the understanding that the images giving substance to the experience of apprehended intentionality take precedence. They originate from an ever present human need, that of communicating with one's universe, whereas the belief in the persistence of souls refers to more specific situations which are of occasional, albeit not altogether infrequent occurrence. This implies that the former necessarily take precedence over the latter and that the belief in the persistence of souls must be considered as just one of the manifestations of the belief in a universe in which personified intentions play a decisive role.

Consequently, the role of the dead as rulers of the hidden world, i.e. as powers influencing the weal and woe of the living, must be the result of secondary development. An argument in favour of the hypothesis can be derived from the fairly insignificant role usually admitted to the recently dead. Among the Marind-anim their role is negligible: they are the object of commemorative rites but they have no important functions in nature or social life. With the Ngad'a the situation is somewhat different. They keep their dead with them, giving them a place to abide and serving them with titbits of food on all festive occasions. Yet their real influence is small. The true rulers of the universe are Déva and Nitu with their retinue, and a great number of ancestors whose importance is defined by their rank high up in the genealogical order of ascendents, the recently dead occupying the lowest ranks. Although Ngad'a religion may be called a typically animistic religion, the highest power is vested in beings of non-human origin (mythologically speaking). And not only this: some of the ancestors who are the main characters of mythology, are akin to demi-deities who can be formally described as magnified souls but who can with equal right be recognised as the relics of a naturalistic pantheon. In conclusion we state that among the Ngad'a the dead are primarily vehicles for easy daily access to communication with one's universe; their role as rulers of the universe is of secondary importance.

Who then are the ancestors? Formally of course they are the souls of forbears who died long ago, but does this formal description cover the facts? Are the totem-ancestors of the Marind-anim and the dream-time ancestors of the Australian tribes the true forbears of the present clans? Among the Ngad'a who live in a kind of symbiosis with all their dead, the supposition that the first ancestors are the first genitors of the clan has a certain measure of probability because an uninterrupted chain of ancestors connects the first among them with the present members of the living generation. Nevertheless, this formal argument is a weak one. It does not give a single reason why this ancestorship should be recognised as factual. Among the Marind-anim the situation is different; the dead are sent off to the country of the dead and have very little to do with the totem-ancestors of the clan, and the souls of the dead are called by another term than the clan-ancestors. The déma are recognised as ancestors even if they did not have off-

271

spring. There is every reason for rejecting the interpretation of the term ancestor as a reference to a genealogical reality, and to admit that it is simply a symbol of a specific relation between the being concerned and the members of his clan or totem-group. Ancestorship is as obvious a means of expressing communicability as the father-symbol with which it is closely related. Instead of deriving the ancestor-concept from the soul-concept we should give full scope to the possibility that the soul-concept owes a great deal of its development to an ancestor-concept of wholly independent origin.

4. Myth and ritual in two religious systems. Conclusion

The two religious systems summarily described in section 1 are consistent wholes, each adhering to a strict pattern. They differ profoundly; they belong to two different worlds, the Marind-anim one weird and savage, the Ngad'a world reasonably well ordered. A few peculiarities of either of them deserve of further examination and comment, at least as far as this is possible in the context of this condensed survey.

First of all Marind-anim myth. It has the home country as its field of action and almost continuously refers to the details of the landscape, vitalising the country with the exploits of the ancestors. A few of these are even identified with some of the landscape's features. Geb is the beach and the dry land along the coast, his decapitated body stretching from west to east; Geb's head is the sun which is also Waba, one of the two central characters of the mayo-ritual. The sea is Yorma, a dangerous and powerful déma. Yet, all these identifications are of a vague and elusive kind. Geb is a man with an acorn-shell covered body; Waba is always represented in human shape and Yorma is a young man not yet initiated who originated far away in the interior, the son of Depth and Groundwater. If these déma are dry land, moon, sun and sea respectively, they certainly are so not in a literal sense. They are not even the makers or creators of these natural phenomena, and we could perhaps as well say that Waba belongs to the sun and Yorma to the sea as the reverse. Yet they are identified with them in a ritual sense, they represent the essence of otherness and communicability of these phenomena in a way which cannot further be analysed for the simple reason that the déma represent the mystery in them: the challenge, the threat and the invitation combined.

In principle it is not so much different with déma representing certain animals or plants, such as Nazr, the pig-déma, or Yawi, the coconut-déma. Nazr assumed the shape of a pig and is the creator of pigs; he is the headhunter of mythology but also the déma of thunderstorms who hurls his children, the flashes of lightning, downwards. Yawi is quite another character; he was the first victim of sorcery and from his head the first coconut originated. If Nazr is the pig and Yawi the coconut, they are these as

272

representatives of everything mysterious in pig and coconut, of what is tricky or unreliable and at the same time useful and promising in them.

All these déma are also human; they are ancestors and they act as Marind-anim are supposed to act, even though these déma act in a more impressive, more powerful way than human beings can. Nevertheless, they set the rules of Marind-anim cultural life and their fights and adventures mirror its conflicts and difficulties. The myth of Waba is a case in point; it is a perfect illustration of the conflicts inhibiting the sexual life of the Marind-anim male. In mythology the universe is represented as a universe subject to the same order as that appertaining to their social life. The order of nature and the order of mankind are united by the déma, the ancestors of the clans and the originators or representatives of the relevant departments of nature. Marind-anim mythology expresses the unity of mankind with its universe. They belong together and the great rituals and festivals with their elaborate shows of déma and of dancers in an attire which is best described as a déma-attire, do not really re-enact the myth but bring about the revival of the universe, reconstituting it in its essential shape.

The ritual is an act in unison with the cosmos and the society as a whole. The two are of the same structure and it is the merit of totemism that it grants every member of a society his own specific place in the social fabric and in nature. In ritual each performer not only *plays* a part, but *is* a part, demonstrating how and why he is a part and what that part is. Marind-anim ritual has this in common with the rituals of the Central- and North-Australian tribes. The meticulous care the Australians devote to the correct adornment of the dream-time beings who enter the ritual scene, the clan-relationship between actor and ancestor impersonated, and the pathetic attachment to their native territory of which every landmark is connected with an ancestral myth, bear witness of a worldview closely akin to that of the Marind-anim.

Yet, the communion of man and universe brought about by ritual is not a simple act of identification with the déma. Although the actor is said to be the déma the performers are well aware that they are not really the déma. When under the weight of his paraphernalia a performer faints and must be brought round, then everybody feels convinced that the déma has entered into him. Consequently, the performance is only partially an identification, but nevertheless one which by its unusual splendour has the power to persuade actors and public of its intrinsic value as a demonstration and experience of the unison of man and universe.

The mediators between man and universe are the déma. Although ancestors they are also powers to be feared. Only clan-members may impersonate a déma and the act is always a serious one for which precautions must be taken. In the cult, prayer is of minor importance; it only plays a role in the magical formulas in which the performer may address himself to the déma. However, even in magic the role of prayer is restricted. Really in-

273

significant is that of sacrifice. One or two poorly described cases have been reported of a sacrifice brought to a déma, but it is not a common practice. The one form of sacrifice very commonly practised on festive occasions is that of putting aside little morsels of food for the dead, actually more a form of social intercourse with invisible guests than one of homage or worship.

A final remark must be made on the role of conscious deliberation and exchange of ideas in myth and ritual. Marind-anim mythology has in common with other mythological systems that many of its mythical patterns are not specific. They may have been borrowed or made part of their original cultural heritage before they came to this part of the country. Nevertheless, there are quite a few myths which apparently are wholly genuine. They are probably the products of visions or dreams of medicine-men. A point of greater interest is that these genuinely Marind-anim myths have been amalgamated with old cultural heritage and newly borrowed mythical material into a comprehensive system of myths which cannot be explained as the pure product of the unconscious or the subconscious of the people concerned. The myths are acted out and the performance of a ritual is a matter of elaborate deliberation among the leaders. We know that sometimes new items or changes of old ones are introduced, but such introductions are always subject to previous consultations. The total ritual is undoubtedly a matter of age-long development and through the years this development has been supervised by tribal leaders who discussed innovations among themselves. A thorough analysis of their myths has brought to light that the confrontation of the Mayo- with the Imo-Marind has led to ritual and mythological adaptations which in turn caused minor changes even in the structure of clans and subclans (cf. Van Baal, Déma pp.941-948). We conclude that the borrowing of myths and the ensuing adaptation to the cultural pattern are matters of a conscious interchange of ideas and speculative thought. The fact itself does not exclude the possibility — and we can surely say, the probability — that the adaptation follows certain unconscious 'grammatical' rules of the kind as suggested by Lévi-Strauss. The evidence brought forward in the 'Mythologiques' to demonstrate the presence of such rules is convincing. Yet, it leads to an oversimplification of the state of affairs if the impact of conscious deliberations is minimised. A myth and its meaning are cultural achievements, the results of a conscious reshaping of materials presented originally by the products of the subconscious, or collected from elsewhere by the bricoleur on occasional visits to a foreign tribe.

Similarly, a classificatory system cannot be the pure product of the unconscious or the subconscious. On the contrary, its close interconnection with ritual is evident; the classificatory system as such is actually an abstract of every clan's role in ritual. The distribution of roles is a matter of continuous adaptation because the unequal effect of population growth or decline on the number of the various co-operating clans makes repeated adaptations a necessity. The coastal Marind of Buti even shifted a certain subclan from one moiety to the other in order to ensure conformity between the mayo- and imo-systems of classification. Such things require a considerable amount of mutual consultation. All-inclusive systems of this kind are so elaborate and sophisticated that they can be confidently considered as the products of a philosophy devoted to the consideration of the communicability of their universe as revealed by religious experience. That such a philosophy is subject to the rules of a 'meta-grammar' is not denied. It is the one as well as the other, and the question may be legitimately raised as to whether the opposition between the conscious and the unconscious is really an adequate tool for the analysis of the process.

A religion based on the recognition of the universe as a universe full of secret meaning and intentions does not necessarily lead to the conception of an always menacing world. Such a world has its kind and friendly aspects as well. It can be and often is a universe of great intimacy. Yet, the notion that there is an intention or meaning behind everything also has its adverse effects. The worst among these is that every death — except that of the very old or the very young — must have a specific cause stemming from that world of secret intentionality. In some cases the Marind will blame the déma for it, more especially so in case of epidemics. However, not every death can be attributed to the déma without casting them in a more invidious role than is compatible with their role of ancestors who care for their descendants. The recently dead cannot be blamed either, because in the attitude vis-à-vis the dead loving memory dominates. The only remaining solution is that of sorcery. Accusations of sorcery are a recurring scourge of Marind-anim society, in fact of every society in which their way of ascriptive thinking prevails. Anthropologists often hold the view that the belief in sorcery is the result of discord and hostility stemming from social conflicts. There is ample reason for revising this view. Many conflicts are caused by the belief in sorcery which is the effect of a worldview capitalising on apprehended intentionality, without being checked by the redeeming notion of a higher power so sublime that resignation becomes an acceptable solution. However, we may see this also the other way round. Accusing or suspecting each other of sorcery, the Marind-anim again identify themselves with their universe, finding in themselves the cause of part of its malice just as human ritual action contributes to its goodness.

Completely different is the religious system of the Ngad'a. Their gods are not powers to be impersonated but to be addressed. Yet, their universe is as much alive with supernatural beings as that of the Marind-anim and, formally at least, many of these beings are of a similar kind, viz. ancestors. However, whereas the Marind-anim ancestors are primarily reifications of certain aspects or departments of the physical universe, those of the Ngad'a are intrinsically human. Next to these ancestors and spirits of the dead the Ngad'a have a multitude of other spirits but on the whole they have a great likeness to human beings. Frightening demons are relatively few; they resemble witches or are witches, and witches indeed are the beings most feared. They bring sickness and death and the prayers pronounced on the occasion of a sacrifice usually end with the exhortation that the *polo*, the witches or witch-like demons, be chased away. The relation with these beings is a negative one; the Ngad'a avoids contact with them. He simply prays that they may be prevented from damaging him.

The fact that the spirit world of the Ngad'a has a rather human character does not imply that it is thought of as having predominantly human origin. The human origin of the ancestors who play a prominent part in Ngad'a myth is decidedly doubtful. What is more, the leading powers of the spirit world, Déva and Nitu, are clearly non-human in origin and scope and the same can be said of their emanations, the lower déva and noa, nitu and ngebu, all spirits who are representatives of these supreme beings.

The nature of these supreme beings is extremely complicated. On the one hand we are told that there is in fact one really Supreme Being, Déva, who is the creator of the world and even of his female counterpart in the underworld, Nitu. The two seem to make a pair but we are not told that they are as husband and wife. The superiority of Déva as creator and ruler of the world is maintained. At the same time the distance between him and mankind is mitigated by his retinue, the legion of lower déva who attend on the Supreme Being and mediate between him and his creatures, every human being having his own déva tending him. The human beings are herded by Déva like men herd their buffaloes. The fundamental notion is that mankind is cared for by Déva who represents the universe in its ultimate totality.

The first thing to be noted in this context is the fact that among the Ngad'a the total universe is symbolised by Déva and Nitu who are called upon as Father and Mother, the Mother being the lesser of the two but in invocations the one who is always mentioned first. The terms are a prelude to communication, a communication which takes the form of a sacrifice. We shall return to this point presently. We must for a little while dwell upon the relations between the Ngad'a and their physical universe. These relations are not wholly devoid of more material symbols than those of the parenthood of Déva and Nitu. Mythology has draped the more important ancestors with moon-symbols, i.e. symbols of that specific item of nature which is also the symbol of the essence of human life, that of passing through the successive stages of youth, maturity and old age. The moon-symbols characterising these ancestors confirm the fundamental unity linking men, gods and nature. Even Déva's image is well equipped with moon-symbols.

A second point requiring attention is the fact that Déva is called father, and in connection with Nitu, usually Mother and Father. The father-symbol has been discussed in an earlier chapter of this book. There we pointed out that this symbol is the most logical and even most probable image for symbolising a relationship characterised by fear and confidence, hope and anxiety, love and hatred (above, pp.153 and 163). There is no symbol imaginable as fit as the father symbol for characterising and impersonating a man's relations with, and his situation in his universe. The father-symbol must be very old in religion, much older indeed than the idea of creation, an idea so often presented as logical and probable, but an idea which in fact presupposes a fairly high developed measure of sophisticated thinking on the one hand, a daring fantasy on the other. The idea of creation is not as simple or obvious as some theologians prefer to believe. A study of so-called creation-myths gives ample evidence of the fact that non-christian peoples have had the greatest difficulty with the problem of origin. Maori myth is revealing in this respect. If, for once, the present author may indulge in theological discussion, he may be allowed to state that theologians show a lack of respect in trying to explain what is really a wonder, what is unfathomable, with a word, an empty cry: creation. Who shall describe what creation is? It is a word easily used and equally easily suggested to other people. What is true in the oftentimes repeated assurance that this or that people believe in a Creator-god? Do they, or is the word creation an addition of the ethnographer who projected the image of the father-god who is a ruler of the universe on the screen of his own theological concepts? We shall never know it for certain; missionaries have implanted the notion of creation so firmly in the minds of the tribesmen whose fathers or grandfathers once believed in a ruling father-god as to make it impossible ever to find out what the content of their pristine faith really was. The one thing we know for certain is that the father-image is the most obvious symbol for a universe which is a gift as well as a scourge, a challenge as well as a prison, a source of plenty and one of hardship.

A more promising object for scrutiny is sacrifice. Ngad'a sacrifice does not fit the 19th century concepts of sacrifice by any means. It can be understood in the context of the gift, the form of communication prevalent among people who are near enough to each other to become partners in a reciprocal relation of gift and return-gift, yet as members of separate groups far enough removed from each other to justify the performance of formal acts of exchange as a means of bridging the gap. Actually, sacrifice has two forms among the Ngad'a, the formal one of a solemn ceremonial presentation of a gift of food in which at a later stage the human members of the community are allowed to have a share, and the simple presentation of titbits brought home from a formal sacrifice to the spirits who are the house-mates of the sacrificers and the receivers of food. The latter form is more an act of recognition that the spirits concerned make part of the family and share its weal and woe, than a presentation performed with a definite purpose in mind. The Marind-anim offerings to the dead come into this same category.

The Ngad'a and their spirits constitute a large community and that this community has communication as its most essential purpose is highlighted by that amazing process of bargaining called divination. The silent guardians of the universe are forced to speak and to give an unequivocal answer to the questions harassing their human offspring. It is not a simple matter of question and answer; the drawn-out consultations almost resemble an interview. In no other form of ritual is the two-way character of real communication so closely approximated as in divination. An aspect of secondary importance phenomenologically, but nevertheless of great psychological impact, is the more or less public character of divination. As a matter of fact the religious acts of the Ngad'a are practically always public acts which unite the participants in common worship, thus contributing to a togetherness which strenghtens their mutual solidarity as well as each individual's awareness of real partnership.

The form and content of the symbols for communication differ from one culture to another. The study of religion necessarily results into a study of religions, of the diversity of the total complexes of symbols permitting man to enter into discourse with his culturally defined universe. The cases cursorily surveyed in this chapter may have given an impression of their diversity, they certainly do not suffice to give a full picture of the variegation of forms and attitudes even within each of the two religions discussed. To that end a more complete analysis would have been called for than is in place in the context of the present introduction into religious thought which aims at disclosing fundamental motives rather than at depicting the diversity of solutions realised in the history of culture.

We shall not try to sum up these motives. They all converge on one point, the need for communication fostered by human beings who, whatever their state of civilisation, all lack the proper means to meet this need. In our need for communication we are all bricoleurs, looking for signs which can 'explain' our universe. Unfortunately, signs are open to contestation; by their very nature they are signs 'to be spoken against'. It is the problem of our time that we have lost confidence in these symbols for communication. Exactly one hundred years ago Tylor named the science of culture a reformer's science and called upon its students "to expose the remains of crude old culture which have passed into harmful superstition, and to mark these out for destruction" (above, p.42). The students have answered the call with unsurpassed throroughness. The discourse of modern man with his universe has been silenced, not because his universe has stopped to address him, but because he is unable to identify the speaker. Vis-à-vis his universe he still is a bricoleur, *mais un bricoleur sans trésor*. He has lost his symbols because he has lost faith in their relevance and truth.

278

The trouble is that in Western religion, religious truth has become identified with scientific truth (cf. Bellah, Christianity and symbolic Realism, 1970). The identification, based on the consideration that there can only be one truth, necessarily led to conflicts, both in the church and in the consciences of the faithful who considered doubt as synonymous with unfaithful, a sin in the religious sense of the word. Although modern Christianity has revolted against this view and makes allowance for doubt, the close connection between religious and scientific truth has persisted, among non-believers as well as among believers. It is in effect a most undesirable connection. Our study of symbols has taught us to place the symbols of religion and science at opposite ends of the scale of lucidity (above, pp.159 ff.). The pious effort (if pious it be) to claim for religion the lucidity and the kind of certainty proper to scientific truth, necessarily ends in failure. The engineer cannot work with the bricoleur's trappings.

Must we conclude that modern man has to give up religion altogether? If he were the perfect engineer in each and every respect, this would be the answer. But with regard to his universe he invariably is a bricoleur and he cannot be anything else. His need for communication with his universe persists undiminished, and we know of no substitute which can fully take the place of the religious symbols. What shall man do in this position? He has a choice to make. Considering the uncertainties inherent in the concepts and representations presented as religious truth, or objecting to the personalisations common to most of the forms of religious communication, he may prefer to try a substitute of some sort, or make an endeavour to forget his problems by indulging in an active way of life. Unfortunately, we have little adequate knowledge of the implications of irreligiosity and under these circumstances all opinions expressed on the suitability of any of these solutions of the existential problem are necessarily impressionistic, that is unscientific. We must confine ourselves to the statement that so far there is little evidence that the human need for communication can be more satisfactorily met by non-religious means than by religious ones. This leads us to the other possibility, that of re-considering the religious solution, a choice which commends itself in so far that (in spite of its errors and failures) it proved its worth in the past and that, consequently, a little more can be said about it. Modern man, if he decides to try the religious solution, shall have to take stock of his own position as well as of the state of his discarded treasury.

An inspection of the old treasury is not very encouraging. There is much to be discarded, among others the absolute truths, ultimate answers and perfect certainties emphasised in the superlatives of which certain types of Christian religious language are so distressingly rich. Religious and scientific symbols belong to opposite ends of the scale of lucidity. The certainties and truths offered by religion necessarily are of the bricoleur's type: imperfect, defective and fragile; an additional peculiarity is that they may have

279

served other ends in bygone days. The conclusion may seem hard, perhaps even cruel to some. In fact there is nothing in it which anyone could not have found out by himself. The intuitive knowledge stored in language gives irrefutable evidence that the speech-making community has always been aware of it. In language religion is associated with belief and faith, the former a term with a definite connotation of uncertainty, the latter one intimating that the certainty implied can never exceed the certainty on which confidence, a personal act of trust, is based. When all is said and done, the credibility of a religious idea or representation (our problem throughout this book) is not a matter of scientific knowledge or certitude, but of the credit which it can be given by an act of trusting confidence based on intuitive agreement.

Modern man has great difficulties with the old treasury. He is up against a universe other than that of his forbears who bequeathed most of the parts of his treasury to him. Scientific knowledge has disclosed a new universe which differs substantially from the old one. Yet, in one respect it remained its old self. The universe of modern man, though signifying differently to him than it did to his ancestors, still signifies to him as well; it still invites him to answer the call with a signified.

At this point modern man has to take stock of his own position, and to recognise that religion is not a gift bestowed on mankind once and for all by an act of grace, but a never ending task which, in a period of rapid culture change, each generation has to shoulder anew. If he accepts this task, modern man may find solace and encouragement by taking the example of primitive man who does not make a secret of it that he is not always sure of his ground, that is, of the precise content of his religious belief and sometimes even of the effect of his rites. However different our situation, we too are up against mystery and enigmas. On the cover of this book a photograph of an Asmat shield is reproduced. Nobody knows what the savage artist (a member of a New-Guinea tribe of headhunters and cannibals) had in mind when he carved its front-side. Is it despair? wonder? adoration? All three in one? The one thing we can be sure of is that in his carving he expressed his mind on man, and that this symbol of man in Asmat is as perfectly a symbol of man in the modern world as it is of man in the stone age. We are all bricoleurs, sitting in wonder beholding our universe.

Bibliography

ABBREVIATIONS

A.A.   American Anthropologist
A.S.   l'Année Sociologique
Bijdragen Bijdragen tot de Taal-, Land- en Volkenkunde
I.A.   Internationales Archiv für Ethnographie (International Archives of Ethnography)
J.A.F.L. Journal of American Folk-lore
J.(R.)A.I. Journal of the (Royal) Anthropological Institute of Great-Britain and Ireland
ZfE   Zeitschrift für Ethnologie

ANKERMANN, B.
1905 Kulturkreise und Kulturschichten in Afrika. ZfE 37;54-84.

ARNDT, F. PAUL, SVD.
1929/31 Die Religion der Nad'a (West-Flores, Kleine Sunda-Inseln). Anthropos 24:817-861, 26:353-405, 697-739.
1932 Die Megalithenkultur der Nad'a (Flores). Anthropos 27:11-63.
1936/37 Déva, das Höchste Wesen der Ngadha. Anthropos 31:894-909, 32:195-209, 347-377.

BAAL, J. VAN
1947 Over Wegen en Drijfveren der Religie. Een godsdienstpsychologische Studie. Amsterdam, Noord-Hollandsche Uitgeversmaatschappij.
1965 (Review of) Claude Lévi-Strauss, Totemism. Bijdragen 121:147-152.
1966 Dema. Description and Analysis of Marind-Anim Culture (South New Guinea). With the Collaboration of Father J. Verschueren MSC. The Hague, Martinus Nijhoff.
1970 The Application of the Concept of Structure. Anniversary Contributions to Anthropology. Twelve Essays published on the Occasion of the 40th Anniversary of the Leiden Ethnological Society W.D.O. Leiden, E. J. Brill.

BAAREN, TH. P. VAN
1960 Wij Mensen. Religie en Wereldbeschouwing bij schriftloze Volken. Utrecht, J. Bijleveld.

BACHOFEN, J. J.
1861 Das Mutterrecht. Eine Untersuchung über die Gynaikokratie der alten Welt nach ihrer religiösen und rechtlichen Natur. Stuttgart, Krais & Hoffman.

281

BASTIAN, ADOLF
1860 Der Mensch in der Geschichte. Zur Begründung einer psychologischen Weltanschauung. 3 vols. Leipzig, Otto Wigand.
1866/71 Die Völker des östlichen Asien. Studien und Reisen. 6 vols. Vols 1-2: Leipzig, Otto Wigand. Vols 3-6: Jena, Hermann Costenoble.

BATESON, GREGORY
1936 Naven. A Survey of the Problems suggested by a composite Picture of the Culture of a New Guinea Tribe drawn from three Points of View. London, Cambridge University Press.

BATESON, GREGORY and MEAD, MARGARET
1942 Balinese Character. A photographic Analysis. Special Publications of the New York Academy of Sciences Vol. II. New York, Academy of Sciences.

BELLAH, ROBERT H.
1970 Christianity and symbolic Realism. Journal for the scientific Study of Religion 9:89-96.

BENEDICT, RUTH
1935 Patterns of Culture. London, Routledge.

BERGSON, HENRI
1932 Les deux Sources de la Morale et de la Religion. Paris, Félix Alcan.

BERNDT, R. M.
1947 Wuradjeri Magic and "Clever Men". Oceania 17:327-365, 18:60-86.

BETH, KARL
1914 Religion und Magie bei den Naturvölkern. Ein religionsgeschichtlicher Beitrag zur Frage nach den Anfängen der Religion. Leipzig/Berlin, Teubner.

BOAS, FRANZ
1916 The Origin of Totemism. A.A. 18:319-326. (Reprinted in Race, Language and Culture: 316-323).
1940 Race, Language and Culture. New York, MacMillan Company.

BORNEMANN, F. FRITZ, SVD.
1938 Die Urkultur in der kulturhistorischen Ethnologie. Eine grundsätzliche Studie. Sankt Gabrieler Studien VI. Mödling bei Wien, Missionsdruckerei St. Gabriel.

BREYSIG, KURT
1905 Die Entstehung des Gottesgedankens und der Heilbringer. Berlin, Georg Bondi.

BROMFIELD, LOUIS
1924 The green Bay-tree. London, T. Fischer Unwin. (Quotations from the Pocket Edition).

BROSSES, CHARLES DE
1760 Du Culte des Dieux fétiches ou Parallèle de l'ancienne Religion de l'Égypte avec la Religion actuelle de la Nigritie.

BUCK, P. H. (TE RANGI HIROA)
1939 Anthropology and Religion. New Haven, Yale University Press.

282

CASSIRER, ERNST
1923/31 Philosophie der symbolischen Formen. 3 vols. 1 Die Sprache (1923); 2 Das mythische Denken (1925); 3 Phänomenologie der Erkenntnis (1929). Berlin, Bruno Cassirer Verlag.
English Translation (1953): The Philosophy of Symbolic Forms. Translated by Ralph Mannheim. Preface and Introduction by Charles W. Hendel. New Haven, Yale University Press (2nd ed. 1957).
1944 An Essay on Man. An Introduction to a Philosophy of Human Culture. New Haven, Yale University Press.

COCQ, A. P. L. DE
1968 Andrew Lang, a nineteenth century Anthropologist. Tilburg, Zwijzen.

CODRINGTON, J. H.
1881 Religious Beliefs and Practices in Melanesia. JAI 10: 261-315.
1891 The Melanesians. Studies in their Anthropology and Folk-lore. Oxford, Clarendon Press.

DARWIN, CHARLES
1859 The Origin of Species by means of natural Selection. London, John Murray.

DEURSEN, A. VAN
1931 Der Heilbringer. Eine ethnologische Studie über den Heilbringer bei den Nordamerikanischen Indianern. Groningen/Den Haag, Wolters.

DOUGLAS, MARY
1966 Purity and Danger. London, Routlege & Kegan Paul.

DURKHEIM, ÉMILE
1893 De la Division du Travail social. Étude sur l'Organisation des Sociétés supérieures. Paris, Félix Alcan.
1895 Les Règles de la Méthode sociologique. Paris, Félix Alcan. (References to the 13th ed.).
1897 Le Suicide. Étude sociologique. Paris, Félix Alcan.
1912 Les Formes élémentaires de la Vie religieuse. Le Système totémique en Australie. Paris, Félix Alcan. (References to the 2nd ed.).

DURKHEIM, ÉMILE et MAUSS, MARCEL
1901/02 De quelques Formes primitives de Classification. Contribution à l'Étude des Représentations collectives. A.S. VI: 1-72.

DUYVENDAK, J. Ph.
1926 Het Kakean Genootschap van Seran. Almelo, Hilarius.

EHRENREICH, PAUL
1906 Götter und Heilbringer. Eine ethnologische Kritik. ZfE 38:536-610.
1910 Die allgemeine Mythologie und ihre ethnologischen Grundlagen. Leipzig, Mythologische Bibliothek IV, 1. J. C. Hinrichs'sche Buchhandlung.

ELIADE, MIRCEA
1948 Traité d'Histoire des Religions. Bibliothèque scientifique. Paris, Payot.
English Translation (1958): Patterns in comparative Religion. Translated by Rosemary Sheet. London/New York, Sheet & Ward.
1951 Le Chamanisme et les Techniques archaïques de l'Extase. Bibliothèque scientifique.

Paris, Payot.

English Translation (1964): Shamanism. Archaic Techniques of Ecstasy. Translated by William R. Trask. London, Routledge & Kegan Paul.

1952   Images et Symboles. Essais sur le Symbolisme magico-religieux. Paris, Librairie Gallimard.

English Translation (1961): Images and Symbols. Studies in religious Symbolism. Translated by Philip Mairet. London, Harvill Press.

EVANS-PRITCHARD, E. E.
1937   Witchcraft, Oracles and Magic among the Azande. Oxford, Clarendon Press.
1956   Nuer Religion. Oxford, Clarendon Press.

FAHRENFORT, J. J.
1927   Het hoogste Wezen der Primitieven. Studie over het "Oermonotheïsme" bij enkele der laagste Volken. Groningen/Den Haag, Wolters.
1930   Wie der Urmonotheismus am Leben erhalten wird. Groningen/Den Haag, Wolters.

FIRTH, R.
1940   The Analysis of Mana: An empirical Approach. Journal of the Polynesian Society 49:483-510. (Reprinted in Tikopia Ritual and Belief).
1940   The Work of the Gods in Tikopia. 2 Vols. Monographs on social Anthropology no. 1 & 2. London, Percy Lund, Humphries & Co. Ltd. (2nd ed. 1967).
1967   Tikopia Ritual and Belief. London, George Allen and Unwin Ltd.

FISCHER, HANS
1968   Negwa. Eine Papua-Gruppe im Wandel. München, Klaus Renner Verlag.

FLETCHER, ALICE C.
1910   Wakonda. Handbook of American Indians North of Mexico. Frederick Webb Hodge ed. Part 2:897-898. Bureau of American Ethnology, Bulletin 30. Smithsonian Institution, Washington, D.C.

FRAZER, J. G.
1887   Totemism. Edinburgh, A. & C. Black. (Reprinted in Totemism and Exogamy I).
1890   The Golden Bough. A study in comparative Religion. 2 vols. London, Macmillan & Co. (See also 1911/15, 1922, 1936).
1910   Totemism and Exogamy. A Treatise on certain early Forms of Superstition and Society. 4 Vols. London, Macmillan & Co. (See also 1937).
1911/15   The Golden Bough. A Study in Magic and Religion. 3rd. ed., revised and enlarged. 7 Parts, 12 Vols. London, Macmillan & Co.
1913/24   The Belief in Immortality and the Worship of the Dead. 3 Vols. London, Macmillan & Co.
1918   Folk-lore in the Old Testament: Studies in comparative Religion, Legend and Law. 3 vols. London, Macmillan & Co.
1922   The Golden Bough. Abridged ed. London, Macmillan & Co. (References to this edition).
1936   Aftermath. A Supplement to The Golden Bough. London, Macmillan & Co.
1937   Totemica. A Supplement to Totemism and Exogamy. London, Macmillan & Co.

FREUD, SIGMUND
1901   Zur Psychopathologie des Alltagslebens. Monatschrift für Psychiatrie und Neurologie. Band X, Heft 1, 2.
1913   Totem und Tabu. Einige Übereinstimmungen im Seelenleben der Wilden und der Neurotiker. Leipzig/Wien, Hugo Heller & Cie.

284

1916/17 Vorlesungen zur Einführung in die Psychoanalyse. 3 Vols. Leipzig/Wien, Hugo Heller & Cie.
1939 Der Mann Moses und die monotheistische Religion. Drei Abhandlungen. Amsterdam, Albert de Lange.
English Translation (1939): Moses and Monotheism. Translated by Katherine Jones. London, The Hogarth Press/New York, A. A. Knopf.
1940/68 Gesammelte Werke. Chronologisch geordnet. 18 Vols. Vol. 1-17 London, Imago Publishing Co. Ltd. Vol. 18 (Index) Frankfurt am Main, S. Fischer Verlag.

FROBENIUS, LEO
1898 Die Masken und Geheimbünde Afrikas. Nova Acta. Abh. der Kaiserl. Leop.-Carol. Deutschen Akademie der Naturforscher. Band 74 nr. 1:1-278.
1898 Der Ursprung der Afrikanischen Kulturen. Berlin, Gebr. Borntraeger.

FUSTEL DE COULANGES, N. D.
1864 La Cité Antique. Étude sur le Culte, Le Droit, les Institutions de la Grèce et de Rome. Paris, Durand.

GEERTZ, CLIFFORD
1966 Religion as a cultural System. Anthropological Approaches to the Study of Religion. A.S.A. Monographs 3. Michael Banton ed.: 1-46. London, Tavistock Publications.

GENNEP, ARNOLD VAN
1909 Les Rites de Passage. Étude systématique des Rites. Librairie Critique. Paris, Émile Nourry.
1920 L'État actuel du Problème totémique. Paris, Éditions Ernest Leroux.

GOODENOUGH, WARD H.
1963 Cooperation in Change. An anthropological Approach to Community Development. New York, Russell Sage Foundation.

GRAEBNER, F.
1905 Kulturkreise und Kulturschichten in Ozeanien. ZfE 37:28-53.
1911 Methode der Ethnologie. Kulturgeschichtliche Bibliothek 1. Reihe: Ethnologische Bibliothek 1. Heidelberg, Winter.

GOLDENWEISER, A. A.
1910 Totemism, an analytical Study. Journal of American Folk-lore 23:179-293. (Reprinted in History, Psychology and Culture).
1918 Form and Content in Totemism. A.A. 20:280-295. (Reprinted in History, Psychology and Culture).
1933 History, Psychology and Culture. London, Kegan Paul, Trench, Trubner & Co. Ltd.

GRIMM, JACOB und GRIMM, WILHELM
1812/22 Kinder- und Hausmärchen. 3 Vols. Berlin, Reimer. (Reprinted in the Series Miniatur-Ausgaben, not dated. Leipzig, Verlag Philipp Reclam jun.).

HADDON, A. C.
1902 Presidential Address to the Section of Anthropology, delivered on 11 September 1902 at Belfast. Report of the 72nd Meeting of the British Association for the Advancement of Science, held at Belfast in September 1902: 738-752. London, John Murray.

HALL, C. S. and LINDZEY, G.
1957   Theories of Personality. New York, John Wiley and Sons.

HARRINGTON, CHARLES
1968   Sexual Differentiation in Socialization and some male genital Mutilations. A.A. 70:951-956.

HELD, G. J.
1935   The Mahabharata. An ethnological Study. Amsterdam, Holland.

HERTZ, ROBERT
1905/06   Contribution à une Étude sur la Représentation collective de la Mort. A.S. X: 48-137. (Reprinted in Mélanges de Sociologie religieuse et Folklore).
English Translation (1960): Death and The right Hand: 25-86. Translated by Rodney and Claudia Needham. London, Cohen and West.
1909   La Pré-éminence de la Main droite. Étude sur la Polarité religieuse. Revue philosophique de la France et de l'Étranger 34 (2): 553-580. (Reprinted in Mélanges de Sociologie religieuse et Folklore). Death and The right Hand: 87-113.
1928   Mélanges de Sociologie religieuse et Folklore. Paris, Félix Alcan.

HEWITT, J. N. B.
1902   Orenda and a Definition of Religion. A.A. 4: 33-46.
(Reprinted in Selected Papers from the American Anthropologist 1888-1920, Frederick de Laguna, ed. 1960: 671-684, Evanston/Elmsford, Row, Peterson & Co).

HILL-TOUT, C.
1901/02   The Origin of Totemism among the Aborigines of British Columbia. Proceedings and Transactions of the Royal Society of Canada. 2nd. Ser. Vol. VII: 6ff.

HUBERT, H. et MAUSS, M.
1899   Essai sur la Nature et la Fonction sociale du Sacrifice. A.S. II: 29-138. (Reprinted in Mélanges d'Histoire des Religions: 1-130).
1902/03   Esquisse d'une Théorie générale de la Magie. A.S. VII: 1-146. (Reprinted in Sociologie et Anthropologie par Marcel Mauss: 1-141, 1950).
1909   Mélanges d'Histoire des Religions. Paris, Félix Alcan.

HUMBOLDT, WILHELM VON
1836/40   Über die Kawi-Sprache auf der Insel Java. Nebst einer Einleitung über die Verschiedenheit des menschlichen Sprachbaues und ihren Einfluss auf die geistige Entwicklung des Menschengeschlechts. 3 Vols. Berlin, F. Dümmler.

JACHMANN, FRIEDEGARD
1967   (Review of) J. van Baal, Dema. ZfE 92:305-308.

JACOBI, JOLANDE
1939   Die Psychologie von C. G. Jung. Zürich, Rascher Verlag.

JAMES, WILLIAM
1902   The Varieties of religious Experience. A Study in Human Nature. Being the Gifford Lectures on Natural Religion delivered at Edinburgh in 1901/02. London, Longmans, Green & Co.
1912   Memories and Studies. London, Longmans, Green & Co.

286

JASPERS, KARL
1919 Psychologie der Weltanschauungen. Berlin, Julius Springer. (References to the 2nd ed., 1920).

JENSEN, A. E.
1951 Mythos und Kult bei den Naturvölkern. Religionswissenschaftliche Betrachtungen. Wiesbaden, Frank Steiner Verlag G.m.b.H.

JESPERSEN, OTTO
1922 Language, its Nature, Development and Origin. London, George Allen & Unwin, Ltd.

JONES, ERNEST
1925 Mother-Right and the sexual Ignorance of Savages. International Journal of Psycho-Analysis 4:109-130.

JONES, WILLIAM
1905 The Algonkin Manitou. Journal of American Folk-lore 18:183-190. (Republished in Source Book for Social Origins, William L. Thomas ed.: 683-693. Chicago, University of Chicago Press/London, T. Fisher Unwin 1909).

JONG, A. J. DE
1917 Afgoderye der Oost-Indische Heydenen door Phillippus Baldaeus. 's-Gravenhage, Martinus Nijhoff.

JOSSELIN DE JONG, J. P. B. DE
1913 De Waardeeringsonderscheiding van "levend" en "levenloos" in het Indogermaansch vergeleken met hetzelfde verschijnsel in enkele Algonkin-Talen. Ethnopsychologische Studie. Leiden, Gebroeders van der Hoek.
1929 De Oorsprong van den goddelijken Bedrieger. Mededeelingen der Koninklijke Akademie van Wetenschappen, Afd. Letterkunde, deel 68 serie B, no. 1. Amsterdam.
1935 De Maleische Archipel als ethnologisch Studieveld. (Inaugural Address). Leiden, J. Ginsberg.
1952 Lévi-Strauss's Theory on Kinship and Marriage. Mededelingen Rijksmuseum voor Volkenkunde, deel 10. Leiden, E. J. Brill.

JUNG, C. G.
1912 Wandlungen und Symbole der Libido. Beiträge zur Entwicklungsgeschichte des Denkens. Wien, F. Deuticke. 4th revised ed. (1952): Symbole der Wandlung. Analyse des Vorspiels zu einer Schizophrenie. Ausgewählt und zusammengestellt von Jolande Jacobi. Zürich, Rascher Verlag.
1928 Die Beziehungen zwischen dem Ich und dem Unbewussten. Darmstadt, Otto Reich.

KARDINER, ABRAM
1939 The Individual and his Society. The Psychodynamics of primitive social Organization. Foreword and two ethnological Reports by Ralph Linton. New York, Columbia University Press.

KLEMM, GUSTAV
1843/51 Allgemeine Cultur-Geschichte der Menschheit. 10 Vols. Leipzig, B. G. Teubner.

KRISTENSEN, W. B.
1928 De goddelijke Bedrieger. Meded. der Kon. Akademie van Wetenschappen, Afd. Letterkunde, deel 66, serie B, no. 3. Amsterdam.

KRUYT, ALBERT C.
1906   Het Animisme in den Indischen Archipel. 's-Gravenhage, M. Nijhoff.
1918/20   Measa, eene Bijdrage tot het Dynamisme der Bare'e-sprekende Toradja's en enkele omwonende Volken. Bijdragen 74:233-262, 75:36-133, 76:1-116.
n.d.   Van Heiden tot Christen. Oegstgeest, Zendingsbureau.

LANG, ANDREW
1898   The Making of Religion. London, Longmans, Green, and Co. (2nd ed. 1900).

LEACH, E. R.
1957   The epistemological Background to Malinowksi's Empiricism. Man and Culture. An Evaluation of the Work of Bronislaw Malinowksi. Raymond Firth ed.: 119-137.
1970   Lévi-Strauss. London, Collins.

LEEUW, G. VAN DER
1924   Inleiding tot de Godsdienstgeschiedenis. Volks-Universiteitsbibliotheek 26. Haarlem, De Erven F. Bohn. (2nd ed. 1948: Inleiding tot de Phaenomenologie van den Godsdienst).
1933   Phaenomenologie der Religion. Tübingen, Mohr.

LEHMANN, ALFRED
1898   Aberglaube und Zauberei von den ältesten Zeiten an bis in die Gegenwart. German Translation: Dr. Petersen. Stuttgart, Ferdinand Enke Verlag (References to 2nd ed. 1908).

LEHMANN, F. R.
1922   Mana. Der Begriff des "auszerordentlich Wirkungsvollen" bei Südseevölkern. Leipzig, Otto Spamer.

LÉVI-STRAUSS, CLAUDE
1949   Les Structures élémentaires de la Parenté. Paris, Presses Universitaires de France. (2nd revised ed. 1967. Paris, La Haye, Mouton et Co.). References to 2nd ed.
       English Translation from the 2nd revised ed. (1969): The elementary Structures of Kinship. Translated by James Harle Bell, John Richard von Sturmer. Rodney Needham ed. Boston, Beacon Press.
1950   Introduction à l'Oeuvre de Marcel Mauss. Sociologie et Anthropologie par Marcel Mauss. Paris, Presses Universitaires de France.
1955   Tristes Tropiques. Paris, Librairie Plon.
1958   Anthropologie Structurale. Paris, Librairie Plon.
1962   Le Totémisme Aujourd'hui. Paris, Presses Universitaires de France.
       English Translation (1964): Totemism. Translated by Rodney Needham. London, Merlin Press.
1962   La Pensée sauvage. Paris, Librairie Plon.
1964   Mythologiques. Le Cru et le Cuit. Paris, Librairie Plon.
1966   Mythologiques. Du Miel aux Cendres. Paris, Librairie Plon.
1968   Mythologiques. l'Origine des Manières de Table. Paris, Librairie Plon.

LÉVY-BRUHL, LUCIEN
1910   Les Fonctions mentales dans les Sociétés inferieures. Travaux de l'Année sociologique. Paris, Félix Alcan.
1922   La Mentalité primitive. Travaux de l'Année sociologique. Paris, Félix Alcan.
1927   L'Ame primitive. Travaux de l'Année sociologique. Paris, Félix Alcan.
1935   La Mythologie primitive. Le Monde mythique des Australiens et des Papous. Paris, Félix Alcan.

288

1949 Les Carnets de Lucien Lévy-Bruhl. Préface de Maurice Leenhardt. Paris, Presses Universitaires de France.

LINTON, RALPH
1936 The Study of Man. An Introduction. New York, London, D. Appleton-Century Company.
1945 The cultural Background of Personality. New York, London, D. Appleton-Century Company.

LOCHER, G. W.
1932 The Serpent in Kwakiutl Religion. A Study in primitive Culture. Leiden, E. J. Brill.

LONG, J.
1791 Voyages and Travels of an Indian Interpreter and Trader, describing the Manners and Customs of the North American Indians, Account of the Posts and Vocabulary of the Chippeway Language.

LOWIE, ROBERT H.
1924 Primitive Religion. New York, Boni & Liveright. (References to the 1960 ed.).
1937 The History of ethnological Theory. London, George G. Harrap & Co Ltd.

Mc LENNAN, J. F.
1869/70 The Worship of Animals and Plants. The Fortnightly Review 6:407-427, 7:194-216.

MAINE, SIR HENRY J. S.
1861 Ancient Law: its Connection with the early History of Society, and its Relation to modern Ideas. London, John Murray.

MALINOWSKI, BRONISLAW
1924 Psychoanalysis and Anthropology. Psyche 4:293-332.
1925 Magic, Science and Religion. Science, Religion and Reality. J. Needham ed. New York/Toronto, the Macmillan Company. (Reprinted in Magic , Science and Religion: 1-71).
1926 Myth in primitive Psychology. The Frazer Lectures 1922-32. W. R. Dawson ed.: 66-119. London, Kegan Paul, Trench, Trubner and Company. (Reprinted in Magic, Science and Religion: 72-124).
1927 Sex and Repression in savage Society. London, Kegan Paul, Trench, Trubner and Company.
1934 Introduction to H. Ian Hogbin: Law and Order in Polynesia. London, Christophers.
1935 Coral Gardens and their Magic. A Study of the Methods of tilling the Soil and of agricultural Rites in the Trobriand Islands. 2 Vols. London, George Allen & Unwin.
1944 A scientific Theory of Culture and other Essays. Chapel Hill, University of North Carolina Press.
1948 Magic, Science and Religion and other Essays by Bronislaw Malinowski. Selected, and with an Introduction by Robert Redfield. Trade ed. Boston, Mass., Beacon Press. Text ed. Glencoe, Illinois, The Free Press.

MANNHARDT, W.
1875/77 Wald- und Feldkulte. 2 Vols. Berlin, Gebrüder Borntraeger.

289

MARETT, R. R.
1909 The Threshold of Religion. London, Methuen & Co (2nd revised and enlarged ed. 1914). References to the 2nd ed.

MAUSS, MARCEL (See also HUBERT et MAUSS and DURKHEIM et MAUSS)
1923/24 Essai sur le Don. Forme et Raison de l'Échange dans les Sociétés archaïques. A.S. nouvelle Série I: 30-186.
(Reprinted in: Sociologie et Anthropologie par Marcel Mauss: 143-279. Paris, Presses Universitaires de France. 1950).
English Translation (1954): The Gift. Forms and Functions of Exchange in archaic Societies. Translated by Ian Cunnison. London, Cohen & West Ltd.

MEAD, MARGARET (See also BATESON and MEAD)
1928 Coming of Age in Samoa. A psychological Study of primitive Youth for western Civilisation. New York, William Morrow & Company.
1930 Growing up in New Guinea. A comparative Study of primitive Education. New York, William Morrow & Company.
1935 Sex and Temperament in three primitive Societies. New York, William Morrow & Company.

MEINERS, CONRAD
1806/07 Allgemeine kritische Geschichte der Religionen. 2 Vols. Hannover, Helwingische Hof Buchhandlung.

MORGAN, LEWIS H.
1871 Systems of Consanguinity and Affinity of the human Family. Smithsonian Contributions to Knowledge, Vol. XXVII. Washington City, Smithsonian Institution.

MORIER, JAMES
1824 The Adventures of Hajji Baba of Ispahan. 3 Vols. London, John Murray. (Republished in the World's Classics. Oxford University Press, London 1923 and since repeatedly reprinted).

MÜLLER, F. MAX
1867/75 Chips from a German Workshop. 4 Vols. London, Longmans, Green and Co.
1873 Introduction to the Science of Religion. Four Lectures with two Essays. London, Longmans, Green and Co.
1878 Lectures on the Origin and Growth of Religion as illustrated by the Religions of India. The Hibbert Lectures 1878. London, Longmans, Green and Co. Williams and Norgate.

NORBECK, EDWARD
1961 Religion in primitive Society. New York, Harper & Brothers.

OSSENBRUGGEN, F. D. E. VAN
1916 Het primitieve Denken zoals dit zich uit voornamelijk in Pokkengebruiken op Java en elders. Bijdrage tot de prae-animistische Theorie. Bijdragen 71:1-370.

OTTO, RUDOLPH
1917 Das Heilige. Über das Irrationale in der Idee des Göttlichen und sein Verhältnis zum Rationalen. Breslau, Trewendt & Granier. (References to the 12th ed.).

PERRY, W. J.
1923 The Children of the Sun. A Study in the early History of Civilisation. London, Methuen & Co. Ltd.

290

PREUSZ, K. Th.
1904/05 Der Ursprung der Religion und Kunst. Globus 86: 321-327, 355-363, 375-379, 388-392; 87: 333-337, 347-350, 380-384, 394-400, 413-419.
1914 Die geistige Kultur der Naturvölker. Leipzig/Berlin, B. G. Teubner.
1926 Glauben und Mystik im Schatten des höchsten Wesens. Leipzig, C. L. Hirschfeld.
1930 Tod und Unsterblichkeit im Glauben der Naturvölker. Tübingen, J. C. B. Mohr (Paul Siebeck).
1933 Der religiöse Gehalt der Mythen. Tübingen, J. C. B. Mohr. (Reprinted in Religions-Ethnologie. C. A. Schmitz ed.: 119-153).

RADCLIFFE-BROWN, A. R.
1942 Sir James Frazer, O.M., F.R.S., F.B.A., 1 jan. 1854 — 7 May 1941. Man 42:1-2.
1951 The comparative Method in social Anthropology. Huxley Memorial Lecture for 1951. JRAI:15-22.
      (Reprinted in: Method in social Anthropology. Selected Essays by A. R. Radcliffe-Brown. M. N. Srinivas ed. 108-129. Chicago, University of Chicago Press, 1958).
1952 Structure and Function in primitive Society. Essays and Addresses. London, Cohen & West.

RADIN, PAUL
1927 Primitive Man as Philosopher. New York/London, D. Appleton and Company.
1938 Primitive Religion. Its Nature and Origin. London, Hamish Hamilton.
1951 Die religiöse Erfahrung der Naturvölker. Zürich, Rhein-Verlag.

RATZEL, FRIEDRICH
1882/91 Anthropo-Geographie oder Grundzüge der Anwendung der Erdkunde auf die Geschichte. 2 Vols. Stuttgart, J. Engelhorn Verlag.
1885/88 Völkerkunde. 3 Vols. Leipzig/Wien, Bibliographisches Institut. (2nd ed. in 2 Vols. 1894/95).
1897 Politische Geographie oder die Geographie der Staaten, des Verkehrs und des Krieges. München, Berlin, R. Oldenbourg.

RIVERS, W. H. R.
1914 The History of Melanesian Society. Percy Sladen Trust Expedition to Melanesia. 2 Vols. Cambridge, University Press.

ROBERTSON SMITH, W.
1885 Kinship and Marriage in early Arabia. Cambridge, University Press.
1889 Lectures on the Religion of the Semites. First Series. The fundamental Institutions. Edinburgh, A. & C. Black.

ROHEIM, GEZA
1925 Australian Totemism. A psychoanalytic Study in Anthropology. London, George Allen & Unwin.
1930 Animism, Magic and the Divine King. London, Kegan Paul, Trench, Trubner & Co.
1945 The eternal Ones of the Dream. A psychoanalytic Interpretation of Australian Myth and Ritual. New York, International University Press.

SAPIR, E.
1916 Time Perspective in aboriginal American Culture. A Study in Method. Canada Department of Mines. Geological Survey, Memoir 90. Anthropological Series 13:1-50. Ottawa, Government Printing Bureau (Reprinted in Selected Writings of Edward Sapir).
1932 Cultural Anthropology and Psychiatry. Journal of Abnormal and Social Psychology 27:229-242. (Reprinted in Selected Writings of Edward Sapir).

1934   The Emergence of the Concept of Personality in a Study of Cultures. Based on a Paper to the National Research Council Conference on Studies in Child Development at Chicago on June 22, 1933. Journal of Social Psychology 5:408-415. (Reprinted in Selected Writings of Edward Sapir).

1949   Selected Writings of Edward Sapir in Language, Culture and Personality. David Mandelbaum ed. Berkeley and Los Angeles, University of California Press.

SCHMIDT, F. WILHELM, SVD.

1908/10   l'Origine de l'Idée de Dieu. Étude historico-critique et positive. (French Translation by F. P. J. Pietsch, OMI.). Anthropos 3:125-162, 336-368, 559-611, 801-836, 1081-1120; 4:207-250, 505-524, 1075-1091; 5:231-246. (German edition in Vol. I of Der Ursprung der Gottesidee).

1910   Die Stellung der Pygmäenvölker in der Entwicklungsgeschichte des Menschen. Stuttgart, Strecker & Schröder.

1926/55   Der Ursprung der Gottesidee. Eine historisch-kritische und positive Studie. 12 Vols. Münster (Westf.), Assendorffsche Verlagsbuchhandlung.

1928   Ein Versuch zur Rettung des Evolutionismus. I.A. 29:99-126.

1930   Handbuch der vergleichende Religionsgeschichte. Ursprung und Werden der Religion. Theorien und Tatsachen. Münster (Westf.), Asschendorffsche Verlagsbuchhandlung.
       English Translation (1931): The Origin and Growth of Religion. Facts and Theories. Translated by H. J. Rose. London, Methuen & Co.

1937   Handbuch der Methode der kulturhistorischen Ethnologie. Mit Beiträgen von Wilhelm Koppers. Münster (Westf.), Assendorffsche Verlagsbuchhandlung.
       English Translation (1939): The Culture Historical Method of Ethnology. Translated by S. A. Siebel. New York, Fortuny's.

SCHMITZ, C. A.

1960   Beiträge zur Ethnographie des Wantoat Tales, Nordost Neuguinea. Kölner ethnologische Mitteilungen 1. Köln, Kölner Universitäts Verlag.

1964   (ed.) Religions-Ethnologie. Frankfurt a.M., Akademische Verlagsgesellschaft.

SCHURTZ, HEINRICH

1902   Altersklassen und Männerbünde. Eine Darstellung der Grundformen der Gesellschaft. Berlin, Georg Reimer.

SELIGMANN, C. G.

1910   The Melanesians of British New Guinea. Cambridge, University Press.

SÖDERBLOM, NATHAN

1916   Das Werden des Gottesglaubens. Untersuchungen über die Anfänge der Religion. German Translation: Rudolf Stübe. Leipzig, J. C. Himrich'sche Buchhandlung.

SIMONIS, YVAN

1968   Claude Lévi-Strauss, ou la "Passion de l'Inceste". Introduction au Structuralisme. Collection Recherches économiques et sociales. Paris, Aubier Montaigne.

SINGER, PHILIP and DESOLE, DANIEL E.

1967   The Australian Subincision Ceremony reconsidered: Vaginal Envy or Kangaroo Bifid Penis Envy. A.A. 69:355-358.

SPENCER, HERBERT

1876/96   The Principles of Sociology. 3 Vols. London, William & Norgate.

STANNER, W. E. H.

1959/63   On Aboriginal Religion. Oceania 30:108-127, 245-278; 31:100-120, 233-258; 32:79-108; 33:239-273. (Reprinted as Oceania Monograph no. 11).

TURNER, VICTOR W.
1969 The ritual Process. Structure and Anti-Structure. Aldine Publ. Cy, Chicago.

TYLOR, EDWARD B.
1861 Anahuac: Or Mexico and the Mexicans, ancient and modern. London, Longmans, Green, and Co.
1865 Researches into the early History of Mankind and the Development of Civilization. London, John Murray.
1871 Primitive Culture. Researches into the Development of Mythology, Philosophy, Religion, Language, Art and Custom. 2 Vols. London, John Murray. (References to the 4th ed.).
      Paperback edition 1958 (Paul Radin ed.). New York, Harper's Torchbooks.
1881 Anthropology, an Introduction to the Study of Man and Civilization. London, MacMillan & Co.

VRIES, JAN DE
1961 Forschungsgeschichte der Mythologie. Freiburg/Müchen, Karl Alber Verlag.

WAITZ, THEODOR
1859/72 Anthropologie der Naturvölker. 6 Vols. (Vol. 5(2) and 6 by Georg Gerland after the author's death in 1864). Leipzig, Friedrich Fleischer.

WARNER, W. LLOYD
1937 A black Civilization. A social Study of an Australian Tribe. New York, Harper & Brothers. (Revised ed. 1957). References to revised ed.

WEBSTER, HUTTON
1908 Primitive secret Societies. A Study in early Politics and Religion. New York, The Macmillan Company.

WILKEN, G. A.
1884/85 Het Animisme bij de Volken van den Indischen Archipel. Amsterdam, J. H. de Bussy. (Reprinted from De Indische Gids 1884/85).
1886/87 Über das Haaropfer und einige andere Trauergebräuche bei den Völkern Indonesiens. Revue Coloniale Internationale 1886(2): 225-279, 1887(1):345-426.
1912 De verspreide Geschriften van Prof. Dr. G. A. Wilken. Mr. F. D. E. van Ossenbruggen ed. 4 Vols. Semarang, Soerabaja, 's-Gravenhage, G. T. C. van Dorp & Co.

WINCKLER, H.
1901 Himmels- und Weltbild der Babylonier als Grundlage der Weltanschauung und Mythologie aller Völker. Der Alte Orient, Gemeinverständliche Darstellungen herausgegeben von der Norder-asiatischen Gesellschaft. Jahrgang 3, Heft 2/3. Leipzig, J. C. Hinrichs'sche Buchhandlung.

WINTHUIS, J.
1928 Das Zweigeschlechterwesen bei den Zentralaustraliern und anderen Völkern. Lösungsversuch der ethnologischen Hauptprobleme auf Grund primitiven Denkens. Leipzig, C. L. Hirschfeld Verlag.

WOUDEN, F. A. E. VAN
1935 Sociale Structuurtypen in de Groote Oost. Leiden, J. Ginsberg. English Translation by Rodney Needham (1968): Types of Structure in Eastern Indonesia. The Hague, Martinus Nijhoff.

WUNDT, WILHELM
1900/20 Völkerpsychologie. Eine Untersuchung der Entwicklungsgesetze von Sprache, Mythus und Sitte. 10 Vols. Leipzig, Vols. 1-6 Wilhelm Engelmann, Vols. 7-10 Alfred Kröner Verlag.
1912 Elemente der Völkerpsychologie. Grundlinien einer psychologischen Entwicklungsgeschichte der Menschheit. Leipzig, Alfred Kröner Verlag.

Index of authors

Ankermann, B. 97 f, 100.
Arndt, P. 250-254, 256-258.

Baal, J. van 137, 182, 202 f., 211, 238, 243, 246 f., 249 f., 260, 274.
Baaren, Th. P. van 91.
Bachofen, J. J. 28.
Bastian, A. 54, 94-96.
Bateson, G. 179.
Bellah, R. H. 279.
Benedict, R. 131, 179-181.
Bergson, H. 126, 131-133, 229.
Berndt, C. 171.
Berndt, R. M. 171, 258.
Beth, K. 74.
Boas, F. 27, 43, 59, 83, 100, 140 f., 178, 199.
Bornemann, F. 173.
Breysig, K. 78 f.
Bromfield, L. 162, 224.
Brosses, Ch. de 11-13, 214.
Buck, P. H. 5.

Cassirer, E. 93, 144, 157-160, 196, **222**.
Cocq, A. P. L. de 59-62.
Codrington, J. H. 25, 64-66.

Darwin, Ch. 28.
Desole, D. E. 136.
Deursen, A. van 79.
Douglas, M. 213.
Durkheim, E. 81, 109-114, 117-119, 121-127, 129, 133, 139-142, 166, 171 f., 178, 185 f., 190, 193, 216.
Duyvendak, J. Ph. 186.

Ehrenreich, P. 78-80.
Eliade, M. 165, 177 f.
Elkin, A. P. 143, 171.
Elliot Smith, G. 101 f.
Evans-Pritchard, E. E. 58, 170.

Fahrenfort, J. J. 106.
Firth, R. 66, 143, 168, 170.
Fischer, H. 219.
Fletcher, A. C. 71.
Frazer, J. G. 1, 34, 45, 48, 53-59, 62, 68, 70, 73 f., 85 f., 113, **139**, **146**.

Freud, S. 51, 85, 130, 144-149, 151-155, 190.
Frobenius, L. 97 f., 100.
Fustel de Coulanges, N. D. 28, 49.

Geertz, C. 2, 214.
Gennep, A. van 74, 123, 126 f., 133-139, 141-143, 189.
Gillen, F. J. 48.
Goodenough, W. H. 179, 268.
Graebner, F. 97-101, 106 f., 173.
Goldenweiser, A. A. 126, 133, 139-141, 143, 153.
Grimm, J. and W. 19 f.
Gusinde, M. 106.

Haddon, A. C. 43, 139.
Hall, C. S. 179.
Harrington, Ch. 136.
Heine-Geldern, R. 100.
Held, G. J. 187.
Hendel, Ch. W. 157.
Hertz, R. 114, 122, 125 f., 138 f., 159.
Hewitt, J. N. B. 71.
Hill-Tout, C. 139.
Hogbin, I. 166.
Hubert, H. 114, 116-119, 121-123, 138 f., 189.
Humboldt, A. von 19, 27.
Humboldt, W. von 19.

Jachmann, F. 177.
Jacobi, J. 154.
James, W. 62 f., 83, 132, 168, 229.
Jaspers, K. 222.
Jensen, A. E. 73, 173-176.
Jespersen, O. 18 f.
Jones, E. 151.
Jones, W. 71.
Jones, Sir W. 18 f.
Jong, A. J. de 18.
Josselin de Jong, J. P. B. de 78, 185-187, 193.
Jung, C. G. 91, 144, 154-157, 159, 212.

Kardiner, A. 179.
Klemm, G. 27 f.
Koppers, W. 106.

Kristensen, W. B. 186.
Kruyt, A. C. 71-75, 176, 219.

Lang, A. 26, 59-62, 77, 103 f., 141, 146.
Leach, E. R. 168, 213.
Leenhardt, M. 130.
Leeuw, G. van der 89-91.
Lehmann, A. 62.
Lehmann, F. R. 65 f.
Lévi-Strauss, Cl. 89, 125, 143, 152, 182, 184-186, 188-213, 223, 240, 274.
Lévy-Bruhl, L. 76, 91, 93, 126-132, 156.
Lindzey, G. 179.
Linton, R. 131, 179.
Locher, G. W. 187.
Long, J. 45.
Lowie, R. H. 27, 82 f., 85, 102.

McLennan, J. F. 28, 45.
Maine, H. J. S. 28.
Malinowski, B. 37, 66, 113, 150-152, 166-171, 193.
Mannhardt, W. 20.
Marett, R. R. 66-70, 73 f., 76, 83, 85, 169.
Mauss, M. 111, 114, 116-119, 121-123, 125-127, 138 f., 183-185, 187, 189 f., 193, 195, 197.
Mead, M. 131, 178 f., 181.
Meggitt, M. J. 48, 171.
Meiners, C. 13 f., 26.
Mommersteeg, A. 250 ftn.
Morgan, L. H. 28 f.
Morier, J. 26.
Müller, F. M. 12 f., 20-26, 34 f., 45, 59, 64, 79.

Nadel, S. F. 182.
Needham, R. 126, 201.
Nieuwenhuys, A. W. 37.
Norbeck, E. 65, 137.

Ossenbruggen, F. D. E. van 44, 74.
Otto, R. 81, 85, 87-89.

Perry, W. J. 102.

Preusz, K. Th. 75-77, 91-93, 100, 268.

Radcliffe-Brown, A. R. 54, 123, 143, 166, 171-173, 182, 185, 187 f., 201.
Radin, P. 31, 82-86.
Ratzel, F. 94, 96 f.
Redfield, R. 166, 170.
Rivers, W. H. R. 43, 101.
Robertson Smith, W. 45, 48-53, 58, 76, 114, 116 f., 121, 146, 148 f.
Roheim, G. 149 f.

Sapir, E. 101, 131, 178 f.
Schleiermacher, F. E. D. 1, 83, 87.
Schmidt, Wilh. 26, 54, 59, 62, 77, 81, 102-108, 173.
Schmitz, C. A. 73, 93, 176.
Schurtz, H. 133 f.
Seligman, C. G. 43, 47.
Söderblom, N. 12, 79-82, 87.
Simonis, Y. 190, 193-195, 197, 211, 213.
Singer, P. 136.
Spencer, B. 43, 48.
Spencer, H. 43-45, 139.
Stanner, W. E. H. 139, 171, 188 f.

Thurnwald, R. 100.
Tiele, C. P. 44.
Turner, V. W. 213.
Tylor, E. B. 13, 27-45, 49 f., 53, 56-59, 61 f., 65-67, 70, 95, 103, 113 f., 146, 168, 192, 214, 218, 267 f., 270, 278.

Verschueren, J. 238, 259 f.
Vries, J. de 16.

Waitz, Th. 25, 27 f.
Warner, W. Ll. 171, 238, 258 f.
Webster, H. 134 f.
Wilken, G. A. 37, 44, 72, 139.
Winckler, H. 101.
Winthuis, J. 106.
Wouden, F. A. E. van 186.
Wundt, W. 94, 96.